NEW SECURITY CHALLENGES IN

POSTCOMMUNIST EUROPE

MANCHESTER
UNIVERSITY PRESS

NEW SECURITY CHALLENGES IN POSTCOMMUNIST EUROPE

Securing Europe's East

EDITED BY

ANDREW COTTEY AND DEREK AVERRE

Manchester University Press

Manchester and New York

distributed exclusively in the USA by Palgrave

Copyright © Manchester University Press 2002

While copyright in the volume as a whole is vested in Manchester University Press, copyright in individual chapters belongs to their espective authors, and no chapter may be reproduced wholly or in part without the express permission in writing of both author and publisher.

Published by Manchester University Press
Oxford Road, Manchester M13 9NR, UK
and Room 400, 175 Fifth Avenue, New York, NY 10010, USA
www.manchesteruniversitypress.co.uk

Distributed exclusively in the USA by
Palgrave, 175 Fifth Avenue, New York,
NY 10010, USA

Distributed exclusively in Canada by
UBC Press, University of British Columbia, 2029 West Mall,
Vancouver, BC, Canada V6T 1Z2

British Library Cataloguing-in-Publication Data
A catalogue record for this book is available from the British Library

Library of Congress Cataloging-in-Publication Data applied for

ISBN   0 7190 6131 8 *hardback*
       0 7190 6132 6 *paperback*

First published 2002

10 09 08 07 06 05 04 03 02   10 9 8 7 6 5 4 3 2 1

Typeset by
D R Bungay Associates, Burghfield, Berks

Printed in Great Britain
by Biddles Ltd, Guildford and King's Lynn

Contents

Contributors

Derek Averre, Research Fellow, Centre for Russian and East European Studies, University of Birmingham

Andrew Cottey, Jean Monnet Chair in European Political Integration, Department of Government, University College Cork and Lecturer, Department of Peace Studies, University of Bradford

Stuart Croft, Professor of International Relations, Department of Political Science and International Studies, University of Birmingham

Sergiy P. Galaka, Associate Professor, Institute of International Relations, Kyiv Taras Shevchenko University

Mark Galeotti, Director, Organised Russian and Eurasian Crime Research Unit, Keele University and Editorial Consultant, *Jane's Intelligence Review*

Vladimir Handl, Research Fellow, Institute of International Relations, Prague

Adrian Hyde-Price, Professor of Politics and International Relations, Department of Politics, University of Leicester

Viktor Kremenyuk, Deputy Director, Institute for United States and Canadian Studies of the Russian Academy of Sciences

Kerry Longhurst, Lecturer in German and European Security, Institute for German Studies, University of Birmingham

Dov Lynch, Lecturer in War Studies, Department of War Studies, King's College London

Richard Sakwa, Professor of Russian and European Politics, University of Kent at Canterbury

James Sperling, Professor of Political Science, University of Akron

Mark Webber, Senior Lecturer in Politics, Department of European Studies, Loughborough University

Marcin Zaborowski, Lecturer in Politics and European Studies, School of European Studies and Languages, Aston University

Preface

This book draws together papers originally presented at a conference entitled 'Ten years after 1989: the changing nature of security relations in
Central and Eastern Europe' held at the University of Birmingham in
November 1999. A decade after the dramatic revolutions of 1989 in Central
and Eastern Europe and the break-up of the Soviet Union, it explores the
nature of the new security challenges facing the countries of postcommu-
nist Europe, the implications of these challenges for the emerging post-
Cold War European order and the policy issues they raise. The conference
on which this book draws was organised by the Centre for Russian and East
European Studies and the Institute for German Studies, University of
Birmingham, and the Department of Peace Studies, University of Bradford.
The conference was made possible by financial support from the School of
Social Sciences, University of Birmingham, NATO, the UK Ministry of
Defence, the UK Foreign and Commonwealth Office, the British
International Studies Association, the Jean Monnet Scheme and the
University Association for Contemporary European Studies. The editors
wish to extend their thanks to all those who provided assistance in the
organisation of the conference and the production of this book.

Andrew Cottey and Derek Averre

Abbreviations

CESDP	Common European Security and Defence Policy
CFE	Conventional Armed Forces in Europe (Treaty)
CIS	Commonwealth of Independent States
CSBMs	confidence- and security-building measures
CSCE	Conference on Security and Cooperation in Europe
EAPC	Euro-Atlantic Partnership Council
EU	European Union
FBI	Federal Bureau of Investigation
G7	Group of Seven
G8	Group of Eight
GUUAM	Georgia, Ukraine, Uzbekistan, Azerbaijan and Moldova
HCNM	High Commissioner on National Minorities
ICTY	International Criminal Tribunal for the Former Yugoslavia
IFOR	Implementation Force
IMF	International Monetary Fund
INF	Intermediate-range Nuclear Forces (Treaty)
IPTF	International Police Task Force
KFOR	Kosovo Force
KLA	Kosovo Liberation Army
NACC	North Atlantic Cooperation Council
NATO	North Atlantic Treaty Organisation
NIS	newly independent states
NMD	National Missile Defence
OECD	Organisation for Economic Cooperation and Development
OSCE	Organisation for Security and Cooperation in Europe
PACE	Parliamentary Assembly of the Council of Europe
PCAs	Partnership and Cooperation Agreements
PfP	Partnership for Peace
PJC	Permanent Joint Council
REACT	Rapid Expert Assistance and Cooperation Teams
SFOR	Stabilisation Force
START	Strategic Arms Reduction Treaty
UN	United Nations
UNPROFOR	UN Protection Force
WEU	Western European Union

1

Introduction: thinking about security in postcommunist Europe

Derek Averre and Andrew Cottey

From intervention in the former Yugoslavia, through the eastward enlargement of the North Atlantic Treaty Organisation (NATO) and the European Union (EU) and the troubled attempt to build a working partnership between Russia and the West, to the less traditional security challenges of mass migration and transnational organised crime, the security problems of postcommunist Europe have been among the most controversial international issues of the post-Cold War era. The collapse of the communist order in Eastern Europe and the Soviet Union between 1989 and 1991 created enormous opportunities but also real dangers. It raised the hope of overcoming the Cold War division of the continent and creating a 'Europe whole and free' based on common democratic values. At the same time, the disintegration of a nuclear-armed superpower, the problems of postcommunist transition and the region's many potential disputes over borders and minorities created the spectre of instability and conflict. The violent dissolution of Yugoslavia indicated that the security problems of postcommunist Europe were very real indeed and posed challenges not just for the region itself but also for the West and the wider international community.

The diversity in political, economic, social, cultural and technological terms across Europe is tremendous and the contrast between a stable and institutionally integrated western half of the continent and a relatively fragmented and, in places, highly unstable eastern half is stark. As a consequence, establishing common, Europe-wide approaches to the security problems of the continent's eastern half has proved deeply problematic. While Central European states see membership of NATO and the EU as vital to their security, Russia and other states unlikely to join these organisations view the eastward enlargement of NATO (and to a lesser the EU) as undermining their own security. At the individual level, the gap between contemporary notions of human rights anchored in the rule of law and the threat posed to people by the institutions of organised violence of the state itself, or by a breakdown of political and legal order within the state, has been dramatically highlighted by the conflicts in the Balkans and the Soviet successor states. While there has been significant progress in the process of what might broadly be termed 'demilitarisation' – reducing the weight of the military factor in international affairs and building on arms control, disarmament, non-proliferation and confidence- and security-building measures (CSBMs), and, in internal affairs, changing the relationship between society, the 'instruments of violence' and the state – this process is far from complete and may face setbacks. Further, the economic dimension of security – though difficult to conceptualise – poses massive challenges in postcommunist Europe. The fundamental changes in economic and social circumstances – a dramatic decline in standards of living, the breakdown of old patterns of social relations, social stratification, migration, resource depletion and environmental damage, technological modernisation and organised criminal business – in many respects pose much greater security problems for most of the people of postcommunist Europe than the political–military relations of the major European powers.

This chapter introduces the security problems of postcommunist Europe, placing them in the context of recent theoretical thinking about international security. Many of the theories and concepts which inform our understanding of security have been modified or challenged by the end of the Cold War and the transformation of communist Europe.[1] During the Cold War, mainstream, orthodox thinking about security focused on the territorial integrity and political independence of states, the shifting balance of power between East and West, and the military problems of defence, deterrence and arms control. Newer approaches to international relations and security have focused on cooperation and community rather than rivalry, conflict and violence, suggesting that interdependence, international institutions and regimes and the 'democratic peace' are key characteristics of world politics. Most recently, a growing number of academics have adopted social constructivist approaches, arguing that international politics can best be understood in terms of the ideas, beliefs and identities that shape state behaviour. Debate on what exactly should constitute the security agenda – what can be considered threats or challenges to collective and individual security – was also given fresh impetus by the end of East–West Cold War confrontation. Scholars have attempted to broaden and deepen the narrow 'orthodox' conception of security – safeguarding the territorial integrity and core values of a state from primarily military-political threats emanating from outside its borders – to include a wider range of potential threats – for example, economic and environmental issues, migration and transnational crime – and switch the focus from the state to individual and societal security. Against this background, postcommunist Europe provides an important test case of how far 'real world' security relations and practices can indeed be transformed as some academics suggest.

Identity and security: in search of Europe

The end of the Cold War and the collapse of the Soviet order raised fundamental questions about the nature of 'Europe', the extent to which the
postcommunist eastern half of the continent forms a distinct region (or
subregion), the relationship between Western and Eastern Europe, and
where the eastern border of Europe lies or should lie. Any consideration of
the new security challenges facing postcommunist Europe cannot be separated from these broader questions of identity. The Cold War provided
clear, if brutal, answers to these questions. Western Europe ended at the
inner-German border and for most Westerners, as long as Soviet communist hegemony held sway to the east, there was little point in debating the
hypothetical eastern borders of Europe. 'Eastern Europe' was those countries lying between the West and the Soviet Union: the non-Soviet Warsaw
Pact allies (Bulgaria, Czechoslovakia, Hungary, Poland and Romania),
Yugoslavia and Albania, defined by their communist systems and common
geostrategic position. While these definitions sometimes hid a more
complex picture – Yugoslavia's and Albania's splits with the Soviet Union,
the diverse adaptations of communism in the Eastern European states, the
calls of dissidents for the re-establishment of a distinct 'Central European'
identity and culture – they nevertheless reflected the crude way in which
the Cold War determined regional identities.

In the 1970s and 1980s issues of identity began to exercise growing
influence on politics within these countries. Dissidents in East Germany,
Czechoslovakia, Hungary and Poland began to reassert the existence of a
distinct Central European region with a history, culture and identity of its
own – a call which received support from an influential section of opinion
in the West.[2] At the same time, pan-European human rights and peace
movements brought together citizens from both East and West, asserting a
common European identity and calling for an end to the division of the
continent into two opposing blocs. Towards the end of the 1980s Soviet
President Mikhail Gorbachev drew on these sentiments with his calls for a
'common European home'.

In the pivotal year of 1989 these debates intensified dramatically. In
Budapest, Prague and Warsaw the revolutions brought to power the dissidents who had championed the idea of Central Europe. These leaders
rejected the definition of their countries as Eastern European, or even East-
Central European; the term 'Eastern Europe' was part of the baggage of
Yalta, Soviet communism and the Cold War and perpetuated their artificial
separation from the rest of Europe. Their countries were Central European
and wished to return to the Europe of democracy and prosperity from
which they had been separated in 1945.[3] Fearing that they might otherwise

be cast into some outer darkness of exclusion from mainstream Europe, leaders in other countries, such as Romania and the Baltic states, rapidly asserted that their nations too were Central European.

The disintegration of the Soviet Union at the end of 1991 created fifteen new states in the former superpower's place, adding a new dimension to this identity debate. The leaders of the newly independent Baltic states rapidly rejected the epithet 'former Soviet', a rhetoric translated into reality by their rejection of inclusion in the Commonwealth of Independent States (CIS) and by their subsequent bids for membership of the EU and NATO. Wary of exclusion from the emerging new Europe and of possible reintegration within a Russian-led union, some Ukrainian leaders also began to argue that their country is Central European – a claim which has greater historical legitimacy for the western half of Ukraine (with its earlier close connections with Poland and the Austro-Hungarian empire) than for the eastern half of the country. Ukraine's ambivalence towards the CIS was demonstrated by its refusal to sign the 1992 Tashkent collective security treaty.

The Russian Federation that emerged from the ruins of the Soviet state has arguably faced the greatest problems in defining its international identity. The Yeltsin, and more recently Putin, administrations have consistently asserted Russia's European identity, based on its major contributions to European culture, its long history as a European great power alongside Germany, France and Britain, and its new acceptance of democracy and market economics. This claim has been cemented through membership of key international institutions shaping the political norms of post-Cold War Europe – in particular the Organisation for Security and Cooperation in Europe (OSCE) and the Council of Europe. However, influential Russian politicians also proclaim distinctive Russian, Slavic or Eurasian identities; this, together with attempts to maintain a dominant political role and pursue a degree of reintegration within the former Soviet space, has suggested an ambivalent relationship with the new Europe. Leaders in Armenia, Belarus, Kazakhstan and Kyrgyzstan have, for varying reasons, been supportive of Russian leadership with the former Soviet space and sought close cooperation with Moscow. The informal group of GUUAM states (Georgia, Ukraine, Uzbekistan, Azerbaijan and Moldova) have, again for divergent reasons, opposed Russian regional leadership. In addition, important political leaders in Ukraine and Georgia assert that their countries are European – as distinct from post-Soviet or Eurasian – and stake claims to eventual membership of the EU and NATO. As a result, the former Soviet space has fragmented.

The violent break-up of Yugoslavia added further actors and complexities to this regional identity debate. The most brutal conflicts in Europe since 1945 reinforced the historical reputation of the Balkans as a by-word for political instability, extreme nationalism and violence. Slovenia and Croatia have cemented the break with Belgrade by asserting that they are Central European, not Balkan, countries. Nationalist leaders in largely Catholic Croatia have also emphasised their country's European identity by contrasting their roots in the Western Church with Orthodox Serbia and the Muslim population of Bosnia. While Slobodan Milosevic successfully played on Serbia's distinct identity as part of his nationalist politics throughout the 1990s, Serbian opposition activists – with the support of Western leaders – argued that their country was European and must not be excluded from the broader mental map and political project of the continent. More recently, leaders in the region and beyond have adopted the term 'South-Eastern Europe' to emphasise inclusion in Europe and help overcome the negative connotations of 'the Balkans'.

This discussion illustrates the way in which the collapse of communism and the end of the Cold War has reopened fundamental debates about the identity of Europe, the difficulty of determining where Europe's eastern border lies and the lack of consensus on where we should locate borders between regions (or subregions) within Europe. While Samuel Huntington's prediction of a clash of civilisations along the faultlines between Europe's Western, Slavic and Muslim cultures may be superficially appealing as a way of understanding the new international politics of postcommunist Europe, the above analysis suggests that regional and national identities are not immutable givens which inevitably generate conflict but rather much more fluid, overlapping expressions of community.[4] Thus the transitions of the postcommunist states have been accompanied by ongoing shifts in national, regional and international identities, and it does not appear likely that these identity debates will settle down in the foreseeable future.

These debates also show that international political and security issues in postcommunist Europe are inseparable from questions of identity. During the 1990s the psychological shift from Eastern to Central Europe became closely intertwined with the eastward enlargement of NATO and the EU. Russia's postcommunist foreign policy – torn between cooperation with the West and the assertion of distinctive national interests and policies – reflects a broader debate about Russian national identity and the country's place in the world. The dynamics of Yugoslav disintegration similarly cannot be understood without reference to the uses and abuses of national identity by political leaders. As NATO and EU enlargement has moved from discussion to reality since the mid 1990s, further, the debate on what constitutes Europe has gained a new salience and substance. As William Wallace reminds us, 'Geopoliticians need not be too concerned with defining exact boundaries within an international system marked by spheres of influence, heartlands and border regions. Institutionalisation however requires hard decisions'.[5]

Thus the location of the boundary between a core defined by the EU and NATO and a periphery of those states remaining outside these organisations, and the consequences of exclusion from core Europe, has become one of the key issues of the continent's post-Cold War international politics.

This book focuses on the postcommunist states which are affected most directly by European developments, in particular the enlargement of the EU and NATO: the Visegrad (the Czech Republic, Hungary, Poland and Slovakia) and Baltic states; Romania and Bulgaria; the former Yugoslavia republics and Albania; and Russia, Ukraine, Belarus and Moldova. In contrast, while the Caucasian (Armenia, Azerbaijan and Georgia) and Central Asian states (Kazakhstan, Kyrgyzstan, Tajikistan, Turkmenistan and Uzbekistan) are members of the OSCE (and in the case of the three Caucasian states the Council of Europe), their history is very different from that of the other postcommunist states, their role in European politics is at best peripheral and they are affected less directly by the processes of EU and NATO enlargement. The eastern half of Europe, however, is likely to remain an area where issues of European, regional and national identity and boundaries remain both blurred and contentious.

Rethinking security

Defining what is meant by security and understanding how security is best achieved are problematic. The exigencies of the Cold War, following the experiences of the Second World War, tended to promote concepts of security which focused on maintaining the territorial integrity, political independence and value systems of states through the manipulation of power and force. Security was largely conceived in terms of zero-sum bargaining relationships and discussed in the language of balance of power, alliances, deterrence and defence. Such thinking reflected a realist or neorealist theoretical model of international relations, with its assumption of self-interested states competing for power in an environment defined by international anarchy. From the 1970s, however, a fundamental debate about the security agenda emerged, calling into question the orthodox understanding of security and how it may best be achieved.

Three strands in this debate on security may be identified. First, arguments were made for moving away from the orthodox confrontational approach to security towards the pursuit of security through cooperation with potential rivals or enemies – what became defined as common security, cooperative security or security regimes. More radically, observers argued that it was possible to go further and establish security communities in regions where cooperation has developed to such an extent that war has become inconceivable. The political reconstruction of a previously war-prone Western Europe after 1945 provided the primary example of just such a community. Subsequent academic analysis has sought to explain the circumstances and factors which facilitate the development of security regimes and security communities, such as the relative balance between offensive and defensive military technology, the extent of military transparency and the role of institutions in security cooperation, and the impact of international interdependence and the role of common values as a basis for cooperation.[6]

The second strand in the debate has revolved around how far one should broaden the concept of security beyond primarily political-military issues to include a wider range of potential threats and challenges to human security. Advocates of a broader definition of security argue that economic inequality or instability, environmental degradation, mass migration, organised crime and other non-military problems can represent serious threats to the security of societies and individuals and may pose fundamental challenges to the institutional capacity and sometimes even survival of states. These 'soft', non-military issues, furthermore, can be just as difficult to deal with as 'hard', political-military security threats.

The third strand relates to the shift away from a state-centric conception of security to thinking about security in terms of the welfare of individual human beings and societies. It is argued that, in many parts of the world, states do not function effectively in terms of providing the basic political order and economic welfare necessary for human security, and may even constitute the main threats to individuals' security, for example through serious human rights abuses and oppression of minorities:

> The doctrines of national sovereignty and national security become a
> justification for the use of state institutions against political opposition:
> citizenship paradoxically becomes a source of insecurity, and the claims
> of citizenship become the justification of violence … This dynamic of
> state formation and the reciprocal relationship of threat and insecurity
> between regimes and citizens are difficult to accommodate within the
> statist assumptions of neorealism.[7]

While generating much new thinking about international relations these attempts to deepen and broaden our understanding of security have proved contentious. There is no consensus on the circumstances or factors that make the establishment of common security or security communities possible, or on how far policies to bring them about can replace more traditional approaches to statecraft. The counter-argument to broadening the security agenda is that it produces conceptual confusion and risks making security a catch-all concept embracing almost all of humanity's problems with no clear analytical focus: 'If security is specified in terms of threats to all acquired values of a state, it becomes almost synonymous with national welfare or national interest and is virtually useless for distinguishing among policy objectives.'[8] Debate has centred on whether non-military problems should be considered as security problems *per se* or primarily as causes of more traditional security problems such as violent conflict. Finally, while there may be a case for a less state-centric approach to security, critics point out that states remain the primary basis for national and international political order, while individual and societal security again risk extending the concept of security to almost all problems faced by people.

More recently, attention has focused on securitisation, the process by which particular issues are 'taken out of the sphere of everyday politics' by particular groups of people, particularly state elites, and defined as security problems or 'presented as an existential threat … justifying actions outside the normal bounds of political procedure'.[9] This idea highlights the point that security is not something that can be objectively defined but is rather a subjective, essentially contested concept dependent on the perceptions of the actors involved. Securitisation also suggests that the definition of an issue as a security problem or threat involves social and political action – a decision (whether conscious or not, explicit or not) to define that issue as a security problem or threat.

These theoretical debates on security have relevance for postcommunist Europe in several ways. The challenge to the traditional balance-of-power approach by those favouring common or cooperative security resonates strongly with the debate over emerging patterns of international relations in a Europe formerly divided between East and West, and over which institutions should be charged with building security; it also lies at the heart of the evolving relationship between post-Soviet Russia and the West. The enormous problems of economic dislocation, environmental degradation, transnational organised crime and mass migration facing countries in the region raise questions about how far these should be considered security threats and, consequently, about the means which should be employed to combat them. The problems of establishing and maintaining effective state and governmental structures, the mismatch between state and (ethnic) nation borders, and the authoritarianism and human rights abuses in some states suggest that debates over state, societal and individual security are also acutely relevant for postcommunist Europe. These issues are discussed in more detail in the rest of this chapter.

Searching for security: beyond the balance of power

Despite the end of the Cold War, traditional security concerns over states' territorial integrity and political independence remain very much alive in the countries of postcommunist Europe. The elites of the majority of these states – from the Baltic states in the north, through the Visegrad states in Central Europe, to Bulgaria and Romania in the south and Ukraine and Moldova in the east – believe that Russia represents at least a potential threat to their countries' security and independence. Russian attempts, albeit inconsistent and with limited success, to maintain a dominant role in the former Soviet space have fuelled these perceptions. The Russian political establishment believes that NATO poses a similar potential threat to Russia's security and political influence, and that the Atlantic Alliance's eastward enlargement and intervention in the former Yugoslavia reflect its aggressive potential and intentions, as Viktor Kremenyuk shows with great clarity in chapter 6 of this book. These perceptions are shared by political elites in some of the postcommunist countries, notably by Belarusian President Alexander Lukashenka. Though less prominent or immediate, there are also residual concerns about German power and influence in the region (Germany's role in the region is examined by Vladimir Handl, Kerry Longhurst and Marcin Zaborowski in chapter 4 of this volume). Many states remain wary of potential conflicts with, or territorial claims by, their neighbours. The Yugoslav wars have indicated that conflicts over state sovereignty, borders and ethnic minorities remain a real possibility in at least parts of postcommunist Europe.

In the late 1980s and early 1990s significant progress was made in overcoming the legacy of confrontation and establishing pan-European common or cooperative security. This new security framework had its roots in the Gorbachev era and was based on political dialogue, arms control and disarmament initiatives, a switch in the offensive–defensive balance towards the latter and efforts to build institutions to underpin cooperation. This new approach reflected a clear effort to use cooperation, partnership and transparency as a means of overcoming the traditional security dilemma whereby uncertainty about other states' intentions and capabilities drives competition for power. Key milestones included the 1986 CSBM document which emerged from the Stockholm Conference; the 1987 Intermediate-range Nuclear Forces (INF) Treaty; the 1990 Conventional Armed Forces in Europe (CFE) Treaty and Conference on Security and Cooperation in Europe (CSCE) Charter of Paris for a New Europe; and the 1991 US–Soviet Strategic Arms Reduction Treaty (START I).

Since the early 1990s this East–West common security agenda has been entrenched and strengthened in some ways, undermined or come under threat in others and, arguably, rendered redundant in yet others. The INF, CFE and START agreements have been largely implemented and, in some cases, built upon; for example, through the separate withdrawal of short-range land-based nuclear weapons from Europe; the 1993 START II agreement; the decision by Belarus, Kazakhstan and Ukraine to give up the nuclear weapons they inherited from the Soviet Union; and further reductions in conventional forces under 1999 modifications to the CFE Treaty. Disputes between Russia and the West over NATO enlargement, intervention in the former Yugoslavia and US plans for a National Missile Defence System have, however, threatened to undermine the progress achieved to date – although the threat has so far not been translated into a withdrawal from key agreements. At the same time, new security challenges have emerged – in particular, the conflict in the former Yugoslavia – to which this East–West cooperative security agenda has been able to provide few, if any, answers.

After the revolutions of 1989 some felt that the time had come to go a step further and establish a pan-European security system. Such a system, it was argued, would overcome the continent's Cold War division, integrate the countries of postcommunist Europe – including Russia – into the new Europe, prevent the re-emergence of traditional balance-of-power dynamics and allow new security problems to be addressed collectively. Given the breadth of its membership and its record as a security-building forum, the CSCE provided the obvious institutional framework within which to implement such a vision. Its November 1990 Paris summit affirmed that international cooperation, respect for existing borders and democracy constituted the basic principles of relations in the new Europe and put in place a modest set of CSCE institutions. More radical ideas for a CSCE Security Council, security guarantees and peacekeeping forces were, however, rejected. Whether these ideas could or should have been acted upon, and whether such a framework might still form the basis of an alternative European security system, remain contentious.

A series of events between 1989 and 1991 – the growing backlash by Soviet hardliners against Gorbachev's reforms culminating in the August 1991 coup attempt in Moscow, the use of force by the Soviet military in the Baltic republics in January 1991 and the outbreak of war in Yugoslavia in the summer of that year – led to growing security concerns in the region. The majority of governments – led by the Visegrad states and followed by Romania, Bulgaria, the Baltic states and Slovenia – concluded that only integration with the core Western institutions of NATO and the then European Community could provide their countries with security. The limitations of the CSCE were sharply illustrated by its failure to respond effectively to the Soviet army's action in the Baltics and the war in Yugoslavia.

The West responded to growing pressure from these countries with a series of incremental steps designed gradually to open up Western institutions. In 1991 NATO's North Atlantic Cooperation Council (which later

became the Euro-Atlantic Partnership Council) established an initial
dialogue with the postcommunist states. The Partnership for Peace (put in
place in 1994) offered more substantive cooperation with NATO to all postcommunist European states on the basis of differentiated individual relationships with the Alliance. The EU's Association Agreements with the
Visegrad four, the Baltic states, Bulgaria, Romania and Slovenia, opened up
the longer-term prospect of EU membership for these countries and were
accompanied by EU Partnership and Cooperation Agreements (PCAs) with
Russia and other former Soviet republics and the Western European
Union's own outreach arrangements. These measures, however, failed to
satisfy the Central European states, which stepped up their claims to full
membership of both NATO and the EU. By the mid 1990s the stage was set
for debates over the eastward enlargement of these organisations.

In 1997 both NATO and the EU took their first decisive steps towards
enlargement. Despite vehement opposition from Russia, NATO invited the
Czech Republic, Hungary and Poland to join the Alliance while committing itself to an 'open door' to further enlargement (the three Central
European countries formally joined the Alliance in March 1999). The
dynamics behind NATO enlargement are discussed further by Stuart
Croft's in chapter 2 of this book. The EU agreed to open membership
negotiations with the Czech Republic, Estonia, Hungary, Poland and
Slovenia; has since initiated membership negotiations with Bulgaria,
Latvia, Lithuania, Romania and Slovakia; and sponsored the Stability Pact
for the countries of South-Eastern Europe. Parallel to this, both NATO and
the EU adopted measures to deepen their relations with the major countries outside the circle of prospective members, namely Russia (through
the NATO–Russia Founding Act and the EU–Russia PCA) and Ukraine. At
the time of writing the questions of which countries will join the EU, and
whether and how far NATO will enlarge further, remain both uncertain
and controversial. The events of the 1990s have, however, made clear that
post-Cold War European politics and security are increasingly being
shaped by the eastward enlargement of NATO and the EU and the
resulting dynamics of 'inclusion' and 'exclusion'.

Behind enlargement is a larger debate about the very definition of
Europe. Here, the concept of a security community has relevance. Emanuel
Adler, developing Karl Deutsch's influential ideas from a couple of generations ago, defines a security community as an entity which preserves the
legal independence of component states while integrating them and fostering a sense of community, together with strong institutions and practices, to
a point where they have 'dependable expectations of peaceful change'.
Adler argues that the central element of a security community is 'legitimacy
... based on collective identity'.[10] Such collective identities are socially

constructed by institutions and individual agents, facilitated by communication (through trade, migration, tourism, cultural and educational
exchanges as well as through more traditional state-to-state activities such as
diplomacy and arms control negotiations) and the existence of a 'core of
power' that attracts weaker states, and then internalised by the elites of the
states that make up the community.[11]

In the context of post-Cold War Europe it increasingly appears that the
EU and NATO form the 'core of power' around which an enlarged security
community based on a new concept of European identity is emerging.
Those postcommunist countries with a realistic prospect of membership of
the EU and/or NATO are becoming part of this security community, while
Russia and most of the Soviet successor states remain firmly on the periphery of, or even outside, this community. The close institutional and functional ties that are developing and deepening between current and future
EU and NATO members will probably reinforce this sense of collective
identity. In contrast Russia does not accept the legitimacy of a European
security community with a powerful NATO as one of its core institutions.
While predictions of a new Cold War have proved exaggerated, Russia's
opposition to NATO enlargement and intervention in Kosovo, and its calls
for a 'multipolar' world in opposition to US 'hegemony', suggest that its
attitude to the enlarging European security community is likely to remain
ambivalent at best, and hostile at worst. Thus the limits of the eastwards
expansion of the security community and relations between the enlarging
'Europe' of EU/NATO and Russia and other 'excluded' countries will be
central questions for European security in coming decades. The overall
situation of those states remaining outside the EU and NATO is explored by
Mark Webber in his contribution to this volume (chapter 3), while the
specific dilemmas of Ukraine and Russia are discussed in chapters 5 and 6
by Sergiy Galaka and Viktor Kremenyuk, respectively.

Domestic politics, statehood and 'new' security challenges

As discussed above, the countries of postcommunist Europe also face a wide
range of less traditional security problems stemming from the enormous
challenges posed by political transition, state building and economic
restructuring. Indeed, for most societies and individuals in the region these
problems are at least as urgent, and probably much more so, than traditional political-military security concerns.

All the countries in the region face problems relating to postcommunist
political transition. After decades of one-party communism – preceded by
various forms of feudalism, empire and authoritarianism – they face the challenge of establishing new political institutions (governmental structures,

constitutions, electoral systems and political parties) and developing civil
societies and political cultures to underpin these new institutions. In most of
the countries of postcommunist Europe there has been a broad consensus in
favour of democracy in terms of free elections and representative government, but building stable and effective political systems has proved more difficult. In a few, most notably Belarus and the rump Federal Republic of
Yugoslavia under Slobodan Milosevic (as well as most of the Central Asian
states on the periphery of the region), the transition has so far been marked
by a new form of postcommunist authoritarianism, drawing heavily on the
communist system which preceded it.

Whether these domestic political challenges are correctly understood as
security problems in their own right or have an overt security dimension is a
matter of debate. Domestic politics, however, can be an important factor
shaping states' foreign and security policies. A state's foreign policy is not
simply a response to its international environment but reflects the way in
which that environment is mediated by domestic politics and the outcome
of struggles between competing political parties and other interest groups
(such as state bureaucracies and economic lobbies).[12] Domestic politics has
had a significant impact on the development of foreign policies in postcommunist Europe. The shift in the centre of gravity in Russian politics
away from the Westernisers who were influential in the early 1990s to the
pragmatic nationalists who now hold power has had an important impact
on Russian foreign and security policy. The domestic politics of nationalism
in Serbia and Croatia played a central role in the Yugoslav conflicts.
Differences between eastern and western Ukraine help to explain ambiguities in that country's foreign policy.

At the same time, as Richard Sakwa explores in his contribution to this
book (chapter 8), the external environment can also impact on domestic
politics and the prospects for democracy. The limitations of Western policies in the 1990s arguably undermined the liberals and strengthened the
more statist and nationalist elements within Russia. Serbian and Croatian
nationalism both fed off the external threat posed by the other. Thus the
complex relationship between domestic and international politics must be
factored into any understanding of the region's new security dynamics. We
would push the argument further and suggest that the longer-term development of stable international relations in postcommunist Europe will
depend crucially on the development of internally stable states with political elites capable of cooperating with one another.[13]

Many of the countries of postcommunist Europe also face classical problems of state building, similar to those faced by Third World countries
which have gained independence since 1945.[14] The Soviet and Yugoslav
successor states have faced the problems of establishing new state and

governmental structures, negotiating disputed borders, settling potential conflicts with neighbouring states and ethnic minorities, and 'nation building' (in terms of building the collective identity and social and political capital necessary to sustain the newly independent state). In these circumstances, pessimists might foresee the collapse of political structures, mass migration and dependency on exploitative relations with the developed world, combining to engender a permanent cycle of weak institutions, predatory rule and (occasionally violent) communal conflict. Alternatively, optimists might point to the positive lead provided by the normative structure of international society with its stress on human rights and representative institutions, the emergence of global networks supportive of nascent domestic civil institutions and the role of international institutions in creating structures of domestic governance.[15]

The problems of state building are sometimes described in terms of weak or even failed states, where state structures do not function effectively (or have collapsed entirely), in contrast to internally strong states where effective and representative state structures are underpinned by a high degree of social cohesion. Weak states (such as Bosnia in the 1990s) tend to be vulnerable to both internal conflict and external intervention. Strong states tend to be successful at peacefully managing domestic conflicts and maintaining their international independence (such as West Germany after 1945). The majority of the countries of postcommunist Europe fall somewhere between these extremes. Longer-term stability will depend to a considerable degree on the establishment of reasonably strong – in the sense outlined above, as distinct from strong authoritarian – state structures throughout the region.

Focusing only on central state structures, however, obscures other levels of governance. Through a multiplicity of programmes linked with the EU at its external borders and through regional initiatives (such as the Council of Baltic Sea States, the Black Sea Economic Council, the Barents Euro-Arctic Council and the Central European Initiative) most postcommunist states are already becoming integrated into multilateral governance structures which work above the nation-state level.[16] These structures primarily deal with 'soft' (non-military) security issues, which are perhaps addressed more effectively at a regional level, although there is a link with political-military security in that the economic and environmental legacy of the Cold War features on their agendas. Relations at the subnational level across borders are also developing, mainly via the establishment of Euroregions. Some Russian regions have taken the lead in promoting regional cooperation and engaging directly with the outside world, prompted by the realisation that Moscow can no longer solve all problems of governance. This may be seen as a positive development, although difficulties stemming from uncertainty about the division of authority between the federal and regional levels remain.

Economic insecurity is arguably the single greatest problem facing the majority of people in postcommunist Europe, with a dramatic collapse in economic production and trade in the early 1990s producing large reductions in real incomes and standards of living, and market-oriented economic reforms imposing further hardships. While some countries (most notably the Visegrad and Baltic states) are now showing high economic growth rates and can reasonably expect relative stability in the future, many continue to face massive economic problems. James Sperling's chapter in this volume (chapter 10) explores the security dimension of these problems. Postcommunist political and economic liberalisation has allowed organised crime to become a major factor in the region, often in association with corrupt politicians and economic reform policies. Mass migration also poses a major challenge. The conflicts in the former Yugoslavia and the Caucasus have produced hundreds of thousands of refugees, imposing additional economic and political burdens on these countries and their neighbours. Though less dramatic in scale, other countries in the region also face the problem of illegal westward migration in search of jobs and prosperity. Environmental security is also part of this picture: the extensive industrial and military-related production of the communist period has left a legacy of environmental hot spots across the region, endangering the health of many people and requiring large clean-up costs and resources for investment in new technologies.

The question of economic security, and how and to what extent it is achievable, is complex. In the contemporary market economy, characterised by risk and uncertainty, a state's ability to control long-term structural factors affecting economic performance is limited.[17] This is particularly the case for the relatively weak postcommunist transition economies. Furthermore, the state's authority in the economic sphere is much harder to define than in the military or political spheres. Deciding when economic problems become a threat to national security, and how to deal with them without closing off avenues of economic transaction and thereby jeopardising prospects for growth, is a difficult task.

How far it is appropriate to define these non-military problems as security issues remains contentious. There may be dangers in importing the dynamics of traditional security thinking into other areas. Defining a problem as a (national) security issue pushes it up the political agenda and may thereby be a means of mobilising political support to address it, but risks adverse consequences in the longer term. Migration, for example, has frequently become associated with crime, and fears about waves of immigrants from the East have been stirred up by politicians and media (both in Western and postcommunist countries) for their own ends; whereas the actual scale of the problem is limited and the potential benefits of free movement of people and labour are often overlooked.[18] At minimum, however, as Mark Galeotti argues in this volume in chapter 9, these non-military issues add further dimensions to the already complex nexus between security, political transition and state building in postcommunist Europe.

New conflicts, new responses

With the Yugoslav wars of the 1990s postcommunist Europe has become one of the main foci of a wider debate about how the international community (itself a problematic concept) should respond to major conflicts within states. There is a growing trend towards intra-state, rather than inter-state, conflict. Such conflicts have multiple underlying causes (necessitating multi-variant responses), are often 'intermestic' (blurring the boundary between international and domestic conflict), are internationalised (through media coverage, their wider international repercussions and the involvement of aid agencies) and usually trigger significant political – and sometimes military – intervention by external powers. In this context, the international community's intervention in Bosnia and Kosovo, and in particular NATO's part in it, has proved highly controversial and has arguably set very important precedents.

The concept of sovereignty is at the heart of these debates. Since the Second World War, and especially since the end of the Cold War, there has been growing acceptance in the West that state sovereignty is not absolute and that states can be subjected to certain fundamental legal obligations relating not only to their international behaviour but also to their domestic behaviour:

> where once legitimacy in international society required primarily the ability to demonstrate control over a specified territorial area and to perform certain limited international obligations, international legitimacy today is coming increasingly to involve considerations that were once deemed to be entirely matters of domestic concern for states, considerations that may be summed up by the term 'good governance': a set of norms embracing democracy, human rights, the rule of law and deregulated economies ... any state participating in or aspiring to participate in the international politico/economic order encounters pressures to internalise the norms, institutions and practices that are now believed to characterize the fully legitimate state.[19]

Developments in international human rights law, together with the laws of war, laws governing war crimes and international environmental law, form part of an emerging framework that increasingly constrains states' internal behaviour. In the European context, the various OSCE agreements (although politically rather than legally binding) are a powerful statement of commitment to democracy and human rights and acknowledgement that states' domestic behaviour is a matter of legitimate international concern. Emerging human rights regimes and law, however, 'sit uneasily with the idea of accepting state sovereignty alone as the sole principle for the organization of relations within and between political communities', and the tensions between the two are very far from being resolved.[20]

It is against this background that the wars in the Balkans and the former Soviet Union have unfolded, raising fundamental questions about how the international community should respond to conflicts occurring primarily within states. Building on the principles laid down in its documents, the OSCE has led the way in developing what may be termed 'soft' political intervention. It has monitored and reported on elections across the region. In an effort to prevent and resolve conflicts it has also deployed a series of semi-permanent missions to regions of tension (from the Baltic states to Macedonia, from Crimea to Chechnya) and established a High Commissioner on National Minorities mandated to address ethnic conflicts. While these innovative practices have arguably had a number of quiet successes, they also have significant limitations, in particular their dependence on the cooperation of the state(s) concerned and the OSCE's inability to enforce or impose any decisions on recalcitrant parties.

The conflicts in Bosnia and Kosovo posed the dilemmas of intervention in their most acute form. Since 1945, United Nations (UN) military intervention in internal conflicts has most commonly taken place with the agreement of the government of the state concerned, with a direct mandate from the UN Security Council and on the basis of peacekeeping (usually to help implement an already agreed settlement) rather than to impose peace by force of arms. In Bosnia and Kosovo these conditions did not apply. In Bosnia, a (primarily European) UN peacekeeping force was deployed with the consent of the recognised government of Bosnia and a Security Council mandate, but in a situation where no peace existed. From 1992 to 1995 war raged in Bosnia, atrocities were committed, UN peacekeepers were humiliated and the international community appeared impotent. Bosnia provoked heartfelt debate about whether the international community should intervene more forcefully to impose a settlement, whether the UN, NATO or other organisations should act, what mandate was required, and the utility of airstrikes and ground forces. In 1995 the combination of NATO airstrikes (under a broadly interpreted Security Council mandate), the strengthening of Croatian and Bosnian government armed forces *vis-à-vis* their Bosnian Serb enemies and US-led diplomacy produced a peace settlement. These events set significant precedents in terms of forceful intervention by a military organisation in an internal conflict in Europe.

NATO's intervention in Kosovo proved even more controversial. By early 1999 violence was escalating in Kosovo, with the Kosovo Liberation Army engaged in low-level guerrilla warfare and Yugoslav forces attacking the province's primarily Albanian population. Following the failure of the Rambouillet peace talks, on 24 March NATO launched airstrikes against Yugoslavia. These continued, accompanied by a growing debate about a possible ground invasion if air power failed to force President Milosevic to back down, until June when a peace settlement was agreed. NATO leaders argued that they had acted – after all alternatives had been exhausted – to prevent a humanitarian disaster and further destabilisation of the region. NATO's action was internationally legal, they argued, because Yugoslavia had violated 1998 UN Security Council resolutions calling for dialogue between Belgrade and the Kosovar Albanians and the withdrawal of Serb forces; those forces were inflicting further violence and Milosevic had rejected an ultimatum to sign the Rambouillet peace agreement. Some international legal experts also argued that non-intervention would entail non-observance of obligations imposed by the 1948 Convention Against Genocide and the 1949 Geneva Convention on the Laws of War that can override the need to preserve the sovereignty and territorial integrity of governments committing such crimes. The majority of postcommunist European states aspiring to membership of NATO and the EU supported the Alliance's action, though not without reservations.

Russia placed a sharply different interpretation on events, arguing that NATO had fundamentally breached international law since it had forcefully intervened in the internal affairs of a sovereign state and done so without a Security Council mandate (as required by the UN Charter). According to Moscow, NATO had violated other international agreements on cooperation between the UN and regional organisations on maintaining peace and international security, a 1974 General Assembly resolution defining aggression against sovereign states, OSCE principles and even NATO's own founding document, the North Atlantic Treaty. Russia's position was backed unconditionally by Belarus, reflected concerns in the Ukrainian political establishment and received support from China, India and other influential non-European countries. These differing interpretations of the Kosovo war contributed to a growing polarisation of views between the NATO powers, especially the US, and Russia.

The Kosovo conflict sent shock waves throughout Europe and beyond. NATO had intervened by force in the internal affairs of a sovereign state without an explicit mandate from the UN Security Council – a dramatic break with previous international practice. NATO's new strategic concept, adopted in April 1999 during the Kosovo war, affirmed the Alliance's willingness 'to engage actively in crisis management, including crisis response operations' without specific reference to any requirement for UN Security Council authorisation.[21] Supporters of humanitarian intervention argue that state sovereignty should no longer be an obstacle to international action to avert massive humanitarian crises and terrible internal conflicts. Given that Russia and China – mindful of their own problems with internal secession movements – would undoubtedly have vetoed any Security Council resolution explicitly authorising the use of force in Kosovo and would in all probability do likewise in similar situations where the use of force might be viewed as morally justified, it may also be argued that the absence of a UN Security Council mandate should not in all circumstances preclude humanitarian military intervention.

The counter-argument is that humanitarian intervention without a specific Security Council mandate is a violation of the core international legal principle of state sovereignty and of the UN Charter, and sets a potentially dangerous precedent for less benign intervention by major powers, coalitions and alliances in the internal affairs of other states. Indeed, Moscow has argued that NATO's action was far from benign and motivated more by traditional power concerns than humanitarianism. There is a widespread perception in the Russian political establishment that humanitarian principles and collective security are being used as a cover for the enforcement of NATO's interests by Alliance firepower. Russia, China, India and other states from outside the region fear that the precedent set in Kosovo could be used against them by the US and its allies in places such as Chechnya, Tibet and Kashmir.

The questions raised by Kosovo, in particular the balance between state sovereignty and intervention in cases where contemporary international norms are breached, are still being digested.[22] Massive violations of basic human rights are regarded by an increasing number of states as impermissible, but the issues of under what circumstances intervention may be justified, who has the right to intervene and what form that intervention should take remain extremely controversial. There are lacunae in contemporary international law where the principle of state sovereignty and the regulation of humanitarian intervention are concerned. Some argue that it is now necessary to change international law to reflect the growing support for humanitarian intervention; for example, by incorporating in the UN Charter an explicit right to intervention in extreme circumstances and limiting the veto power of the five permanent members of the Security Council. Whatever their merits, however, such changes are unlikely in the foreseeable future. In the meantime, as Dov Lynch illustrates in chapter 7 of this volume, postcommunist Europe and Eurasia remain key areas of the world where the tension between the principles of state sovereignty and intervention may be worked out in practice.

Conclusion

The first postcommunist decade witnessed a rapid transformation of the European political system and generated a massive and complex new security agenda. After 1989, Western Europe, preoccupied with its own grand project of union, was suddenly confronted with the problems brought about by the collapse of the political, economic and security order of the continent's eastern half and by demands from the postcommunist states and peoples for support in addressing their security problems.

In the shadow of the Cold War, traditional political-military security challenges – the disengagement of the former Warsaw Pact states from Soviet influence, the entrenchment of arms control, disarmament and confidence-building processes, and the management of conflicts arising from the break-up of the Soviet Union and Yugoslavia – have remained important. Here, the reinvention of NATO as an organisation concerned not just with the defence of its members against external threats but also with 'security and stability throughout the Euro-Atlantic area' has been the key development.[23] Since the early 1990s, however, attention has also turned to less traditional challenges to the security of individuals, societies and states. In particular, economic weakness or failure has been a major problem across postcommunist Europe. Economic problems not only pose major challenges to the individual security of people throughout the region, but also undermine political stability and exacerbate other problems such as environmental degradation, organised crime and migration. Against this background the EU, with its promise of economic and social stability, has begun to play a major role in addressing these non-traditional security challenges.

The EU and NATO, therefore, have taken on the central role in addressing the security challenges of postcommunist Europe. While these two core institutions have begun the process of integrating the weak states of postcommunist Europe into a new political order, however, there has been no clear strategic plan for the region as a whole. Despite proclamations of a new European security architecture at the beginning of the decade, the 1990s was characterised by the incremental development of a new political and security order, competing visions of what that order should look like and which institutions should play the leading role within it, and a mismatch between declared goals and the political commitment and material resources available to achieve those goals.

Part of the problem resides in the nature of the institutions themselves. If the EU is a prototype of some form of transnational or 'post-sovereign' European political system, with multiple levels of governance, then the postcommunist states must be integrated accordingly. Given the long-term nature of the development of the Western European community, this process is likely to take generations and will entail a radically new way of thinking about problems of political order in the postcommunist states. Where the borders of the 'post-sovereign' system are located, the nature of those borders and what lies on the other side are all highly contentious questions in a region in which ideas of state, nation and society are still being formed or rethought.

The role of NATO as an 'exporter of stability' is even more contentious. As Stuart Croft argues in this book (chapter 2), while NATO enlargement may not have been designed to change the balance of power in Europe, the Russian political establishment remains deeply wary of NATO's intentions and perceives the Alliance's enlargement in balance-of-power terms. NATO's intervention in Kosovo raised even more sensitive questions about who has the authority and legitimacy to intervene in internal conflicts. The differences between NATO and its aspiring members on the one hand and Russia and other non-Western states on the other over Kosovo, further- more, reflect deeper tensions over fundamental questions of European and international order, in particular over the extent to which the terms of the post-Cold War international order are being determined – even dictated – by the West.

In the absence of an overarching security system covering the whole of the European continent, the roles of the principal institutions – NATO, the OSCE and the EU (particularly in view of recent steps towards a Common European Security and Defence Policy (CESDP)) – and their relationship to each other are still very much a matter of debate. It is generally accepted that the EU is the institution best suited to managing many of the economic and social challenges which constitute the new European security agenda. By enlarging into Central and Eastern Europe while also assuming greater responsibility for its defence and military security through CESDP, the EU may also be better placed to develop a more coherent set of policies linking hard and soft security. Eastward enlargement to include many of the coun- tries of Central and Eastern Europe over the next decade, however, may intensify concerns about exclusion from the new Europe among those countries remaining outside, not least Russia, possibly even generating more traditional security problems. The fact that the economic interests of Russia and the other states likely to remain outside the EU are now closely bound up with the Union may encourage the maintenance of cooperative relations, but it may also exacerbate some of the problems of exclusion.

As Adrian Hyde-Price argues in the conclusion to this book (chapter 11), however, developing a wider European security community extending beyond the future borders of the EU and NATO is likely to be difficult. The development of such a community will require the development not only of closer institutional and functional ties between an enlarged EU/NATO and its eastern neighbours, but also common approaches to crucial questions such as the balance between state sovereignty and the international community's right to intervene (whether in terms of monitoring and encouraging democracy, respect for human rights and good governance or in terms of military intervention in violent conflicts).

Engaging those states on Europe's new eastern periphery is thus a key challenge, particularly in the case of Russia. The failure of Russian elites to understand or accept certain trends in Western security politics and develop policies to engage with them mirrors the failure of Western policy makers to develop a coherent vision of the future international order and engage conceptually with Russian security concerns. Thus Russian foreign policy is shaped by an uneasy balance between the rhetoric of collective security – pursued through the OSCE, with a grudging acknowledgement of the role played by NATO – and balance-of-power realpolitik.[24] It remains for Russia and its European partners to develop the underlying basis of common perspectives necessary for stable, long-term cooperation.

While there is growing recognition that economic stability is vital to long-term security in postcommunist Europe, the political economy/security relationship remains poorly understood in the context of the transition economies. As James Sperling argues in this book (chapter 10), the acknowledgement of economic security as a policy problem suggests that issues of political economy must be treated as elements of the new security architecture and not simply as traditional economic problems subject to the simple calculus of welfare maximisation with little relevance to issues of war and peace. A closer examination of the formation of social capital, formal and informal economic institutions and good governance in the transition economies is vital in the security context. This is part of what other commentators have identified as a wider global phenomenon – a move away from 'a once hegemonic neoliberal discourse' towards 'a visible awareness among policy communities of a need for a new "development paradigm" that is more reflective of the centrality of politics in global and domestic processes of economic change'.[25]

This chapter has placed due emphasis on the importance of the dual enlargement of NATO and the EU for future security relations in Europe. We should, however, equally emphasise the danger of limitations stemming from 'the reluctance of most international relations scholars to examine the regional international relations of Europe in much detail, and the predisposition of most students of European integration to start from Brussels and work outwards, rather than start from the changing European context and work in'.[26] Close study, both on the scholarly and policy levels, of regional relations in postcommunist Europe – in other words, 'working in' – is vital to understanding the landscape of the emerging European system, the links between the international and the domestic, and the sources of security policy in the countries concerned. Nor should this be limited to the study of political elites in the capitals, who by their nature may be too preoccupied with national security issues; it is becoming increasingly important to consider subnational and transnational elites and non-governmental, civil society actors.

The question of borders, and their potential impact on regional and sub-regional security relations, is a central aspect of this new agenda. The problems posed by tighter controls on the EU's external borders stemming from the Schengen Agreement are likely to increase with enlargement. The effect on local economies as a result of more restrictive regimes, and uncertainties about visa arrangements – prompting fears of the return of the kind of restrictions imposed on cross-border travel by the 'iron curtain' – have featured in recent scholarly and policy-related research. Balanced against this are the arguments that in practice borders in postcommunist Europe are increasingly defined by a 'fuzzy logic' of looser, overlapping identities and that open borders may be a necessary condition for a free, pluralistic society.[27] Thus a recent study by academics and officials of the European Commission concluded that a 'fortress Europe' approach undermines the broader foreign policy role of the EU and will not work in practice. It suggested that an enlarged EU will need to show greater willingness to engage with eastern neighbours in support of their economic development, administrative reform and political stability; show greater sensitivity to the existing economic and cultural links between the new member states and their eastern neighbours; and adopt a more flexible visa regime as part of a comprehensive immigration policy, so that the burden of managing the EU's eastern border is not left to the new member states alone.[28] The future stability of the periphery, and consequently the security of postcommunist Europe as a whole, will depend on the successful management of these problems.

Notes

1 The literature on this subject is vast. A useful source describing these trends is K. Holsti, 'Scholarship in an era of anxiety: the study of international politics during the Cold War', *Review of International Studies*, 24: special issue (1998), 17–46.

2 G. Schopflin and N. Wood (eds.), *In Search of Central Europe* (Oxford, Polity Press, 1989); and T. Garton Ash, *The Uses of Adversity: Essays on the Fate of Central Europe*, rev. edn. (London, Granta/Penguin, 1991).

3 This was the primary motivation behind the establishment of the Polish–Czechoslovak–Hungarian 'Visegrad group' in the early 1990s. See 'Text of the Visegrad Summit Declaration', *Report on Eastern Europe*, 2:9 (1991), 31–2.

4 S. P. Huntington, 'The clash of civilizations', *Foreign Affairs*, 72:3 (1993), 22–49.

5 W. Wallace, 'Europe after the Cold War: interstate order or post-sovereign regional system?', *Review of International Studies*, 25: special issue (1999), 213.

6 R. Jervis, 'Security regimes', *International Organization*, 36:2 (1982), 357–8; and L. Reychler, 'A pan-European security community: utopia or realistic perspective?', *Disarmament*, XIV:1 (1991), 42–52.

7 K. Krause and M. C. Williams, 'From strategy to security: foundations of critical security studies', in K. Krause and M. C. Williams (eds.), *Critical Security Studies* (Minneapolis, University of Minnesota Press, 1997), pp. 44–5.

8 D. Baldwin, 'The concept of security', *Review of International Studies*, 23 (1997), 17–18.

9 K. Krause, 'Theorizing security, state formation and the "Third World" in the post-Cold War world', *Review of International Studies*, 24:1 (1998), 134.

10 E. Adler, 'Condition(s) of peace', *Review of International Studies*, 24: special issue (1998), 167 and 184.

11 Adler, 'Condition(s) of peace', 180.

12 B. Buzan, *People, States and Fear: An Agenda for International Security Studies in the Post-Cold War Era* (London, Harvester Wheatsheaf, 1991), p. 348.

13 Buzan, *People, States and Fear*, p. 360.

14 M. Ayoob, *The Third World Security Predicament: State Making, Regional Conflict and the International System* (Boulder, CO, Lynne Rienner, 1995).

15 Krause, 'Theorizing security', 132.

16 On the role of the regional (or subregional) initiatives see A. Cottey (ed.), *Subregional Cooperation in the New Europe: Building Security, Prosperity and Solidarity from the Barents to the Black Sea* (Houndmills, Macmillan/EastWest Institute, 1999); and A. Cottey, 'Europe's new subregionalism', *Journal of Strategic Studies*, 23:2 (2000), 23–47.

17 Buzan, *People, States and Fear*, p. 124.

18 G. Amato and J. Batt, *The Long-Term Implications of EU Enlargement: The Nature of the New Border (Final Report of the Reflection Group)* (Florence, Robert Schuman Centre for Advanced Studies, 1999), pp. 52–6.

19 D. Armstrong, 'Law, justice and the idea of a world society', *International Affairs*, 75:3 (1999), 560.

20 D. Held and A. McGrew, 'The end of the old order? Globalization and the prospects for world order', *Review of International Studies*, 24: special issue (1998), 234.

21 'The Alliance's Strategic Concept, approved by the Heads of State and Government participating in the meeting of the North Atlantic Council in Washington D.C. on 23rd and 24th April 1999', *NATO Review*, 2 (1999,) para. 10.

22 See O. Bring, 'Should NATO take the lead in formulating a doctrine of humanitarian intervention?', *NATO Review*, 3 (1999), 24–7; and N. Chomsky, 'Now it's a free for all', *The Guardian* (17 May 1999).

23 'The Alliance's Strategic Concept', para. 33.

24 On the continuing arguments for collective security see M. Shelepin, 'Equal security for OSCE countries', *International Affairs (Moscow)*, 46:3 (2000), 170–82.

25 R. Higgott and N. Phillips, 'Challenging triumphalism and convergence: the limits of global liberalization in Asia and Latin America', *Review of International Studies*, 26:3 (2000), 370–1.
26 Wallace, 'Europe after the Cold War', 201–2.
27 E. Bort, *Illegal Migration and Cross-Border Crime: Challenges at the Eastern Frontier of the European Union*, EU Working Paper No. RSC 2000/9 (Florence, Robert Schuman Centre for Advanced Studies, 2000), p. 20.
28 Amato and Batt, *The Long-Term Implications of EU Enlargement*.

2
Rethinking the record of NATO enlargement

Stuart Croft

The debate over the enlargement of the North Atlantic Treaty Organisation (NATO) has been extraordinary. Within a period of five years the Alliance moved from a clear position of rejecting the expansion of its membership to a policy that could best be described as 'open door minus Russia'. How could this have happened? Clearly, had there been a massive external shock – akin to the Berlin blockade perhaps, or to the outbreak of the Korean War – one could see how such change could have been brought about. But no such shock occurred. Russia fought poorly in an internal conflict within its borders, and the lesson of the Chechen conflict was that the Red Army could not pose any kind of serious threat to the rest of Europe, even should its political leaders have wanted to. The shock to the European security system of the 1990s – the violent and bloody collapse of the former Yugoslavia – could not really be used as an explanation of such dramatic policy change on the part of NATO.

Conventional explanations are simply not sufficient to explain why NATO has embarked upon a process of enlargement. Simply put, one can discern three types of explanation in the Western literature. These relate to the dangers of a Russian threat, the possibilities of spreading stability, and to the value of binding the United States further into European security structures.[1]

The first argument suggests that enlargement is a strategic response to possible adverse developments to the east of the Alliance. Should Russia re-emerge as a threat – due to the shallowness of the democratic process in that country – it would be best to acquire as many allies as possible now and to deny Russia strategic depth by a process of moving the Alliance eastwards. Russia may threaten again, so the argument suggests that Moscow's current vulnerability must be exploited.[2] This would certainly stop pressure from Moscow leading to the re-emergence of communist governments in the region; at the very least, in 'old-speak' it would prevent the Finlandisation of Central Europe.

The second set of arguments concerns democratisation and marketisation in Central and Eastern Europe. In the same way that the Washington Treaty provided the security backdrop for democratisation in West Germany (and Italy and France) and for the economic miracle of the

1950s, so a similar guarantee was needed to ensure the same for Central Europe. As US Secretary of State in the second Clinton administration, Madeleine Albright, put it:

> Now the new NATO can do for Europe's east what the old NATO did for Europe's west: vanquish old hatreds, promote integration, create a secure environment for prosperity, and deter violence in the region where two world wars and the Cold War began. Just the prospect of NATO enlargement has given Central and Eastern Europe greater stability than it has seen in this century.[3]

Of course, the European Union (EU) has a role to play here as well, but it is quicker and easier to enlarge NATO first. The provision of such security to the Central Europeans provides for a measure of stability that would be as much in the interests of Russia and Ukraine as it would be of Germany.

The third and final set of arguments relates to the engagement of the United States in Europe. NATO enlargement ties America very firmly into European security, at the end of a period in which the United States' future role in Europe has been frequently questioned.[4] If US leadership is important to NATO in the post-Cold War world, enlargement is vital. It lessens strategic arguments in the US Senate that the Western Europeans can now look after their own interests; it trumps the argument that NATO has lost an enemy but not found a role; and it can be portrayed as giving the Alliance a moral purpose – the ethical duty to fulfil a responsibility towards those countries that suffered during the fifty years of the Cold War – that provides a clear issue around which American political leaders can gather.

Such arguments often shape analyses of NATO's role in postcommunist Europe. Dismissing these arguments with such brevity is not meant to disparage them, for there is weight here. It is also not meant to imply that the arguments against enlargement are more powerful than those in favour. The problem is instead with the form of analysis. Each of these approaches implies that NATO enlargement has been a product of carefully weighed strategic options. The central thesis of this chapter is that this is not so. NATO enlargement is obviously a product of deliberate policy; but it was brought about by an inevitable logic stemming from the refusal to create alternative structures for European security other than NATO. That is, policy choices in the early 1990s, ones that did not even consider the possibility of NATO enlargement, held within them the seeds of that enlargement. This chapter will argue this case in the following manner. First, it will suggest that enlargement can be separated from a logic of the balance of power. Second, an argument will be put forward that suggests that enlargement is a product of ideas, not of notions of objective interest.

The analysis will then demonstrate this by arguing that enlargement decisions were taken at great speed, and with great variation from previous
ideas, in the period 1993–94. The chapter will then argue that in fact
enlargement had been inevitable from 1991, once no alternative pan-
European institution to NATO was built in the security area. The chapter
then concludes that this process of NATO enlargement will continue.

Enlargement and the balance of power

The starting point for this analysis is an assertion: NATO enlargement is not
designed to change the balance of power in Europe. The European security
discourse that dominates debate in the NATO countries can best be
described as post-balance of power; that is, no one in NATO headquarters,
no policy makers in the major European capitals nor key decision makers in
the US government have believed that balance-of-power politics should be
the order of the day in Europe. Of course, there are outliers to this. Many in
Russia argue that enlargement is precisely about changing the balance to
Moscow's detriment. But Russia is excluded from the dominant discourse
on the west of the continent, whether deliberately or not, and whether self-
imposed or not – as disagreement over language and concepts over the
former Yugoslavia and the NATO–Russia Permanent Joint Council demonstrates. Balance-of-power thinking can still be found in Warsaw and Prague;
but perhaps that indicates simply the time it takes to integrate new
members fully into the dominant discourse. And, of course, there are
outliers in the United States, especially on the Republican right in Congress
and among old Cold Warriors such as Henry Kissinger. But to admit that
there are those outside the consensus is not to question the dominance of
that consensus, and the dominant Western security discourse wants to allow
for the enlargement of NATO without that process leading to a renewed
discussion of the balance of power on the continent.

How can this be? To explain to colleagues in Russia that a process of
enlargement that excludes Russia is not part of some plan to divide Europe
to Russia's detriment is an impossible task. But enlargement is not about a
future Russia; indeed, in many ways it is not about Russia at all. As
Aleksandr Golts eloquently argued,

> Alliance and NATO country leaders quite recently state in all sincerity
> that Russia's refusal to accept the plans for NATO expansion is not a
> rational but an emotional refusal. The Russians are allegedly being
> influenced by the outdated stereotypes of the Cold War. You only have
> to explain everything properly to the Russians for them to immediately
> consent. But each time Solana, Kohl, and Clinton have heard
> completely rational arguments in response.[5]

The issue is not that one side is being irrational, but that there are two rationalities at work. For the Western security consensus, as Ole Waever has argued, 'Europe's "other", the enemy image, is today to no very large extent "Islamic fundamentalism", "the Russians" or anything similar – rather Europe's Other is Europe's own past which should not be allowed to become its future.'[6] This is a crucial insight to which this analysis will return, but for now the key point is to stress the difference of this perspective from the one from Moscow. As James Sherr put it, 'It is ironic that much of Russia's political, defence and security establishment re-legitimised geopolitics just at the time that the West de-legitimised it.'[7] Of course, this allows narratives to be (re)constructed about Russia's difference from 'Europe': Gennady Zyuganov tells us that 'from the historical point of view, Russia presents a special type of civilisation which follows and continues the thousand-year tradition of Kievan Rus, old Muscovy, the Russian empire, and the USSR'.[8] Different assumptions reinforce different perceptions of identity. If Europe's enemy image is its past – and one can argue that this was incredibly powerful in shaping the response to the Kosovo crisis – then it is perfectly possible to hold that NATO enlargement does not necessarily lead to a renewal of the balance-of-power model of politics in Europe.

The ideational nature of NATO enlargement

So far it has been asserted that there is a dominant set of assumptions in the Western security discourse that now holds enlargement of NATO to be a process, and one that does not seek to re-establish a balance of power in Europe. From this point, the argument proceeds to suggest that the enlargement of NATO may be said to have been inevitable. Of course, this is somewhat controversial. It is certainly not what the neorealist (and realist) theorists of international relations predicted, and security studies is dominated by neorealism, is it not? John Mearsheimer predicted that NATO would fade, along with the EU, to be replaced by the uncertainties of great power politics mitigated by German nuclear weapons.[9] Precisely a vision of the enemy image identified by Waever, though to a different end. Kenneth Waltz argued that 'NATO's days are not numbered, but its years are.'[10] Rather than see the validation of the realist thesis concerning the marginality of international institutions, however, what we have seen instead is a debate over the enlargement of most of Europe's major institutions: the EU, NATO, the Western European Union (WEU), the Council of Europe and – although it is too often passed over – the Organisation for Security and Cooperation in Europe.[11] Perhaps we should not be too harsh in this assessment of neorealism; after all, prediction is the most difficult demand of positivist social science. But the point is that neorealism of the Mearsheimer–Waltz variety tells us nothing about NATO enlargement; only that the Alliance will, contrary to all the evidence, fade away.

One therefore cannot fall back upon realist theory to explain NATO enlargement. Perhaps to many this will make the central thrust of this chapter – that the enlargement of NATO was inevitable from early 1991 – seem an extreme argument. It will be suggested that NATO enlargement was inevitable because ideas matter in international relations. Of course, in a discipline so heavily influenced by the realist paradigm for so long it is easier to speak of interests than it is of ideas. This is particularly the case in security studies. Yet ideas are clearly of importance. How else can we explain why, for example, the UK government and military establishment was so hostile to military involvement in the former Yugoslavia in 1991 and 1992, and yet that same government and establishment became such an important actor in the region in the United Nations and NATO operations in Bosnia, before – following the general election of 1997 and a change of government – becoming deeply involved in NATO's intervention in Kosovo? Did UK interests change fundamentally in that time? Or was it the influence of ideas that led to a changing notion of how the UK should act?

Perhaps strangely, the influence of ideas on foreign policy is not yet widely accepted among scholars of international relations. Probably the most significant work in this area is Goldstein and Keohane's *Ideas and Foreign Policy: Beliefs, Institutions and Political Change*, and yet that work does not really address security issues. The influence of ideas over interests is probably seen to be weakest in security policy. Certainly much of the work published has been on political economy.[12] Security and ideas have really only been brought together in the literature on the issue of Soviet New Thinking.[13] Yet it is with the development of constructivist thought that the role of the ideational comes to the fore most clearly.

Whereas realists and neorealists seek to identify objective material factors to explain NATO's role, the constructivist approach is rather different. Consider the three crucial insights put forward by Thomas Risse-Kappen.[14] First, he explains that constructivists reject the notion of an objective threat, as 'Threat perceptions do not emerge from a quasi-objective international power structure, but actors infer external behaviour from the values and norms governing the domestic political processes that shape the identities of their partners in the international system.' Risse-Kappen then argues that, once functioning, alliances are shaped by shared values and are not simply bound together by an objective external threat: 'the Western Alliance represents an institutionalisation of the transatlantic security community based on common values'. Third, for Risse-Kappen, this institutionalisation of common values is robust in the face of political change: 'It is easier to adjust an already existing organisation, which encompasses an elaborate set of rules and decision-making procedures, to new conditions than it is to create new institutions of security cooperation.'[15]

To the extent that there has been a debate between the constructivists and neorealists, it has been about explaining NATO's survival rather than its enlargement. One may, however, draw clear constructivist implications for understanding institutional enlargement. Most significantly, constructivism draws the attention of the analyst away from purely objectivist accounts of security, based on material notions of the national interest, and instead raises in importance the role of language and ideas. It is not the case that NATO has embarked upon a rational process of enlargement driven by strategic considerations. Rather, it is a process that has been driven by ideas. The next section will argue that the decision to enlarge the Alliance only occurred after the 1994 Brussels summit; but that the language used at that summit made that decision inevitable. The following section will argue that the language used at the summit was itself inevitable, due to a series of decisions made in 1991 and 1992.

The significance of post-1994 summit decisions

A central part of the rationalist explanation of the enlargement of NATO is that the Alliance came to a decision at its January 1994 summit to increase its membership. NATO and the NATO governments seek to portray the enlargement process as a rational one, in which options were examined in an incremental fashion, and in which movement towards enlargement was not driven by any forces other than the desire to spread stability without creating new dividing lines, a desire which could be presented to be in Russia's interests. But the enlargement process has not been a rational one; it has been intensely political, a product of shifting ideas and alliances.

The January 1994 summit did not mark the decision point. This is because the essential idea behind that summit was not enlargement but delay: hence the Partnership for Peace (PfP). To see the power of interpretations over objectively defined interests in this process, it is useful to look at the period from the summer of 1993 to the summer of 1994. During this time opinion among NATO decision makers swung violently from support for a move towards enlargement, to the creation of a policy of delay, to a move to decrease the shelf-life of that policy of delay. The summit was only one marker in this story.

In the first phase, in the summer of 1993, the central idea had been to move towards enlargement. Consider three pieces of evidence. First, most notably, is the reaction to the joint Russian–Polish statement on 25 August

1993, in which Russia recognised Poland's right to join NATO, stating that such membership would not be against Russian security interests.[16] Subsequently, the Polish Prime Minister, Hanna Suchocka, said that 'Any further delay in this question does not seem possible', a position to which the Hungarian Foreign Minister, Geza Jeszenszky, immediately subscribed.[17] This led Senator Lugar, an influential member of the US Senate Foreign Relations Committee, to press for the inclusion of the Visegrad countries (the Czech Republic, Hungary, Poland and Slovakia) in NATO at the forthcoming January summit.[18] Chancellor Kohl stated that 'At these talks in January I will raise the question of how we can give these countries not only the feeling but also a guarantee that they have a security umbrella.'[19] A concession (or mistake) by Yeltsin seemed to open the way to enlargement for those who supported the idea in Central Europe and in the West. Second, the publicity given to the circulation in NATO and Western European governmental and semi-official circles of a paper written by Ronald Asmus, Richard Kugler and Stephen Larrabee of the RAND Corporation in America. The paper argued for the immediate expansion of NATO to Poland, Hungary, the Czech Republic and also possibly Slovakia.[20] A version of the paper was later published in *Foreign Affairs*, in which the authors argued that the North Atlantic Cooperation Council, created by NATO in December 1991 as a framework for cooperation with the countries of postcommunist Europe, 'does not go far enough. It is essentially a holding operation that provides only meagre psychological reassurance.'[21] Third, the Defence Minister of one of the most important NATO countries – Germany – was a loud proponent of early enlargement. The immediate expansion of NATO, he argued, was in Germany's interests in order to create further stability on its eastern borders. Volker Rühe argued that 'The Atlantic Alliance must not become a "closed shop". I cannot see one good reason for denying future members of the European Union membership in NATO.'[22]

Thus in the summer of 1993 it became clear that a decision to enlarge NATO could have been openly stated at the January 1994 Brussels summit without equivocation. The Western security discourse made this possible by the change of orientation over this period. But this momentum was reversed by the dominant interpretation within NATO countries given to two events. First, the repudiation of Yeltsin's acceptance that the Poles could join NATO. Yeltsin's 'official statement, however, was soon counteracted by Foreign Minister Kozyrev and other Russian politicians'.[23] In the aftermath of the violent defeat of the conservatives in the Russian Parliament Yeltsin, perhaps to appease those in the military who had stood by him in the attack on Parliament, wrote to several Western governments suggesting that the time was not right for the extension of NATO.[24] Second, in Poland general elections removed the Solidarity-oriented coalition government from power and replaced it with the Democratic Left Alliance (SLD), the former communist party. The Chair of the SLD, Wlodzimierz Cimoszewicz, had argued that 'There was never any debate on Poland's future security possibilities or about NATO membership and its implications ... We don't say no, but we believe it would be wise to explore other possibilities.'[25] This was combined with the general reticence of two major Western European countries. For countries such as Britain, it was not clear that stability would be enhanced by enlargement, while the cohesion of NATO might, it was feared, be damaged.[26] The French were still concerned that the EU, and the WEU, should be allowed to play a significant role in the European security debate.[27] Thus it was deemed that the Russians had not accepted enlargement; the Poles were moving against NATO membership; the risks of enlargement to NATO itself were too great; and other alternatives still had to be considered. None of this was objective reality; each was an idea that contributed to the opposition to enlargement.

How can it be that an alliance such as NATO can see its dominant security discourse shift so rapidly in such a short period of time, without a clear external and objective shock? Three issues need to be borne in mind. First, to the summer of 1993 the enlargement issue had not been taken seriously. It was only over this relatively short period that it began to rise in importance on the ladder of NATO priorities. Thus the intellectual and political environment was fluid. Second, there was no clear idea as to why NATO should be maintained; enlargement began to appear to give some possible justification, if it could be seen to be making a contribution to the promotion of that nebulous concept, stability (hence the importance attached to Yeltsin's Warsaw comments). Third, no one knew what to say to the Central Europeans. When Clinton and Central European leaders met at the Holocaust memorial at the end of 1993, a romantic vision apparently emerged. 'Somehow the occasion gave Bill Clinton a sense of history for the first time and planted the seed that the Alliance had to embrace Eastern Europe so war could never start again there.'[28] Whether or not such a retrospective interpretation can be justified, what is clear is that Clinton and other NATO leaders had no alternative to offer the Central Europeans other than NATO membership at some point, except to allow a perception to grow that these countries were to be abandoned to the wrong side of a new Yalta.

Thus at the end of 1993, NATO was divided on the enlargement issue. NATO's policies towards the east at this time were determined by a need to maintain balance within the Alliance itself. The potential for open and bitter public argument, both within NATO and between NATO and the partner countries, had to be minimised. Thus the adoption of PfP at the

Brussels summit was absolutely central to the continued vitality of the Alliance. At this time, NATO faced two deep problems. First, the Alliance was profoundly split over the issue of enlargement. Second, no one could really decide what the purpose of the Alliance was. PfP resolved both problems, for it gave a purpose to NATO – projecting stability into Central and Eastern Europe – and it offered the prospect of both opening up NATO to new members and putting that prospect into the distant future. Volker Rühe commented that, with the endorsement of PfP at the January summit, new members could join the Alliance by the year 2000.[29] In contrast, British Defence Secretary Malcolm Rifkind argued that 'It would be a great mistake if some new line were to be driven through Europe.'[30] The PfP was thus essentially a NATO plan to solve NATO internal problems – the arguments over enlargement within the Alliance and within many of the governments of the Alliance.[31] This was vital, as the summit was taking on ever growing importance. As George and Borawski noted at the time, 'All governments realise that unless the Summit succeeds in rejuvenating the Alliance after the perceived failure of its member nations over Yugoslavia and its slowness in adapting by deed as well as word to the new challenges of European security, support for the Alliance will wane on both sides of the Atlantic.'[32]

While PfP developed a policy of delay, it also held within it the seeds of actual decision. After all, PfP committed the Alliance to 'expect and … welcome NATO expansion that would reach to democratic states to our East, as part of an evolutionary process, taking into account political and security developments in the whole of Europe'.[33] But by not setting criteria for such expansion, the policy of delay was furthered; it would be possible to set up a whole series of barricades to an actual decision, and the general expectation – certainly in Central Europe – was that this would be the case.

The critical moment in the enlargement debate took place later in 1994, as pressure grew in the United States to move away from delay and President Clinton's administration began to lead the Alliance on the issue. The Americans stressed that they were committed to NATO enlargement.[34] Many stated that the issue was not 'if but when'.[35] In January a 'sense of the Senate' resolution had been passed in the US Congress by 94–3, calling on the American government to argue for NATO enlargement. This was followed in April by the introduction of the NATO Expansion Act of 1994 in Congress, which called for the Visegrad states to become members by 1999. Pressure was increased in May when Republican Congressman Henry Hyde introduced the NATO Revitalisation Act, which urged NATO 'to establish benchmarks and a timetable for eventual membership for selected countries', which were identified as the Visegrad and the Baltic states. Clinton himself promised the Polish Parliament in July 1994 that 'The expansion of NATO will surely come, and Poland's role as the first nation to participate in joint exercises with NATO troops makes Warsaw a prime candidate for inclusion.'[36]

But such a clear American lead on the issue was only possible due to a bridging of the differences in the German government. In the period immediately after Chancellor Kohl's coalition was returned to power in the 1994 German elections, agreement was reached in Bonn that NATO enlargement should be pursued in parallel with the expansion of the EU. This kept Germany in line with the new American policy direction, and also enabled Bonn to maintain a strong Franco-German policy line, given that Paris had been concerned that a speedy expansion of NATO would sideline European construction.

Thus the move towards enlargement did not come in January, but later in 1994. It was revealed publicly in the communiqué from the ministerial meeting of the North Atlantic Council on 1 December. The ministers confirmed that they 'expect and would welcome NATO enlargement that would reach to democratic states to our East, as part of an evolutionary process ... part of a broad European security architecture based on true cooperation throughout Europe'.[37] The ministers confirmed that NATO enlargement would take place in parallel to the enlargement of the EU, and that therefore there would be differentiation in the accession of new members. They also confirmed that no timeframe for actual admission could yet be set, but 'decided to initiate a process of examination inside the Alliance to determine how NATO will enlarge, the principles to guide this process and the implications of membership'.[38] Hence a study was authorised, under the Council, to include a significant input from the military authorities, particularly on the role of PfP in enlargement, to report the following year.

NATO policy over this twelve month period gave the clear impression of stop–go. Up to the summer of 1993, there was little interest in the NATO countries in pursuing enlargement, with the notable exception of the German Defence Minister. Then, in the summer of 1993, a sudden 'go' emerged, as momentum developed behind the idea of taking a speedy enlargement decision. In the autumn and through to the summit, the trend changed to 'stop', with the development of a policy of delay. But then the following summer, the US itself undermined the policy of delay, and accelerated the process. No wonder there was frustration, within the Alliance as well as outside. In a leaked cable, the German Ambassador to NATO, Baron von Richthofen, decried the

> unilateral changes in US policies towards the ex-Soviet Union and Eastern Europe since the NATO summit in January directly affect the Alliance. There was an abandonment at short notice, without any consultation, of the 'Russia First' concept ... Now the US is applying

political pressure for more speed in the expansion question, without paying attention to how this affects internal alliance positions on eastern policies as well as the military and financial consequences.[39]

By 1993–94, the enlargement issue was tied up with the future of the Alliance. Most members of NATO wanted to keep the Alliance; but they did not have a convincing explanation of why. Enlargement thus became a convenient tool to maintain the Alliance. NATO enlargement would, it was suggested, spread stability into Central Europe. This idea may or may not be persuasive; but it is the only real justification that could be developed and, most importantly, publicly articulated, unless enlargement was to lead to a formal break with Moscow. There was no consensus on this within the Alliance in early 1994; but, by the middle of the year, a functioning consensus was fashioned by US leadership. For after all, the place where the utility of the Alliance would be questioned first would be in the US. It had been the Americans that had suggested that the Alliance had to 'go out of area or go out of business'. The enlargement issue gave one of only two possible rationales for NATO's continuation, and the other rationale – peacekeeping or peace making in Yugoslavia – was seen to be at best a short-term solution and at worst vulnerable (at that time) to appalling failure.

NATO enlargement was, thus, inevitable by the middle of 1994 because it was the only credible way of maintaining a future for the Alliance. It was also inevitable because the policy of delay had to decay over time; it was never possible to maintain the position over time. However, although most focus is on the debates of 1993 and 1994 as the key moments in the enlargement process, the next section will argue that it was the decisions of 1991 and 1992 that really made enlargement inevitable.

The inevitability of enlargement from 1991

The inevitability of enlargement dates not only from 1994, but also back to 1991. This is controversial. No one in NATO wanted enlargement in 1991; there was an extremely firm consensus against it. Yet what will be suggested here is that as soon as the Central Europeans decided that they would seek membership, that membership became only a matter of time unless the perception of the geopolitical situation in Europe, the idea of European security itself, changed fundamentally.

Initially, of course, the Central Europeans did not seek NATO membership. Instead, they sought to build the then Conference on Security and Cooperation in Europe (CSCE) into a pan-European security structure that would include Russia. However, the goals of 1990 faded in 1991, when the Visegrad states turned from the CSCE to NATO.[40] They did so for essentially two reasons.

First, many NATO members were not interested in creating a strong CSCE, certainly not the Americans, British and French. It implied a lessening of NATO and a distraction from creating a defence identity within the EU. This NATO–EU debate was much more comfortable than one involving the postcommunist states. Developing the CSCE required a very close relationship with Russia but, with the exception of the Germans, others feared that the Russian reform process might not produce a stable democracy. During 1991 there was a concern in NATO countries about a reconstitution capability in Russia, an ability to re-create major military forces quickly, which summed up nicely the sense of distrust in the NATO–Russia relationship despite all of the changes.

The second reason was that, once the route to developing the CSCE as a pan-European security organisation was effectively blocked, it was inevitable that the Central Europeans would seek NATO membership, given their perception of their history. How could anyone in Warsaw argue against Polish worst-case analysis and expect to be taken seriously? This does not imply that Russia is inevitably aggressive; but it does recognise that for the Central Europeans instability in Russia is threatening. Thus one might date the change in Central and Eastern European attitudes to 8 January 1991, when Soviet troops were deployed around Vilnius in order to try to impose the conscription of Lithuanians into the Soviet army which had been resisted since the Lithuanian Parliament had voted on 11 March 1990 to re-establish Lithuanian sovereignty. On 11 January 1991, those Soviet forces were involved in violent struggles in the streets of Vilnius in which there were several deaths. It is difficult to overstate the psychological impact that this event had on policy makers in Central and Eastern Europe and, indeed, upon nationalists in the non-Russian republics of the Soviet Union.[41] Whereas in 1990 the Soviet Union had been associated with the peaceful conclusion of the Cold War, in early 1991 pictures of the Soviet use of force alerted many in Central Europe to the dangers of being so close to Russian power. Following these events, a decision was taken to wind up the Warsaw Pact in Budapest on 25 February.[42]

Thus the failure of the NATO countries to pursue the CSCE option seriously made NATO enlargement inevitable. It is perfectly possible and legitimate to argue that the CSCE option could not have been made to work. But this is not at issue here. The point is that it was not seriously considered. And it was the failure to consider this option seriously that made NATO enlargement a reality. The seeds of NATO's discomfort over enlargement were therefore sown by the reluctance of the leadership of the NATO countries to act on a principle of enlightened self-interest in 1990. From that point, it could not have been possible for NATO to permanently defer enlargement. It was vulnerable to pressure on political grounds – the pressure of then Czechoslovak (later Czech) President Vaclav Havel's 'return to Europe' argument. How could NATO, as an alliance of values as well as force – if one accepts the constructivist argument – have rejected the demands of the Central Europeans? In terms of identity, Western Europeans identify with Central Europeans in a way that they do not with Chechens and Tajiks, and Havel's demand to overturn the logic of Yalta played powerfully to the moral crusaders in the US Congress. In addition, NATO had a practice of enlargement – to Greece, Turkey, West Germany, Spain and finally eastern Germany – that could always be turned to.[43] But enlargement, and the 'open door' policy committed NATO to filling much of the politico-security space promised to the CSCE in 1989–90.

Conclusion

This chapter has sought to argue that NATO's enlargement was inevitable, first because of the conservatism displayed by the governments of the Alliance in 1991 and 1992, and second due to the perceived weakness of the Alliance in terms of its purpose in 1993 and 1994. NATO enlargement became inevitable because of the power of the idea that NATO must be preserved. Not that it should be preserved for some defined purpose; simply that it should be maintained as a hedge against an uncertain future, as an insurance policy. Unfortunately, the commitment to that insurance policy has raised the likelihood that a claim will have to be made on that policy, for by disparaging the CSCE alternative, NATO has moved down the path of enlargement which has further deepened the new post-Cold War division of Europe. Thus by clinging so tenaciously to the policy of the past instead of listening to the revolutionaries of Central Europe and building a collaborative future, the idea of preserving NATO helped to create the political and security problems that NATO now faces through the move towards enlargement. Perhaps much of this was natural; the analysis here is not intended to apportion blame. Rather, in order to understand why there seem to be so few options now, it is important to understand how changes in discourse closed alternatives in the past.

The key date in the enlargement process was 1994, for by then enlargement was perceived to be the only way of giving the Alliance a task for the future. Enlargement events from that time, up to the Kosovo war, have been in many ways mere footnotes to this larger picture. In 1993 and 1994 governments and officials looked for alternative justifications for the continuation of NATO other than 'spreading stability'. Willy Claes tried to explain the inexplicable: that the threat to NATO from North Africa was greater than it had been from the Soviet Union.[44] One may argue that neither posed a threat; but once one is inside the logic of threat, Claes' argument, like his political position as NATO Secretary-General, was unten-able. In 1994, some sought a future for NATO in reconstructing Bosnia. But this was derailed by the American fixation first not to get involved on the ground and then, once they got there, the obsession to leave as soon as possible, and preferably earlier. This meant that at that time NATO could not talk about a long-term commitment to the region. Ironically, one of the central implications of the war in Kosovo is likely to be just such a long-term commitment. But, in the middle of the 1990s, the only role left for NATO was to 'spread stability eastwards' through enlargement.

Ideas, and not some notion of objective interest, is what explains the process of NATO enlargement. There is no purpose to outlining the purely strategic implications and objections to the process, for these objective notions carry no independent meaning. The process has been carried by non-objective assumptions and by language that has had more to do with identity than with notions of objectivity. A process of enlargement has been constructed out of the immediate post-Cold War period. It began because of the desire to protect NATO and hence not to build rival pan-European security organisations; it took root because the spreading of stability/enlargement became the only means of articulating a justification for the continuation of the Alliance.

NATO enlargement has been constructed as a speech act: enlargement is to spread stability. How this should be so is not important; what is of sig-nificance is that enlargement and stability are connected. Hence notions of a balance of power are excluded. While a balance of power could bring stability, in the dominant NATO security discourse this is not accepted. The fear is that any NATO–Russian balance of power could not be other than unstable; the fear, as Ole Waever has put it, is a repeat of Europe's past.[45]

The future of NATO enlargement is therefore caught up in these language games. As long as enlargement and spreading stability are connected concepts; as long as Western leaders fear that the Europe of the future might resemble the Europe of the past; as long as no alternative justi-fication for NATO's continuation can be defined and articulated; and as long as there is no institutional alternative to NATO for those still outside the Alliance; under these circumstances, the discourse, and hence practice, of enlargement will continue.

Notes

1 For an excellent summary, see The Report of the Defence Committee by Mr Blaauw on *The United States and Security in Europe* (WEU Parliamentary Assembly, transmitted electronically by both NATO and the WEU, 13 May 1996).

2   See, for example, W. Safire, 'We cannot trust Russia, so let the Alliance grow', *International Herald Tribune* (17 January 1995).

3   M. Albright, 'Enlarging NATO: why bigger is better', *The Economist* (15 February 1997).

4   Of course, some have argued the contrary case; see, for example, F. C. Ikle, 'Why expanding NATO eastwards is a deplorable idea', *International Herald Tribune* (12 January 1995). Ikle commented that, 'If the United States now pressured its reluctant European allies to consent to some scheme of eastward expansion, it would jeopardize the bonds that link America to Europe.'

5   A. Golts, 'NATO: last synchronization of watches', *FBIS-SOV-96–109 Daily Report* (4 June 1996).

6   O. Waever, 'European security identities', *Journal of Common Market Studies*, 34:1 (1996), 122.

7   J. Sherr, *The Dynamics Shaping European Security* (CSRC Sandhurst, document M16, 1998), p. 2.

8   G. Zyuganov, 'Russia and the contemporary world', *Brown Journal of World Affairs*, 2:2 (1995), 123.

9   J. J. Mearsheimer, 'Back to the future: instability in Europe after the Cold War', *International Security*, 15:1 (1990), 5–56.

10 K. Waltz, 'The emerging structure of international politics', *International Security*, 18 (1993), 76.

11 S. Croft, J. Redmond, W. Rees and M. Webber, *The Enlargement of Europe* (Manchester, Manchester University Press, 1999).

12 J. Goldstein and R. O. Keohane (eds), *Ideas and Foreign Policy: Beliefs, Institutions and Political Change* (Ithaca, NY, Cornell University Press, 1993).

13 J. Checkel, 'Ideas, institutions and the Gorbachev foreign policy revolution', *World Politics*, 45:2 (1993) 271–300; and P. Shearman, 'New Political Thinking reassessed', *Review of International Studies*, 19:2 (1993), 139–58.

14 T. Risse-Kappen, 'Identity in a democratic security community: the case of NATO', in P. Katzenstein (ed.), *The Culture of National Security* (New York, Columbia University Press, 1996), pp. 359–99.

15 Risse-Kappen, 'Identity in a democratic security community', pp. 367, 395 and 396.

16 B. George and J. Borawski, 'Sympathy for the devil: European security in a revolutionary age', *European Security*, 2:4 (1993), 488.

17 Quoted in A. Marshall, 'NATO moves to include former enemies', *Independent* (7 September 1993).

18 W. Drozdiak, 'NATO family cool to taking in Warsaw Pact orphans', *International Herald Tribune* (2 September 1993).

19 Quoted in Marshall, 'NATO moves to include former enemies'.

20 F. Kempe, 'NATO: out of area or out of business', *Wall Street Journal* (9 August 1993).

21 R. D. Asmus, R. L. Kugler and F. S. Larrabee, 'Building a new NATO', *Foreign Affairs*, 72:4 (1993), 32.

22 This was the 1993 Alastair Buchan Memorial Lecture. The text is reproduced in 'Shaping Euro-atlantic policies: a grand strategy for a new era', *Survival*, 35:2 (1993), 134–5.

23 G. Wettig, 'Moscow's perception of NATO's role', *Aussenpolitik*, 45:2 (1994), 127.

24 Yeltsin wrote to the Americans, British, Germans and French, apparently taking the 1990 'two-plus-four' talks on German unification as a model for discussions on Central European security and arguing that the 'two-plus-four' agreement made NATO expansion illegal, a view rejected in the West. See 'NATO/East', *Atlantic News*, 2559 (6 October 1993), 3; and W. Drozdiak, 'NATO likely to slow East Europe's entry', *International Herald Tribune* (6 October 1993).

25 Quoted in A. LeBor, 'Polish leaders cast doubt on entry to NATO', *The Times* (21 September 1993). However, on 19 September leaders of the three parties that won the Polish elections had stressed the need for Poland to join NATO 'as soon as possible'. See 'NATO enlargement', *Atlantic News*, 2561 (13 October 1991), 1. Despite this, doubt had already been created in many minds in the West.

26 This was made clear in a 'strictly personal' speech to the Royal United Services Institute by Sir Richard Vincent, the British Chair of NATO's Military Committee. According to Vincent, guarantees for Central Europe had, unlike in the 1930s, to be backed up with political and military resolve and 'I do not see either of these seriously in prospect.' See D. White, 'Military chief fears for NATO expansion', *Financial Times* (10 November 1993).

27 See, for example, D. White, 'Caution urged on NATO expansion', *Financial Times* (23 September 1993); R. Boyes, 'Confusion in NATO ranks as left prepares for power in Poland', *The Times* (16 September 1993); and 'Bonn wants East in updated NATO', *International Herald Tribune* (8 October 1993), which reported that French Foreign Minister Alain Juppé had suggested that the Balladur plan should be explored before NATO expanded its membership.

28 A quote from 'an American official deeply involved in the international debate about enlarging the North Atlantic Treaty Organisation', cited by J. Fitchett, 'Moving cautiously on NATO expansion eastward', *International Herald Tribune* (29 May 1995).

29 See M. M. Nelson, 'NATO officials back plan for closer ties with ex-bloc', *Wall Street Journal* (22–23 October 1993).

30 Nelson, 'NATO officials back plan for closer ties with ex-bloc'.

31 See, for example, 'The World sends NATO back to the drawing board', *The Economist* (25 December 1993–7 January 1994).

32 George and Borawski, 'Sympathy for the devil', 475.

33 NATO, *Partnership for Peace Invitation* (Brussels, NATO, 10 January 1994), p. 1.

34 See, for example, President Clinton's speech to the French National Assembly, 7 June 1994.

35 See, for example, Warren Christopher, cited in 'Christopher', *Atlantic News*, 2631 (11 June 1994), 3.

36 Cited in 'Enlargement of NATO', *Atlantic News*, 2639 (8 July 1994). The Republicans' 1995 NATO Revitalisation and Expansion Act proposed that the Visegrad states should accede to NATO in one group. See, for example, D. Priest and D. Williams, 'Clinton draws line against Republicans on national security', *International Herald Tribune* (16 February 1995).

37 North Atlantic Council Communiqué, 1 December 1994, reproduced in *Atlantic News*, 2676 (annex) (3 December 1994).

38 North Atlantic Council Communiqué, 1 December 1994.

39 A leaked cable from November 1994, see *Financial Times* (2 December 1994).

40 On this, see J. Sedivy, 'From dreaming to realism – Czechoslovak security policy since 1989', *Perspectives (Institute of International Relations, Prague)*, 4 (1994–95), 61–9.

41 For example, J. Urban, 'The Czech and Slovak republics: security consequences of the break-up of the CSFR', in R. Cowen Karp (ed.), *Central and Eastern Europe: The Challenge of Transition* (Oxford, Oxford University Press for SIPRI, 1993), p. 115; also, author's interviews with officials in Prague, 1990 and 1991. For similarities in the Hungarian position, see P. Dunay, 'Hungary: defining the boundaries of security', in Cowen Karp, *Central and Eastern Europe*, p. 148. See also A. Hyde-Price, 'Future security systems for Europe', in C. McInnes, *Security and Strategy in the New Europe* (London, Routledge, 1992), pp. 49–50.

42 Although this did not come into effect until 1 July. The last Soviet units left Hungary and Czechoslovakia in June 1991, while the last Soviet/Russian forces did not leave Poland until November 1992 (although 5,000 logistic troops remained to oversee the withdrawal of the Red Army from eastern Germany). On this, see A. Hyde-Price, 'After the Pact: East European security in the 1990s', *Arms Control: Contemporary Security Policy*, 12:2 (1991), 280–3.

43 Under Article 10 of the Washington Treaty, 'The Parties may, by unanimous agreement, invite any other European State in a position to further the principles of this Treaty and to contribute to the security of the North Atlantic area to accede to this Treaty.'

44 S. Sefarty, 'Algeria unhinged: what next? Who cares? Who leads?', *Survival*, 38:4 (1996–97), 153.

45 Waever, 'European security identities', 122.

3

Security governance and the excluded states of postcommunist Europe

Mark Webber

It is now over a decade since the collapse of communism in Central and Eastern Europe and the dissolution of the Soviet Union.[1] A good deal of analysis concerning the shape of postcommunist, post-Cold War Europe has since emerged. This has not always been positive in its assessment of the changes which have occurred; indeed, in relation to security affairs there are still obvious uncertainties, not least in the Balkan region.[2] Yet while European security remains subject to a number of imponderables, one fixed feature had seemingly emerged by the end of the 1990s; namely, the pivotal role of the North Atlantic Treaty Organisation (NATO) in shaping the discourse and organisation of European security affairs. In this connection its was highly symbolic that 1999, the year which marked the tenth anniversary of the fall of the Berlin Wall, should coincide with the fiftieth anniversary of NATO's formation, and no less symbolic that these twin events occurred during the same year in which the Czech Republic, Hungary and Poland formally acceded to the Atlantic Alliance.

NATO enlargement, particularly when coupled with ongoing accession negotiations between a number of Central and Eastern European states and the European Union (EU), seemed to suggest that by 1999 a more inclusive Europe was emerging.[3] Just how inclusive, however, remains an open question. The accession criteria for membership of NATO and the EU suggest that their enlargement is likely to be incremental rather than sudden and swift.[4] Furthermore, enlargement, even in an incremental fashion, creates new forms of exclusion in its wake as states which want membership are denied it and states which do not seek it look askance at the dominance of the enlarging NATO/EU. As Neal Ascherson has argued, there is a risk of creating a 'post-1989 world' in which 'the old Iron Curtain frontier has simply shifted eastward', with the enlarged NATO/EU divided politically and economically from the rest of the continent, in particular Russia.[5]

Surveying the post-1989 period as a whole, a Europe characterised by these new forms of inclusion and exclusion seems to be a far cry from the vision of a continent 'whole and free' or a 'common European home' proclaimed at the end of the Cold War. Yet it would be inaccurate to suggest that a one-bloc Europe has come into being outside of which all other states stand marginalised and resentful. With rare exceptions, those states excluded from formal membership of NATO and the EU are nonetheless willing participants in arrangements formally linking them to both organisations. This, moreover, is complemented by other inclusive arrangements not formally part of NATO or the EU. Overall, these various structures have not overcome differentiation, nor have they removed certain types of exclusion, but they have meant that the deep schisms that defined Cold War Europe have so far been avoided. In the field of security, this state of affairs is best characterised as one of security governance.

Defining security governance

Security governance may be defined as an intentional system of rule, dependent on the acceptance of a majority of states that are affected, which, through regulatory mechanisms (both formal and informal), governs activities across a range of security and security-related issue areas. This definition implies other important elements: directedness (the pursuit of clearly defined goals);[6] resources, and thus a capacity to act; and a variegated set of power relations. This last feature may at first sight seem incongruous; however, a system of governance does allow for differentiation among its constituent parts. What is important is that governance is suggestive less of strict hierarchy, imposition and coercion than of negotiation, coordination and participation.[7]

One final and important feature underlying security governance is a sense of shared understanding. At its most developed, this equates to the notion of a 'security community' in the Deutschian sense. Here, there is agreement not just on the material components of security governance, but a convergence of values and identity and thus the presence of a sense of 'weness'. This ensures that while differences of interest may exist between states, there is no likelihood that these will be resolved by force.[8] The existence of a community of this sort may characterise part (or, indeed, all) of a system of security governance, but the former is not a *sine qua non* of the latter. A system of security governance could, for instance, be oriented around simple pragmatism – agreement on its basic structures and purposes for the sake of mutual gain. Such was arguably the case with respect to the set of arrangements that characterised détente in the 1970s. That said, the development of security governance is clearly facilitated by a deeper structure of values. It is these that foster consensus and stabilise and legitimise the system, and thus ensure its durability. Where they exist security governance can be said to have an ideational as well as simply an institutional basis.

Security relations in post-Cold War Europe approximate to a form of security governance. This system is multi-layered and *inter alia* encompasses the following: organisations with both formal and informal security-related purposes (principally NATO, but also the EU, the Organisation for Security and Cooperation in Europe (OSCE) and the Council of Europe); treaty-based arrangements (particularly the 1990 Conventional Armed Forces in Europe (CFE) Treaty, the legal provisions surrounding German unification and the peace settlements in Bosnia and Kosovo); bilateral and multilateral interactions (NATO–Russian dialogue as formalised in the 1997 NATO-Russia Founding Act, and initiatives relating to Bosnia and Kosovo); and a set of understandings on what constitutes acceptable inter-state and domestic political conduct (non-aggression, the rule of law, democracy, free markets and individual rights).[9]

Security governance in Europe, however, is only emerging and the reality therefore departs from the ideal in certain important respects. First, there is a tendency to resort to the imposition of order in certain circumstances (as in the case of Bosnia and Kosovo). Second, a less than full consensus exists on the scope and goals of security governance (the obvious cleavage being between Russia and the NATO states). Third, power relations do exhibit distinct principal–agent characteristics (and thus hierarchy), owing to the dominant roles of NATO and the EU (and of certain states within these organisations). Furthermore, the underlying values of political and economic order that have influenced the particular form of security governance, while having served an assimilationist function, still enjoy only shallow roots in much of postcommunist Europe. This unfolding state of affairs can usefully be illustrated by considering the development of the system of security governance at the beginning and the end of the 1990s. This chapter examines this system of security governance, exploring the situations of those postcommunist states which – in different ways and to varying degrees – are excluded from it.

An overview of European security governance: 1989–91 and 1997–99

The period 1989–91 coincided with three monumental developments in the history of the twentieth century: the end of the Cold War, the dissolution of the Soviet Union and the demise of communism as a viable political and economic system. The Cold War European security system – defined by a bipolar division of the continent, superpower 'overlay' and latent military conflict – was transformed overnight.[10] Amid such tumult, Europe's political leaders were hard pressed to conceptualise, let alone control, the process of change. In the security sphere various grand proposals were made on Europe's future. During

1989–90 these ranged from the notion of a 'European security architecture' proposed by US Secretary of State James Baker, through Mikhail Gorbachev's 'common European home' and Czechoslovak Foreign Minister, Jiri Dienstbier's 'European Security Commission', to Vaclav Havel's 'Organisation of European States' and Francois Mitterrand's 'Confederation of Europe'.[11]

What emerged by the end of 1991, however, was not in accord with any grand proposal but reflected rather the pragmatic adjustment of existing security organisations (NATO, the Conference on Security and Cooperation in Europe (CSCE, which later became the OSCE) and the Western European Union (WEU)). Neither was it the outcome of any general political or military settlement among the major powers – there was, in other words, no peace treaty that ended the Cold War. That said, in combination, documents such as the treaties on German unification, the 1990 CSCE Paris Charter and the 1987 Intermediate-Range Nuclear Forces (INF) and CFE Treaties did amount to a settlement of sorts. The *ad hoc* character of this settlement, however, meant that certain critical matters were left undefined. There was no clear agreement on the strategic status of Central Europe in the context of German unification and Soviet troop withdrawals. At the point of the Warsaw Pact's dissolution in 1991, there was also no inter-bloc agreement with NATO on the future of the Alliance.

In retrospect, these two omissions were to underlie the genesis of later controversies concerning NATO enlargement. Although expanding the Alliance was not on the agenda at the time, it was apparent by 1991 that NATO would play a central role within the emerging system of security governance. After 1989 a considerable amount of soul searching had surrounded the future role of the Alliance.[12] NATO had, however, emerged from the Cold War with its political and military credentials intact and could, after all, consider itself the 'victor' of the Cold War.[13] The Alliance's July 1990 London and November 1991 Rome Declarations and 1991 Strategic Concept signalled its readiness to adapt to the new circumstances through a reformulation of its strategy and mission. Furthermore, there was no credible institutional alternative to the Alliance for the majority of European states. Calls to strengthen the CSCE as the core of a pan-European collective security system had been made by German Foreign Minister Hans Dietrich Genscher in 1990, a view articulated outside of NATO's membership by the new postcommunist administrations in Czechoslovakia, Hungary and Poland.[14] This particular vision of the CSCE was, however, easily dispelled. Spearheaded by the American and British governments, the NATO position, outlined in the London Declaration, envisaged giving the CSCE only a modest security role.[15] The institutionalisation of the CSCE at its Paris summit in 1990 largely reflected this position. In light of this outcome, and casting a wary eye also at an unstable Soviet

Union, Central European governments abandoned their own preference for the CSCE and began to request admission to NATO.

The period 1997–99 marked an important watershed in the evolution of post-Cold War security governance in Europe. The previous six years had been marked by a considerable degree of uncertainty concerning the institutional (re)configuration of security structures, as well as by serious challenges to European stability, most obviously in the Balkans but also in the Russian North Caucasus (Chechnya) and in the Transcaucasus more generally (the civil war in Georgia and the Armenian-Azeri conflict over Nagorno-Karabakh). These problems have not been removed – as illustrated by the 1999 crisis in Kosovo and the ongoing conflict in Chechnya. Yet amid these ongoing challenges, the institutional bases upon which security governance in Europe rests are now clear. The principal feature in this respect is the leading and defining roles of NATO and the EU.

This is the culmination first and foremost of the Alliance's ability during the 1990s to see through a far-reaching transformation of organisational and strategic goals. The more obvious features in this regard include: a reform of command and force structure; the adaptation of strategic thinking, including a restatement of NATO's core tasks and the articulation of new missions; the enlargement of membership; and the establishment of cooperative arrangements with non-members, including the institutionalisation of bilateral ties with Russia and Ukraine.

These various initiatives can be regarded as contributing to security governance in at least four ways. First, they have a regulatory component, in the shape of the organisational and military infrastructure of NATO itself, coupled with the variety of arrangements linking NATO with non-members. Second, these initiatives have meant a continuation and, indeed, a broadening of the political purpose of the Alliance – facilitating defence/security coordination and manufacturing consensus among a core of European states which now includes not only NATO's members but also Central and Eastern European states aspiring to membership. Third, they demonstrate the assumption of authority in a range of security-related issues. NATO has, in other words, begun to transform itself from a collective defence organisation concerned with the straightforward military protection of its members to a nascent collective security organisation which claims a responsibility for the 'security and stability of the Euro-atlantic area' as a whole.[16] Fourth, they reflect the fact that NATO has reaffirmed its position as upholder of the ascendant set of values associated with security governance in Europe. As Frank Schimmelfennig has recently argued, NATO cannot simply be understood as a military alliance or the provider of shared security goods. It is equally 'an organization [that represents] an international community of [liberal] values and norms'.[17]

The effects of NATO's transformation have been nowhere more evident than in the Balkans. Here NATO has attempted to impose forcibly a system of security governance upon a region of instability and seeming ungovernability. Although these efforts have highlighted certain political and military limitations of the Alliance, it is clear that, particularly since 1995 when it first used force in Bosnia, NATO has become increasingly robust in its determination to act. In so doing it has taken a number of path-breaking steps. These have included: the use of force in circumstances other than those involving a direct attack on a NATO member state (Operation Allied Force against Serbia in March–June 1999); the deployment of long-term peacekeeping forces under direct NATO command (in Bosnia and Kosovo); and the deliberate disregard (again in Operation Allied Force) of the absence of an explicit United Nations (UN) Security Council mandate for military intervention. Furthermore, Operation Allied Force was, however disingenuously in the eyes of some, justified by an explicitly humanitarian (value driven) as opposed to a military purpose.[18]

Despite its importance, NATO does not represent the sum total of European security governance. The EU has taken significant steps towards the development of a Common European Security and Defence Policy (CESDP). To this end, at the June and December 1999 European Councils in Cologne and Helsinki the EU outlined the development of a military capability (involving absorption of the WEU) geared to undertaking crisis management tasks.[19] The OSCE has also established a niche in the civilian/political aspects of conflict management and post-conflict stabilisation, as well as providing a forum for discussions on a 'Common and Comprehensive Security Model' and 'Charter for European Security' (the latter being adopted at the OSCE's Istanbul summit in November 1999). The Council of Europe, meanwhile, has elaborated the notion of 'democratic security' as a political route to regional stability.[20] The CFE Treaty continues to determine post-Cold War conventional military force levels in Europe. Subregional initiatives have also flourished. Some of these, such as the Commonwealth of Independent States (CIS), claim quite explicit traditional security functions of military cooperation. Others, such as the Black Sea Economic Cooperation group, are engaged in non-traditional security areas relating to international crime, terrorism and environmental concerns.[21]

In the main, however, these various regional and subregional arrangements cannot in any sense be regarded as constituting a form of security governance that is either an alternative to that defined by NATO or outside of its purview. Virtually all have a clear connection to the Alliance, whether this be in the shape of a formal organisational link, the need to call upon NATO assets and capabilities (as in the case of the EU's CESDP) or the preponderant influence of NATO member states. The CIS is an exception in this respect and it does provide a vehicle for a form of Russian hegemony in the former Soviet Union. It is, however, at present far too weak to play any meaningful role in the security affairs of continental Europe.[22]

Inclusion and exclusion in security governance

To talk of security governance as constituting a system is to suggest the existence of boundaries.[23] In a system of security governance that is multi-layered, the outer boundary is not necessarily an exact one. Because the system of security governance comprises a range of international organisations, practices and regimes it has the potential to accommodate the vast majority of European states. Indeed, even if only through participation in some of the more embracing manifestations of security governance (the CFE Treaty and the OSCE), there are very few European states that are not included in the system to some degree. That said, given the determining role of NATO in the recent development of security governance, membership of the Alliance is the single most important criterion of inclusion (and thus, conversely, a marker of exclusion). Formal membership constitutes the core of the system of security governance – that part of Europe that approximates a security community (in institutional terms membership of this community also overlaps with that of the EU).[24] Beyond this, involvement in the system of security governance is diffuse and variegated.

It is possible to identify the states involved in the system of security governance and to quantify the extent of their involvement. In short, one can posit parameters or dimensions of inclusion and exclusion:

- The normative dimension: relating to how far a state accepts the system of security governance and, by extension, the principles and norms that underpin it, and perceptions of compliance with these norms by the state concerned and by other states.
- The intentionality dimension: the extent of the state's involvement in the purposeful creation of that system.
- The regulatory dimension: the degree to which the state participates in the institutional mechanisms of the system in terms of membership of formal security-related structures and compliance with treaty and related commitments in the security field.
- The geopolitical dimension: the state's geopolitical location – a demarcation less rigid than in the Cold War but nonetheless still relevant to states at the geographic periphery of Europe.[25]

These parameters should be seen as cumulative in effect. To be amiss in one does not in itself suggest complete exclusion, only a degree of exclusion. Indeed, almost without exception exclusion is a relative rather than an absolute condition. In the system of security governance in contemporary Europe at least six types of (relative) exclusion are apparent, five of which are of relevance here (the sixth type of exclusion refers to the European 'post-neutrals' of Austria, Finland, Ireland, Sweden and Switzerland, states which are closely involved in many aspects of security governance but which hold no desire to join formal military alliances such as NATO). These are ranked in descending order.

The first type of exclusion refers to states such as the Federal Republic of Yugoslavia/Serbia (until the overthrow of President Slobodan Milosevic in 2000) and Belarus. These depart from the system of security governance on almost every count. They disagree with it in principle, have been detached from (indeed, actively opposed to) its formation and development, and have not been involved (other than when forced) in its regulatory mechanisms. Their domestic political orders, further, hardly correspond to the underlying norms that characterise the core states of that system.

The second type is an exclusion that follows partly from distance, and refers to those states on Europe's geographic periphery such as Moldova and the Transcaucasian states of Armenia, Azerbaijan and Georgia. These hold an ambiguous disposition towards the operational principles and format of the system (a function both of distance and calculations regarding their more immediate, Russian-influenced security environment) and tend to be only partially involved in its regulatory mechanisms. These states have also faced major problems in terms of postcommunist democratisation and marketisation and have experienced profound political crises stemming from unresolved internal ethno-regional antagonisms.

The third type, constituting the Balkan states of Bosnia, Albania and, to a lesser degree, Macedonia, shares certain features of the second group. These states too have experienced profound civil strife (or, in Macedonia's case, the threat of it) and problems of fashioning postcommunist political and economic orders. The major and crucial difference, however, is their status as *de facto* protectorates of NATO, something that accords them a unique relationship to the system of security governance.

The fourth type of exclusion relates to the special cases of Russia and Ukraine. Although geographically removed from the heart of Europe they have developed an important relationship with the system of security governance. Russia, in particular, even though it holds an ambivalent position towards the normative dimension has, by dint of size, history, geostrategic importance and the absence of a realistic alternative, helped to define the system's evolution and retained a significant involvement in its regulatory mechanisms.

The fifth type is a form of exclusion that derives not from any lack of commitment to the system of security governance by the state concerned, but instead from hesitance on the part of core states in involving it more fully in that system's mechanisms (through membership of NATO and the EU). Slovenia, Romania (since November 1996), Bulgaria (since May 1997), Slovakia (since September 1998) and the Baltic states of Estonia, Latvia and Lithuania fall into this category. The status of these states can, however, be regarded as transitional to the extent that they have realistic future prospects of NATO and/or EU membership.

Case studies of exclusion

Yugoslavia

In many respects, Yugoslavia under Milosevic constituted the acme of exclusion from Europe's system of security governance. It departed from the normative basis of security governance, refused to recognise its underlying organisational premises and subverted the system in the Balkan region. Under Milosevic, Yugoslavia's domestic political order was authoritarian and the political leadership committed gross human rights violations. On all these counts, it was in open dispute with the major European and Euroatlantic organisations and, almost alone among European states, enjoyed virtually no formal links to them. Under Milosevic, Yugoslavia was expelled from the CSCE in 1992, was not a member of the Council of Europe and had no partnership arrangements with either the EU or NATO.

In other respects, however, Yugoslavia was linked to security governance in a rather unique manner – it was subject to a form of coercive imposition of governance. NATO's 1995 Operation Deliberate Force compelled the Milosevic regime in Serbia and Serb forces in Bosnia to accept the Dayton Agreement, which provided a formal guarantee of Bosnian sovereignty and thus independence from the former Yugoslavia. It also formed the basis upon which a string of international organisations – the OSCE, the Council of Europe, the EU, the UN, the Contact Group and the International Financial Institutions – established long-term regulation and oversight of political and civil affairs in Bosnia. The activities of these bodies crucially were premised upon the establishment of a more immediate civil order by NATO, first through IFOR and subsequently through SFOR. The upshot was the creation of an international protectorate subsumed within the system of security governance and dependent for that status on NATO's commitment.[26]

Even more clear cut is the case of Kosovo. As with Bosnia, force was used to impose a political settlement and a mandate established for the international oversight of post-conflict political order accompanied by a NATO military presence (KFOR). Kosovo has been transformed into a *de facto* international protectorate. Kosovo differs from Bosnia, however, in that *de jure* it remains part of Yugoslavia, so that imposition has been of a qualitatively different order.

The recourse to force and imposition had obvious implications for Yugoslavia's relationship to the system of security governance, suggesting as it did a condition of subordination. It also implied much about the nature of the system itself. While governance is not usually associated with imposition and coercion, these features – extending to the direct use of military force – have been very much on display in Bosnia and Kosovo. In this light, it may seem perverse to speak of a system of security governance at all. Yet governance, while it may imply a condition of peace, does not require that peace be present in the system as a whole. What matters when talking about security governance in Europe is the security condition of the region in its widest sense. Local wars – be these in Kosovo, Bosnia, the Caucasus or, for that matter, Northern Ireland or the Basque country – detract from security governance in the territories immediately and indirectly affected and even have knock-on effects on certain broad aspects of the system as a whole. The system as such, nonetheless, endures. Governance, furthermore, need not be totally incompatible with coercive practices. Although governance usually refers to something distinct from government, with the latter being seen as more appropriately associated with formal authority and force, this does not rule out situations where the two may coexist in a situation of 'government within governance'.[27] Here the system as a whole enjoys a legitimacy, rests on consensus and operates through non-coercive practices (governance); aspects of the system, however, may be regarded as dysfunctional to the whole and require more telling and forceful interventions (government) for the sake of system stability. Thus in the Bosnian and Kosovan cases, the system's resources were mobilised to correct what, in the form of Serb action, was seen as a destabilising and system-threatening element. With the fall of the Milosevic regime in autumn 2000, Yugoslavia will provide an important test case of how far and how quickly a formerly recalcitrant state can be reintegrated into the system of security governance.

Georgia

The position of Moldova and the Transcaucasus states puts them on the geopolitical (and, indeed, the economic and cultural) edge of Europe. Their involvement in European security governance has, therefore, been less than full. This, however, cannot be seen as a geographic phenomenon alone. It reflects also the legacies of their recent past and the traumas of postcommunism. These have placed the four states in question in the invidious position of having to face turbulent domestic politics (civil war and the threat of territorial secession), economic collapse and interference on the part of neighbouring Russia. These multiple challenges have led to three contrasting strategies of foreign policy: alliance with Russia (as in the case of Armenia), resistance to Russia (Azerbaijan) and compromise with Russia (Moldova and Georgia).[28] The latter two courses have been accompanied by the assiduous cultivation of Euro-atlantic states and organisations.

Since 1991 Georgia has been preoccupied with giving expression to a European orientation and, by extension, with distancing itself from Russia.[29] This reflects, in part, a cultural-historical legacy, but has been buttressed by an unenviable record of Russian encroachment. Moscow has effectively converted the Georgian regions of South Ossetia and Abkhazia into Russian protectorates. It has also secured – in the face of local opposition – access to four Soviet-era military bases. In November 1999 Russia agreed to the closure of two of these bases by June 2001 and to reduce its CFE Treaty-limited military equipment in Georgia by the end of 2000, but even if these reductions are carried out Russian forces in Georgia will be greater than the Georgian armed forces.[30] Some evidence also exists to suggest that maverick forces within the Russian military have had a hand in the various assassination attempts mounted against Georgian President Eduard Shevardnadze. Interference of this sort, particularly when coupled with Georgia's internal civil conflicts, has been partly managed by Tbilisi through begrudging concessions to Moscow. As well as granting access to bases, Georgia has agreed to the presence of Russian/CIS peacekeepers in South Ossetia and Abkhazia, reluctantly joined the CIS in 1993 and in January 2000 agreed to joint Russian–Georgian patrols along the Georgian–Chechen border.

Georgia has sought to ameliorate the effects of its proximity to Russia through actively diversifying its foreign ties. This trend has become increasingly evident since the mid 1990s, reflecting the general weakening of Russia's position in the Soviet successor states and efforts by NATO (and in particular the US) to enhance cooperation with states on Russia's periphery. Georgia has thus cultivated links with other disaffected post-Soviet states (through the Georgia–Ukraine–Uzbekistan–Azerbaijan–Moldova GUUAM group) and sought closer integration with Western institutions (engaging with NATO's Partnership for Peace (PfP) and Euro-Atlantic Partnership Council and receiving American arms as well as Turkish, British and American military training).[31] Shevardnadze, moreover, has outlined some fairly bold ambitions with regard to NATO, arguing in favour of the Bosnia/Kosovo option (the use or threat of force by NATO to impose peace) in Abkhazia and publicly favouring Georgia's eventual membership of the Alliance.[32] Diversification has been assisted in Georgia's case by its geographic location. Bordering the Black Sea and Turkey means that it has much to gain from the development of energy pipelines and transit routes that establish it as a link with the Caspian Sea and Central Asia. This has clear security-related implications, insofar as it has spurred the development of the GUUAM group, provided Georgia with leverage against Russia and been part of the geoeconomic subtext to NATO/EU and other Western activities in the region.

The case of Georgia illustrates the fact that security governance can have effects on peripheral states by orienting them towards the core. It would be perhaps too generous to argue that this has been a consequence of the attraction of the system's underlying norms. Georgia may well have posited European ideals as an alternative to a Russian orientation but sincerity on this score owes much to Shevardnadze personally and less to the particulars of geography or post-Soviet political development (as illustrated by Georgia's neighbour Azerbaijan, which has been equally anti-Russian and pro-Western but under President Heidar Aliev has been distinctly out of touch with liberal political norms). The extent of Georgia's involvement rather reflects historical accident (its inclusion in the CFE Treaty regime and the CSCE in 1992 stemmed from its position in the Soviet Union) and the strategic calculation that diversification was the best route to undermining Russian influence. Despite the clear preference of the Shevardnadze leadership for incorporation, however, Georgia's relationship to the system of European security governance is likely to retain telling aspects of exclusion. While proximity to Russia in itself need not rule out membership of either NATO or the EU, there is no likelihood of Georgia obtaining such exalted status in the foreseeable future. Unlike Poland, Georgia is much more firmly within a Russian sphere of influence. It also shares little history with the European core, is much more distant from that core's main foci of power and enjoys little political patronage in Western Europe or the US. Notwithstanding the energy issues noted above, Georgia's geopolitical location thus remains marginal for NATO and the EU. Not only does this preclude membership of either organisation, it also rules out NATO action in Bosnia and Kosovo as a precedent for an externally imposed settlement of Georgia's internal strife.

Albania

Following breaks with the communist states of Yugoslavia (in 1949), the Soviet Union (1961) and China (1978), Albania entered a state of almost total international isolation. This state of oblivion – as an Albanian defence adviser put it[33] – was underpinned by a notably harsh form of communist authoritarianism, an exaggerated sense of nationalism and a military posture of defensive self-sufficiency.

Since the removal from power of the communist regime in 1991, Albania has pursued a foreign policy that has sought to break out of such isolation through integration in Euro-atlantic structures, the development of bilateral ties with Western states (the US, Italy and Germany in particular) and the improvement of relations with regional neighbours (Greece, Macedonia and Turkey). This is a policy based upon a recognition of the importance of Western military and economic assistance for the promotion of Albanian political stability, economic recovery and military development, and the desire to promote stability within a troubled regional setting. These two priorities are, in turn, connected – cultivating external patronage is seen as a route to protection against very real domestic and regional threats.[34]

With regard to its Euro-atlantic orientation, Albania has developed a wide-ranging relationship with the EU based on trade preferences and various forms of economic, technical and humanitarian assistance (it is not, however, a formally recognised applicant country and therefore does not have an EU Association Agreement). It has also joined the Council of Europe and the OSCE (the latter providing crucial mediation during a major civil and political crisis in 1997). As for NATO, in 1992 Albania lodged a formal application for membership (the first postcommunist state to do so) and after 1994 enthusiastically pursued an Individual Partnership Programme under the PfP.

Tirana's enthusiasm, however, is unlikely to compensate for the reluctance of both NATO and the EU to begin the process of formal accession owing to Albania's shaky political and economic credentials. That said, Albania has managed to establish strong connections with these bodies. Indeed, the very weakness of the Albanian state has encouraged external involvement, NATO and the EU viewing the shoring up of Albania as a means of staunching instability in the Balkan region. Albanian integration has, in other words, been facilitated by domestic and regional crises. The near civil war of 1997 resulted in the temporary deployment of a Multinational Protection Force in the country (led by Italy and involving other NATO states such as France, Greece, Spain and Denmark). The deployment, moreover, proved a catalyst for a comprehensive programme of assistance under the PfP geared towards a total refashioning of the Albanian armed forces (complemented by WEU assistance in training the Albanian police). This programme, although it has no formal mandate to promote disarmament, entails oversight of military budgeting and ordnance disposal and has acted as a partial redress for Albania's non-participation in the CFE Treaty. Albania demonstrated its strategic significance to NATO during the war in Bosnia, providing the Alliance with aircraft facilities and, following the 1995 Dayton Accord, transit bases for the deployment of US IFOR contingents. During the Kosovo crisis, Albania was used as a base for two large-scale NATO air and ground deployments aimed at

deterring Serb attacks against Kosovar Albanians in 1998, was the recipient
of a NATO Albanian Force tasked with refugee protection under
Operation Allied Harbour in 1999, and later became an important staging
post for the deployment of KFOR. [35] Albania is also likely to be a key benefi-
ciary of the EU-led Stability Pact for South-Eastern Europe developed after
the 1999 Kosovo crisis.[36]

Albania has thus been transformed from an isolationist and effectively
non-aligned state to a virtual protectorate of NATO. Its status of dependency is not as great as that of Bosnia or Kosovo – there is no semi-permanent military presence along the lines of SFOR or KFOR, and NATO and
the EU are not directly involved in the oversight of domestic governmental
arrangements. Albania's defence capability has, however, been increasingly linked to NATO assistance and its security has, since at least 1995,
been contingent upon NATO's defining role in the broader regional security context. Furthermore, whether out of pragmatism or principle, the
post-1991 Albanian leadership has willingly (even enthusiastically) aligned
itself with the norms and, by extension, the practices of both the EU and
NATO, and has proven material to the strategic objectives of the Alliance
in both Bosnia and Kosovo. It thus has a strong link to the system of security governance even though it is likely to remain excluded from its core
membership.

Russia

Russia is related to European security governance in a rather unique way.[37]
In some respects, it has been in broad concurrence with the normative
underpinnings of the system. The manner in which security governance
has developed over the last ten years owed much initially to the interaction
between Mikhail Gorbachev's Soviet regime and the West. Many of the key
changes in European security to which Gorbachev contributed have, moreover, not been challenged by the subsequent post-Soviet leadership in
Moscow. A unified Germany, the removal of the Russian military presence
from Central Europe and the elimination of intermediate range nuclear
forces are considered legitimate and, thus, have not become sources of
conflict with the West.

One major difference with the Gorbachev period, however, is striking.
Gorbachev's acceptance of changes in Europe was based on an assumption
that the Soviet Union was, and would remain, an important component of
the new set of arrangements that emerged with the Cold War's demise. In
the Russian case, however, there is a profound sense that these arrangements have evolved during the 1990s in a manner that is inimical to
Moscow's interests. The key source of Russian anxiety in this area is NATO.
Despite the rhetoric of some politicians, Russian analysts have developed a

relatively sophisticated set of arguments against NATO's post-Cold War development. Specifically they argue that: a NATO-centrism has developed, establishing the Alliance as the core European security body and overriding the OSCE and, in the Kosovo crisis, the UN; NATO remains a primarily military organisation, and one which has enlarged its membership; the Alliance has developed a military-political orientation to undertake tasks beyond NATO territory; and NATO has elevated itself above international law.[38]

Underlying these specific charges is a sense that Russia has been marginalised by NATO's ascendancy in Europe. The dominance of the Alliance (and, indeed, other Western organisations such as the EU) has capped a decade of Russian geostrategic decline and the creation of a European (and global) order that has been defined by the West and in particular the US. The degree to which Russia has exaggerated this sense of isolation by its own foreign (and domestic) policies, and the extent to which NATO and its member states have sought and should seek to accommodate Russia and thereby ameliorate its isolation are, of course, matters of considerable controversy. What is obvious, however, is that a growing sense of estrangement characterises Russia's relation with the US and Europe, compounded by a growing feeling of impotence in Russia. There is now a sense of clear frustration in Moscow that it is, in fact, powerless to stop Alliance actions such as enlargement or the air campaign against Yugoslavia.

Despite its problems with the manner in which security governance has developed, Russia has remained engaged with that system. Its participation has, however, become less enthusiastic, notably from the mid 1990s as NATO came to play the leading role in European security affairs. Yet recognising the material limitations of its military and economic position in Europe, and aware also of the unattractiveness of isolation, Russia has been unwilling to withdraw totally from cooperative practices. In policy terms, Russia has continued its involvement in important security-related initiatives, but has done so in a manner designed to project specific Russian national interests often in juxtaposition to positions held by NATO. Thus Russia has, to a point, actively shaped security governance (the intentionality dimension outlined above) while also being involved in its institutional mechanisms (the regulatory dimension).

Russia's active engagement in European security governance can be seen in four areas. First, Russia has been an active, indeed principal participant, in the implementation and adaptation of the CFE Treaty. Second, Russia has supported the denuclearisation of the post-Soviet states through the removal of nuclear weapons from Belarus and Ukraine, the START strategic arms control process, bilateral cooperation with the US and upholding the 1968 Nuclear Non-Proliferation Treaty. Third, despite its opposition to NATO's use of force in Bosnia and Kosovo, Russia has been an active and cooperative participant in international actions in the Balkans, through its engaging in framing and implementing the Dayton Accords and the 1999 Kosovo peace agreement and involvement in IFOR/SFOR and KFOR.[39] Fourth, Russia has retained or assumed membership of bodies that have played a central or indirect role in European security, including the UN Security Council, the OSCE, the Council of Europe, the Group of Eight (G8) and the Contact Group. It has also enjoyed a relatively favoured status in various *ad hoc* arrangements and initiatives (such as diplomatic contacts with the US, the EU and the G8 during the 1999 Kosovo crisis and the March 1998 troika summit of the French, German and Russian Presidents).

In a system of security governance increasingly dominated by NATO, however, what really matters is how far Russia is involved in, and attuned to, Alliance-related mechanisms. Presidents Yeltsin and Putin both recognised that NATO's key role in European security necessitated Russian engagement with the Alliance. The particular type of engagement demanded offers Moscow a privileged place in NATO arrangements. Prior to 1997, demands of this nature had only a limited impact. NATO mechanisms such as the North Atlantic Cooperation Council and the PfP treated partner states in a largely egalitarian manner. Russian claims that its greater international weight needed to be taken into account won only symbolic concessions and Russian participation within these fora was less than enthusiastic.[40]

The terms of the relationship underwent a qualitative change in 1997 with the signing of the NATO–Russia Founding Act and the subsequent formation of the Permanent Joint Council (PJC). While the basic disagreement on NATO expansion was not resolved by the Act, Russia was heartened by specific pledges relating to the modalities of enlargement (statements that NATO had no plans to deploy nuclear weapons on the territory of new members and would maintain transparency regarding their military integration with the Alliance) and the PJC's institutionalisation of mechanisms of consultation then unparalleled for a non-NATO member. The Founding Act and the PJC soon became objects of contention as the two sides disputed just how constraining (for NATO) or how empowering (for Russia) they should be. This whole set-up was, in turn, endangered by the Kosovo crisis as Russia, in protest at NATO action, withdrew from the PJC as well as from the PfP and other NATO-related activities. With the halt of the bombing campaign, however, ties were gradually restored. Russia was an early participant in KFOR and a fairly reliable command mechanism for NATO–Russia cooperation on the ground was soon established.[41] More formal, high-level contacts were cemented during the early months of

Putin's presidency in 2000, with NATO Secretary-General Lord Robertson meeting Putin in Moscow, Foreign Minister Igor Ivanov attending a ministerial meeting of the restored PJC and regular PJC meetings of ambassadors and military representatives being re-established. It remains moot how constructive and far reaching these interactions will be. Indeed, their resumption occurred against a backdrop of new disputes between Moscow and NATO (over the Russian campaign in Chechnya and rival interpretations of the Russian military doctrine adopted in April 2000). Yet their mere existence adds something, however minor, to Russia's involvement in European security governance.

In short, Russia's relationship to the system of security governance exhibits features of both exclusion and inclusion. Insofar as the main engine of security governance is NATO and the prospect of Russian membership of that organisation is slim, then a definite exclusion exists. This is compounded by Russia's parallel exclusion from the EU and the fact that the activities of the OSCE, the one pan-European organisation it has championed, offers Russia scant compensation. As well as being inimical to the interests of Russia, this state of affairs has potentially destabilising consequences for Europe as a whole. NATO's preponderance on the continent and the implicit subordination of Russia have created incentives on Russia's part to defect from those aspects of European security governance in which its participation might otherwise be important. As the oscillating NATO–Russia relationship illustrates, this danger has yet to be fully realised. However, further NATO expansion (particularly to incorporate the Baltic states) or the repetition of a Kosovo-type campaign elsewhere in the former Yugoslavia (over Montenegro, for instance) could well trigger such an eventuality. This would result in a type of security governance incomplete in several respects. Geographically, it would not extend to a major part of European territory. Politically it would be denied the small (but at times still significant) diplomatic influence Russia wields in some quarters (in Minsk, Yerevan and Belgrade). Institutionally it would freeze the contribution of the UN and the OSCE, owing to the wielding of a Russian veto. Militarily it would jeopardise the major gains achieved within the CFE framework. In this light, security governance would come to be more appropriate as a concept for understanding what is missing in the organisation of Europe than what is present.

One may, however, also take a more sanguine view of Russia's involvement in European security. While a degree of competition and estrangement has emerged between Russia and the West, this has occurred in a European setting that remains conducive to cooperative behaviour and the peaceful management of differences between Russia and its western neighbours. The main precondition for this state of affairs was the winding down of the Cold War in the late 1980s and early 1990s. Although sometimes held responsible for the existence of a 'long peace' on the continent of Europe, the Cold War was in essence destabilising in that it represented a conflict *in potentia* between two rival military blocs.[42] Although the end of the Cold War did entail a victory for the West, this was accompanied by path-breaking security measures that promoted amity rather than enmity between the great powers. The INF and CFE Treaties, Confidence- and Security-Building Measures and the package of measures that attended German unification meant that by 1991 the former Cold War adversaries, rather than being poised at the point of aggression, had embraced arms reduction, military transparency and the renunciation of offensive military postures.[43]

The subsequent rise to primacy of NATO may well have had the unintended effect of undermining the principles of mutual confidence inherent in these measures, but this has not yet constituted for Moscow sufficient cause to subvert the whole post-Cold War system of security governance itself. While Moscow has challenged the precise institutional form of security governance and the terms of its own participation in it, Russia's position owes little to ideology and even less to territorial ambition or popular nationalist mobilisation.[44] Given this, plenty of scope remains for the involvement of Russia in security governance. Despite Russian–NATO tensions in the 1990s, there have been many cases of joint action and cooperation. Russia has won concessions over the implementation and adaptation of the CFE Treaty, NATO enlargement, the institutionalisation of relations with the Alliance and the development of the OSCE, and a role in the settlement in Kosovo. At a time of domestic crisis and international decline, Russia has succeeded in preserving a sense of self-importance and asserted the continuing legitimacy of its interest in the continent's affairs.

Of course, this practical cooperation may be a consequence of Russian weakness and a militarily and economically strong Russia might be much bolder in asserting its interests. In this context, however, several points are worth noting. First, a revival of this sort is unlikely in the short or even medium term. Indeed, Russia may never fully recover from its current prostrate position. As Thomas Graham has put it, we may face 'a world without Russia', where Russia is reduced permanently to the ranks of a middle power and its involvement in international affairs is of less and less consequence.[45] A Russia of such stature could still play a spoiling role in Europe but would also be compelled to seek continued accommodation with the other European powers in order to compensate for its decline in status. Second, even should a Russian revival occur it need not subvert security governance as such, only alter the terms upon which it is based (since Russian objections to the existing system of security governance are largely pragmatic in nature and Russia benefits from its engagement in that system). Third, Russia is presently experiencing an unprecedented externalisation of its economy and has benefited from reinforcing political cooperation (through partnership arrangements with the EU and Russia's incorporation into the G8). The fact that the US and Western Europe are now Russia's main sources of external finance and trade creates an obvious incentive for Moscow to maintain favourable relations with the West.

The Baltic states

The Baltic states of Estonia, Latvia and Lithuania have made an unambiguous bid for the fullest possible degree of inclusion in the system of security governance. Since the resumption of their independence in 1991 the Baltic states have pursued determinedly pro-Western/European foreign policies. They have aimed to differentiate themselves from the other post-Soviet states, distance themselves from Russia (which they regard as a potential threat) and boost their credentials as candidates for membership of the EU and NATO. This policy has been buttressed by the steady progress all three states have made in consolidating post-Soviet political and economic reforms and efforts to boost subregional integration within the broader Baltic Sea and Nordic areas.

The position of the Baltic states is symbolic of the revolution in European security affairs in the last decade. Before 1991, not only were these denied international statehood, but there was very little notion that the Baltic area itself constituted a self-contained geopolitical and economic region owing to its incorporation in the Soviet Union.[46] By the turn of the century, the orientation and identity of the region were of a quite different order. Estonia, Latvia and Lithuania are full members of the OSCE and the Council of Europe, are associate partners of the WEU and have Association Agreements with the EU and well-developed political and military ties with NATO. All three are entwined in a dense network of subregional activities through the Council of Baltic Sea States and 'five-plus-three' Nordic–Baltic cooperation. The latter has taken on a distinct security dimension. Sweden and Finland, along with NATO members Norway and Denmark, have assisted in the formation of regional structures such as the Baltic Peacekeeping Battalion and the joint Baltic Naval Squadron.

These changes reflect a significant process of inclusion within nascent European security governance. The Baltic states, however, remain excluded from formal membership of NATO, the core organisation of that system. That said, among the excluded states the Baltics enjoy a relatively privileged position in that the Alliance collectively and the US specifically have made explicit reference to the possibility of future membership.[47] Should the Baltic states gain entry into NATO this will not only prove crucial to the

states concerned but also carry significant implications for the development of security governance more broadly. The Baltic states currently
occupy a strategic niche between the Nordic countries, Central Europe and
Russia. Since the early 1990s, the Baltic states' relations with their Nordic
and Central European neighbours have been based on openness, integration and cooperation. The regional stability this has fostered has helped to
promote the Baltic states' case for wider integration. The Baltic states'
accession to the Alliance would further transform the region, converting it
into a demarcation line between an enlarged NATO and the rest of the
former Soviet Union. The strategically sensitive position of the Baltic states,
a desire within the West to avoid a confrontation with Russia and the possibility (in the wake of the Kosovo crisis) of prioritising a southern enlargement, however, may well delay the Baltic states' membership of NATO.[48] All
of this does not foreclose Baltic inclusion, but it may well be delayed, differentiated and/or dependent on a wider process of multilateral integration
involving Russia.

EU membership appears, at first sight, to be more straightforward.
Estonia has been viewed as a first-wave candidate and accession negotiations opened with Latvia and Lithuania in February 2000. The security
implications of EU accession have in some respects already become apparent. Alterations in domestic legislation to the benefit of Russian speakers in
Latvia and Estonia (and thus to the benefit of Baltic–Russian relations)
have been prompted by EU cajoling. Somewhat more problematic are the
implications of the EU's CESDP. While it does not involve a binding security
guarantee, EU membership has been interpreted by some as constituting *de
facto* enjoyment of protection not just by the EU's own nascent military
capability, but also by NATO. Thus EU membership appears to offer security assurance to states such as the Baltic countries likely to enter the EU
before joining NATO. There are, however, two caveats to this. First, the
nature of this assurance is not well articulated, let alone agreed, within the
EU (or NATO). Second, what the Baltics may gain from a sense of assurance through the EU, they may lose through a deterioration of relations
with Russia if that membership is accompanied by the opening up of
discord between the EU and Russia stemming from incautious security
pledges. Given this, EU membership when it arrives for the Baltic states is
unlikely to be accompanied by clarity or forthrightness in terms of the security status of these new members.

Conclusion

Since 1989 security governance in Europe has developed in a manner that
reflects the dominance of what Norman Davies has termed the 'Allied

Scheme'. This is a view of Europe (and the international system more broadly) that is derived from Allied victories in 1918, 1945 and 1989. It encapsulates a belief in the superiority of Western values (democracy, the rule of law and the free market) and an assumption that institutions of Western European and Euro-atlantic origin embody tried and tested practices of international cooperation and should thus continue to form the basis of Europe's organisation.[49] If this scheme triumphed in 1989 by offering a more robust alternative to communism, then its viability (and thus the viability of the particular form of European security governance of which it is part) thereafter has rested on the ability of its core organisations (NATO and the EU) to assimilate or manage relations with the states of postcommunist Europe. Their efforts in this regard have led to the presence within Europe of two conflicting processes of change – the dynamics of inclusion and exclusion.

The dynamic of inclusion is defined as a process that acts to mitigate the forms of exclusion detailed above. This process is determined ultimately by NATO and the EU. Although security governance is multi-layered, these two organisations, and in particular NATO, have nonetheless played the pivotal role in its development. The enlargement of NATO has created a domino effect whereby the Alliance is compelled to respond to demands for inclusion from non-members. Granting membership to the Czech Republic, Hungary and Poland has had the effect of raising the expectations of those states which perceive themselves to be in the second wave (the Baltic states, Bulgaria, Romania, Slovakia and Slovenia). Their claims, in turn, fuel a fear of losing out among other states (Albania and Macedonia), leading to an exaggeration of their own case for inclusion. In this light, enlargement can be viewed as having a direct bearing on security governance. It expands the core of NATO states, creates incentives towards good behaviour (both domestically and externally) on the part of aspirant NATO members, and is a magnet for the assertion of Western norms and values in states long cut off from the West by communist rule.[50] In this sense some states, while not formally NATO members, can nonetheless be said to observe the obligations of membership. As in the case of Albania they have enjoyed a certain commitment on the part of NATO in return.

In contrast, the dynamic of exclusion is a process whereby the ascendancy of NATO in European security governance has generated a sense of separation between the Alliance and states remaining outside NATO. This dynamic has manifested itself with varying degrees of intensity. It was most acute in the case of Yugoslavia, resulting in a NATO strategy of imposition. The dynamic has been somewhat less marked in the case of Russia. Russia has, to a point, been included in security governance. This, however, has not resolved some of the fundamental issues surrounding the terms of that inclusion. Nor has it overcome perceptions of exclusion in Russia that stem from the pivotal position of a NATO that does not count Russia among its members. *Ipso facto*, so long as NATO continues to enjoy primacy, Russia's relative exclusion will endure. Elsewhere, NATO's dominance in Europe has been less of an issue. A relatively benign (even favourable) attitude towards the Alliance, however, has not necessarily meant the overcoming of geopolitical distance (as the cases of Georgia and, to some degree, Ukraine make clear). Although less explicitly directed towards security issues than NATO, the process of EU enlargement is generating a similar dynamic of inclusion and exclusion.

These dynamics of inclusion and exclusion suggest that Europe cannot be viewed as divided along a single axis as in the Cold War. True, a boundary does exist in Europe that approximates the formal membership of NATO and the EU, but it is a boundary that is malleable.[51] The expansion (actual or mooted) and transformation of these two organisations have elided the distinction between included and excluded states. This distinction has been blurred still further by the presence and development of other, more truly pan-European, arrangements such as the CFE Treaty and the OSCE. Europe is still far from united and, arguably, is never likely to be completely so. Yet a decade on from 1989, the year in which the demand for a 'return to Europe' provided a rallying call for the dismantling of communism, the deep schism that beset the continent for most of the post-war period has at least begun to heal.

Notes

1 This chapter is derived partly from research for a project entitled 'Security governance in the new Europe', funded by the Economic and Social Research Council's 'One Europe or Several?' programme (award no. L213 25 2008).

2 T. Rosenberg, 'The unfinished revolution of 1989', *Foreign Policy*, 115 (1999), 91–105.

3 R. Rose, 'Another great transformation', *CSD Bulletin (Centre for the Study of Democracy, University of Westminster, London)*, 6:2 (1999), 6–8.

4 Membership Action Plan (issued at the meeting of the North Atlantic Council, 23–24 April 1999), *NATO Review*, 47:2 (1999), D13–16; and European Commission, 'Agenda 2000: for a stronger and wider Union', *Bulletin of the European Communities*, 5 (1997).

5 N. Ascherson, 'The balloon goes up', *The Observer* (11 April 1999), 28.

6 R. Rhodes, 'The new governance: governing without government', *Political Studies*, 44:4 (1996), 664.

7 J. Rosenau, *Along the Domestic–Foreign Frontier. Exploring Governance in a Turbulent World* (Cambridge, Cambridge University Press, 1997), p. 146; and M.-C. Smouts, 'The proper use of governance in international relations', *International Social Science Journal*, 155 (1998), 86.

8 E. Adler and M. Barnett, 'Security communities in theoretical perspective', in E. Adler and M. Barnett (eds.), *Security Communities* (Cambridge, Cambridge University Press, 1998), pp. 6–7.

9 J. Sperling and E. Kirchner, 'The security architectures and institutional futures of post-1989 Europe', *Journal of European Public Policy*, 4:2 (1997), 163; and D. Deudney and G. J. Ikenberry, 'The nature and sources of liberal international order', *Review of International Studies*, 25:2 (1999), 193.

10 B. Buzan et al., *The European Security Order Recast. Scenarios for the Post-Cold War Era* (London and New York, Pinter, 1990), especially chapter 3.

11 A. Rotfeld, 'New security structures in Europe: concepts, proposals and decisions', in SIPRI (ed.), *SIPRI Yearbook 1991: World Armaments and Disarmament* (Stockholm, SIPRI, 1991), pp. 585–600.

12 P. Corterier, '*Quo vadis* NATO?', *Survival*, 32:2 (1990), 141–56.

13 J. J. Holst, 'Pursuing the durable peace in the aftermath of the Cold War', *NATO Review*, 40:4 (1992), 9–13.

14 Rotfeld, 'New security structures in Europe', pp. 594–6.

15 NATO, 'The London Declaration on a Transformed North Atlantic Alliance' (6 July 1990), para. 22 (www.nato.int/docu/comm/49-95/c900706.htm).

16 NATO, 'The Alliance's Strategic Concept', *NATO Review*, 47:2 (1999), D7–D13.

17 F. Schimmelfennig, 'NATO enlargement: a constructivist explanation', *Security Studies*, 8:2-3 (1998–99), 213.

18 A. Roberts, 'NATO's "humanitarian war" over Kosovo', *Survival*, 41:3 (1999), 103–4.

19 M. Oakes, *European Defence: From Portschach to Helsinki*, House of Commons Research Paper 00/20 (London, House of Commons Library, 2000).

20 D. Tarschys, 'The Council of Europe: strengthening European security by civilian means', *NATO Review*, 45:1 (1997), 4–9.

21 I. Bremmer and A. Bailes, 'Subregionalism in the Newly-Independent States', *International Affairs*, 74:1 (1998), 131–48.

22 R. Sakwa and M. Webber, 'The Commonwealth of Independent States, 1991–98: stagnation and survival', *Europe-Asia Studies*, 51:3 (1999), 379–415.

23 R. Dahl, *Modern Political Analysis* (Englewood Cliffs, NJ, Prentice-Hall, 3rd edn, 1976), p. 6.

24 T. G. Ash, 'Europe's endangered liberal order', *Foreign Affairs*, 77:2 (1999), 61.

25 M. Smith, 'The European Union and a changing Europe: establishing the boundaries of order', *Journal of Common Market Studies*, 34:1 (1996), 14–15.

26 A. Agh, 'Processes of democratisation in the East-Central European and Balkan States: sovereignty-related conflicts in the context of Europeanisation', *Communist and Postcommunist Studies*, 32 (1999), 274–7.

27 G. Stoker, 'Governance as theory: five propositions', *International Social Science Journal*, 155 (1998), 24.

28 H. E. Hale, 'Independence and integration in the Caspian basin', *SAIS Review*, 19:1 (1999), 177.

29 B. Coppieters, 'Conclusions: the failure of regionalism in Eurasia and the Western ascendancy over Russia's near abroad', in B. Coppieters, A. Zverev and D. Trenin (eds.), *Commonwealth and Independence in Post-Soviet Eurasia* (London and Portland, Frank Cass, 1997), pp. 209–10.

30 *Moscow Times* (29 January 2000).

31 *Izvestiya* (24 June 1999).

32 *Johnson's Russia List* (1 February 1998); *Novye Izvestiya*, 15 July 1999, trans. in
    Current Digest of the Post-Soviet Press, 51:29 (1999), 15; and *Moscow News* (12–18
    May 1999).

33 A. Copani, 'The new dimensions of Albania's security posture', *NATO Review*,
    44:2 (1996), 24.

34 R. Lani and F. Schmidt, 'Albanian foreign policy between geography and
    history', *International Spectator*, 33:2 (1998), 79–103; and F. Nano (Prime
    Minister of Albania), 'Security in Southeastern Europe: an Albanian perspec-
    tive' (www.csdr.org/98Book/nano98.htm).

35 R. C. Hendrickseon, 'Albania and NATO. regional security and selective inter-
    vention', *Security Dialogue*, 30:1 (1999), 109–16.

36 'Chairmens' conclusions: regional funding conference', Brussels, 29–30 March
    2000 (www.seerecon.org/Calendar/2000/Events/RC/conclusions.htm).

37 This section is drawn, in part, from M. Webber, 'A tale of a decade: European
    security governance and Russia', *European Security*, 9:2 (2000), 31–60.

38 I. Ivanov, 'Europe on the threshold of the 21st century', *International Affairs
    (Moscow)*, 1 (1999), pp. 1–6; B. Kazantsev, 'Serious concern over New NATO
    strategy', *International Affairs (Moscow)*, 45: 2 (1999), 23–8; and E. Primakov,
    'The world on the eve of the 21st century', *International Affairs (Moscow)*, 5–6
    (1996), pp. 2–14.

39 M. Andersen, 'Russia and the former Yugoslavia', in M. Webber, (ed.), *Russia
    and Europe. Conflict or Cooperation?* (Houndmills, Macmillan, 2000).

40 See 'Protocol on the results of discussions between Russian Foreign Minister
    Andrei Kozyrev and the NATO Council', reprinted in M. Mihalka,
    'European–Russian security and NATO's Partnership for Peace', *RFE/RL
    Research Report*, 3:33 (1994), 44.

41 Andersen, 'Russia and the former Yugoslavia', pp. 203–4.

42 L. Freedman, 'Military power and political influence', *International Affairs*, 74:4
    (1998), 763.

43 M. Mandelbaum, *The Dawn of Peace in Europe* (New York, The Twentieth Century
    Fund Press, 1996), pp. 76–109; and J. Sperling and E. Kirchner, *Recasting the
    European Order* (Manchester and New York, Manchester University Press, 1997),
    pp. 1–23.

44 A. Fedorov, 'New pragmatism of Russia's foreign policy', *International Affairs
    (Moscow)*, 45: 5 (1999), 47–52; and A. Lieven, 'The weakness of Russian national-
    ism', *Survival*, 41:2 (1999), 53–70.

45 T. Graham, 'A world without Russia?', paper presented to a conference of the
    Jamestown Foundation, Washington, DC, 9 June 1999, carried on *Johnson's
    Russia List* (11 June 1999).

46 Z. Ozolina, 'Baltic Sea region – a test case for European integration', in D.
    Bleiere et al., *The Impact of European Integration Processes on Baltic Security* (NATO
    Fellowship Final Report, Brussels, NATO, 1999), p. 12.

47 'Washington Summit Communiqué', paragraph 7, *NATO Review*, 47:2 (1999),
    D3;   speech   of   S.   Talbott   in   Tallinn,   January   2000
    (www.talbott.mfa.ee/Talbott_Frasure.html); and the letters of US presidential

contenders A. Gore and G. W. Bush addressed to a conference of nine NATO applicant states in Vilnius and reported in *The Washington Post* (20 May 2000).

48 W. Drozdiak, 'NATO sets its sights on the Balkans', *The Washington Post* (7 July 1999), p. A15.

49 N. Davies, *Europe: A History* (London, Pimlico, 1997), pp. 39–40.

50 Schimmelfennig, 'NATO enlargement', 217.

51 Smith, 'The European Union and a changing Europe'; and L. Friis and A. Murphy, 'The European Union and Central and Eastern Europe: governance and boundaries', *Journal of Common Market Studies*, 37:2 (1999), 211–32.

4

German security policy towards Central Europe

Vladimir Handl,[1] Kerry Longhurst and Marcin
Zaborowski

> 'We have lived with our neighbour Germany for 1,000 years, but always
> back to back. Never face to face.' Edward Pietrzyk, Polish military officer
> on his nation's admission to NATO[2]

Germany has always been a key, defining player in Central and Eastern
Europe. During the Cold War, relations between Germany and its eastern
neighbours were determined almost entirely by the bipolar international
context. The implosion of the Soviet bloc and the unification of Germany
therefore created new opportunities for a fundamental redefinition of relations. These developments prompted a debate, both within and outside of
Germany, as to whether the country would resume its historically hegemonic role in the region or whether a new, more cooperative paradigm of
relations would emerge, grounded in multilateral institutions and fora.

In response to the changes of 1989–90 Germany has sought new, cooperative relations with all the countries of postcommunist Europe and has
put particular energy into fostering cooperation with its Central European
neighbours (Poland, the Czech Republic, Hungary and Slovakia – the so-
called 'Visegrad countries'). It is with these countries (although to a lesser
extent in the case of Slovakia) that qualitatively better and deeper forms of
cooperation have been fostered, principally because of their geographical
proximity to Germany, but also because these states have made more rapid
progress in restructuring their political and economic systems than others
in the former communist bloc.

The shape and form of post-Cold War relations between the Visegrad
four and Germany, it will be argued here, confirm the idea that Germany
has not slipped into its historical hegemonic role in the region, but has
instead sought to replicate the highly institutionalised forms of cooperation the Federal Republic developed with its Western allies during the Cold
War. This chapter explores Germany's role in Central and Eastern Europe
over the past decade, focusing on its relations with the Visegrad states, with
particular reference to Germany's role in the enlargement of the North

Atlantic Treaty Organisation (NATO) and military cooperation with these countries.

Germany and Central and Eastern Europe after 1989

The Central and Eastern European region has grown in importance in German foreign and security policy over the past decade. Although Germany's relations with its Western partners in the EU and NATO remain its first foreign policy priority, developing a new eastern policy has become the second most important area of foreign policy action for the country.[3]

After the dramatic events of 1989–90, Germany's particular role in post-communist Europe first became controversial with its 'defection from the rules of the game' when it recognised the independence of Croatia and Slovenia in 1991. This apparent deviation from (West) Germany's usual policy of acting through multilateral fora was viewed by many as signalling the emergence of an assertive new unilateralism in foreign policy. It appeared to be a reversal of the multilateralism which had been the trademark of the Federal Republic's foreign policy since 1949. This deviation from existing patterns of behaviour, however, was followed by consistent efforts on the part of Germany to stabilise the region as a whole. Germany provided much of the impetus for the reform and regeneration of international fora, most notably through the adoption of NATO's new strategic concept and the creation of the North Atlantic Cooperation Council (NACC) in 1991, the establishment of NATO's Partnership for Peace (PfP) in 1994, the reform of the European Union (EU) and the development of its security role, and the renewal of the Conference on (now Organisation for) Security and Cooperation in Europe (C/OSCE). The return to multilateralism was also apparent in the crucial role played by Germany in determining the evolution of both NATO and the EU's enlargement policies.

On balance, after some initial blunders, Germany's role in the region since 1989 has been characterised by the exporting of her Western policy style to Central and Eastern Europe. Although German interests have been voiced more confidently since the end of the Cold War, they have been conceived of and promoted along European lines, compatible with multilateral structures and pursued through cooperation with allies and neighbours.[4]

NATO enlargement

In the immediate wake of the end of the Cold War Germany's approach to Central and Eastern Europe was defined primarily in terms of its

relationship with Russia. Guided by a traditionally 'Russia first' policy and
wary of the still sizeable Russian military presence in the region, Germany
maintained this stance. Early German diplomacy viewed Central and
Eastern Europe as rife with the same types of risks and instability as in
Russia and thus pursued a cautious, incremental path in establishing relations with the region, not yet prepared to articulate the prospect of NATO
membership for Central and Eastern European states. At this point Bonn
focused on promoting the development of the CSCE as a pan-European
security structure. Germany proposed a CSCE European Security Council,
comprising representation from major countries and regional groups,
including the Visegrad four and the EU. The most immediate security
problems of the region, Bonn argued, were the need for access to Western
markets and soft security issues – the environment, migration and crime.
These new soft security problems could not be addressed by NATO
enlargement. Hence Germany's relatively early pledge to support the
enlargement of the EU to include Poland, Hungary and Czechoslovakia,
together with financial assistance to help alleviate the region's socio-
economic problems.

Until 1991 these policies broadly mirrored the expectations of the
Central European states, which – since these countries were still formally
members of the Warsaw Pact – were focused predominantly on dismantling
the Cold War division between the two military alliances. At this point various ideas for transforming European security architecture were put
forward by new Central European leaders. During his first visit to NATO's
headquarters in March 1990, for example, Polish Foreign Minister
Krzysztof Skubiszewski argued in favour of a pan-European security system,
including both NATO and Warsaw Pact members.[5] A similar argument was
voiced by the Czechoslovak President Vaclav Havel during a speech to the
Council of Europe in May 1990.[6]

External developments, however, soon put NATO at the centre of the
post-Cold War reorganisation of European security. In particular, the
August 1991 coup attempt by hardliners in the Soviet Union sent a chilling
message to other Central and Eastern European states and the West.
Reacting to these events German Foreign Minister Hans-Dietrich Genscher
and American Secretary of State James Baker proposed a new organisation
– the NACC, formally established at NATO's December 1991 Rome summit
– to bring together members of NATO and Central and Eastern European
states, including the Soviet Union.[7] In response to this initiative the leaders
of the Visegrad group, gathering in Krakow in October 1991, issued a joint
declaration which, although stopping short of a formal application for
NATO membership, pleaded for intensified cooperation between the
group and the Alliance. Polish President Lech Walesa warned against the

emergence of a 'grey security sphere' in Central and Eastern Europe following the break-up of the Warsaw Pact and the recent events in the Soviet Union.[8] In the meantime Germany, France and Poland established a trilateral consultative forum, the Weimar Triangle, which included regular meetings between defence ministers. Such interim solutions, however, did not satisfy the ambitions of the Central European countries, which sought NATO membership above all else – a goal formally declared by the Polish Foreign Minister in 1992.[9]

A number of mutually reinforcing factors, most importantly the dissolution of the Soviet Union and the war in Yugoslavia, began to make NATO membership a real possibility for the Central European states. Meanwhile in the West, although the Maastricht Treaty had formally established a Common Foreign and Security Policy for the EU, that policy lacked substance and the Union's credibility was undermined by its floundering during the break-up of Yugoslavia. Consequently, the Visegrad four's resolve to become full members of NATO was bolstered and their diplomatic efforts focused on this goal.

The momentum behind the possible enlargement of NATO was seized upon by the new German Defence Minister Volker Rühe, who emerged as one of the few voices in the West promoting the Alliance's expansion at this time. In March 1993 Rühe delivered a speech arguing that Central and Eastern Europe could not remain a 'conceptual no-man's land'; that the region was increasingly a zone of instability, threatened by ethnic wars, nationalism and fragmentation, and that the means to prevent this was through the eastward extension of Western institutions. Rühe, moreover, stressed the urgency of this task, stating that Europe did not have time to postpone such actions.[10]

By promoting NATO, as opposed to the enlargement of the EU, Rühe's thinking was in line with US policy but at odds with the current orthodoxy in Germany and elsewhere in Western Europe. Thus, unsurprisingly, his argument was challenged by the German Foreign Ministry and, more importantly, was not supported by Chancellor Kohl, whose thinking at the time remained focused on addressing Russia's concerns.[11] Rühe did, however, succeed in planting the seed-corn for an internal German debate on NATO enlargement. In addition, the case for NATO enlargement was soon to receive a decisive boost after the December 1993 electoral success of the Russian ultra-nationalist Vladimir Zhirinovsky, who promised that Russia would soon expand westwards to the internal Polish river Vistula. It was this event which triggered a substantial shift in German perspectives on NATO enlargement.

Feelings in Germany at this time were illustrated by an issue of the influential magazine *Der Spiegel*. The magazine put on its cover a picture of

Zhirinovsky dressed in his favourite combat uniform posing in Hitler's shadow. This was accompanied by a ferocious article in favour of Polish membership of NATO written by the magazine's founder Rudolf Augstein and entitled 'Poland in danger'. The publication was striking not only because of the strength with which the argument was advanced – 'Poland belongs to us, and in the future it will belong to Europe, whatever kind of Europe it will be, and this is the way it must be!' – but also because *Der Spiegel* had not previously advocated the enlargement of NATO.[12] The Zhirinovsky factor also served to strengthen calls for NATO enlargement within the governing Christian Democratic Union, the security policy spokesperson of which, Friedbert Pflüger, appealed to the Bundestag for the rapid accession of the Visegrad states to NATO.[13] In the wake of these developments Bonn's official security policy towards the Visegrad four evolved into active support for NATO enlargement. Once the issue was put on the political agenda and formally accepted as an objective of the Alliance at the Brussels summit in January 1994, Germany became a full and active advocate of enlargement.[14] For Germany, enlargement would, it was hoped, alleviate the potential problems of being the Western border state facing an unstable east.[15]

Thus, from the mid 1990s onwards, the broad perspectives of the Visegrad four on cooperation with the West came to coincide with those of Germany. For both the Visegrad states and Germany, the eastward enlargement of NATO became one of the key means of supporting independence, stability and prosperity in Central Europe, and of overcoming the region's historic problem of being a *Zwischeneuropa* – of belonging neither to East nor West. Although in the early 1990s the ambitions of the Visegrad states far outstripped what was then on offer from the West, closer cooperation with Germany was nevertheless viewed in Central Europe as vital to achieving the goal of integration with the West. In March 1992 the Polish newspaper *Obserwator* welcomed the then German Defence Minister Gerhard Stoltenberg with the headline, 'Through Germany into NATO'. A new Polish military doctrine of August 1992, which included NATO membership as a prime objective, also described cooperation with Germany as 'one of the most important paths to integration into Western Europe'.[16] Indeed, Polish–German reconciliation and NATO enlargement were seen as intimately linked. Poland emphasised that NATO membership would make Germans and Poles allies for the first time and further the process of rapprochement and reconciliation between the two countries.[17]

Germany's relatively early conversion to the inclusion of the Central European states as full members of the Alliance therefore played an important role in the process of NATO enlargement. As a consequence, when

Poland, the Czech Republic and Hungary joined NATO on 13 March 1999, both the form and substance of the enlargement were entirely in line with German expectations and interests.

Military cooperation

Even before NATO enlargement became an express goal of German security policy, a variety of mechanisms were put in place to foster military cooperation with Germany's eastern neighbours, particularly the Visegrad states. As with German policy towards Central and Eastern Europe more generally, this military cooperation was developed within the context of broader multilateral Western policy frameworks such as NATO's PfP. The development of bilateral military cooperation with postcommunist states also reflected a longer-standing practice of developing such cooperation with partners outside Europe.[18]

The general goals of German military cooperation are:

- to contribute to the security of Germany and its allies, to enhance confidence through partnership and cooperation, and to strengthen crisis prevention and management;
- to add another important dimension to the web of ties between Germany and other countries;
- to contribute to the transformation of armed forces and defence administrations;
- to share German experiences and models in the military sphere, and to enhance democratic stability and political control over, and transparency of, military structures;
- to create a solid basis for permanent ties with countries and to increase their understanding of German policy;
- to increase cooperation in arms procurement and/or production and thereby enhance the prospects of German and European arms production programmes competing effectively with the US.

The first military contacts between Germany and the Visegrad four were established early in 1990, closely followed by a number of agreements aimed at expanding working contacts among higher ranks of the military. More general agreements on military cooperation followed in 1993. Supplementing these, Germany has concluded specific agreements with individual neighbours on cooperation in a variety of fields, including air defence, the exchange of information on military flights in border areas, rescue operations at sea and the status of national troops on the territory of partner countries.[19] The main forms of cooperation between Germany and the Visegrad states are in the fields of civil–military relations, the

organisation of defence policy making, military budgeting, the organisation of armed forces, and – in the run-up to Polish, Czech and Hungarian
membership of NATO – the inter-operability of armed forces. German
military cooperation with Poland, the Czech Republic and Hungary has
developed more deeply than with most other countries. Germany defines
its military cooperation with partner states in terms of 12 distinct areas.
Cooperation has been developed with Poland, the Czech Republic and
Hungary in 11 of these areas. Of the 125 countries with which Germany
has military relations, only France, Russia, Romania and Slovenia also have
cooperation in 11 of these 12 areas.

The essence of Germany's role in military cooperation has been
dubbed by some German analysts as providing 'an example' of modern,
democratic armed forces.[20] The German approach, however, does not seek
to impose a German model on other countries' armed forces and defence
policies. Experts from the Visegrad states confirm that their countries'
bilateral military relations with Germany are a consensual encounter and
that Germany does not push its partners into particular activities or models
of behaviour, impose specific aspects of German know-how or press for the
procurement of German arms.

Annual programmes

Underlying Germany's approach to military cooperation with the countries
of Central and Eastern Europe has been the introduction of bilateral
'annual programmes' detailing cooperative activities. These annual
programmes cover a wide range of issues: exchanges of information on
international security, in particular relating to areas of crisis (such as the
Balkans); arms control and disarmament; military education; personnel
and social issues; the German civil–military relations concepts of *Innere
Führung* (moral leadership) and *Bürger in Uniform* (Citizen in Uniform);
military training, including bilateral and multilateral exercises; armed
forces reforms; air traffic control and air defence; military budgeting,
research and development and arms production; and democratic control
of armed forces.[21] Annual programmes work on the basis of equality, with
the two defence ministries involved formulating their national positions
regarding the development of their armed forces which then form the basis
for negotiation with the partner. Implementation of the agreements is then
dependent upon the current priorities of the respective defence administrations and armed forces and the financial resources available to each side.
For Poland, the Czech Republic and Hungary, the content of these annual
programmes is at present geared to bringing the new NATO members up
to NATO standards and therefore benefits from additional financial
support. By 2003, however, the new NATO members are expected to have

achieved NATO standards and cooperation is likely to be based on the principle of these states covering their own expenses.

The number of activities undertaken under the annual programmes
with Poland, the Czech Republic and Hungary is relatively high compared
with those with other countries. In 1997, for example, 47 per cent of the
specific activites undertaken in the framework of annual programmes with
21 postcommunist states were with these 3 countries (249 of a toal 529 activities, of which 104 were with Poland, 78 with the Czech Republic and 67
with Hungary).[22] Moreover, the success of the annual programme formula
developed with the Visegrad countries has subsequently been developed by
German planners and used in promoting military cooperation with other
countries, including some of Germany's existing NATO partners (specifically Belgium, Denmark, France, Italy and the United Kingdom). By 1997
bilateral military cooperation with Poland, the Czech Republic and
Hungary was effectively deeper than with some of Germany's long-standing
NATO partners.

Assistance in military education and training

Military education and training has been an essential component of
Germany's military cooperation with the countries of postcommunist
Europe. Much of this cooperation is conducted in the field of language
training. Germany admits officers from partner countries to the Hürth
(Federal Institute of Foreign Languages), as well as sending its own teach-
ers abroad. The Bundeswehr also runs special courses to prepare military
personnel from partner countries to work at NATO Headquarters (this also
includes language training). In addition, officers from partner countries
study at the Führungsakademie der Bundeswehr (the Bundeswehr
Leadership Academy) in Hamburg (in 1998, for example, 97 officers from
48 countries attended the Academy).

Such education programmes are, however, relatively expensive (costing
6.8 million DM in 1999 and 7.3 million DM in 2000). With growing pressure on the German defence budget, spending on this element of military
cooperation is likely to shrink rather than grow in future. In this situation,
the three new NATO member states sought more assistance prior to 2002,
since after this date they will have to finance any training and education
activities in Germany themselves. A decrease in the numbers of applications
and participants from Poland, the Czech Republic and Hungary can thus
be expected. In addition, the German Ministry of Defence is shifting its
focus towards longer-term projects.

There is also a reciprocal dimension to military education. While it is
rare for German officers to study in a partner country, it is more common
for future defence attachés to take part in training and education

programmes in these states. So long as military education in the Visegrad states is not fully compatible with NATO standards, however, their courses are likely to have only limited attractions for Germany.

Advising partners

The provision of advice on general military matters, civil–military relations, the development of defence administration and other specific issues has been one of the most frequent forms of military cooperation between Germany and the states of postcommunist Europe. Most of these contacts are integrated into annual programmes, although some take place on an *ad hoc* basis.

By 1999 fourteen German military advisers were working in eight Central and Eastern European countries.[23] Such advice is based on the interests of the partner concerned and therefore involves different tasks in different countries. One example of such cooperation was the placement of a German adviser to the Czech Military Academy in Brno to work on education and language training. More importantly, Bundeswehr advisers were also sent to Hungary to assist the airforce in formulating and implementing a new air defence concept. More generally, senior German officers with long-term NATO experience have helped NATO applicants and new members to meet Alliance standards in various areas.

Cross-border military cooperation

For obvious reasons of geography, the Bundeswehr's relations with the Polish and Czech armed forces differ from those with other partner countries. Direct contacts between troops in border areas add a further dimension to military cooperation with Poland and the Czech Republic. Relations in this area are quantitatively and qualitatively different from those with other postcommunist states, reaching far beyond military issues, including cooperation in civilian areas (such as the prevention of natural disasters) and involving not only close ties between military personnel but also between their families, as well as local populations. The extent of cross-border military cooperation is seen in the numbers of joint activities. In 1998 there were 350 joint German–Polish or German–Czech military activities.[24] There are also 10 'bilateral patronage' relations between German and Polish units and 7 between German and Czech units.[25] Poland and the Czech Republic's bilateral military cooperation with Germany, furthermore, has been more extensive than with each other – despite their previous shared experience of cooperation within the Warsaw Pact, the largely compatible equipment and shared civil–military culture of their armed forces and their common postcommunist transformations. Germany has also promoted trilateral Czech–German–Polish military cooperation through contacts between the three armed forces in the Nysa/Neisse Euroregion, although most ties remain bilateral.[26]

Germany's cross-border military cooperation with Poland and the Czech Republic has produced close relations between troops in border regions, facilitating direct communication and mutual understanding and helping to spread Western norms regarding the conduct of military matters and especially civil–military relations. Even when direct relations do not include joint military exercises, partner units exchange observers in the interests of enhancing understanding and communication. Cross-border military cooperation has proved to be one of the most important tools of German policy in helping to integrate the Czech and Polish armed forces into NATO.[27]

Multilateral military cooperation

Germany has also sought to multilateralise military cooperation with its Central European neighbours. Polish–German cooperation, in particular, has been enhanced in this way. The Weimar Triangle cooperation includes regular contacts between the Polish, German and French Defence Ministers and has been extended to involve Directors of Planning Departments within Ministries of Defence. Similar arrangements have been established between the Danish, Polish and German Defence Ministries.

A German–Polish–Danish Multinational Corps Northeast has also been established, with its headquarters in Szczecin, which became operational in September 1999. Although the corps is assigned to NATO, its headquarters are not part of the integrated NATO command structure. The corps' defined missions include NATO Article V-type collective defence operations, crisis management and natural disasters response. Importantly, the corps serves as an organisational basis for military exercises which will involve other Baltic states. The corps also bears an important political message – one of reconciliation and integration, attempting to bring former adversaries together.[28]

The participation of a Czech unit in one of the German–US corps and the development of a Czech–German–Polish NATO corps have also been mooted. The multilateralisation of German–Czech military cooperation has not, however, been viewed as a priority by Berlin or Prague and these ideas had not been taken further by 2000.[29]

Arms production and procurement cooperation

In the first half of the 1990s Germany donated a considerable supply of former East German weapons and military equipment to Hungary (partly in gratitude to Hungary for opening its borders to East German asylum seekers in 1989 and thereby triggering the events which made German unification possible a year later). Since then, however, the Visegrad states have not received assistance from Germany in the form of military material.[30]

In the general area of arms production and procurement Germany is committed to pursuing the 'European option' wherever possible and resisting US defence industrial dominance. In the context of NATO enlargement and the likely future purchase of new fighter aircraft by the Central European states, therefore, Germany has been encouraging NATO's new members to postpone procurement decisions and consider buying the Euro-fighter once it becomes available.

To date, the financial constraints facing the Central European states have meant that no major procurement agreements have been concluded since the collapse of communism. The potential for cooperation betweeen Germany and the Visegrad states in the area of arms production and procurement, however, is immense. Greater cooperation would help the Visegrad states to obtain modern weapons systems and find a niche for their own armaments industries. To this end permanent bilateral committees and coordination groups on arms cooperation have been established and meet on an annual basis. Although present levels of armaments cooperation are not very high, a number of joint ventures may emerge. Germany and Hungary have cooperated on the maintenance of MiG-29 aircraft, and some Czech–German research and development projects have been established.

Civil–military relations

Germany's post-war experience with, and particular model of, civil–military relations have also been of relevance to the countries of Central and Eastern Europe. Although critics argued that the German model of civil–military relations would be of little use to postcommunist states since the Bundeswehr would be ineffective in combat missions, German politicians and the military now argue that the Bundeswehr has proved its mettle in Bosnia and Kosovo and should be viewed as a viable framework for adaptation in postcommunist Europe. The German model of civil–military relations, centred around the concepts of *Innere Führung* and *Bürger in Uniform* has, indeed, attracted considerable attention in Central Europe.[31] While this model has not been fully adopted by any of the Central European states, the idea of the citizen in uniform has resonated in the region and German personnel/staff development policies have been influential. The German model of a mixed armed force, combining a sizeable conscript element together with soldiers in extended service and professional soldiers, has also found interest in the region.

All indicators suggest that military cooperation between Germany and the Visegrad states has been a success. In particular, Germany and the Bundeswehr became a vehicle for the smooth entry of Poland, the Czech Republic and Hungary into NATO.[32] Moreover, cooperation in the military sphere appears to have developed ahead of wider political ties. In the case of Polish–German relations military cooperation has been one of the most successful aspects of the two countries, post-1989 rapprochement.[33]

Conclusion

This survey demonstrates that since 1989–90 Germany has developed an active *Ostpolitik* towards Central and Eastern Europe as a whole and particularly close relations with the Visegrad countries. This new German *Ostpolitik* has taken place very much within a framework of multilateral institutions, in particular the EU and NATO. The development of close relations with Germany's eastern neighbours, furthermore, has not progressed at the expense of existing relations with Western partners. Nor has Germany's especially close cooperation with the Visegrad states undermined relations with other Central and Eastern European countries. These developments highlight both the key role Central Europe now plays in German security policy and the importance the countries of Central Europe now attach to Germany in their own foreign and security policies.

A number of features of Germany's policy towards its eastern neighbours are particularly notable. Germany has consistently avoided unilateralism and has sought to multilateralise and institutionalise its relations with the countries of postcommunist Europe. Since the end of the Cold War, Bonn has approached Central and Eastern Europe with a strong institutional emphasis, viewing the EU, NATO and the OSCE as central elements of its policy towards the region. Since 1994, further, the eastward enlargement of NATO has been a key component of German security policy towards Central Europe. In essence, German security policy towards its eastern neighbours has followed the same approach that the country developed in its relations with its Western partners after the Second World War, namely the avoidance of unilateral action, the moderation of national interests and the promotion of multilateral fora.

The Central European Visegrad region has been a particular priority for Germany. Once the Visegrad states are part of the integrated structures of NATO and the EU, however, the region's importance to Germany is likely to decrease. As this 'second normalisation' is consolidated, German policy is likely to focus on other priorities. The one exception is likely to be Poland, given its role not only as a major power in Central Europe itself but also *vis-à-vis* its former Soviet eastern neighbours (Russia, Ukraine and Belarus) and in the Baltic region. Differentiation is therefore likely to become more visible in Germany's policies towards Central Europe. Due to geographical proximity the Czech Republic and Poland enjoy particularly deep cooperation with Germany – as shown by the extensive cross-border element in both relationships. Beyond this, Poland is likely to emerge as

Germany's key partner in the east and it can be anticipated that the two countries will expand cooperation in developing relations with the former Soviet countries further east.[34] Trilateral cooperation with France and Denmark may also develop in this way. Warsaw seems to be more than willing and able to assume this more prominent role in assuring the security and stability of the region.[35] In this context, German policy makers view Central European states as important partners in developing military cooperation with countries further east (Poland has been active in developing military cooperation with Ukraine and Lithuania along these lines, as has the Czech Republic with Slovakia).[36]

Although Germany has developed particularly close cooperation with its immediate Central European neighbours, it is premature, and probably misleading, to see Germany and the Visegrad states constituting a distinct regional identity. Although the convergence of German and Central European interests shaped the first wave of NATO enlargement, there was no particular convergence of perspectives with regards to the 1999 Kosovo conflict. The contrast between Poland's full support for NATO's action and the more reluctant Czech position demonstrates that geographical proximity, intensive military cooperation, comparable histories and shared security concerns do not mean that Central European states will always adopt similar positions. It is also clear that there are no particular similarities between German and Polish perspectives on the development of European defence cooperation. While Germany is a keen proponent of developing an EU-based European security and defence identity, Poland prioritises Atlanticism and ties with the United States.

In conclusion, whether or not Germany and Central Europe (or post-communist Central and Eastern Europe more widely) one day become a modern-day *Mitteleuropa* is probably less important than the transformation in relations that has already occurred. Germany's principal security interests and those of its eastern neighbours now run in parallel and are largely complementary. The security policy perspectives of the Central and Eastern European countries, furthermore, are now intimately tied up with Euro-atlantic structures – a decisive shift in focus that German diplomacy has played a key role in promoting and facilitating.

Notes

1 Vladimir Handl's contribution to this chapter draws on research on military cooperation between Germany and the Visegrad countries, including extensive interviews with officials in the Foreign and Defence Ministries of these countries. This research was financed by a Manfred Wörner Stipendium from the German Federal Ministry of Defence and by an Economic and Social Research Council on

'Germany and the Reshaping of Europe' (Project L213252002). Handl extends his gratitude to a number of officials at the German Ministries of Defence and Foreign Affairs; the Universität Bundeswehr (Hamburg); Professor August Pradetto, Director of the Institut für Internationale Politik; and Ivon Hassenstein of the Fachinformations-zentrum der Bundeswehr in Bonn.

2 Quoted in *Time Magazine* (22 March 1999), p. 15.

3 W. von Bredow and T. Jäger, *Neue deutsche Außenpolitik: Nationale Interessen in Internationalen Beziehungen* (Opladen, Leske und Budrich, 1993), p. 212.

4 Rede von Bundeskanzler Gerhard Schröder zur offiziellen Eröffnung des Sitzes der Deutschen Gesellschaft für Auswärtige Politik am 2 September 1999 in Berlin, 'Verlässlichkeit in den internationalen Beziehungen', *Bulletin* (20 September 1999) (www.bundesregierung.de/pressf.htmllf); and R. Scharping, 'Grundlinien deutscher Sicherheitspolitik', Rede an der Führungsakademie der Bundeswehr, 8 September 1999, Hamburg (www.bundeswehr.de/presse/reden/bm_990908.html).

5 *Atlantic News* (23 March 1990).

6 *Atlantic News* (12 May 1990).

7 A. Krzeczunowicz, *Krok po Kroku: Polska Droga do NATO 1989–1999* (Znak, Warszawa, 1999), p. 66.

8 *Atlantic News* (9 October 1991).

9 K. Skubiszewski, Foreign Minister of Poland, in *Polska Zbrojna* (1–2 June 1992).

10 H. Tewes, *Germany as a Civilian Power: The Western Integration of East-Central Europe 1989–1997* (PhD thesis, Institute for German Studies, University of Birmingham, October 1998), pp. 242–53.

11 *Der Spiegel*, 52 (1993); and *Frankfurter Allgemeine Zeitung* (8 January 1994).

12 R. Augstein, 'Bedrohtes Polen', *Der Spiegel*, 2 (1994).

13 F. Pflüger, *Die Zukunft des Ostens liegt im Westen: Beiträge zue Aussenpolitik* (Düsseldorf und Vienna, Econ taschenbuch Verlag, 1994), pp. 106–17.

14 F. M. Alamier, *Die Öffnung der NATO nach Osten: Retrospektive und Ausblick*, WIFIS-Aktuell (Hamburg, Wissenschaftliches Forum für Internationale Sicherheit e.V., 1999), p. 23.

15 C. Royen, 'Kongruenzen und Divergenzen in der Politik Deutschlands und seiner westlichen Partner gegenüber den ostmitteleuropäischen Transformations-staaten', in W. Kühne (ed.), *Problemfelder deutschen Aussenpolitik: Gemeinsamkeiten und Konkurrenz deutscher, europäischer und amerikanischer Interessen und Gestalltungsvorstellungen* (Ebenhausen, Stiftung Wissenschaft und Politik, 1997), p. 23.

16 T. Budnikowski et al. 'Stosunki Polsko-Niemiecki', in B. Wizimirska (ed.), *Rocznik Polskiej Polityki Zagranicznej 1992* (Warsaw, PISM, 1992), p. 176; and Tewes, *Germany as a Civilian Power*, pp. 234–44.

17 P. Seydak, 'Was erwartet Polen von der Mitgliedschaft in der NATO?', *Der Mittler-Brief. Informationsdienst zur Sicherheitspolitik*, 1 (1998), 6.

18 Bundesministerium der Verteidigung, *Friedenssicherung durch Vertrauensbildung. Zusammenarbeit mit anderen Streitkräften. Stichworte für die Öffentlichkeitsarbeit und Truppeninformation* (Bonn, Bundesministerium der Verteidigung, August 1999).

19 A. Sverák, 'Germany's military policy vis-à-vis the Central and East European region', in V. Handl, J. Hon and O. Pick (eds.), *Germany and East-Central Europe since 1990* (Prague, Institute for International Relations, 2000), pp. 133–44.

20 A. Uzulis, 'Neuer NATO-Partner – Polen', *Der Mittler-Brief. Informationsdienst zur Sicherheitspolitik*, 1 (1998), 1.

21 Sverák, 'Germany's military policy', pp. 137–8.

22 Bundesministerium der Verteidigung, *Kooperation – ein entscheidender Faktor für Stabilität und Frieden in Europa: Die militärische Zusammenarbeit zwischen Deutschland und seinen Partnern im Osten: Stichworte für Öffentlichkeitsarbeit und Truppeninformation* (Bonn, Bundesministerium der Verteidigung, July 1998), p. 9.

23 Bundesministerium der Verteidigung, *Friedenssicherung durch Vertrauensbildung*, p. 6.

24 Bundesministerium der Verteidigung, *Friedenssicherung durch Vertrauensbildung*, p. 7.

25 L. Schreiber, 'Vojenska spoluprace Nemecka s Ceskou Republikou', *Alliance*, 1:3 (1999), 6.

26 M. Graf, 'Przygraniczna Wspolpraca Wojskowa Polski z Panstwami Sasiedzkimi na Przykladzie Slaskiego Okregu Wojskowego', *Studia i Materialy*, 13 (Warsaw, PISM, 1998), p. 10.

27 Graf, 'Przygraniczna Wspolpraca Wojskowa Polski', p. 19.

28 Brigadegeneral Hans-Joachim Sachau, Chief of Staff of the Multinational Command Northeast, 'Standort mit hoher Symbolkraft', *www/Bundeswehr/Streitkräfte/Multinationales Korps*.

29 Graf, 'Przygraniczna Wspolpraca Wojskowa Polski', 10, 24.

30 L. Keresztes, 'Partner mit Zukunft. Hungarisch-deutsche militärische Beziehungen gewinnen an Kontur', *Information für die Truppe*, 2 (1997), 13.

31 R. Moniac and U. Schmidla, 'Bundeswehr für Armee von Polen Vorbild', *Die Welt* (26 January 1993), p. 3.

32 Seydak, 'Was erwartet Polen', 6.

33 C. Royen, 'United Germany and its Central-East European neighbours', *Polish Quarterly of International Affairs*, 6:1 (1997), 37.

34 M. E. Zaborowski, 'The Europeanisation of Polish–(West) German Relations 1944–2000', Unpublished PhD Thesis (University of Birmingham, Institute for German Studies, 2001).

35 See, for example, interview with Andrzej Karkoszka, First Deputy Minister of Defence of Poland, 'Klichees verlieren an Bedeutung', *Europäische Sicherheit*, 11 (1997), 6–8; and K. Myszczak, 'Der neueste deutsch–polnische Sicherheitsdialog', *Europäische Sicherheit*, 8 (1994), 392–5.

36 E. Feldmann and S. Gareis, 'Polen und seine Nachbarn', *Reader Sicherheitspolitik (Beilage zu Informationen für die Truppe)*, 3 (1998), 15–16.

5

Nuclear-weapon-free Ukraine: between the two poles of power

Sergiy P. Galaka

The break-up of the Soviet Union and the establishment of the CIS

The demise of the Soviet bloc in Eastern Europe, the break-up of the Soviet Union and the collapse of the communist system have had a profound impact on the destiny of hundreds of millions of people and left many countries searching for a new place in the international system. This is particularly true of Ukraine. Ukraine's geopolitical situation and close ties with Russia and other former Soviet republics mean that it is of special importance to the processes of domestic and international change underway in postcommunist Europe.

Any understanding of Ukraine's move towards independence in the late 1980s and early 1990s should start with a recognition of the deep sense of dissatisfaction prevalent in Ukrainian society by this time. For historical reasons – in particular western Ukraine's earlier connections with Poland and Central Europe rather than Russia – such dissatisfaction was more prominent in the west of the country than in the east and the south. Unless they actively identified themselves as Ukrainians rather than Soviet citizens, most Ukrainians did not ordinarily face discrimination within the Soviet Union. The Ukrainian political elite was, however, unhappy with the highly centralised Soviet system under which virtually all power was concentrated in Moscow. The professional classes were dissatisfied with the limited possibilities for professional growth or active participation in decision making. The reform-minded part of the Ukrainian political and economic establishment viewed the Soviet centre as the main obstacle to economic reform and social transformation. Popular opinion blamed the central Soviet leadership for falling living standards and the failure to bring about the long-awaited and promised improvement in their lives.

By the late 1980s and early 1990s the situation within the Soviet Union was characterised by deepening political and socio-economic crises. Soviet leader Mikhail Gorbachev's failure to introduce deep political and economic reforms and the progressive disintegration of the existing political and economic system polarised the country's political forces, weakened the central authorities and produced a crisis of power within the country. Republics struggled to devolve power away from Moscow, while conservative forces gained strength within the upper echelons of the central power apparatus. The disintegration processes culminated in the August 1991 coup attempt in Moscow. These events frightened Ukraine's ruling elite since the attempted coup threatened to undermine its power. Leaders of the Ukrainian national-democratic forces exploited the opportunity created by the unique post-coup period and formed an unofficial alliance with the more nationally oriented part of the ruling elite.

On 24 August 1991 the Ukrainian Parliament, the Verhovna Rada, adopted an Act of Proclamation of Ukraine's Independence, creating an independent Ukrainian state and stressing the indivisibility and inviolability of Ukraine's territory.[1] Subsequent attempts by Mikhail Gorbachev and his allies to re-establish the power of the central authorities and revitalise the Soviet Union in the form of a new Union of Sovereign States faced opposition not only from Russian President Boris Yeltsin and the new Russian elite but also from the leadership of several republics. Ukraine's role in the process was central. The refusal by the Ukrainian leadership to join any new union resembling the USSR and the endorsement of this decision by almost 92 per cent of the popular vote in a referendum on independence on 1 December 1991 were among the most decisive factors leading to the final break-up of the Soviet Union.

An examination of the creation of the Commonwealth of Independent States (CIS) reveals the divergent motives of its founders. While the various republican leaders had been allies in their efforts to wrest power from Mikhail Gorbachev, they initially viewed the CIS very differently. The distinguished Ukrainian historian Sergiy Kulchyzky argues that Russian leader Boris Yeltsin agreed to sign the documents establishing the CIS because 'he appeared to be the head of a new superpower in the making' and that his intention was 'to move the still existing union structures under the "roof" of the CIS, seemingly not a remote possibility'.[2] This approach was unacceptable to more nationalist and reformist Russian leaders who favoured a strong *independent* Russia which could influence its neighbours by virtue of its economic strength and the dynamism of its reforms. Ukraine's leaders assessed the situation differently. From the very beginning they viewed the CIS not as a state or a body potentially capable of becoming a state, but rather as an instrument for a civilised divorce from the Soviet Union and transitional to the consolidation of Ukrainian independence. The divergent views of the two major Soviet successor states meant that future disputes about the nature of, and prospects for, the CIS were inevitable. Nevertheless, on 8 December 1991 Russia, Belarus and Ukraine signed the agreement formally stating that the Soviet

Union 'ceases its existence as a subject of international law and geopolitical reality' and establishing the CIS.[3] Article five of the agreement states that all parties 'recognise and respect the territorial integrity of each other and the inviolability of borders existing within the Commonwealth'.[4] These last words were included at Russia's insistence and highlighted the intention of the Russian leadership to make recognition of existing borders conditional on former Soviet republics' membership of the CIS. Eight of the other former Soviet republics rapidly joined the new CIS, with Georgia following more reluctantly after Russian pressure in 1993, while the three Baltic states chose to remain outside the CIS.

Developing a Ukrainian foreign policy

In contrast to the Central Asian former Soviet republics, which were, in the words of Martha Olcott, 'catapulted to independence', Ukraine appeared better prepared to establish a foreign policy to reflect its new situation.[5] A founder member of the United Nations (UN) in 1945, Ukraine had had a small Ministry of Foreign Affairs since 1944. Several hundred specialists were trained in Kyiv University for the Ministry of Foreign Affairs and several dozen Ukrainian diplomats gained experience working in Ukrainian missions to the United Nations, UNESCO and other international bodies. With independence, however, the Ukrainian institutions designed to develop and implement foreign policy faced problems of an entirely different nature and scale. In the Soviet Union, with its highly centralised and ideological system of rule, foreign and defence policy was the prerogative of Moscow. Article twenty-eight of the Constitution of the Ukrainian Soviet Socialist Republic stated that Ukraine's international activity was to be 'guided by the goals, tasks, and principles of the foreign policy determined by the Constitution of the USSR.'[6] The Ukrainian quasi-state, in fact, had no foreign policy in Soviet times. Its Ministry of Foreign Affairs was simply a branch of Moscow central office.

Ukraine thus faced great problems in establishing foreign policy-making structures. The country lacked the hundreds of specialists needed to man its diplomatic service and foreign policy-making institutions. Few experts of Ukrainian origin from the former Soviet institutions or diplomatic service returned to Kyiv. The emerging vacancies had to be filled either by people invited from academic institutions or, in most cases, from unrelated governmental bodies and institutions, sometimes after short-term retraining courses. The practice of appointing people with no experience in the field to some key diplomatic posts adversely affected Ukraine's foreign policy, with the (often politically motivated) promotion of non-professionals to such posts proving particularly counterproductive.

More generally, the broader realities of Ukraine's post-independence transition have created a number of problems in terms of foreign policy decision making. With democratic traditions non-existent in both Ukrainian society at large and the political elite, decision making has been characterised by both inertia and the concentration of power in one centre (focused on the President). Actions and decisions by the Verhovna Rada are often coloured by political power struggles motivated not only by the personal ambitions of politicians at all levels, but also very strongly by the socio-economic interests of different leaders and groups. With the country in deep economic crisis and social tensions growing, many foreign policy problems tend to become issues in the political struggle within Ukraine.

The Verhovna Rada formally adopted Ukraine's foreign policy concept – the 'Guidelines of the Foreign Policy of Ukraine' – in July 1993. The concept stresses that Ukraine will conduct an open foreign policy, avoid dependence on any state or group of states, and is against the presence of foreign troops on its territory.[7] Listing Ukraine's foreign policy priorities, the concept puts them in the following order: neighbouring states, member states of the European Community (now the European Union (EU)) and the North Atlantic Treaty Organisation (NATO), Asia, Africa and Latin America. The concept stresses that due to historic, geopolitical and economic reasons relations with Russia constitute a 'special partnership', the character of which will greatly influence stability in Europe and the world, and that Ukraine will build this partnership on the basis of good neighbourly relations, mutual respect and partnership. At the same time, Ukraine will counter any attempts to interfere in its internal affairs or claims on its territory.[8] The foreign policy concept also indicates that the long-term goal of Ukrainian foreign policy is membership of the EU and other European structures.

Ukraine, Russia and the CIS

In 1992–93 a pragmatic approach prevailed in Russian policy towards the other former Soviet republics. This approach was based on an assessment that Russia should concentrate its efforts on the domestic economic, social and political transformation necessary to join the international community as an equal partner as rapidly as possible. This approach presumed that Russia should avoid unnecessary commitments to, or pressure on, the former Soviet republics since these might drag Moscow into complex regional conflicts and involve a potentially enormous financial burden which might undermine the positive results of economic reforms. This policy was personified by Prime Minister Yegor Gaidar and Foreign Minister Andrei Kozyrev. These leaders generally favoured a strong, independent Russia focusing primarily on domestic reforms, with much less emphasis on the development of a strong CIS.

An alternative approach was pursued by the Russian parliamentary leadership (symbolised by Vice-President Aleksandr Rutskoi) and part of the Russian military establishment. This approach aimed to re-establish a dominant role for Russia in the former Soviet space by pressurising other former Soviet republics to join the CIS (as in the cases of Georgia, Moldova and Azerbaijan), increasing the dependence of these states on Russian trade and energy supplies (as in the cases of the Baltic states and the Central Asian states) and providing incentives to create close political–military alliances (as with Belarus). This neo-imperial approach was fuelled by other problems in relations between Russia and its former Soviet neighbours. The most acute and complicated of these problems was the situation of the twenty-five million ethnic Russians living outside Russia – an issue that Russian actively exploited in its relations with countries such as the Baltic states, Moldova and Kazakhstan.

Ukraine viewed the establishment of new institutions within the CIS as unacceptable if their functions resembled those of the old, centralised Soviet Union, instead preferring to develop relations with the CIS countries on a bilateral basis. This policy led to Ukraine's refusal to join the 1992 Tashkent CIS Collective Security Treaty or to sign the CIS Statute. Similarly, at the April 1994 Moscow CIS summit, Ukraine insisted that it would only join the CIS Economic Union as an associate member. At that summit Ukrainian President Leonid Kravchuk, speaking on the CIS' future and the prospects for Kazakh President Nursultan Nazarbayev's proposed Eurasian Union, argued that if some countries seek closer ties, such as those between Russia and Belarus, 'the need for a Eurasian Union or even for the CIS will disappear'.[9]

This position of relative independence from Russia and the CIS, however, has created problems for Ukraine. Ukraine's refusal to join the Tashkent Treaty, in essence rejecting a Russian nuclear umbrella, has left Ukraine in a potentially vulnerable situation between the two poles of power in the Euro-atlantic area – Russia and NATO. While NATO's Partnership for Peace, which Ukraine joined in 1994, and the NATO–Ukraine Charter on Distinctive Partnership, signed in July 1997, open new possibilities for cooperation with NATO they do not provide Ukraine with security guarantees.

The election in 1994 of a new President, Leonid Kuchma, came as a surprise to many observers in the West. By winning over 52 per cent of the vote (compared with 45 per cent for Leonid Kravchuk) Kuchma received a mandate for change.[10] Immediately after his election President Kuchma proclaimed changes in relations with the CIS. Kuchma argued that 'historically

Ukraine is part of the Eurasian economic and cultural space' and 'vital Ukrainian national interests are concentrated on the territory of the former Soviet Union'. Listing these vital interests, he mentioned 'sources of necessary goods, raw materials and energy, and the most realistically accessible market for Ukrainian producers'. He stressed that

> self-isolation of Ukraine, its voluntary refusal from the active competition for its own interests in the Eurasian area was a serious political mistake. We have to actively influence the policy within the Commonwealth, defending our interests ... I am sure that Ukraine can play the role of one of the leaders of the process of Eurasian economic integration.[11]

At the same time, Kuchma expressed caution towards Nazarbayev's proposal to develop some kind of supranational body within the CIS.[12] Evidently, Kuchma also bore in mind that any move towards closer integration within the CIS would cause an outcry in western Ukraine. He pledged to work for an independent, sovereign Ukraine and pointed out that Ukraine's return to the old union was impossible.[13]

Since Kuchma's accession to power in 1994, relations with the CIS have undergone a significant evolution. The CIS failed to fulfil Russian expectations and its significance as an instrument of Russian policy declined. Integrationist plans, popular in the first half of the 1990s, remained unimplemented.

During the January 2000 CIS summit in Moscow President Kuchma stressed that the Commonwealth 'has to change' in order to survive. The extent of the crisis within the CIS is illustrated by an annual 15–20 per cent decrease in the volume of trade within the Commonwealth. The free trade area agreement that Ukraine was hoping would re-vitalise economic and trade relations with Russia and give an impetus to the Ukrainian economy by providing cheap oil and natural gas supplies was not even ratified by Russia. Since the mid 1990s, the fragmentation of the CIS into several groups has become increasingly evident. Aside from the Union of Russia and Belarus, other structures – a customs union between Russia, Belarus, Kazakhstan, Kyrgyzstan and Tajikistan; the GUUAM (Georgia, Ukraine, Uzbekistan, Azerbaijan and Moldova) group; and the Central Asian Economic Community (comprising Kazakhstan, Uzbekistan, Kyrgyzstan and Tajikistan) – have gained momentum.[14] In October 2000 the existing customs union of the five was transformed into the Eurasian Economic Community and declared goals similar to those of the earlier European Economic Community.[15] In September 2000, during the UN millennium summit in New York, the GUUAM countries decided to transform the group into an international organisation, based on free trade.[16] Since then, there have reportedly been discussion of plans to include Romania as a member of GUUAM, which, if implemented, would extend the group beyond the borders of the CIS.[17]

The shadow of energy dependence, predominantly natural gas debts, has hung over Ukraine's relations with Russia since the early 1990s. In the late 1990s and 2000 Ukraine's dependence on Russian energy supplies assumed a new importance as Moscow sought to increase pressure on Kyiv. Regular seasonal pressure was introduced after Russian President Vladimir Putin's accession to power, with insistent demands that Ukraine either repay its energy debts to Russia (an impossibility under current economic conditions) or cede control of strategic energy facilities – mainly gas-transit pipelines – to Gazprom and other Russian companies. Such pressure also appeared designed to force Ukraine to deviate from its pronounced foreign policy of integration with European and Euro-atlantic structures. Surrendering control of gas pipelines would further increase Ukrainian dependence on Russian energy sources and deprive it of an important part of its natural gas supplies (which are given by Russia as payment for the transportation of Russian gas westward).

These problems were further complicated for Ukraine by the announce-ment of plans by Gazprom to by-pass Ukrainian territory by constructing an alternative pipeline through Belarus, Poland and Slovakia. In October 2000 Gazprom signed a protocol with Gaz de France, Ruhrgaz, Wintersthal and ENI confirming its intention to create a consortium to build a new gas pipeline via Poland and Slovakia.[18] If this project is successful, Gazprom will gain a new lever over Ukrainian policy in this strategically important area and Russia will have a new instrument, designed to make Ukrainian foreign policy manageable from the Russian perspective. Ukraine would not only be deprived of the possibility of counter-balancing its dependence on supplies from Russia with Russia's dependence on a reliable transit route via Ukraine to Central and Western Europe, but also risks losing, even if the gas pipeline remains Ukrainian property, the thirty billion cubic meters of natural gas it receives annually as transit payment from Gazprom.[19]

Ukrainian Minister of Fuel and Energy Sergiy Yarmilov has said that Ukraine's dependence on Russia for 80 per cent of its natural gas supplies and 90 per cent of its oil supplies makes the 'situation with energy supplies in Ukraine dangerous from an economic point of view, and diversification of energy sources is one of the main components of economic independ-ence'.[20] However, Ukraine's inability to assure alternative sources of oil and gas supplies (illustrated by the failure to construct on schedule an oil termi-nal in Illichevsk on the Black Sea) puts it in a very difficult situation and makes future concessions to Russia likely. Events in 1999–2000 demon-strated that the new Russian leadership was inclined to use natural gas and oil as a tool in a wider geostrategic game. Ukraine appears to be one of the objects of this game. Ukrainian economic dependence on Russia, furthermore, extends into other areas. Over 60 per cent of Ukrainian factories also depend upon cooperation with Russian industries.[21]

Ukraine's failure to create the conditions for economic cooperation with EU countries and the EU's cautious policy towards Ukraine will further push Ukrainian industry towards closer cooperation with Russia. This is best illustrated by the Antonov-70 transport aircraft project. Rejected by Germany and France, this project is now likely to be realised by joint Russian–Ukrainian efforts and the main market, aside from CIS countries, will be in China, India, and some other Asian and African countries.

Ukraine's relations with Russia were complicated for much of the 1990s by the problems of dividing the former Soviet Black Sea fleet and the related issue of a basic treaty between the two countries. Both issues were used by Russia as a means of pressuring Ukraine to accept closer cooperation between the two countries, but were finally resolved by a series of compromises in 1997. The Russian Black Sea fleet is to stay in Sebastopol until 2017 and will therefore remain a major foreign policy and security factor in relations between the two countries and the Black Sea region more generally. The 'big treaty' between Russia and Ukraine, signed on 31 May 1997, was based on mutual recognition of existing borders and established a legal foundation for relations between the two countries. The treaty, however, has not resolved underlying differences between the two countries. Russia continues to react nervously to any sign of rapprochement between Ukraine and the West, while Ukraine continues to refuse to participate in regional security efforts initiated by Moscow (such as the Tashkent Treaty on collective security). The growing differences between those CIS states with close relations with Russia on the one hand and the GUUAM group on the other were highlighted by the decision of Azerbaijan, Georgia and Uzbekistan not to prolong the Tashkent Treaty in 1999.[22]

Following the election of Vladimir Putin as Russian President in May 2000, however, Ukrainian–Russian relations became more pragmatic. The proof of this new approach was demonstrated during the meeting of the two countries' Presidents in Sochi in October 2000, when it was agreed that Russia would take part in the privatisation of the Ukrainian gas transportation system in return for which Ukraine's debt to Russia for gas and oil would be treated as a state debt of Ukraine (and hence partly written off).[23]

Ukraine and the West: developing closer ties

The West's unequivocal support for Russia's claim to be the primary successor state of the USSR created complications in its relations with the other newly independent states (NIS), in particular Ukraine. The 'Russia first' approach which prevailed in Western policy towards the NIS in the early 1990s, and the tendency to seek simple solutions to complicated problems, were arguably counterproductive and taught other NIS some bitter lessons. In Ukraine it resulted in increased support for a *realpolitik* approach to foreign policy in general and security issues in particular.

The issue of former Soviet nuclear weapons remaining on Ukraine's territory after independence strained Kyiv's relations with the West in the early 1990s. The experience gained in negotiating on the nuclear issue had a decisive impact on broader Ukrainian foreign policy. The Verhovna Rada had first proclaimed Ukraine's intention to become a non-nuclear weapon state in the declaration of sovereignty adopted in July 1990. This stance was designed to distance Kyiv from Moscow and gain public support for independence by exploiting the strong anti-nuclear feelings in the country in the aftermath of the Chernobyl disaster. In the period after the August 1991 Moscow coup the Verhovna Rada reiterated the country's intention to become a non-nuclear state, apparently seeking to gain support from the West and calm Russian suspicions. The Ukrainian leadership's 1991 decision to implement the proclaimed intention to remove all nuclear weapons was motivated not only by the need to gain international recognition of Ukraine's independence but also by the desire to make a breakthrough in its relations with the West, in particular the United States and the EU, and to distance itself from Russia. Denuclearisation was initially viewed by the Ukrainian leadership as an essential precondition for achieving Ukraine's declared intention of integration into European structures, especially the EU.

It quickly became clear, however, that the West was not willing to offer Ukraine great economic support at this stage and that integration with Western structures was at best a distant prospect. Ukrainian leaders and politicians thus began to explore alternative options for dealing with the nuclear weapons on the country's territory and exploiting the nuclear asset at its disposal. The Verhovna Rada, in particular, began to take a hard line on the issue, arguing that Ukraine should receive compensation for surrendering the nuclear weapons. In the West this provoked fears that Ukraine was breaking its commitment to abandon the country's nuclear weapon status. The result was a series of accusations and threats from the West in 1992–93 (for example, threats to deprive Ukraine of economic aid).

Under pressure from the West and Russia, Ukraine agreed to surrender the nuclear weapons it had inherited from the Soviet Union. In January 1994 Presidents Bill Clinton, Boris Yeltsin and Leonid Kravchuk signed a joint statement agreeing to the elimination of all nuclear weapons on Ukrainian territory. From a Ukrainian perspective, however, in exchange for the nuclear arsenal that was created with Ukrainian participation and for decades deprived the Ukrainian people of the enormous resources spent on the arms race, the country failed to gain either binding security guarantees from Russia and the West or the scale of economic aid for which it hoped. Having met the requests of the official nuclear powers and their allies to become a non-nuclear state and join existing non-proliferation regimes, Ukraine has found itself between the two poles of power, deprived of the legally binding security guarantees it had sought. In a number of cases, furthermore, Ukraine found both Russia and the West unwilling to take its national interests into consideration, ruthlessly using its dependence on Western financial aid and Russian energy supplies in the wider competition for markets.

This problem was starkly illustrated by the Bushehr project, under which Ukraine had agreed to supply two power generation engines (manufactured by the Kharkiv Turboatom factory) for an Iranian nuclear power plant. The US feared that Iran was clandestinely developing nuclear weapons and believed that the development of the power plant would help Tehran to achieve this goal. Having failed to influence Russia (the main contractor on the project), Washington decided to put pressure on Ukraine (the weaker partner in the project) in order at least to delay its implementation. During a March 1998 visit to Ukraine by US Secretary of State Madeleine Albright an agreement was reached with Ukraine on the project. Ukraine agreed to withdraw from the Bushehr project in return for US support for its membership in the Missile Technology Control Regime and a promise to provide Turboatom and a number of other enterprises in the Kharkiv region with compensation for the business lost.[24] The benefits for Ukraine are largely still to come, while its losses have extended beyond those resulting directly from the abandoned contract. The most significant loss, however, is that of credibility in the eyes of potential economic partners. The whole story vividly illustrates the implications of Ukraine's dependence on US financial aid and International Monetary Fund and World Bank credits assured by US support.

The result of Ukraine's involvement with nuclear weapons and non-proliferation was a bitter lesson in *realpolitik* taught by the great powers. The conclusion was evident: only power matters. In addition, the nuclear issue illustrated how the domestic problems of Ukrainian foreign policy making might impact on the country's international situation. When the nuclear problem became an issue in internal political struggles (as it did in the early 1990s), the West accused Ukraine of inconsistency and unpredictability and the country's international image suffered, while the gains finally achieved from surrendering the nuclear weapons are still to materialise.

It was only after the shocks of the October 1993 violence in Moscow and the December 1993 Russian Duma elections – which saw a majority of votes won by the Communist opposition and the ultranationalist Vladimir Zhirinovsky's Liberal Democrats – that the West started to reconsider its policy towards Russia and the other NIS. Changes in Western policy were strengthened by a parallel hardening of Russian policy towards the West and Russian attempts to regain influence in traditional Russian and Soviet spheres of influence. While differences with the West over Bosnia played a role here, much more important and potentially more dangerous was the tougher Russian policy towards the countries of the so-called 'near abroad', especially Ukraine.

With the honeymoon with Russia apparently over, the West in general, and the US in particular, started looking towards Ukraine as a nation vital to stability in Central and Eastern Europe. Visiting Ukraine in March 1994 former US President Richard Nixon stressed that 'Ukrainian independence is vital', warned of the consequences of possible conflict between Russia and Ukraine, and stated that 'stability in Ukraine is vital'.[25] Nixon advised, however, that US support for Kyiv should remain conditional on the progress of economic reforms in the country.[26] The prospects for rapprochement with the West improved dramatically after the January 1994 trilateral agreement on the elimination of Ukraine's nuclear weapons. A subsequent visit to the US by President Kravchuk in March 1994 opened up new possibilities for cooperation with the West, but further developments remained conditional on the progress of economic reforms in Ukraine.

In the context of the stated goal of integration with European structures, membership of the EU has become the single most important long-term aim of Ukrainian foreign policy. Ukraine's economic and political performance, however, compares poorly to that of the Baltic states and even Moldova, let alone that of Poland, the Czech Republic, Hungary and Slovakia. Ukraine has failed to introduce radical economic reforms and to provide a stable legal environment compatible with EU legal norms. Ukraine's domestic situation has therefore very seriously undermined the credibility of its claim to future EU membership. The EU's Common Strategy towards Ukraine, adopted at the Union's December 1999 Helsinki summit, reflects the belief that Ukrainian movement towards the EU depends mainly upon the country demonstrating progress in domestic reforms. Then Ukrainian Foreign Minister Boris Tarasyuk stressed that Ukraine's approach towards EU membership had to become 'more pragmatic' and that the country had 'to concentrate on internal affairs, on reforms, being a primary task of a new reform-minded government'.[27]

Ukraine's relations with the major countries of Western and Central Europe have generally developed positively since 1991. In this context, strict adherence to the principles of international law, the UN Charter and the Helsinki Final Act – formally proclaimed in Ukraine's foreign policy concept – has been a cornerstone of Ukrainian foreign policy. Respect for these principles is considered vital to Ukraine's security and its existence as an independent state. The Helsinki principle of inviolability of borders is of special importance to Ukraine since all its neighbours (with the exception of Belarus) have in the past held territorial claims to Ukraine (whether formally at the state level or in terms of irredentist demands by political parties and movements).

Ukraine's declared goal in the security sphere is a comprehensive Europe-wide security system, based on existing European structures (the Organisation for Security and Cooperation in Europe, NATO and the Western European Union). Ukrainian membership in such systems is viewed as essential. The formal Ukrainian foreign policy concept adopted in 1993 clarifies that the intention to become a neutral and non-bloc nation (proclaimed at the time Ukraine became independent in 1991) should be adapted to the new realities of the post-Soviet era and the geopolitical situation of the country, and should not be an obstacle to Ukraine's participation in bilateral, subregional, regional and global security structures.[28]

Acting in this direction, Ukraine seized the opportunities for cooperation with NATO countries that emerged as the US attempted to reconcile the desire of the Central European Visegrad countries to join NATO with Russia's strong objections to the Alliance's enlargement. In February 1994 Ukraine was the first CIS country to join NATO's Partnership for Peace programme.

The central paradox of Ukraine's international situation is that while the country is striving for EU membership and closer ties with Euro-atlantic structures it remains economically tied to Russia. Ukraine increasingly finds itself caught between the two poles of power – an expanding NATO and Russia. A number of distinguished Western former policy makers and political scientists have emphasised Ukraine's position between Russia and the West. Zbigniew Brzezinski puts Ukraine on the border between European and Eurasian groups of states.[29] Henry Kissinger argues that from a balance-of-power perspective Ukraine is on the eastern edge of the space separating two poles of power – Europe and Russia.[30] Samuel Huntington calls Ukraine a 'cleft country' between two opposing civilisations, separating those countries seeking to join NATO and Russia.[31]

This situation was made even more acute by the prospect of NATO enlargement in the second half of the 1990s. Adjusting to the new reality, Ukraine's position slowly evolved towards closer relations with the Atlantic Alliance. Describing the drastic choice the country faces, former US Ambassador to the Soviet Union Jack Mattlock stressed that NATO enlargement 'will put Ukraine in almost impossible situation'.[32] If NATO enlargement stops after incorporating Poland, the Czech Republic and Hungary into the Alliance, Ukraine faces the risk of being confined to a Russian sphere of influence. Alternatively, if Ukraine pursues intensive rapprochement with the Alliance, it risks triggering Russian pressure, possibly even direct confrontation with Moscow. In order to neutralise these dangers, Ukraine argued for a gradual, evolutionary approach to NATO enlargement, a nuclear weapon-free zone in Central and Eastern Europe, security guarantees for itself and the possibility of applying for NATO membership in the future. Then Ukrainian Foreign Minister Hennady Udovenko said that the normalisation of relations with NATO was 'a stage on the way to full-scale integration into European and Atlantic structures'. Such an approach reflects the formal Ukrainian National Security Concept, which includes among the country's national security policy goals 'adhering to the existing systems of regional and global security and those under development'.

Intensive negotiations with the Alliance resulted in the signing of the 'Charter on a Distinctive Partnership Between the North Atlantic Treaty Organization and Ukraine' at NATO's Madrid summit in July 1997. The Charter commits NATO 'to support Ukrainian sovereignty and independence' and reaffirms that the Alliance has no intention to deploy nuclear weapons on the territory of its new members.[34] At least as importantly, the Charter appears to be oriented towards the further transformation of NATO–Ukrainian relations, giving Ukraine the possibility of opting for membership of the Alliance in the future. Ukraine thus views NATO as the potential core of a future Europe-wide security system. Given Ukraine's geopolitical position it is doomed to play an active role in developing such a Europe-wide security system.

At the same time, it is highly improbable that Ukraine will join NATO in the foreseeable future. Ukrainian membership of NATO is likely only in the context of larger developments involving either the creation of a comprehensive pan-European security system or a drastic deterioration in Ukraine's security environment provoking an urgent appeal for membership in the Alliance. In the latter case, many analysts question whether NATO would respond positively to such a request.

Looking to the future: problems and challenges

Against the background of the catastrophic state of its economy, the most urgent security problems facing Ukraine come from within not from outside. Ukraine's ability to consolidate its independence will be determined to a very great degree by the success of domestic economic and political reforms. The core foreign policy problem facing Ukraine is its relations with Russia. Ukraine is still closely tied to Russia economically, culturally and by many day-to-day human interactions. The development of the Russian–Belarusian Union demonstrates that Russia's efforts to maintain a sphere of influence on its western border have the potential to complicate Ukraine's already difficult geostrategic situation. While Ukraine's declared foreign policy goal is to integrate into European and Euro-atlantic international structures, and in particular the EU, the failure to introduce the domestic reforms which might make such integration possible has led to serious doubts in Western Europe and the US about the commitment of Ukraine's leaders to the long-term goal of westward integration. In terms of security and *realpolitik*, with the development of a comprehensive pan-European security system only a distant possibility, Ukraine finds itself in a potentially dangerous situation between two poles of power – Russia and an expanding NATO. Unless this situation changes in the near future – which appears unlikely – Ukraine will remain in a vulnerable position, which in the worst case could even threaten its existence as an independent state.

In September 2000 Anatoly Zlenko was re-appointed Ukraine's Minister of Foreign Affairs (having served in that post earlier in the 1990s). He reiterated that integration with Europe remained a priority of Ukrainian foreign policy but also acknowledged the 'low efficiency of purely declarative diplomacy' and declared that Ukraine must now 'seek to materialise the European choice into concrete forms' in order to gain support from the EU.[35]

Since 1991 Ukraine has been successful in securing and even strengthening its independence. Domestic economic and political problems, however, continue to pose major challenges for this democracy in the making. Ukraine now faces the complex challenge of realising its foreign policy objectives against the background of the critical state of its economy. The most immediate potential threat to Ukrainian independence, therefore, now comes from within. Under these circumstances, Ukrainian foreign policy will continue to face the task of pursuing a balanced strategy capable of securing the country's independence and providing for gradual movement towards closer integration with Central and Western Europe, while preserving stable relations with its CIS neighbours to the east, in particular Russia.

Notes

1 *Vechirny Kyiv* (27 August 1991), p. 1.
2 S. Kulchyzky, 'Russian shadow over Ukraine's independence', *Polityka i Chas (Kyiv)*, 12 (1993), 31.
3 *Vechirny Kyiv* (10 December 1991), p. 2.
4 *Vechirny Kyiv* (10 December 1991), p. 2.

5 M. B. Olcott, 'Central Asia: catapulted to independence', RAND-AAAS Course Materials, *Defense Politics. Politics for Peace and Security* (Kyiv, 1992, in Russian), p. 49.

6 'Constitution of the Ukrainian SSR', in *Politizdat Ukrajiny* (Kyiv, 1989), p. 12.

7 *Holos Ukrajiny* (24 July 1993), p. 3.

8 *Holos Ukrajiny* (24 July 1993), p. 3.

9 *Uriadovy Currier (Kyiv)* (19 April 1994), p. 2.

10 *Uriadovy Currier (Kyiv)* (12 July 1994), p. 1.

11 *Holos Ukrajiny* (21 July 1994), p. 2.

12 *Kievskiye Vedomosty* (12 August 1994), p. 2.

13 *Holos Ukrajiny* (15 July 1994), p. 2.

14 *Den (Kyiv)* (26 January 2000), p. 1.

15 *Izvestiya* (11 October 2000), p. 3.

16 *Den (Kyiv)* (13 October 2000), p. 3.

17 *Den (Kyiv)* (13 October 2000), p. 3.

18 *Holos Ukrajiny* (20 October 2000), p. 1.

19 *Izvestiya* (25 October 2000), p. 6.

20 *Uriadovy Currier (Kyiv)* (16 October 2000), p. 1.

21 Kulchyzky, 'Russian shadow over Ukraine's independence', 33.

22 *Izvestiya* (12 October 2000), p. 3.

23 *Den (Kyiv)* (17 October 2000), p. 1.

24 *Den (Kyiv)* (10 March 1998), p. 1.

25 *Izvestiya* (31 March 1994), p. 4.

26 *Izvestiya* (31 March 1994), p. 4.

27 *Uriadovy Currier (Kyiv)* (29 January 2000), p. 5.

28 *Holos Ukrajiny* (24 July 1993), p. 3.

29 Z. Brzezinski, *Out of Control. Global Turmoil on the Eve of the Twenty-First Century* (New York, Charles Scribner's Sons, 1993), pp. 163–4.

30 'A world we have not known', *Newsweek* (27 January 1997), p. 25.

31 S. P. Huntington, *The Clash of Civilizations and the Remaking of the World Order* (New York, Simon & Schuster, 1996), p. 166.

32 Interviewed onC-SPAN television channel (20 November 1995).

33 *Zerkalo Nedely (Kyiv)* (18 January 1997).

34 'NATO–Ukraine Charter: first act or the curtain call?', *BITS Briefing Note 97.1* (Berlin, Berlin Information Centre on Transatlantic Security, 1997), pp. 18–19.

35 *Den (Kyiv)* (12 October 2000), p. 3.

6
Russia's defence diplomacy in Europe: containing threat without confrontation

Viktor Kremenyuk

In the 1990s, when the Cold War was winding down, no one predicted that a short while later the spectre of a new military confrontation would re-emerge in Europe. At that time it seemed that all major controversies had been solved, appetites for militarism had been contained and for the fore-seeable future Europe would be at peace. At the beginning of the twenty-first century, it seems that the possibility of a new round of military rivalry is again on the horizon: in the eyes of some, the gods of war have prevailed, as usual. There are those who doubt this but, irrespective of their views, this alternative view has relevance for contemporary Europe.

The process of ending a military confrontation may be compared to that of releasing a taught spring: slow, careful, step by step, without sudden moves. Otherwise, the spring may fly out of control and injure the operator. If we apply this metaphor to the process of ending the Cold War it shows that special solutions were needed which would have done two things at the same time: end confrontation and create a new non-confrontational regime. The process had to be handled with care and diplomacy and a strong understanding that, if mishandled, it could backfire and unleash a new and much more dangerous conflict.

If we look back at the dramatic events of 1989–92 in Europe which brought an end to the Cold War, it is evident that the end of the military confrontation was more or less negotiated (though after German re-unifi-cation in 1990 it developed spontaneously, without any firm control), while a new non-confrontational regime was the subject of only sporadic discus-sions. What would the future Europe be like – with or without the Warsaw Pact, with or without the North Atlantic Treaty Organisation (NATO), with new or old security arrangements? At that time, no one was able to give direct answers to these questions.

This subject was never discussed in depth, creating the seeds of a possi-ble new confrontation in the future. When this possibility was recognised by responsible parties in the West the only answer suggested was: enlarge NATO. Disregarding the well-known fact that NATO was specifically designed in another historical setting and for other military and political purposes, the West has applied tremendous efforts to revive NATO and to make it the only viable security mechanism in Europe; the West hoped thereby to cope with new threats of conflict, but in the meantime contributed to them through the revival of the Alliance.

The old rule – what was created for war cannot be used for building peace (or, as Napoleon put it, you may do many things with a bayonet but you cannot sit on it) – was completely ignored. As a result, the strategic situation in Europe rapidly deteriorated. Being essentially a military alliance of northern Atlantic nations aimed at a major war in the east of the continent, NATO could not change its nature within a short period of time. Instead, it has added to its initially defensive nature an offensive capability demonstrated in the war against Yugoslavia and, thus, has turned into a major threat in Russian eyes. Somewhat unexpectedly, Russia has come to learn that the strategic setting in Europe has changed completely. Instead of the prospect of living another decade in peace and tranquillity, Russia faces the probability of becoming engaged in a new war in the not-too-distant future.

Strategic changes in Europe after Kosovo: a Russian view

A short answer to the question 'what has changed in Europe after the 1999 Kosovo crisis?' is: everything has changed. The first lesson the crisis brought home is that there is no more trust and confidence, there is a threat of a new large-scale war and there is a need to be prepared for it. Europe after 1999 will never be the post-1989 Europe that seemed to have become a zone of peace and stability. Instead of the post-1989 expectations of reconciliation of former enemies, partnership, the democratisation of international relations and the marginalisation of conflicts, a new reality has come to existence. This shift has raised major questions. Where will the next conflict be? Who will be engaged in it? Will Russia be prepared for it? In what way will Russia force NATO to respect its interests militarily?

The borderline between the two Europes – Europe after 1989 and post-Kosovo Europe – was marked by the NATO air attack against Yugoslavia. NATO's air war did not shatter Yugoslav defences (generally speaking, the results of the air war against Yugoslavia say more about NATO's weakness than about its strength), nor did it make Russia feel exposed to an immediate attack. It simply indicated that a Europe without war is an empty dream, and nothing has changed in the pattern of European security affairs: when there is no prospect of a war between traditional enemies, meaning France and Germany, then there is the possibility of a 'collective war' of the West against a Slavic nation, as happened in 1812 when Napoleon led a

European coalition against Russia or in 1941 when Germany led a coalition of six European nations against Russia. The mainstream of European history has not changed: from war to war, this time after a long pause caused by the Cold War, as happened after the Congress of Vienna in 1815 (which was also ended by a European coalition war against Russia in 1854–56).

The second lesson that Russians learned from the Kosovo crisis was that NATO has ceased to be a purely defensive alliance and has acquired both an offensive capability and the resolve to use that capability. For many years strategic planners in Moscow were accustomed to living with a NATO that was responsible for the security of its members and did not act outside of its zone of responsibility. That is why the Soviet Union could afford to intervene militarily in Hungary in 1956, in Czechoslovakia in 1968 and even plan for a possible advance into Yugoslavia in the event of a crisis. Now NATO has decided to abandon its purely defensive posture and is searching for appropriate targets for its military might. Russia, not being a member of the Alliance and differing from the West culturally and economically, could all too easily become just such a target if it does not take care of its own defences.

The third lesson was that the decision to use military force, which was usually the prerogative of the United Nations (UN) Security Council where Russia could use its veto power (and this was precisely the purpose of the idea of permanent membership), was usurped by NATO. Russia, while still a permanent member of the UN Security Council, could do nothing to avert or to stop the Alliance's action. It was a direct sign of the premature death of the only organisation that could both contain aggression in the years of the Cold War and accommodate conflicting interests. War in Yugoslavia has put an end to its function and, maybe, even to its existence. The hope of being protected by mechanisms of international law has ceased to exist. Instead, only a strong defence capability can be regarded as a means of containing NATO.[1]

The fourth lesson for Russia was that the West may, when it chooses, ignore agreements which helped to improve the security situation in Europe in the last years of the Cold War, such as the Conventional Armed Forces in Europe (CFE) Treaty signed by NATO and the Warsaw Treaty Organisation in 1990. Disregarding provisions of the CFE Treaty, which established strict limits on the numbers of key items of military equipment permitted in different parts of Europe, NATO unilaterally altered force levels in South-Eastern Europe, thus indicating that the considerations which prompted it to attack Yugoslavia were much more valuable than any commitments worked out cooperatively with Russia. In the eyes of Moscow, this has raised strong doubts over the validity of any agreement with the West on security issues.

While there may also be other lessons to be drawn from the Kosovo crisis, the implications for Russia may be condensed as follows. [2] The period of romanticism in security terms, which emerged as a result of the end of the Cold War and consisted of the belief that cooperation between former enemies would preclude the possibility of war in Europe, has ended rather abruptly. Russian leaders were strategically unprepared for such a turn of events in European security. The sense of humiliation as a consequence of weakness and the inability to assist a historically close nation in its hour of need has had an especially profound effect on Russian security policy thinking. This sense of Russian weakness, and the perception that NATO has openly taken advantage of that weakness in order to consolidate its position as the strongest force in Europe, have left Russians with a strong anti-Western sentiment and helped groups associated with military power and advocates of forceful solutions to political problems to come to power in the Kremlin.

The other important conclusion is that the period during which Russia could afford to focus on domestic political and economic reforms has come to an end. Disregarding the fact that many political, economic and social issues are still far from being solved, the Russian government has had to change its attitudes towards privatisation, government control over the economy and subsidies to the military sector of its economy (which is under strict government control with only a limited private element). In a way, the war in Yugoslavia has helped the opponents of democracy in Russia to block further movement of the nation towards democracy. Whether this is a temporary slowdown or a decisive turn in Russian domestic development remains to be seen, but as of 2000 the anti-democratic forces have won.

Re-evaluating the balance of power

In the area of practical foreign policy, the major task for Russia is to re-evaluate the existing balance of power in Europe and look for the means to restore the balance that existed during the Cold War. During the Cold War, the sober understanding that a rough parity existed between the capabilities of the two blocs in Europe helped to keep the continent safe from war for more than fifty years. Since the new, post-Cold War security arrangements have not made it possible to avert a new war in Europe and, instead, are based on a dangerous asymmetry, it is in the Russian interest, as well as the interests of other European nations, to restore a rough parity of military capabilities between East and West or to find other ways to contain the most radical elements in Western security agencies who might be ready to start another war at the moment of their choosing. This does not mean that the balance has to be the same as existed during the Cold War or that it should be based on numerical military parity. This is impossible, at least currently, and a new direct confrontation is unthinkable because economic considerations make it counter to Russian interests. But other means may and must be found: this has become the essence of Russian defence thinking, including that about the country's security interests in Europe.

The last official attempt to frame a power balance in Europe was undertaken in 1990 with the agreement on the CFE Treaty, which mandated a rough parity between the forces of NATO and the Warsaw Pact and indicated that the balance between the two parts of Europe was essential for strategic stability on the continent. The CFE Treaty was one of several major agreements which built a bridge from the Cold War to a peaceful Europe, in particular the 1987 US–Soviet land-based Intermediate-Range Nuclear Forces (INF) Treaty, the 1991 US–Soviet Strategic Arms Reduction (START) Treaty, the 1991 reciprocal unilateral initiatives by Presidents Bush and Gorbachev which led to the removal of tactical nuclear weapons from Europe and, finally, the agreement on the re-unification of Germany which opened the way for a possible withdrawal of foreign troops, including Soviet/Russian forces, from that country. The CFE Treaty not only confirmed the balance between the two parts of Europe but also opened a way to lower ceilings on armaments in Europe.[3]

There are grounds for thinking that the CFE Treaty was more a case of looking back to the years of the Cold War than to a future with new security arrangements, notably under the aegis of the then Conference on (now Organisation for) Security and Cooperation in Europe (C/OSCE) (at that time considered the umbrella organisation for all security efforts in Europe). While it fixed a rough parity between the two blocs – in itself a major achievement – it miscalculated the life expectancy of the blocs, failing to consider the possibility that one of them – the Warsaw Pact – might disintegrate while the other – NATO – might survive and become a rival to the C/OSCE. Nevertheless, it permitted two processes to develop together: enhancing security and reducing armaments levels. Thus a cornerstone principle for European security was laid down, borrowing largely from US–Soviet security dialogue: parity in, and lower levels of, armaments.

This principle came into existence as part of a larger process of change in Europe. When the Helsinki Final Act was signed in 1975 it was more a statement of intentions than a reflection of the existing reality. After the signing of the Act, however, the situation in Europe changed, with progress in military confidence building (which finally led to the Stockholm Document in 1986), the establishment of a permanent consultative mechanism – the CSCE – and the beginnings of a new security system. Together with these innovations, the CFE Treaty laid the foundations for an alternative European security.

These impressive developments brought Europe to the most important decision of the last fifty years: German re-unification. This not only put the final touch to the rehabilitation of Germany as a peaceful nation but also represented the initial act in demolishing the Yalta–Potsdam system that had been sufficiently robust to survive almost fifty years of confrontation without a major war. By the end of the 1980s, the Yalta–Potsdam system was regarded by many in the West and the East, especially among the former Soviet allies, as outmoded, obsolescent and irrelevant. Many wanted it to be destroyed. Only a few, however, tried to insist that something new had to be negotiated instead.

The fact that the European nations decided at that time to wind down the East–West confrontation without making an effort to create a new security system can be explained by the specific experience of the Cold War years. Due to the realities of nuclear confrontation and a shared desire to avoid an inadvertent nuclear war, the United States and the Soviet Union very often spontaneously cooperated in resolving acute issues such as the Cuban missile crisis. This produced the impression that cooperation on acute international issues was an automatic consequence of confrontation between nuclear powers.[4] Some analysts regarded the idea of a 'conflict–cooperation' dichotomy as a universal explanation of the fact that military confrontation had not produced a military conflict.[5] The public at large was confident that there were strong limitations built into the confrontation that worked to save the universe; few understood how close the world came to catastrophe each time there was a crisis.

This attitude may explain why the European powers did not insist that a new European order must be negotiated and agreed upon in the crucial years 1990–92, when both the Warsaw Pact and the Soviet Union disintegrated with the end of ideological rivalry and military confrontation. Failure to negotiate a new security arrangement and an unfounded belief that membership in NATO would help to avoid another war have produced an asymmetrical outcome to the confrontation, which has led in turn to an asymmetrical new system of military–strategic relations in Europe. As a result, the situation in the region has become inherently unstable and fraught with the possibility of a new conflict. In conditions where the overall ratio between NATO and Russia in the area of conventional weapons has, according to some assessments, become 4:1 (and in air forces has even reached 5:1), a super-concentration of military power on one side has been achieved, distorting views of the military situation. Fortunately, the real results of the war against Yugoslavia testified that, despite NATO's apparent preponderance of military power, the Alliance is in fact far from capable of projecting genuine power and its preponderance has not translated into a usable military capability. Nevertheless, the unnecessary war

against Yugoslavia and other provocative acts by NATO (such as naval operations in the Black Sea) provide clear evidence of the risky decisions to
which a wrong and distorted view of the military balance may drive the governments of the Atlantic Alliance.

Still, the possibility of a new conflict was far from a probability early in
the 1990s, and both sides concentrated their efforts on avoiding the re-
emergence of such a conflict. The motives of the various actors were far
from identical. The Western nations (possibly under the influence of the
US administration) considered the strategic asymmetry in Europe to be
more dangerous for Russia than for the West. Russian leaders decided that
strategic asymmetry in Europe, if identified to the extent of becoming a
subject for domestic debate in Russia, could cost them the support of the
military. Both sides were eager to find a solution to the situation of asymmetry, and this became the hard core of defence diplomacy efforts in Europe
in the mid 1990s.

The foremost task for Russia in these conditions was to evaluate its new
military position and the prospects for its security. When looking at its new
military posture – which came about as a result of the cuts in military
deployments following the CFE provisions, the disintegration of the Soviet
Union and distribution of the former Soviet armed forces among the
successor states, and the withdrawal of Russian forces from Germany,
Poland and the Baltic states – Russian strategic planners had to draw two
conclusions. First, reflecting the best case scenario, there was a need to
engage in some sort of military cooperation with NATO and, thus, to work
for something like a condominium in Europe of the two largest military
entities. Second, reflecting the worst case scenario, Russia could use the
period of NATO's post-Cold War euphoria to carry out military reform,
restructure its armed forces and make them, if not a peer to NATO's, then
at least the second largest and strongest in Europe in order to resume
containment of the Alliance without undue confrontation. These ideas
were spelled out, though rather vaguely, in the first draft of the new Russian
military doctrine in 1993.[6]

The growth of the disparity in military capabilities between Russia and
NATO was regarded as a sign that Russia would face the necessity of
revising considerably some of the understandings of the previous period in
order to achieve parity in defensive (and offensive) capabilities with the
West. The first of these understandings to be revised would be the
Bush–Gorbachev agreement on the removal of tactical nuclear weapons
from Europe, possibly to be followed later by the INF Treaty. The Russian
leadership has signalled that, if necessary, it is ready to go as far as abro-
gating its commitments under these agreements if it feels that the West is
using its economic leverage and the political turmoil in Russia to further

alter the balance of forces in Europe in its own favour and contrary to Russia's security interests.

It is understandable that, while possessing nuclear weapons, Russia will not passively observe the growth of the imbalance in conventional military capabilities between itself and NATO. Even without direct evidence that NATO would use its leverage against Russian interests, as happened in Yugoslavia, Moscow is still prepared to use its assets in the form of tactical nuclear weapons to prevent this imbalance from encouraging NATO to take provocative decisions which might create a situation fraught with the danger of direct military conflict. After the Kosovo crisis, and in the wake of a possible US decision to deploy a National Missile Defence system which could create a further imbalance in military capabilities, this time in the area of strategic weapons, Russian policy makers concluded that they may have to revise some of the agreements of the previous decade in Russia's favour.

Security structures

The dissolution of the Yalta–Potsdam system and the old East–West balance of power was accompanied by a new political and security factor: the prospect of democratisation in Russia and the other successor states following the fall of the Soviet communist regime. The hope that these changes might lead to the advent of democratic societies in these countries and, logically, to a complete reversal in their foreign and security policies played a crucial role in the transformation of the entire European security landscape.

First, it was thought that these changes would lead to the end of the ideological rivalry that, according to some assessments, played a crucial role in the Cold War military confrontation (although history also suggests that military confrontation may occur without ideological differences). Although the role of ideology in the Cold War remains contentious, the disappearance of the ideological dimension of the Cold War and the decision of the former communist countries to opt for Western-style liberal democracy nevertheless raised hopes that the security situation would change.

Second, the fact that the Warsaw Pact had ceased to exist was regarded as a positive development in principle, though not by everyone. Given that local ethnic, border and territorial issues had played an important role in the origins of the Second World War and might now re-emerge, one of the important issues was to avoid a security vacuum in the eastern part of the continent. The Yugoslav tragedy had, by this point, already started to unfold, the division of Czechoslovakia was being debated and in the former

Soviet Union tensions were evident in the Baltic states, Crimea, Moldova and Georgia. The main political and security task at this time was seen to be to prevent conflict through local mechanisms. Thus the Visegrad group was regarded as a possible approach to Central Europe's security problems, while Russia attempted to play the role of security guarantor in the former Soviet Union via the 1992 Tashkent Collective Security Agreement.[7]

Third, the security negotiations of the 1980s also played a visible role. The January 1993 Russian–US START II Treaty and continuing Russian–NATO dialogue on conventional arms ceilings in Europe, together with the first official political and military contacts between Russia and the Atlantic Alliance, helped to maintain the process of mutual accommodation on security issues. These steps were complemented by Russo–Hungarian and Russo–Czechoslovak agreements on the withdrawal of the former Soviet troops from these two countries and ongoing negotiations on the withdrawal of Russian/former Soviet forces from Germany, Poland and the Baltic states. All in all, the inertia of this process produced a positive start to joint Russian–NATO thinking on European security.

The first, and primary, aim of such a security agreement was to establish a special relationship between Russia and NATO. Such a relationship would achieve several purposes: the avoidance of conflict between the two, the establishment of a security shelter (or umbrella) for the countries of Central and Eastern Europe and the former Soviet Union, and the establishment of cooperative mechanisms to meet non-military security problems such as terrorism, drug trafficking and illegal immigration. For the majority in NATO and for the Russian leadership such an arrangement was regarded as desirable and optimal. Negotiations on what later became the NATO–Russia Founding Act were prepared.[8]

An alternative scenario was discussed at that time as a distant possibility. This was first suggested by Polish President Lech Walesa and subsequently supported by Czechoslovak (and later Czech) President Vaclav Havel and the Hungarian leadership. The Central European leaders argued that their countries should become full members of NATO, thus refocusing security policy in the West towards the enlargement of NATO and turning the Alliance into the cornerstone of European security. The proposal met with some scepticism and opposition in the West, which permitted Russian President Boris Yeltsin to bless the idea for propagandistic purposes during his visit to Poland in 1993, a blessing later disavowed by the Russian Foreign Ministry.

By late 1994 the two scenarios were floating around European capitals, inviting European leaders to debate their merits. The pros and cons of each scenario were very sensitive for Russia, making Moscow nervous of the outcome of this debate in the West. The dominance of domestic considerations, however, prompted President Yeltsin to start the war in Chechnya in late 1994. The utter disregard by his government of the responses to the intervention in Chechnya in both the West and Central Europe tilted the debate definitively in favour of the enlargement of NATO. During 1995 it became clear that the West had decided to divert its quest for security away from dialogue with Russia to the incorporation of Poland, the Czech Republic and Hungary into NATO. All attempts to present the two things as reconcilable were simply propaganda. The Western choice was humiliating for Moscow, but the message was clear.

The period 1995–97 was wasted in futile attempts by both Moscow and Brussels to sell their ideas of future European security to the other. Moscow was essentially right in its warning that the decision to enlarge NATO would not enhance European security but would only establish a rigid line between East and West and turn it into a possible line of confrontation. In order to understand the essence of the tensions between Russia and NATO one needs to recognise that Moscow views NATO enlargement as a threat to its security. The West tried in vain to persuade Moscow that NATO enlargement would extend the zone of stability without undermining Russia's security. [9] Unfortunately, this became a dialogue of the deaf, with only one slight difference: both sides also wanted to save face and hence pursued a limited *modus vivendi* with regard to NATO's expansion into Central Europe at this point. This possibility of at least partial compromise in relation to the first wave of post-Cold War NATO enlargement may help to explain Western insensitivity to Russia's anxieties.

Two further points may be mentioned here. First, and most importantly, the majority of political leaders and groups in Russia accepted that NATO was relevant and beneficial for European security. From their perspective NATO helped to contain intra-European conflicts and tensions, pave the way to European integration, and contain possible outbreaks of German nationalism and channel German ambitions in a more constructive direction. It also provided an important link between Europe and North America and created a centre of gravity for current global arrangements. All these aspects were appreciated in Russia and only extreme and radical Russian nationalists continued to demand NATO's dissolution.

Second, connected with the question 'how can we live with NATO?', it was clear that Russia had (and has) no chance of becoming a member of NATO. Russia is too big for the bloc, its security interests lie outside the Alliance's zone of responsibility and NATO lacks the resources to address Russia's security problems. Besides, there is no practical need for Russia to join NATO because both militarily and diplomatically it can manage its own security concerns. But, if not a member of NATO, then what? Non-membership of NATO may threaten Russia with isolation in other European and

North Atlantic institutions because Russia will always feel alien to the rest of
Europe, and this may create certain political tensions with the West. Russia,
further, is not a member of the World Trade Organisation or the European
Union. All this could place it in a vulnerable position it its moment of weakness when it most needs substantial support. This is essentially why Russian
leaders regarded and continue to regard NATO's enlargement as essentially anti-Russian.

The signing of the NATO–Russia Founding Act in May 1997, in
exchange for Russian acquiesence to a decision on enlargement in July
1997, permitted both sides at least to pretend that they had paid attention
to, and taken steps to address, the interests of the other. In reality, the
strategic situation in Europe after 1997 has changed dramatically for the
worse. The decision on enlargement produced a false image of a reinvigo-
rated Atlantic Alliance which then pushed NATO further into the Balkan
quagmire. Somewhat unexpectedly, NATO decided that it had the obliga-
tion, commitment and power to intervene in Yugoslavia and force Belgrade
to change its course in Kosovo.

Two points should be mentioned with regard to NATO's intervention in
Kosovo. First, despite having mobilised all the potential air power at its
disposal (at the expense of reducing US force levels in other areas considered vital to the US), NATO could not destroy Yugoslav defences and
armed forces after seventy-eight days of intensive bombing. Second, even
after Kosovo was occupied by NATO peacekeepers, the situation in the
province has arguably not changed for the better. This suggests that NATO
cannot deploy sufficient forces to destroy Yugoslav defences with their
outmoded anti-aircraft capabilities within a reasonably short period of
time. It also suggests that NATO has developed little understanding of what
to do in 'liberated' areas or how to solve ethnic conflicts. Both these conclusions provoke concern in Russia because they testify that NATO is capable
of taking risky, poorly grounded decisions and cannot plan sensibly for the
future. In certain conditions, these tendencies might tempt NATO military
planners and political leaders to take the path which led Charles XII of
Sweden, Napoleon and Hitler to Russia.

Options for Russian defence diplomacy: looking ahead

As a result of these developments, Moscow faces three possible options.
First, Russia may try to develop a reconciliation with NATO, coming to a
modus vivendi that will permit the two to coexist without too much undue
friction. Second, it may try to mobilise what is left of Soviet military power
and to optimise it in order to create a military capability adequate to
contain possible steps by NATO. Third, Russia may try to develop a new

system of relations which will strengthen its sphere of influence in Eastern
Europe (Yugoslavia) and the former Soviet Union (Belarus), as well as
extending its security links with China, India, Iran and other non-European
states that will help Russia to counter-balance NATO's growing importance
in Europe and the Mediterranean.

All these scenarios assume the possibility of a new conflict with NATO.
Recent developments in Russia–NATO suggest three possible foci of
conflict: Yugoslavia, the Black Sea–Caspian Sea region and the Baltic
region. In Yugoslavia, there is no clear and identifiable Western policy.

The West's refusal to deal with then Yugoslav President Slobodan
Milosevic on the pretext of his 'malice' (though he had arguably been a
good partner for the West both in Dayton in 1995 and Rambouillet in 1999)
simply concealed the fact that, having bombed Yugoslavia and occupied
Kosovo, the West had no idea of where to go next. It cannot openly annex
Kosovo and make it an independent state because of some residual respect
for law (otherwise it will have absolutely no grounds for accusing Saddam
Hussein, who annexed Kuwait in 1990) and the risk of intensified demands
for a 'greater Albania' which would ignite crises in Macedonia and
Albanian-populated areas of Greece. Equally, the West is not inclined to
allow the Serb authorities back into Kosovo.

The absence of a sound policy in Kosovo makes conflict with Yugoslavia
inevitable since no leader in Belgrade can afford to forget about the wound
inflicted by NATO's actions in Kosovo. This poses a difficult question for
Moscow: will it help its Yugoslav brethren to restore their defence capabilities, including sophisticated anti-aircraft weapons? As of 2000, there is no
clear answer to that question. Much depends on the domestic situation in
Russia, its relations with the West and its resolve to fight for its previous positions in the Balkans, almost all of which are now occupied by NATO.

Other possible foci of Russian–NATO tensions are the Caspian Sea oil
reserves and the Black Sea. The US has, without prior consultation with
Moscow, identified this vast region as a zone involving its national interests.
While this development may be legally permissible, it ignores Russia's
historic and economic interests in the region – as if there were no Russia at
all – and Moscow's tremendous investment in the region's infrastructure
and economy in recent centuries. Since this region is increasingly regarded
as an important source of oil and gas, Russia has grounds to plan for its
legitimate part in the exploitation of the vast resources of the Caspian Sea.
From this point of view, the numerous military and quasi-military operations of NATO naval forces in the Black Sea are regarded as a campaign of
military pressure on Russia.

Finally, there is the problem of the Baltic states. The desire of these
states, governments to join NATO is well known, as is the reciprocal desire

of many Western states to see them in the bloc. If the Baltic states join
NATO, however, from a military perspective the more or less peaceful life
for the Alliance will be over. The armed forces of Russia and NATO –
navies, air forces and ground forces – will come into direct contact in a way
that has never previously been the case. Their 'coexistence' will produce
numerous and endless small incidents at sea, in the air and on the ground.
Losses will occur and mutual accusations will follow on an almost daily
basis. And all this will take place in a political climate of mistrust and suspi-
cion, since Russia will never agree to the Baltic states' membership of
NATO.

There is a clear understanding in the Russian government and among
the Russian public that, under current conditions, Russia cannot afford a
new confrontation with the West. Such a confrontation would dramatically
overstretch Russia's resources and cut Russia off from supplies of food and
consumer goods from the West, as well as from financial assistance. As a
result, there is a strong trend towards developing a defence diplomacy
which would permit Moscow to use its military assets and diplomatic efforts
in order to contain what is perceived as one of the biggest threats to Russian
security, the North Atlantic Alliance in its present form and with its present
doctrine.

This may be seen from several recent developments. The Russian
Security Council under President Vladimir Putin has decided on the new
elements of the Russian military doctrine.[10] In essence, it follows the lines
of the first draft military doctrine of 1993: a strong emphasis on military
reform that would make the Russian conventional forces equal in capabilities to those of NATO and a stronger emphasis on tactical nuclear weapons
to compensate for Russia–NATO asymmetry in airpower in the event of war.
However, although the new military doctrine follows the same broad lines
as that of 1993, there are important differences. First, the Russian army has
gone through hard lessons in Chechnya and its ground forces may be
regarded as much more combat ready than those of NATO. Second, the
emphasis on the first use of nuclear weapons has become much stronger.
This time nuclear weapons will be used not only as the *ultima ratio* but also
at a much earlier stage of conflict as a weapon to deter large-scale aggression, including 'aggression with the use of conventional weapons in situations critical for the national security of the Russian Federation'.[11]

Russian foreign policy style has also changed. The new foreign policy
concept, which was also discussed in the Security Council in spring 2000, is
much less oriented towards partnership with the West.[12] While it does not
completely reject partnership with the West, it places a much greater
emphasis on Russian national interests, especially in the security field and,
as President Putin has insisted, on the much more aggressive pursuit of

those interests. It underlines the necessity of promoting international multipolarity, which means a much broader spectrum of foreign policy alignments. It also hints at the possibility of building new alliances in areas where Russian national interests correspond with those of local states. Potential allies include countries such as Yugoslavia and Iran.

It seems the Russian government has set itself a difficult task for its security diplomacy in Europe. It has accepted the idea that there is not much room for cooperation with NATO but, equally, that there is no sense in rejecting this possibility altogether. Some middle-of-the-road course must be developed which will give Russia leverage to defend its interests when they are challenged by the West, whether in the Balkans, the Baltic or Caspian Sea region. At the same time, Moscow should at all costs avoid a new war in Europe.

Notes

1   See W. Pfaff's commentary in *International Herald Tribune* (22 August 1999).
2   V. Kremenyuk, 'Rossiya–SShA: pervye uroki balkanskogo krisisa 1999 goda (Russia and the USA: first lessons of the Balkan crisis of 1999)', *SShA i Kanada: ekonomika, politika, kul'tura*, 1 (2000), 5–15.
3   D. L. Averre, 'Russia and issues of demilitarisation', in M. Webber (ed.), *Russia and Europe: Cooperation or Conflict?* (Basingstoke, Macmillan, 2000).
4   R. Kanet and E. Kolodziek (eds.), *The Cold War as Cooperation: Superpower Cooperation in Regional Conflict Management* (Baltimore, The Johns Hopkins University Press, 1991).
5   R. Axelrod, *The Evolution of Cooperation* (New York, Basic Books, 1984).
6   V. Kremenyuk, 'Perceptions russes et reponses aux conflicts futurs', *Defense Nationale*, (April 1996), 191–9.
7   V. Kremenyuk, *Conflicts In and Around Russia: Nation-Building in Difficult Times* (London, Greenwood Press, 1994).
8   V. Kremenyuk, 'Global security conflicts: alliances', in I. W. Zartman (ed.), *Preventive Negotiation: Avoiding Conflict Escalation* (New York, Rowman & Littlefield Publishers, 2000).
9   See, for example, M. Albright, 'Enlarging NATO: why bigger is better', *The Economist* (15 February 1997).
10 *Nezavisimoe voennoe obozrenie*, 15 (2000), 1 and 4–5.
11 *Nezavisimoe voennoe obozrenie*, 15 (2000).
12 *BBC Summary of World Broadcasts, part 1, former USSR*, (12 July 2000), B/5–12.

7
New thinking in conflict management

Dov Lynch

The end of the Cold War gave rise to a resurgence of conflicts across Eurasia, from the Tajik civil war in Central Asia to the Yugoslav wars of dissolution. In these circumstances, conflict management has changed at four levels. First, conflict management has come to encompass a wide spectrum of activities. At the pre-conflict stage, conflict management has included preventive deployment and diplomacy. When conflicts have broken out, conflict management has featured military deployments to ensure the provision of humanitarian aid and to create conditions for negotiated settlements. These activities have included both consensual and enforcement elements, as witnessed in the former Yugoslavia. Following armed conflict, conflict management has included military deployments to support the implementation of peace agreements, as in Bosnia and a number of post-Soviet conflicts. In the former Yugoslavia, such efforts also featured attempts at wider peace building. Conflict management has come to encompass a range of linked activities at all stages of a conflict. The coordination of these levels has created difficulties. Moreover, the use of conflict management as a means of coercion has made the integration of military and civilian components a key problem.

Second, the targets of conflict management have changed. Most post-Cold War European conflicts have taken place within rather than between states, complicating conflict management. These conflicts have featured high levels of violence, increasingly against civilians. Actions undertaken by parties to conflicts have transgressed international legal norms on the conduct of war. A choice has been seen to arise for third parties between the application of justice and the pursuit of conflict resolution. The high levels of violence against civilians have made the task of reconciliation more difficult. Also, conflicting parties have included a range of leadership levels, political and military. Conflict management has faced the difficulty of addressing different leadership levels within each conflicting party, as well as between them.

Third, the actors undertaking conflict management have changed. At a sub-state level, non-governmental organisations have assumed increasingly important roles. At the state level, individual states have deployed unilateral peacekeeping operations, raising, for example, questions about the legitimacy of Russia's role in the former Soviet Union. Coalitions of willing states have also played an important role, as witnessed in the Italian-led Operation Alba in Albania. Finally, international organisations and European regional institutions have become involved at all levels of conflict management. An informal division of labour has emerged between these organisations in terms of 'soft' and 'hard' activities, creating problems of coordination between these organisations. The role of regional organisations has also raised questions about the legitimacy of their activities, particularly if undertaken without the specific approval of the United Nations (UN).

Fourth, the justifications for conflict management have changed. The definition of threats to international peace and security has expanded beyond traditional problems of state aggression to include humanitarian disasters and the massive violation of human rights.[1] On firmer legal ground, the international community has intervened to enforce agreements reached between the parties. The North Atlantic Treaty Organisation (NATO) justified its 1999 military action against Yugoslavia on the basis that Belgrade's forces were using 'unrestrained' force in Kosovo.[2] Russia has justified its peacekeeping operations on several grounds, including the 1992 Commonwealth of Independent States (CIS) Collective Security Treaty (with regard to its intervention in Tajikistan), humanitarian grounds (in order to avert violations of the rights of ethnic minorities) and national interests. The expanding justifications for conflict management have raised problems regarding its legitimacy.

This chapter examines one dimension of new thinking about conflict management, that of peacekeeping intervention. International organisations and states have intervened in seven armed conflicts in Eurasia: in the former Yugoslavia, Albania, the Federal Republic of Yugoslavia, Moldova, on two occasions in Georgia, and Tajikistan. The outbreak of internal, civil conflicts has challenged traditional peacekeeping mechanisms developed during the Cold War. Intervening states and organisations have undergone a painful learning process about the utility of force and intervention. This experience has generated an international debate about the nature of peacekeeping. This ongoing debate has addressed the dilemmas that have arisen because of the increasing use of force in such operations. The militarisation of peacekeeping has created problems for the civilian aspects of conflict management. Intervention also raised problems for the creation of mutually reinforcing conflict management mechanisms. Problems have arisen in the interaction between different security-related organisations – particularly NATO, the Organisation for Security and Cooperation in

Europe (OSCE) and the UN. Problems have also emerged in the interaction between particular states and regional organisations, such as Russia and the OSCE.

New thinking about peacekeeping and intervention: the first phase of the debate

Shifts from traditional peacekeeping

As noted by Sir Brian Urquhart, peacekeeping emerged as a 'series of improvisations to side-step East–West tension and to allow the [UN Security] Council to take at least some action when peace was threatened or when a conflict seemed likely to escalate'.[3] Traditional operations were guided by six principles: operations were established by the UN and under the command of the Secretary-General; operations were set up with the consent and ongoing cooperation of the parties to the conflict; operations were guided by neutrality and impartiality in their deployment and actions; peacekeeping troops were provided voluntarily by member states, generally by small and medium powers; peacekeepers were instructed to use force only in self-defence (not to alter the prevailing distribution of power in an area); and, peacekeepers were deployed only after a cease-fire between the parties to the conflict.[4] Traditional peacekeeping missions were usually deployed in inter-state conflicts as interposition forces. Alan James underlined the secondary role played by traditional peacekeepers as 'inert guarantors whose success relied largely on the effective nature of the political agreements which had been reached prior to their deployment'.[5] The strength of traditional peacekeeping resided partly in a 'hostage effect', 'placing a soldier from an international force between two opposing armies as a hostage to their good behaviour'.[6] The success of this effect depended on the operation's impartiality, neutrality and minimum use of force. The operation had to be seen by all as the legitimate and authoritative expression of the will of the international community.

Peacekeeping since the end of the Cold War has challenged all six principles.[7] Peacekeeping interventions have been organised more by states and organisations other than the UN. Consent from the conflicting parties has been challenged, adding an enforcement element to peacekeeping. Neutrality and impartiality, originally intended towards the parties to a conflict, has been interpreted as relating to the fulfilment of the mandate of an operation. Moreover, peacekeeping has been led by great powers – the United States, Russia, France and Great Britain. The grounds for the use of force have been redefined to include ensuring the fulfilment of a mandate. Finally, peacekeeping troops have been deployed in highly volatile circumstances.

Russian peacekeeping experience in the former Soviet Union high-lights these shifts. Russian peacekeeping operations were deployed under Russian command without the support of the UN.[8] Claims that the conflict-ing parties consented to these operations must be qualified by the fact that Russian forces based in the conflict zones intervened coercively in Moldova and Georgia in support of separatist forces in Transdniestria and Abkhazia. Moreover, the conflicting parties have been integrated into the peacekeep-ing operation as troop contributors. In Tajikistan, Russian peacekeeping forces have undertaken limited counter-insurgency operations.

International peacekeeping actions in the former Yugoslavia are also indicative of the changed nature of such actions. The UN deployed a peace-keeping force (UN Protection Force, UNPROFOR) in Croatia in 1991 to monitor a cease-fire and perform traditional peacekeeping tasks.[9] As the conflict escalated, the geographical responsibility of UNPROFOR was extended to Bosnia-Herzegovina and its mandate came to include enforce-ment components, namely to protect the delivery of humanitarian assis-tance and the security of the 'safe areas', but within a broadly consensual framework. This placed the peacekeeping troops in an impossible position. These forces were not armed appropriately for enforcement actions, were over-exposed in deployment and were vulnerable to coercion by the conflicting parties. The operation was caught between the aim of ensuring consent from the conflicting parties and that of implementing the mandate. The command and control for UNPROFOR was complicated by the UN's interaction with NATO, which was mandated to enforce a no-fly zone and provide air support for the protection of the 'safe areas'.

The first debate about peacekeeping and intervention

This experience stimulated an international debate about the nature of post-Cold War peacekeeping. Then UN Secretary-General Boutros Boutros-Ghali set the tone for the debate, stating: 'The dynamics and prior-ities of a new era, along with the difficulties in working with local authori-ties, have raised profound questions about the absolute need for consent from the parties in the first place'.[10] This debate focused on the nature of consent and the use of force in contemporary operations. The contenders in this phase of the debate can be divided into two groups.

The first group may be called 'traditionalists'. Marrack Goulding under-lined in 1993 that 'creating this kind of gray area between peacekeeping and peace-enforcement can give rise to considerable changes'. He highlighted the distortions that arise as these operations moved into a grey area, making the fulfilment of the mandate all the more difficult and increasing an opera-tion's casualty levels.[11] The traditionalist group argued that there was an absolute distinction between peacekeeping and peace enforcement.[12]

Evoking UN operations during the Congolese civil war, Brian Urquhart stated that 'a peacekeeping force which descends into the conflict may well become part of the problem, instead of the solution to it'.[13] With emphasis on the 'hostage effect', Lieutenant-General Gustav Hagglund also argued that 'weakness is often the strength of the peacekeepers'.[14] The peacekeeping doctrines developed by Scandinavian states followed these lines, maintaining an absolute distinction between peacekeeping and enforcement measures.[15]

'Middle ground' theorists argued that there existed a middle ground between traditional peacekeeping and peace enforcement. John Mackinlay placed contemporary peacekeeping on a spectrum of military activity stretching to enforcement.[16] In this view, the difference between traditional and contemporary peacekeeping resided in the degree of intensity in the use of force. According to Mackinlay, the legitimacy of these operations was based on the extent to which an operation even-handedly upheld its mandate. Similarly, James Gow and Christopher Dandeker argued that consent was no longer a sufficient basis for determining the legitimacy of an operation. In their view, these operations had to 'strive to reconcile the operational needs for a broadly consensual environment, so as not to escalate into war-fighting, with the need in certain circumstances, to ensure compliance through enforcement measures'.[17] In this respect, Mackinlay called for peacekeeping to draw on the experience of former colonial powers in 'keeping the peace' operations.[18]

Given the complexity of contemporary conflicts, middle ground theorists questioned the utility of traditional principles. In order to fulfil its mandate, they argued that an operation must have significant strength in order to alter the prevailing distribution of power in a conflict zone, negotiate from strength and deter any attacks on its forces. In these circumstances, the 'hostage effect' had to be set aside. These analysts argued that the relationship between the use of force and the maintenance of consent and legitimacy was not as simple as the traditionalists assumed. Force could be used in a selective manner to implement a mandate without undermining the legitimacy of an operation or the consent of the conflicting parties.[19] Boutros-Ghali contributed to these discussions in his 1992 *Agenda for Peace*, where he called for heavily armed peace enforcement units to be used in peacekeeping operations.[20]

A parallel debate occurred in Russia. The lines of this debate, however, differed from wider European discussions. In general, Russian analysts opposed those who viewed peacekeeping as a form of combat activity, and others who adopted views similar to middle ground theorists. Moreover, Russian peacekeeping operations were officially linked to the promotion of Russian interests. These differences set Russian operations and the Russian debate on the sidelines of the wider European experience and debate. An important, if minority, view portrayed peacekeeping as a form of combat activity, drawing upon Soviet experience in the Afghan war and Russian counter-insurgency in the Tajik civil war.[21] Russia's experience in Chechnya, however, reinforced the position of more moderate voices in the military leadership and the government. While recognising the role of force, the Ministry of Foreign Affairs presented peacekeeping as the legal *via media* between unilateral coercion and genuine non-intervention in the affairs of the newly independent states, arguing that peacekeeping had to be integrated into a coherent strategy combining 'firmness with restraint and subtlety in its approach'.[22] This policy juxtaposed political and diplomatic measures with the 'carefully considered application of economic and military force ...within the framework of the law'.[23]

At the wider European level, middle ground theorists drew upon positive examples in the former Yugoslavia – such as the limited use of force by certain elements of UNPROFOR – to justify their views.[24] In general, however, initial conclusions from the experience of peacekeeping in the former Yugoslavia, as well as Somalia, led to a retreat from prescriptions for ambitious operations in the middle ground.

Initial conclusions

The 1995 British army field manual *Wider Peacekeeping* was indicative of initial European conclusions drawn from experience in complex conflicts.[25] This approach sought to resolve the problem of combining the use of force and consent in a volatile environment, developing 'wider peacekeeping' as an adjustment of traditional peacekeeping to contemporary circumstances. Wider peacekeeping was defined as the 'wider aspects of peacekeeping operations carried out with the consent of the belligerent parties but in an environment that may be highly hostile'.[26] The concept drew a distinction between peacekeeping and peace enforcement in terms of consent, legitimacy and the use of force, arguing that there was no middle ground in practice between these two activities.

At the same time, it was recognised that consent was not an absolute commodity to be counted on at all times from all parties, and a distinction was drawn between tactical (at the level of the check-point), operational (between the major conflicting parties) and strategic (within the UN Security Council) levels of consent. Wider peacekeeping depended on consent at the operational and strategic levels. The British army field manual stated that wider peacekeeping was a '[peacekeeping] category where the preservation of consent is the principal guide of operational activity'. At the tactical level, wider peacekeeping forces have to build consent through consent-building techniques. These forces may use force at the local level, provided that it is not of such a magnitude that it breaches operational and strategic levels of consent. Force could be used as 'the measured application of violence or coercion sufficient only to achieve a specific end, demonstrably reasonable, proportionate and appropriate and confined in effect to specific and legitimate targets'.[27] The legitimacy of wider peacekeeping resided not only in the fulfilment of a mandate but also in the levels of consent to its activities.

Wider peacekeeping represented an initial diagnosis of the experience of peacekeeping in the former Yugoslavia that sought to remain within the consensual framework of traditional peacekeeping. These concepts were developed at a time of rethinking in the UN.[28] The experience of UNPRO-FOR and the UN operation in Somalia (UNOSOM II) had been sobering events. This experience was exacerbated by the increasing financial over-stretch of the UN in peacekeeping. Boutros-Ghali's 1995 *Supplement to the Agenda for Peace* marked a retreat from ambitious concepts: 'The logic of peacekeeping flows from political and military premises that are quite different from those of enforcement; and the dynamics of the latter are incompatible with the political process that peacekeeping is intended to facilitate'.[29] This statement reflected the end to the first phase of the debate about post-Cold War conflict management.

The second phase in the debate

The second phase of new thinking about post-Cold War conflict management was stimulated by three factors. First, new studies of contemporary operations argued that initial conclusions about this experience were misdiagnosed. As a result, new concepts have been developed, drawing upon points raised in the first phase of the debate. Second, the appointment of Kofi Annan as UN Secretary-General in 1997 contributed to new thinking about peacekeeping. Third, the experience of European states and NATO in the implementation of the Dayton Agreement in the former Yugoslavia led to renewed efforts at conceptualising post-Cold War peacekeeping.

A new diagnosis

New studies of post-Cold War operations have argued that the concept of wider peacekeeping had drawn too heavily from experience in the former Yugoslavia.[30] In their analysis, Donald Daniels and Bradd Hayes argued that misdiagnosed conclusions had been formulated about the effectiveness of a 'third option' between traditional peacekeeping and peace enforcement, that UNPROFOR was not representative of a third option (as it had shifted in an improvised manner between two extremes) and that there existed a 'conceptually distinct, practicable middle option' called coercive induce-ment.[31] Daniels and Hayes drew heavily from concepts developed earlier by

middle ground theorists, arguing that the legitimacy of coercive inducement resided in its even-handed implementation of a mandate and that
consent had to be built at the local level in order to operate within a
broadly consensual framework, although rules of engagement might be
expansive. Daniels and Hayes argued that such operations must be
endorsed by the UN, but commanded by leading states or a coalition of
states. While troop composition for such operations must be as universal as
possible, priority had to be given to troops from states with credible capabilities for effective crisis response. Coercive inducement operations had to
assume only provisional consent and act at the local level to impose the will
of the international community on recalcitrant parties. The use of force
had to be tactical in nature and effect.

This concept was new in its integration of coercive actions on the
ground with the wider diplomatic process. Daniels and Hayes drew from
Thomas Schelling's concept of coercion in order to understand the essential objective of such an operation: 'It aims to persuade rather than to seize
or to bludgeon, and it must form part of a concerted campaign involving a
variety of means – political, diplomatic, economic, hortatory, as well as military – to influence [the conflicting parties'] behaviour,'[32]

James Gow's analysis of international conflict management in the
former Yugoslavia argued that UNPROFOR's weakness resided in the fact
that it became a substitute for ineffective diplomacy at the international
level.[33] In this view, an effective peace support operation may employ force
at the tactical level in order to advance a wider diplomatic process. In such
operations, legitimacy resides in the impartial and even-handed implementation of the mandate. The wider diplomatic process has to be coordinated
between major states and the UN, and be backed by clear political commitment, including a willingness and the capabilities to use force.

Kofi Annan and 'coercive inducement'

The appointment of Kofi Annan as UN Secretary-General also stimulated this
phase of thinking. Annan had been Under-Secretary-General for
Peacekeeping and had well-developed views, maintaining that post-Cold War
operations had to undertake 'tasks that call for "teeth" and "muscle" in addition to the less tangible qualities that we have sought in the past'.[34] As
Secretary-General, Annan developed these views in greater depth, calling for
the use of coercive inducements in peace operations. Coercive inducement
consisted of the 'judicious resort to coercive diplomacy or forceful persuasion by the international community in order to implement community
norms or mandates vis-a-vis all the parties to a particular crisis'.[35] The objective of coercive inducement was to integrate peacekeeping effectively with
conflict resolution.[36] While Annan recognised the role that force may play

when used by troops at the tactical level, in his view the effect of coercive actions eroded over time. Annan stressed the need to coordinate coercion with *positive* inducements to build consent in the conflict zone and enhance the effectiveness and legitimacy of an operation. Peace operations had to undertake 'civic actions' at the local level and provide 'peace incentives' to gain leverage – both of these measures were seen as critical parts of a 'structure of rewards' to further the conflict resolution process.[37]

Annan had previously been Special Envoy of the UN Secretary-General to NATO and argued that UN–NATO cooperation in peacekeeping in European conflicts held 'the promise of a vast qualitative and quantitative expansion of the means for collective action that are at the disposal of the UN'.[38] He played an important role in the shift that occurred in 1995 towards a NATO-led peace operation to implement the Dayton Agreement. The implementation of the Dayton Agreement seemed to provide a model for coercive use of force by the international community, with the integration of different types of peace operation (including the Implementation Force (IFOR) with heavily armed troops under NATO command and control, and robust rules of engagement, and an International Police Task Force (IPTF) under UN control and following traditional guidelines). While IFOR did use force on occasion, it sought to create a consensual climate on the ground.[39]

Peace support operations

The experience of IFOR and the follow-up Stabilisation Force (SFOR) reflected rethinking by NATO and European states about peace operations. This phase of new thinking featured a shift towards operations dominated by military requirements and principles. These official concepts were closer to Daniels and Hayes' work on coercive inducement than Annan's incentives strategy.

NATO thinking about peacekeeping emerged slowly under the experience of its support to UNPROFOR. In May 1993 NATO Secretary-General Manfred Woerner stated that: 'We see more clearly that peacekeeping covers the entire spectrum of operations from humanitarian and police tasks in a non-hostile environment right up to major enforcement actions under Chapter VII of the UN Charter'.[40] In 1993–95 the Peacekeeping Office at NATO's Supreme Headquarters Allied Powers Europe produced a document on NATO military planning for peace support operations.[41] In this document, peace support operations were defined as:

> multifunctional operations conducted in support of a UN or OSCE mandate, including military forces, diplomacy and humanitarian agencies and … designed to achieve along term political settlement or other conditions specified in the mandate. They include peacekeeping and

peace enforcement, as well as conflict prevention, peace-making, peace-building and humanitarian operations.[42]

NATO thinking on peace support operations argued for the capacity for enforcement actions by troops operating under NATO unified command and robust rules of engagement to achieve clear objectives set forth in an internationally endorsed mandate. NATO forces would seek primarily to deter parties from violating agreements, but would, if required, use force in a proportionate and mission-specific manner. A distinction was drawn between peace support operations and peace enforcement operations under Chapter VII – where force structures, mission objectives and the rules of engagement were those of war.[43]

The British wider peacekeeping concept had remained explicitly within the traditional framework of consent and the minimal use of force. Subsequently, British thinking shifted with the peace support concept developed by NATO. The 1997 *Joint Warfare Publication 3.01* set forth new views on peace support operations, with substantial enforcement capabilities in complex emergency situations.[44] Contrary to wider peacekeeping, peace support operations represented a middle ground between traditional peacekeeping and legally defined peace enforcement. The legitimacy of such operations was to be based upon their fulfilment of a mandate. Consent was seen as an objective to be achieved through two types of measure: enforcement actions and consent-building measures. This concept contained elements of Kofi Annan's positive inducement strategy. However, the emphasis clearly resided in the military dimension of such operations and, in particular, coercive inducement.

These concepts have been reflected in other state doctrines. The US joint doctrine of 'Military Operations Other Than War' addresses operations focusing on 'deterring war, resolving conflict, promoting peace and supporting civil authorities' through the selective and coercive use of force.[45] The Danish approach to peacekeeping since 1992 has shifted away from traditional peacekeeping towards NATO-compatible rapid reaction forces, with the Danish International Brigade, consisting of 4,550 combat and support troops with substantial training and heavy weaponry, becoming fully operational in 1997.[46] The French armed forces have also developed new concepts for second-generation peacekeeping (defined as Peace Restoration Operations), where forces may be deployed while a conflict is ongoing and insecurity reigns on the ground, and force is used in a timely and robust manner under national command, although the operation must remain impartial in order to build legitimacy.[47]

The Russian Ministry of Defence has developed formal concepts to guide training and operations along similar lines.[48] Agreements adopted at the CIS summit in January 1996 also allow for greater use of force and leeway for the commander of an operation in deciding when this is appropriate.[49] In theory, the CIS documents focus on operations deployed after a cease-fire on traditional lines. In practice, however, the Russian government has not applied a spectrum approach, limiting Russian operations to traditional inter-position exercises. Even in Tajikistan, where elements of the Russian 201st division were designated as peacekeeping forces in the civil war, Russian forces sought to retain limited operational profiles. After the first Chechen war, Russian operations eschewed spectrum tasks and adopted mainly passive inter-position positions.

Practical and conceptual problems

IFOR, SFOR and KFOR

While Russia has avoided ambitious peace support, the IFOR and SFOR operations put into practice some of these concepts. NATO strategy towards the crisis in Kosovo in 1999 was also indicative of this new phase in thinking. In the former Yugoslavia, NATO evolved from a subcontractor in support of a UN operation to become the leading participant after the Dayton Agreement. Following its negative experience as subcontractor, NATO concluded that its operations would only be undertaken under NATO unified command and control and following robust rules of engagement.[50] The lessons from NATO's initial cooperation with the UN and the apparent success of the use of force against the Bosnian Serbs in 1995 were applied to the design of IFOR to implement the Dayton Agreement. UN Security Council Resolution 1031 contained a unique combination of peacekeeping and peace enforcement elements, attempting to resolve the dilemma of enforcement and consent by building into the mandate the parties' consent to any future use of force against themselves.

The military annexes to the Dayton Agreement provided a series of deadlines for the separation of forces and the creation of a cease-fire line and inter-ethnic boundary line. IFOR had also limited 'supporting tasks' to assist the implementation of the civilian dimensions of the Agreement. The principal military tasks were completed more or less on time in 1996. Following this, IFOR concentrated more on assisting civilian agencies, including providing logistical support to the OSCE in preparing and conducting elections, as well as reconstruction efforts.[51] SFOR, activated in December 1996 with fewer troops (31,000) but a similar mandate, became more involved in providing support to the implementation of the political dimensions of the Dayton Agreement. The Bonn meeting of the Peace Implementation Council in December 1997 strengthened the role of the High Representative Carlos Westendorp and placed emphasis on reinforcing the link between civilian and military activities.[52] These decisions increased SFOR support to the International Criminal Tribunal for the former Yugoslavia (ICTY). SFOR and the IPTF also started limited joint patrols in 1997. Shifts in the US State Department and the British government, as well as the appointment of General Wesley Clark as NATO's Supreme Allied Commander Europe, set the context for increasing civil–military cooperation in the former Yugoslavia.[53]

NATO's 1999 Operation Allied Force against the Federal Republic of Yugoslavia highlighted the Alliance's focus on the coercive dimension of peace support. NATO conducted an air-bombing campaign in an area beyond the Alliance's territorial remit and without direct Security Council approval. The operation had clear coercive intent: the objective was to use force short of war to persuade Yugoslav President Slobodan Milosevic to accept the proposals set forth by the Contact Group at the Rambouillet conference. For this reason, the initial weeks of the operation consisted of limited strikes by a small number of aircraft against limited targets in an attempt to use just enough force to compel the Serbian leadership to acquiesce.[54] For most of the operation, air strikes seemed to have no effect on the Serbian willingness to cooperate. In May, Prime Minister Tony Blair lobbied the US and other allies on the need to prepare for a large-scale ground operation to enter Kosovo even in non-permissive conditions. The increasing possibility of such an operation, combined with Russian compromises to NATO demands, compelled the Yugoslav leadership to accept international conditions in early June, including the withdrawal of Serbian military forces from Kosovo and the deployment of KFOR (the NATO-led Kosovo Force).

Decoupled and over-militarised peacekeeping

The new approach to peacekeeping presents numerous problems. The most fundamental resides in its over-militarised nature, which has given rise to three questions: first, about the use of force as an instrument of coercion; second, regarding the link between military and political aspects of conflict management; and third, concerning the legitimacy of enforcement measures by regional organisations.

The source of the concept of coercive inducement resides in the work of Thomas Schelling in the 1960s and Alexander George in the 1980s and 1990s. According to these works, the aim of coercive diplomacy is compellent: that is, to use coercion (or threaten to) to persuade the target state either to stop doing something that it has already undertaken or to do something that it has not yet undertaken. In theory, there are three conditions for the successful use of coercive diplomacy: 'The coercing power must create in the opponent's mind a sense of urgency for compliance with its demands, a belief that coercing power is more highly motivated to achieve its stated demands than the opponent is to oppose it, and a fear of unacceptable escalation if the demand is not accepted.' Given its psychological dimension, the use of force must be closely coordinated with appropriate signalling and communication from the intervening power to the target in order to make clear the nature of its demand and the strength of its resolution. As argued by George, 'the state that engages in coercive diplomacy can seldom have full or reliable control because so much depends on the adversary's assessment of the situation'.[55]

Operation Allied Force was a coercive strategy that sought to compel Yugoslav acquiescence to NATO demands in Kosovo. In retrospect, the strategy proved successful. However, it took far longer than had been expected and very nearly failed. Before his retirement as Chairman of NATO's Military Committee, General Klaus Neumann drew attention to the weakness of NATO's strategy: 'Quite frankly and honestly, we did not succeed in our initial attempts to coerce Milosevic through air strikes to accept our demands, nor did we succeed in preventing the [Former Republic of Yugoslavia] from pursuing a campaign of ethnic separation and expulsion'.[56] The limited nature of the initial strikes 'cost time, effort and potentially additional casualties'. NATO strategy was conducted without any thought to establish the necessary conditions that increase the chances of successful coercion. As the Alliance ruled out ground operations, the air strikes failed to create a sense of urgency in the Yugoslav leadership of the need to comply with NATO's demands. These self-imposed limitations failed to convince Belgrade that the Alliance would escalate to unacceptable levels. Fundamentally, there was a clear asymmetry of motivations in the Yugoslav favour: Kosovo was seen as integral to the very history of the Serbian people.

The deep miscalculations in NATO's strategy highlight the potential weakness of coercive strategies used as means of peace support. The targets of such strategies are likely to be more deeply motivated than any third party. Moreover, thus far such strategies have not been tested in actual peace support operations on the ground (as opposed to from the air). In complex circumstances it would seem extremely difficult to use coercive inducement successfully, not only because of the problems of calculating the motivations of the conflicting parties, but also because of the difficulty for the intervening states of achieving and utilising sufficient coercive leverage. The history of international efforts to end the Bosnian war from 1991 to 1995 is one of the failed use of coercion and the effective use of counter-coercion by the conflicting parties to undermine the efforts of the international community.[57]

In theory, coercive inducement appears to resolve the dilemma of using force in a manner short of war to advance settlement in a complex conflict. In practice, however, the experience of the international community shows that these concepts may be false solutions. At the very least, European military establishments and political leaders should realise the difficulties involved in using coercion successfully. The conceptual work done so far has failed to devote sufficient attention to the psychological dimension of such strategies, which are based on the target's perception of a given situation, its degree of motivation and its understanding of the third party's commitment.[58]

These new concepts of peace support are also problematic in their predominantly military logic. The emphasis on escalation dominance may ensure force protection and the fulfilment of the military dimensions of peace support. This same logic, however, may de-couple a military operation from the civilian aspects of peace support. The peace support approach may displace the critical importance of the wider political process of peace settlement and post-conflict reconciliation. As Alexander George argued, the 'logic of war as a political act' may clash with the 'logic of the instrument of war itself' in a dynamic that undermines the political objectives that force is intended to further.[59] Michael Pugh has distinguished between vertical (unintended escalation in the use of force) and horizontal (unintended expansion of non-military tasks) mission creep in contemporary operations, arguing that the spectrum approach inherent in peace support allows for the possibility of vertical creep with forces that are heavily armed. This acceptance of vertical creep may have solved the problems that faced the lightly armed and politically limited UNPROFOR. However, the adaptation of a 'combat-oriented ontology' to peace support foreclosed the possibility of horizontal mission creep.[60] This logic creates problems for linking the military aspects of an operation with peace-building activities. As witnessed in the implementation of the Dayton Agreement, the predominantly military logic of peace support may create problems for relating military forces to these wider objectives.

IFOR and SFOR contained several hundred civil–military cooperation specialists to ensure liaison with civilian organisations. Carl Bildt, the first High Representative, was, however, very critical of the lack of integration between the military aspects of the operation and the civilian tasks, contrasting the integrated political–military effort of UNPROFOR with the de-coupled process in IFOR: 'Where the UN had conducted an integrated operation under clear political control, at least on paper, every effort was made at Dayton to construct various firewalls between the military sphere and the political arena'.[61] These firewalls ensured that IFOR effected its military tasks very quickly. However, they prevented the integration of military and political tasks and created serious problems for the lightly armed IPTF, which led to an 'enforcement gap' on the ground.[62] Moreover, the fear of horizontal mission creep led to a conservative reading of IFOR's tasks in support of the ICTY. Some of these problems were rectified by the decisions of the Peace Implementation Council in December 1997. SFOR has played a much more effective role in this respect. In general, the experience of peace support in Bosnia has raised the need to rethink the critical issue of civil-military integration in peace support operations.[63]

The third problem raised by these new concepts resides in the issue of legitimacy. The legitimacy of traditional peacekeeping resided in the fact that these operations represented the will of the international community and were deployed with the consent and cooperation of the conflicting parties. The legitimacy of peace support operations is much more elusive. The consent of the conflicting parties is not assumed. The legitimacy of an operation is seen to reside in its even-handed fulfilment of a mandate. This raises questions regarding the legitimacy of the mandating authority for such an operation.

The spectrum approach requires troops that are able to dominate escalation. NATO member states are dependent on the US for such capability. Only Russian armed forces have such potential within the CIS. As a result, only regional arrangements, and certain states in particular, will be able to undertake peace support operations. By definition, regional organisations cannot claim to represent the will of the international community. Thus the legitimacy of peace support measures undertaken by regional organisations requires clear support from the UN. Operation Allied Force, however, was undertaken without the explicit approval of the Security Council in contravention of Chapter VIII of the UN Charter. None of the Security Council resolutions passed in 1998 allowed specifically for the use of force. These circumstances raised doubts about the legality of NATO actions, particularly for Russia and the People's Republic of China. Russian peacekeeping operations in the former Soviet Union were also deployed without UN mandating legitimacy, placing them under question, particularly as these operations played a role in the pursuit of Russian interests in its so-called 'sphere of vital interests'. The UN and the OSCE have deployed observer missions in many post-Soviet conflicts, but the interaction between Russian forces and these missions has been limited.[64] The experience of Russian peacekeeping and Operation Allied Force has highlighted the need to clarify the relationship between regional and universal organisations and to reaffirm the primacy of the UN Charter in regulating the use of force.

Conclusion

The experience of peacekeeping in European conflicts since the end of the Cold War has been fraught with difficulty. Traditional guidelines have been displaced. As a result, European states and organisations have sought to resolve the dilemma of finding legitimate and efficient measures to advance conflict resolution and peace building. The latest concepts of peace support represent but one more stage in this evolution of thinking about these dilemmas. Both conceptually and in practice, peace support operations present problems in terms of efficiency and legitimacy. These concepts, furthermore, were not really tested in the IFOR/SFOR and KFOR operations, since – while the forces were heavily armed and had robust rules of engagement – these operations have acted as traditional peacekeepers within a consensual framework.

Much more thinking is required to clarify the integration of civilian and military components, as well as the relationship between regional organisations and the UN in peace support operations. Reflecting this need, much recent work on peace support has focused on the need to integrate civilian and military tasks, 'cultures' and dimensions more effectively.[65] As it is, with many post-Cold War conflicts still simmering, peace support in postcommunist Europe remains fundamentally untested.

Notes

1   A. Roberts, 'Humanitarian intervention: military intervention and human rights', *International Affairs*, 69:3 (1993), 429–49.
2   *Statement on Kosovo, North Atlantic Council, Press Release S-1, 62* (Brussels, NATO, 23 April 1999).
3   B. Urquhart, 'Beyond the sheriff's posse,' *Survival*, (1990), 32:3, 196–205; and D. Lynch, *Russian Peacekeeping Strategies towards the CIS: The Cases of Moldova, Georgia and Tajikistan* (London, RIIA and Macmillan, 2000).
4   M. Goulding, 'The evolution of UN peacekeeping,' *International Affairs*, 69:3 (1993), 451–65.
5   A. James, *Peacekeeping in International Politics* (London, Macmillan, 1990), pp. 368–70.
6   J. Mackinlay, *The Peacekeepers: An Assessment of Peacekeeping Operations at the Arab–Israeli Interface* (London, Unwin Hyman, 1990), p. 222.
7   M. Berdal, *Whither UN Peacekeeping? An Analysis of Changing Military Requirements of UN Peacekeeping with Proposals for its Enhancement*, Adelphi Paper 281, (London, IISS, 1993).
8   Lynch, *Russian Peacekeeping Strategies towards the CIS*.
9   On UNPROFOR, see J. Gow, *Triumph of the Lack of Will: International Diplomacy and the Yugoslav War* (London, Hurst and Co., 1997).
10 Boutros Boutros-Ghali, 'UN peacekeeping in a new era: a new chance for peace,' *The World Today*, (April 1993), 66–8.
11 Goulding, 'The evolution of UN peacekeeping', p. 461.
12 A. James, 'UN Peacekeeping: recent developments and current problems,' in D. Bourrantanis and J. Wiener (eds.), *The UN in the New World Order* (London, Macmillan, 1995), pp. 105–23.

13 Urquhart, 'Beyond the sheriff's posse', p. 201.

14 G. Hagglund, 'Peacekeeping in the modern war zone,' *Survival*, 32:3 (1990), 2–40.

15 *Nordic UN Stand-By Forces* (Oslo, NORDSAMFN, 1993); and *Nordic UN Tactical Manual* (Vols One and Two, Oslo, NORDSAMFN, 1992).

16 J. Mackinlay, 'Defining a role beyond peacekeeping,' in W. E. Lewis (ed.), *Military Implications of UN Peacekeeping Operations*, MacNair Paper 17, (Washington, DC, National Defense University, 1993), pp. 26–40.

17 J. Gow and C. Dandeker, 'Peace support operations: the problem of legitimation,' *The World Today*, (August/September 1995), 171–4.

18 Mackinlay, *The Peacekeepers*, p. 245.

19 C. Zorgbibe, 'La France et le Maintien de la Paix: Propositions,' *Cahiers du CEDSI*, 21 (Espace Europe, 1995), pp. 57–64.

20 Boutros-Ghali, 'UN peacekeeping in a new era', 484–5.

21 *Krasnaya zvezda*, (20 November 1992); and I. Vorob'ev and A. Raevskii, *Russian Approaches to Peacekeeping Operations* (New York, UNIDIR, 1994).

22 *Izvestiya*, (30 June 1992).

23 *Rossiiskie vesti*, (3 December 1992).

24 Gow, *Triumph of the Lack of Will*, pp. 128–9.

25 *Wider Peacekeeping* (Army Field Manual, Vol. 5, Part 2, HMSO, 1995).

26 C. Dobbie, 'A concept for post-Cold War peacekeeping,' *Survival*, (Autumn 1994, 121–48.

27 *Wider Peacekeeping*, pp. 2–6.

28 A. Roberts, 'The crisis in UN peacekeeping,' in C. A. Chester and F. Osler (eds.), with P. Aall, *Managing Global Chaos: Sources of and Responses to International Conflict* (Washington, DC, US Institute of Peace Press, 1996), pp. 297–319; and T. G. Weiss, 'Military–civilian humanitarianism: the age of innocence is over,' *International Peacekeeping*, (Summer 1995), 157–74.

29 Quoted in S. Tharoor, 'Should peacekeeping go back to basics?', *Survival*, (Winter 1995–96), 55–64.

30 J. Mackinlay and R. Kent, 'A new approach to complex emergencies,' *International Peacekeeping*, 4:4 (1997), 31–49.

31 D. C. F. Daniels and B. C. Hayes with C. L de Jonge Oudraat, *Coercive Inducement and the Containment of International Crisis* (Washington, DC, US Institute of Peace Press, 1999), p. 21 and pp. 169–88.

32 Daniels and Hayes, *Coercive Inducement*, p. 22.

33 Gow, *Triumph of the Lack of Will*, p. 8.

34 K. Annan, 'UN peacekeeping operations and cooperation with NATO,' *NATO Review*, 41:5 (1993), 4.

35 K. Annan, 'Peace operations and the UN: preparing for the next century,' *Conflict Resolution Monitor*, 1 (1997).

36 T. Woodhouse, 'The gentle hand of peace? British peacekeeping and post cold war conflict,' *Cahiers du CEDSI* 21 (Espace Europe), pp. 45–55.

37 Annan, 'Peace operations and the UN'.

38 Annan, 'UN peacekeeping operations', p. 6.

39 D. A. Leurdijk, *The UN and NATO in the Former Yugoslavia, 1991–1996: Limits to Diplomacy and Force* (The Hague, Netherlands Atlantic Commission, 1996).

40 Quoted in M. A. Smith, *On Rocky Foundations: NATO, the UN and Peace Operations in the Post-Cold War Era*, Peace Research Report No. 37, (Bradford, University of Bradford, 1996), p. 61.

41 S. R. Rader, 'NATO,' in T. Findlay (ed.), *Challenges for the New Peacekeepers* (Stockholm, SIPRI and Oxford University Press, 1996), pp. 142–58.

42 Quoted in D. Zandee, 'The use of force in peace support', in B. Huldt, A. Hilding and A. Eriksson (eds.), *Challenges of Peace Support into the 21st Century* (Stockholm, Swedish National Defence College, 1998), p. 79.

43 D. Zandee, 'The use of force in peace support', p. 82.

44 Woodhouse, 'The gentle hand of peace?'; and M. Pugh, *From Mission Cringe to Mission Creep? Implications of the New Peace Support Operations Doctrine* (Oslo, Institutt for Forsvarsstuddier, 2, 1997).

45 *Joint Doctrine for Military Operations Other Than War* (Joint Publication 3-07, 16 June, Washington, DC, US Department of Defence, 1995), p. I–1.

46 P. Viggo Jakobsen, 'The Danish approach to UN peace operations after the Cold War: a new model in the making?', *International Peacekeeping*, 5:3 (1998), 106–23.

47 T. Tardy, 'French policy towards peace support operations,' *International Peacekeeping*, 6:1 (1999), 55–78.

48 *The Programme for the Training of Peacekeeping Units* (Moscow, Russian Federation Ministry of Defence, 1992); and *Temporary Instructions for the Training of Military Contingents for the Formation of Groups of Military Observers and Collective Forces for Peacekeeping of the Member States of the CIS* (Moscow, Russian Federation Ministry of Defence, 1993).

49 L. Jonson, 'In search of a doctrine: Russian interventionism in conflicts in its near abroad', *Low Intensity Conflicts and Law Enforcement*, 5:3 (1996,) 440–65; and L. Jonson, *Keeping the Peace in the CIS: The Evolution of Russian Policy*, Discussion Paper 81, (London, Chatham House, 1999), p. 26.

50 Smith, *On Rocky Foundations;* and Rader, 'NATO', pp. 155–7.

51 Zandee, 'The use of force in peace support', p. 82.

52 M.-J. Colic, 'Post-SFOR: towards the Europeanization of the Bosnian peace operation,' in M.-J. Colic, N. Gnessotto, J. Sharp, S. Woodward and S. Clement (eds.), *The Issues Raised by Bosnia and the Transatlantic Debate*, Chaillot Paper No. 32, (Paris, WEUISS, 1998), pp. 10–22.

53 J. Sharp, 'Prospects for peace in Bosnia: the role of Britain,' in Colic, et al. (eds), *The Issues Raised by Bosnia*, pp. 33–43.

54 *Statement on Kosovo, North Atlantic Council, Press Release S-1, 62* (Brussels, NATO, 23 April 1999).

55 A. L. George and G. A. Craig, *Force and Statecraft: Diplomatic Problems of our Time* (New York, Oxford University Press, second edn, 1990), pp. 197–211; and A. L. George, *Forceful Persuasion: Coercive Diplomacy as an Alternative to War* (Washington, DC, US Institute for Peace, 1991), p. 198 and p. 211.

56 'General admits failure of air strikes,' *The Independent*, (5 May 1999), p. 4.

57 James Gow, 'Coercive cadences: the Yugoslav war of dissolution,' in L. Freedman (ed.), *Strategic Coercion: Concepts and Cases* (Oxford, Oxford University Press, 1998), pp. 276–96.

58 P. Viggo Jacobsen, 'The strategy of coercive diplomacy: refining existing theory to post-Cold War realities,' in Freedman (ed.), *Strategic Coercion*, pp. 37–61.

59 A. L. George, 'The role of force in diplomacy: a continuing dilemma for U.S. foreign policy,' in Chester and Osler (eds.), *Managing Global Chaos*, pp. 209–22.

60 Pugh, *From Mission Cringe to Mission Creep?*, p. 9.

61 C. Bildt, *Peace Journey: The Struggle for Peace in Bosnia* (London, Weidenfeld and Nicolson, 1998), pp. 384–6.

62 J. Sharp, 'Dayton report card,' *International Security*, 22:3 (1997-98), 101–37.

63 There is evidence that this is underway; see *Doctrine for Joint Civil–Military Operations, First Draft*, US JP 3–57 (Washington, DC, US Department of Defence, 26 February 1999).

64 D. Lynch, 'Russia and the OSCE,' in M. Webber (ed.), *Russia and Europe: Cooperation or Conflict?* (London, Macmillan, 1999).

65 C. Dandeker and J. Gow, 'Military culture and strategic peacekeeping', *Small Wars and Insurgencies*, 10:2 (1999), 58–79; J. Mackinlay, 'Beyond the logjam: a doctrine for complex emergencies,' *Small Wars and Insurgencies*, 9:1 (1998), 114–31; and M. J. Dziedzic, 'Policing the new world disorder: addressing gaps in public security during peace operations,' *International Peacekeeping*, 9:1 (1998), 132–59.

8

The keystone in the arch: inclusion, democracy promotion and universalism in Central and Eastern Europe

Richard Sakwa

> The old sovereign nation state has destroyed itself, as the feudal nobility destroyed itself in the Wars of the Roses ... The nineteenth century had already built up a higher order than any of its predecessors achieved. The democratic state on the national scale, with its deepened sense of public responsibility, still conserving regard for personal freedom, was the highest political organisation yet known to the world, and the [first world] war has proved it tougher and firmer than its autocratic rival. But the states, considered together, were an arch without a keystone, and they fell to pieces. We have now to rebuild them into a world-order, and in doing so, in dispelling fear and hostility between nations, we shall remove the main obstacles to the growth of equal freedom and brotherly comradeship.[1]

Ten years after the end of communism in Eastern Europe we can begin to undertake an interim audit and evaluation of democratisation in the region. To what degree has democracy become consolidated in postcommunist Eastern Europe, and what are the dynamics behind subregional differentiation? While most of Central Europe appears to have achieved democratic consolidation, although with some notable ambiguities, most of the post-Soviet world is suffering aspects of what may be called the 'failed transition syndrome'. These disparities themselves are the source of profound insecurity. At the same time, the role of the European dimension is crucial. This involves not only institutional aspects of Europe, above all the European Union (EU) and the Council of Europe, but also the broader question of identities and developmental paths. Among the plethora of institutions structuring the postcommunist security area, all want to be the keystone, none the arch. A very strange architecture of the new Europe has emerged, top heavy and with endless overlapping jurisdictions and concerns. To understand the dynamics of post-Cold War security, therefore, we need to identify the many dimensions of Europe, with differential politics of inclusion and exclusion at work. If there are 'ins' and 'pre-ins', there are also 'outs'. As Neumann argues, 'there is no inclusion without exclusion'.[2]

Representation and inclusion

For historical and geopolitical reasons Russia appears to be the furthest 'out' of all the postcommunist countries, a perception sharply accentuated as a result of the 1999 Kosovo war and the second Chechen war. Russia faces distinctive problems in the face of modernisation, state building and democratisation. From the civilisational, and indeed the security, perspective, Russia implicitly is the bearer of a counter-European project. If this becomes explicit, then a new post-ideological Cold War may begin. As of 2000–01, however (and this continued in the first period of Vladimir Putin's presidency), Russia tried once again to find a middle way between uncritical Westernism and xenophobic nationalism.

The dilemma of countries in the new borderlands of Europe, the new marches between an expanding EU and Eurasia, is no less keen. Ukraine, for example, finds itself torn between an Eastern and a Western orientation in its foreign and domestic policies as a result both of 'path dependent' issues and because of the very structure of post-Cold War European international politics. President Leonid Kuchma, in response, talked in terms of a multivector foreign policy for Ukraine, facing both East and West simultaneously. As Sherman Garnett notes, 'The problems of Ukrainian stability and of the stability of Ukraine's relations with Russia are part of the European security agenda – whether we want them to be so or not.'[3] He goes on to argue that 'Ukraine is the keystone in the new security arch that stretches from the Baltic Sea to the Black Sea.'[4] Paradoxically, Ukraine's very nature as a borderland propels it to the centre of post-Cold War security concerns. Some, like Zbigniew Brzezinski, have tried to use it as the cornerstone of an anti-Russian *cordon sanitaire*,[5] while Poland and its neighbours, which are successfully negotiating the road to Europe, have tried to ensure that no new 'paper curtain' will divide the 'ins' from the 'outs'.

This chapter takes a broad view of the concept of democracy promotion, but focuses ultimately on two key aspects: internal democratisation and inclusion in the broader European system. In the post-Cold War world these two aspects are intimately connected. The traditional division between domestic and foreign policy in the European arena is being eroded, and thus democratisation has become an 'intermestic' issue.[6] Accession to the EU, for example, requires the fulfilment of a transformatory programme focusing above all on good governance and liberal economics. At the same time, representation in both the external and domestic spheres is not quite the same as inclusion. In Russia, for example, the rudiments of a liberal democracy have been established, with a functioning Parliament, regular elections and a relatively free media. The population has achieved representation, but the inclusion of these democratic institutions and of the people in policy formulation and lines of accountability leaves much to be desired.

Similarly, just as representation can take many distinctive forms within a state, inclusion within the community of nations is also a highly ambiguous phenomenon. The fundamental question remains: on whose terms does inclusion take place? While Russia has stressed the need for a multipolar world order, it fears that instead a unilateral system dominated by the United States is emerging. Russia's promotion of a multipolar approach to international politics, however, is predicated on strength and resources that it no longer enjoys, and thus attempts to establish a strategic partnership, a new triple alliance of Russia, China and India, reveal more about Russia's illusions of leadership than they do a serious and credible foreign policy goal. Nevertheless, the attempt to challenge unipolarity in a situation where the universalist agenda of human rights and security through democratisation is perceived to have been appropriated by the hegemonic power and its allies does make sense. A more imaginative response by Russia, and one that would place it on the high moral ground, would be to call for the genuine universalisation of the universalist agenda, bringing on board China and other countries that at present, despite having signed the United Nations' (UN's) 1948 Universal Convention on Human Rights and later Acts, are distinctly uncomfortable with the way that these tend to undermine national sovereignty.

Three Europes or one?

The concepts of inclusion and representation provide a fruitful way of approaching the security dilemmas of postcommunist Europe. The slogan of the Central European anti-communist revolutions in 1989 was 'return to Europe', but what Europe did the demonstrators have in mind? The EU is only one vision of Europe, and is itself divisive in that it is unlikely in the near future to encompass Russia and Turkey (despite the decisions taken at the Helsinki EU Council in December 1999), and an enlarged Europe is in danger of hardening the frontier between Central Europe and countries such as Ukraine.[7] Are the outsider countries to remain eternal supplicants grateful for whatever crumbs might fall from the European table? This is not a recipe for European solidarity or for the long-term consolidation of European security. There remain fundamental tensions between the dynamics of official European integration, processes of pan-European unity that bring together the whole of the continent, and forms of cultural coherence that reflect the distinctive features of a separate continent-wide

European civilisation. Three concepts of European solidarity, of inclusion if not unity, can be identified.[8]

1 OFFICIAL EUROPE

Western European integration is central to what is sometimes termed 'official Europe'. The EU is only one form of European integration, although by far the most important. The fifteen members of the EU of the late 1990s had become one of the most successful supranational institutions in European history. The principles on which the EU itself will be built are still not entirely clear, with no formal constitution enshrining principles of federalism and political accountability. The extent of its eastward enlargement remains problematic with, as we have seen, Ukraine, for example, left out of official definitions of what constitutes Europe. While Russia has sought to make the Commonwealth of Independent States (CIS) an official counter-Europe, most of its members have distanced themselves from this idea, which they view as a way of projecting Russian hegemony over the former Soviet space. The enlargement of the North Atlantic Treaty Organisation (NATO) and the EU threatens to isolate Russia, a concern voiced by the Russian Prime Minister Sergei Stepashin, warning the EU not to marginalise Russia as it brings Eastern Europe into its fold.[9]

The programmes for EU and NATO enlargement have been powerful catalysts of change in Eastern Europe, and in turn have fed back and forced an agenda of reform and adaptation on the enlarging institutions themselves. EU enlargement has challenged the whole continent to rethink what it means to be European.[10] Deepening (i.e., the intensification of the pace of institutional integration within the existing membership) has taken precedence over widening (the incorporation of new members), a priority that many have argued was wrong, leaving the Eastern Europeans in the lurch. According to Garton Ash, the EU's member states caught the wrong bus in the 1990s: 'Instead of seizing the opportunities, and preparing to confront the dangers, that would arise from the end of communism in half of Europe, they set about perfecting the internal arrangements of an already well-functioning, peaceful and prosperous community of states in Western Europe.'[11]

Official Europe is based on the following principles: exclusive membership where entrance is by invitation only and requires a long period of adjustment; a tendency towards supranationalism rather than intergovernmentalism; internal adaptation and adjustment as a condition of accession; and the emergence of a distinctively particularistic type of universalism, aspiring to achieve an expansive form of capitalist democracy yet constrained by the very vessel in which it is contained, the Western European 'region-state'. In this context, the notion of 'returning to Europe' is a thoroughly misleading one. As Thurman puts it:

'Europe' today is less a geographical than a cultural notion possessing a univocal definition of the past, present and future based on a single currency, 'ever closer union', the single market, and Hegelian end-of-history arguments. The countries of the former Eastern Bloc have never been part of this new Europe, so to speak of a return is nonsense. As is most evident in the debate raging in the Czech Republic, at the bottom of the controversy lies the desirability of exchanging one universalistic worldview based in Moscow for a new one based in Brussels.[12]

In addition to processes of inclusion and exclusion, accession to official Europe also involves renouncing elements of a country's past and reshaping its present.

2 PAN-EUROPE

The idea of the establishment of a Europe-wide federation has long been part of the European intellectual agenda, and was most eloquently advocated by Count Coudenhove-Kalergi in his 1923 book *Pan-Europa*.[13] Soviet President Mikhail Gorbachev's espousal of a 'common European home' from the Atlantic to the Pacific (the trans-Urals region of Russia is European in all but name) appeared to signal a new reconciliation of all parts of the continent, not opposed to North America but separate from it, in a deepening process of pan-European integration. President François Mitterrand in early 1990 floated the idea of a European confederation, and the idea was later taken up by other French leaders and President Vaclav Havel of the Czech Republic. The Gorbachevian ideal of pan-European unity and a 'common European home' has, however, been eclipsed in the post-Cold War era. Instead, while some pan-European institutions continue to develop, the ideal itself has been marginalised.

While most democracy assistance has been conducted in the framework of a bilateral donor–recipient relationship, there is also a multilateral framework that has perhaps been of even greater effect. This is the dense network of civil and human rights organisations. In the pan-European context this is above all the Council of Europe and the Organisation for (until 1994 Conference on) Security and Cooperation in Europe (O/CSCE). The Council of Europe, established in May 1949, together with its European Commission on Human Rights and the European Court of Human Rights, are together responsible for the enforcement of the 1950 European Convention on Human Rights whose social aspects are now formulated in the European Social Charter. The Council of Europe is a robust body with legal enforcement mechanisms and sanctions, above all the European Court of Human Rights. The Council of Europe and like organisations, however, are at best what Jeffrey Checkel calls 'soft mediation', trying to impose a human rights regime before the outbreak of violence. These bodies are not very good at 'hard mediation', as demonstrated by their poor performance in the Balkans.[14] The Council of Europe is above all preventive and normative, whereas NATO after Dayton has increasingly taken on an interventive and separative role.

Russia formally acceded to the Council of Europe in January 1996, breaking the stranglehold formerly exerted by the Russian Ministry of Foreign Affairs on human rights issues. The Council of Europe quickly moved to establish links with a variety of governmental and non-governmental organisations in Russia. By September 1997 the Russian government had submitted for ratification by the Duma the European Convention on Human Rights, one of the most powerful documents of its type in the world, allowing citizens recourse to a court beyond the borders of the country in which they live. Membership of the Council of Europe allows non-governmental organisations concerned with human rights issues a measure of protection. Formal guarantees are supplemented by a joint EU–Council of Europe programme to support civil society actors in Russia, crafted by one of the most visionary of the Council's leaders, Daniel Tarschys. Relatively small sums were used to great effect when channelled to grassroots civil and educational bodies in postcommunist countries. Human rights integration at this level empowered new social actors, whereas economic and security cooperation only legitimated and reinforced the powerful corporate actors already deeply entrenched in the Soviet era.

The pan-European space is now a uniquely intense arena of human rights development. The Parliamentary Assembly of the Council of Europe (PACE) brings together deputies from all forty-two member states. With the fall of communism the Council has gradually extended its reach to the east as countries are deemed to have fulfilled certain conditions of democracy and human and civil rights, including the abolition of the death penalty. PACE acts as one of the most effective instruments for the political socialisation of a whole generation of politicians in the postcommunist world. This vigorous human rights agenda has raised sharp questions about the balance to be drawn between national and supranational rights. The Russian government, for example, encouraged the Council of Europe to establish human rights-monitoring agencies in Russia's regions and republics, particularly the more recalcitrant ones, as a way of exerting pressure on them and bringing them into line with the federal constitution. In effect, the disciplinary mechanisms lacking in the Russian state are now being exerted by external agencies. The Council of Europe here acts as a new type of representative body to which governments and subnational bodies are accountable. The case of the environmental activist Alexander Nikitin, who after four years of prison and harassment by the Federal Security Service was finally acquitted in January 2000, provides one of the more powerful examples of new patterns of representation and inclusion. The judge in St Petersburg, Sergei Golets, based his decision to dismiss the case in part on Russia's status as a signatory to the European Convention on Human Rights.[15]

Another of the founding blocs of pan-Europe is O/CSCE. The 1975 CSCE Helsinki Final Act set the stage for the transcendence of communism, first ratifying Yalta (the borders agreed at the Yalta summit in the Crimea between Stalin, Roosevelt and Churchill, in effect allowing Soviet dominance of Eastern Europe) and then transcending it by formalising the agenda of international public law (sovereign equality of states, territorial integrity, non-intervention in internal affairs and inviolability of frontiers) in relations between states. It reinforced human rights and fundamental freedoms as part of European inter-state relations, including the idea of equal rights and the self-determination of peoples. The CSCE played a crucial part in the final days of communism, above all at its Vienna follow-up meeting from November 1986. By 1989 Gorbachev had accepted the whole agenda of human rights and civil society formulated by the concluding document of the Vienna conference. He assumed that this universalistic agenda based on ethical individualism could be grafted on to the communist system to create a more humane form of socialism that could easily be integrated into the international system. Perhaps in different circumstances this might have been possible, but by the late 1980s the repressive legacy of communism and its systematic denigration of representative democracy meant that few were willing to give this new experiment the benefit of the doubt.

At its Paris meeting in 1990 the CSCE created a number of institutions designed to give it a more permanent form and to make it a more effective instrument of democratisation: a Council made up of foreign ministers; a permanent Secretariat and a Conflict Prevention Centre in Vienna; an Office of Democratic Institutions and Human Rights in Warsaw; and a Parliamentary Assembly. The wars in the Balkans, however, starkly revealed the C/OSCE's inadequacies. Above all, the tension between the core OSCE principles of national self-determination and the inviolability of borders has still to be reconciled. Russia hoped to make the OSCE the main security body in Europe to replace NATO, but these aspirations were not fulfilled. Instead, NATO became the dominant security body, and in the sphere of integration the EU began the long process of enlargement.

The institutions of pan-Europe are intergovernmental rather than supranational; they tend to be governed by principles of consensus rather than majority voting; they are pluralistic rather than hegemonic; and they are relatively more inclusive than the bodies associated with official Europe. The universalism associated with pan-Europe is less particularistic than that of official Europe, but is still bounded by the notion of Europe itself. The boundaries of this Europe, however, are more readily expansive than those of official Europe while acting as the advance guard, as it were, for the latter, socialising and integrating borderlands for possible future inclusion in official Europe. The danger that pan-Europe will be perceived as a second-best option to the 'real' inclusion represented by official Europe is a real one.

3 Civilisational Europe

While Europe during the Cold War was divided politically, and new sources of division remain, there can be no doubt that the countries of postcommunist Europe, including Russia, are part of a broader European civilisation. Russia's literature and art have embellished European culture, its music and philosophy are part of the currency of European thinking, and its people are firmly part of the European tradition. This cultural unity transcends political divisions and geographical barriers. Mass tourism, electronic communications, student exchanges, cheaper air flights and much else are gradually creating a single European people.

Of the three Europes, the civilisational one is perhaps the weakest. Economic globalisation and the Western-centred process of European integration cannot conceal an underlying unease about the loss of national and regional identities. With the end of overt organised ideological conflict, above all between capitalism and socialism, and despite rhetorical support for the view that there were no winners or losers at the end of the Cold War, Europe remains divided, but in new ways. Ideological conflict has given way to amorphous culture wars where issues of identity and separateness come to the fore.

In a landmark article Samuel Huntington suggested indeed that the new era would be characterised by 'the clash of civilisations'.[16] In Europe he identified an Orthodox civilisation and a Western European one. While this division might be questionable, the fact of tensions between the various parts of Europe, in particular in the Balkans and in the former Soviet Union, confirmed the view that just as one set of conflicts came to an end, new ones emerged. Although Huntington failed to address those elements that unite Europe culturally, he raised important issues. Above all, the end of the Cold War division of the continent allowed its peoples to argue that 'we are all Europeans now'; but the history of the post-Cold War years has brought home that there is no unanimity over who *we* are, quite apart from the question of what is distinctively *European* about Europe. For Neumann, Huntington's basic argument about civilisational conflict entailed a process of 'othering': 'Integration and exclusion are two sides of the same coin, so the issue here is not *that* exclusion takes place but *how* it takes place'.[17]

These three conceptions of Europe are in tension. One, the official Europe represented by European integration in the form of the EU and its predecessors, has traditionally served to fulfil French strategic aims, the German search for rehabilitation after the war and Italian hopes for good governance and participation in Europe, while providing the Benelux countries with markets and a political stature quite incommensurate with their size. Only Britain has not perceived any vital national interest in membership, other than fear of exclusion from the most dynamic market in Europe, and thus has traditionally been Europe's 'awkward partner'.[18] Western Europe, and above all the EU, has become the ideal to which the rest of the continent aspires. Enlargement after the fall of communism, however, has been a concession granted, as it were, by sufferance rather than conceded as a right, and thus represents a very different political dynamic. This is official Europe at its starkest, contrasted with the more pluralistic although universalist concept embedded in the pan-European ideal. The conception associated with pan-Europe is based on inclusivity and the principle of the universal applicability of human rights and democratic aspirations. Although the Council of Europe was established in Western Europe, it became a genuinely pan-European body after the fall of communism and is not dominated by any single state or alliance of states. The origins of the OSCE were even more genuinely pan-European, having originally been sought by the Soviet Union (and its allies) to enshrine by treaty what it had achieved at the end of the Second World War by force, but then going on to become one of the main instruments to overcome the Cold War. By contrast with official Europe, pan-Europe was inclusive and consensual. The third Europe is that of peoples and cultures, where gradually the outline of a single cultural space not only at the elite but also at the mass level is beginning to emerge.

Democracy promotion and universalism

Democracy assistance to the postcommunist world is torn between whether the emphasis should be on the development of market economies and the associated capital infrastructure, or whether the emphasis should be on democratisation – good governance, non-governmental and third-sector development, and technical assistance. Putnam stresses a third option, the development of 'social capital'. As Putnam puts it:

> proposals for strengthening market economies and democratic institutions center almost exclusively on deficiencies in financial and human capital (thus calling for loans and technical assistance). However, the deficiencies in social capital in these countries are at least as alarming. Where are the efforts to encourage 'social capital formation'?[19]

The promotion of democracy in any particular country requires, as it were, an institutional peg on which to hang. Democracy assistance has often been criticised as involving no more than a technical exercise in the transfer of techniques and procedures from one country to another.[20] Although democratisation is often explicitly an interest of foreign policy, it can only be effective in the distinctive conditions of receptivity. This applies to most postcommunist European countries, but works with declining force the further east one goes, and does not operate at all in China. Receptivity is both a question of culture, but also one of social development. In the Russian, and indeed the Serbian case, there are individuals, social groups and socio-cultural interests who have a vital stake in the democratisation of their own societies, and for whom Western democracy assistance can be crucial. A measure of the threat that such groups pose to authoritarian leaders and the depth of the fear of democracy assistance programmes can be seen in Alexander Lukashenka's attempts to undermine both in Belarus and to characterise the democratic opposition as foreign-inspired 'fifth columnists'.

Democracy promotion and security

The concept of democracy promotion or, more narrowly, democracy assistance, immediately frames discourse in terms of an agent and a recipient, a subject and an object. As far as security is concerned, it is clear that much Western action in the postcommunist world works implicitly within the terms of the democratic peace concept.[21] This is not the place to discuss the merits of the thesis that democratic states do not go to war with each other, but clearly there is an assumption that by encouraging the development of democracy, above all in Russia, the security of all countries is thereby enhanced. The basic argument is that liberal democracies encourage consensus building and non-violent means to resolve political questions in domestic politics, and since other democracies operate according to the same principles they are unlikely to go to war with each other. The promotion of democratic regimes is therefore assumed to provide the basis for long-term peace in Eurasia. There is, however, a view that while democratic states may not go to war with each other, the situation is very different with democratising states. Long ago Huntington argued that states undergoing economic or political transitions were unstable and prone to violence.[22] This thesis has subsequently been reinforced by scholars examining recent transitions.[23]

A less state-centric view of democracy and democratisation is needed. A type of collective, if not virtual, citizenry has emerged on behalf of whom an increasingly dense network of human and civil rights agencies claim to speak. The nation-state is thus only one community of inclusion; and as a complement to it a type of universal representative state is emerging, still unformed but nevertheless a recognisable keystone in the arch.

The universalistic agenda marginalises geopolitics, renders borders porous and transparent, elevates communities of citizens and civil society above so-called national interests, and seeks to replace fear with trust as the guiding principle in international politics. So far these are little more than tendencies, but universalism is beginning to take on the attributes of an institution, defined as a set of formalised practices, rather than a formal bureaucratic organisation. Universalism in the European context is both advanced and constrained by the institutions of official Europe and even, although to a lesser extent, by those of pan-Europe. As with communism earlier, there is a contradiction between internationalist aspirations and the form in which they are contained, the nation or regional state.

A type of universal policy state is emerging. This, of course, raises issues of accountability and the problem of genuine universality. It would be easy for any one single dominant superpower to appropriate the institutions of universality and to cloak its own hegemony in a spurious universalism. This, of course, is what the West, and above all the United States, is accused of having done in launching the aerial bombardment of the Federal Republic of Yugoslavia in March 1999. The universalistic agenda has been operationalised in a partial and instrumental way by states and coalitions of states, and thus there remains a tension between universalistic theory and sectarian practices. Russia's appeal to genuine universalism, however, represented above all by the UN and to some degree by the pluralistic multipolarity of the OSCE, was undermined by its inability to move beyond old-fashioned geopolitical thinking, reflected in its partisan support of Slobodan Milosevic's Serbia and thus its inability to act as a genuine honest broker that could facilitate a multilateral solution to the problem.[24]

Democratisation requires a viable state, but the relationship between state building and democratisation requires more study. Democratisation in Russia, to take perhaps the most vivid example, has been accompanied by the dramatic loss of state capacity (here defined as the ability to impose the state's will on, and extract resources from, society). In turn, the weakening of the state cannot but undermine not only the viability but the very legitimacy of democratisation. While participation has formally been extended to include the whole population, only a very small proportion of winners has effectively been included in the new order. The shallowness, if not fragility, of representative institutions – elections, parties and legislatures – reflects the process of partial inclusion. Where these institutions are more robust, as in most of Central Europe, then one can see more effective inclusionary processes and, in turn, a more effective state. It is clearly misleading to equate authoritarianism with stability, as the case of Serbia under Slobodan Milosevic clearly illustrates. But the achievement of durable forms of democratic stability is a trick that does not come to all countries.

Western support for democracy and market transition in postcommunist countries has served a foreign policy agenda. We have already noted the debate over the relationship between democratisation and security. The point has been made forcefully by Andrzej Karkoszka, a former State Secretary in Poland's Ministry of Defence, who has stressed that while Russia no longer represents a military threat to NATO, European security still hinges on developments in Russia:

> The outcome of pan-European continental security is much more dependent now on what's going on in Moscow than on what will be done with NATO enlargement or in Brussels. NATO is very effective in helping and building up and opening up and engaging Russia. But finally, we will be secure only when Russia is democratic, [when] Russia is secure, Russia is affluent, Russia is friendly and peaceful.[25]

Thus support for democracy serves a crucial security-building purpose. The very notion of democracy assistance suggests a one-way flow within the framework of an established hierarchy of donor and recipient, yet there is a crucial reverse flow measured in terms of political utility, security and ultimately the expansion of the capitalist market. As Sonja Licht, Director of the Fund for an Open Society Yugoslavia, put it, 'Democracy assistance is not charity. It is an investment in our common European future'.[26] The argument that democratisation is a security issue could not be put more forcefully.

One area that is particularly important is support for military modernisation; that is, the conversion of the Russian military into an institution operating within the modern conventions of civil–military relations. The military has become more politicised, with officers serving as parliamentary deputies (although formally they are not allowed a second occupation) and active in various political organisations, accompanied by the de-professonalisation of the armed forces in the face of chronic under-funding. Hunger, corruption, suicide, engagement in commercial activities, food growing and illicit arms sales all characterise the Russian army today. The military is not only the least democratised institution in Russia, but it also poses the greatest threat to democracy as a whole.

Western institutions have supported various programmes to assist military reform. The largest is the US-funded Cooperative Threat Reduction programme, established in 1991 by Senators Sam Nunn and Richard Lugar, that has focused on the denuclearisation of Belarus, Kazakhstan and Ukraine and the destruction and safe storage of nuclear weapons in Russia.

Between 1992 and 1999 $2.7 billion was spent on deactivating nuclear warheads, destroying intercontinental ballistic missiles and the construction of safe storage facilities.[27] However, of the $1.8 billion spent on projects in Russia, only $50 million was devoted directly to democracy enhancement aspects of civil–military relations. There are numerous partnership and other schemes allowing Russian officers to travel to the West to observe and learn about Western practices. Although these seldom lead to any Damascene conversion in the attitudes of Russian officers, experience suggests that a valuable positive residue remains from these visits that could, at the margins, be crucial.

The deeper assumption is that countries such as Russia are amenable to influence and, more fundamentally, to change: that Russia does not always have to be an authoritarian and expansive power, however troublesome it may be in the interim. The observation about the not entirely disinterested nature of Western intervention does not delegitimate democracy assistance programmes. At base, it is clear that democracy assistance is premised on the view that there are constituencies in Russia itself for a democratic evolution of the polity that can be assisted by judicious assistance, and that the outcome, while benign from the Western perspective, is above all of benefit for the Russian people themselves.

There is a deeper problem, reflected sometimes in George Soros' thinking, that without Western support democracy in Russia, and perhaps in some other countries, would wither away, suggesting that the West's role was decisive.[28] In the Russian case this is probably an exaggeration: ultimately democracy will be made or broken by Russia itself. Western democracy assistance is useful, but marginal. Democracy assistance is probably most effective early on in a democratic transition, but since this opportunity was effectively squandered in the early 1990s, efforts now are largely ameliorative. The appointment of Yevgenii Primakov as Prime Minister (however short-lived his premiership, lasting from September 1998 to May 1999) suggested the indigenisation of Russian reform, and this tendency remains strong, despite Russia's indebtedness to the West.

Support for democratisers and civil society can, however, help to marginalise those advocating authoritarian and messianic solutions. As Grigorii Yavlinskii put it, 'Only Russia can save itself, but the West can help', and he insisted on strict conditionality linking assistance to 'deep structural as well as political reform'.[29] Here the support does not necessarily have to take the form of assistance programmes but can be expressed through diplomatic support for reformers and above all the establishment of a supportive political environment for democratic forces. This challenge, too, was not grasped in the early 1990s, and instead support was given to Yeltsin personally and not to the institutional development of a democratic polity. Every state has a personalised face to its power structure, but the degree to which this power is institutionalised and de-personalised marks the extent to which a modern state has emerged. In Russia we have a structural personalisation in the form of the presidency in tension with the development of countervailing institutions – above all Parliament, the judiciary and the regions. Everywhere there is a tension between institutionalisation and personalisation, suggesting that Yeltsin's patriarchal characteristics are not just a feature of Yeltsin's personality but a structural characteristic of postcommunist Russian politics. We will only be able to judge this question once the character of Vladimir Putin's presidency becomes clear.

The larger strategic aim of democracy assistance appears to be to turn 'them' into 'us', to transform the erstwhile enemy into a replica of the West. It is here that the tension between universalism and particularism emerges. Russia and other postcommunist countries may well strive to become 'us' in general, but if they lose their particular 'them-ness', they cannot effectively be 'us' either. Thus there is a delicate balance to be drawn between general democratic goals and the specific way democracy is interpreted in a local environment. Any strategy that fails to take this into account is fundamentally misconceived, leaving out of account Russia's specific civilisational trajectory and distinctive culture. The problem that has plagued Russia for the last three centuries, however, is how to go its own way when there is no consensus over what this way entails and where it leads.

Foreign democracy assistance in this context cannot be anything but ambiguous, since by its very definition it is seeking to import experience gleaned from elsewhere. An analogy may be drawn between economic policies that forced Russia to open its markets to the flood of Western goods, squeezing out on grounds of cost and quality whole swathes of Russian production, and the opening up of the Russian political market place to Western ideas, for example on individualism, the rule of law and representative party government. The problem here is not whether the Western ideas are correct or not, but the way in which they are promoted. Tensions remain between universal principles and the idiom in which they are presented and the institutions in which they are framed in any particular country. Universal principles need to find a native form in which they can be couched. Only if they are nativised or inculturated can these universal principles take root.

Universalism and nativisation

There is an increasingly dense market relationship between the postcommunist world and the West; there is an intense, although not always warm, direct security relationship (NATO's Partnership for Peace and other forms of security cooperation); but a third strand must not be forgotten, the intensifying integration of human rights and civil standards. Of this, Jeffrey Checkel has noted: 'Integration with human rights institutions, in contrast with that in the economic and security spheres, is empowering a different and broader set of Russian domestic actors'.[30] Paradoxically, he goes on to argue that this integration on the level of human rights is being driven forward by two apparently negative stimuli: NATO enlargement and the regionalisation of Russia. NATO enlargement has encouraged Russia to promote non-military forms of multilateral integration in the European sphere, above all the Council of Europe. At the same time, the emergence of what some have called regional despotisms in Russia has encouraged the federal authorities to use the stick of human rights to attempt to bring regional authorities back into line.

In this context it is clear that Andrew Linklater has been quite right to question the boundedness of citizenship to the traditional national-state.[31] One does not have to be a Hegelian to understand that elements of what we may call transcitizenship have emerged. It has been suggested above that there is an emerging virtual universal policy state, and, furthermore, its membership comprises transcitizenship, an intermediary stage between traditional state citizenship and membership of the universal state mentioned earlier. Transcitizenship is not just transitional citizenship; it also takes on the characteristics of dual citizenship, facing both down to the nation-state but also up to the emerging universal state. Although state citizenship may remain central, it is increasingly complemented (if not challenged) by trans-state obligations and recourses. The most obvious is the ability to appeal to the European Court of Human Rights for citizens of those countries that have incorporated the European Convention on Human Rights (and its many subsequent protocols) into national law. Against the particularism of the state there is a trend not only towards what some have taken to calling globalisation but, for our purposes of greater importance, a human rights-based process of universalism that is eroding state sovereignty with the insistence and patience of lapping water.

One should here distinguish, as Stephen Chan has done in his review of Linklater's work, between the exclusivity of political citizenship and forms of 'moral universal citizenship'.[32] From being an abstract ethical category, universal citizenship is increasingly taking on political forms. The political forms of this universalism are at present rudimentary and embryonic, and do not yet contain the full armoury of cultural allegiances, political passions and identity-making instruments that are traditionally the property of the nation-state; yet to argue that transcitizenship is as yet a thin concoction is not to be confused with the argument that it does not exist. It is precisely the tension between the narrow political citizenship of the state and the emerging ethical universal citizenship of transnational practices that defines the contemporary security situation in Eurasia. In between we have transcitizenship, something that allows citizens of any particular state recourse to bodies outside of that state, but which as yet lacks any sustained formalised institutional expression and which at present is largely constituted by a set of normative principles whose practices are very much being tested in contemporary international politics. Humanitarian intervention, for example, clearly infringes the traditional sovereign rights of a state, as do plans for an International Criminal Court and the establishment of particular war crimes courts such as the International Criminal Tribunal for the former Yugoslavia. This was a tension built into the founding documents of the UN, the OSCE and, in a different way, the Council of Europe, but whose resolution may finally be at hand. There is no Hegelian dialectical inevitability about this, only practical responses to the limitations of the bounded nation-state in the technologically mobile postcommunist era.

Transcitizenship represents both an enhancement and a diminution of citizenship rights. They are enhanced because they become the responsibility of more than a single state, and individual states themselves are constrained by the emergent universalistic order. They are diminished because of the amorphousness of the new universal order. In a sense, transcitizenship is no citizenship at all, lacking institutional accountability. The institutions that represent the universalistic agenda are 'soft' ones, such as the Council of Europe, the OSCE and the UN, although they do at times have a hard edge.

The body that has been at the cutting edge of intermestic developments, linking political–military concerns with the 'human dimension' of security, from the very beginning, is the OSCE. The tensions and contradictions between its own 'ten basic principles' are those that characterise the emergence of the universalistic transcitizenship agenda in general.[33] How respect for human rights could be squared with non-intervention in countries' internal affairs has not yet been resolved, while the declared right to national self-determination and the inviolability of borders provides a rich morass of confusion in which the Chechens and Kosovars find themselves mired. Nevertheless, the OSCE has devoted itself in the post-Cold War era to ensuring that its member states (now numbering over fifty) comply with democratic norms. To this end it established missions to Latvia and Estonia to encourage the integration of Russians in the citizenship community of these two newly independent nations.

The Russian government's support for these OSCE missions, as for the activities of the Council of Europe noted above, was based not only on the desire to see natural justice done to its compatriots who now found themselves abroad, but also as a crucial device for deflating some of the extremist rhetoric of Russian nationalists at home. The OSCE has also deployed a mission to Belarus, where the issue is not ethnic conflict but a straightforward struggle between the basic facets of liberalism and the power of the traditional administrative *nomenklatura* reconstructed with a populist turn by President Alexander Lukashenka. The key point is that in all cases, albeit mostly with some reluctance, the OSCE's *droit de regard* was regarded as legitimate and thus the erosion of state sovereignty was enshrined as fact. The normative principles of universalism were accepted as superior and as taking precedence over narrow definitions of state particularism.

Ethnic conflicts are pre-political, in the sense that they are not easily amenable to settlement through a formal negotiating process but can be ameliorated, if not resolved, through a variety of problem-solving techniques. It is these in which the OSCE, and in particular its High Commissioner on National Minorities Max van der Stoel, have accumulated a rich experience in the postcommunist world. By acting as an impartial third party and mediator the OSCE has helped defuse potential intra-state conflicts. However, it is the OSCE's very multilateralism that has undermined it as a useful instrument of policy in American eyes; they prefer to use NATO or to act unilaterally. While willing to use it as an instrument to attack human rights abuses in the communist world, with the fall of the wall the OSCE lost much of its usefulness as an instrument in US policy. This does not undermine the argument about the development of an embryonic ethical univeralist structure to international affairs. What is at stake here is the danger that the universalist agenda could be hijacked to become a proprietary concern of the West in general, or even of America in particular.

If ethnic conflicts are pre-political, then in a certain sense the universalist agenda is post-political. Certain principles are considered absolutes, and the definition of these, together with the conditions and circumstances under which they can be implemented, are aggregated by a section of the international community on behalf of the rest of that community. The challenge today is to ensure that universalism becomes a genuinely political process, and thus one whereby all of its constituent parts are equally susceptible to the bargaining process. It is precisely because politics is usually bounded by the state, with, traditionally, realist views of state-centred relations taking over thereafter, that any discussion of Eurasian security must think of ways of politicising international relations in general, and questions of universality in particular. It is not enough simply to argue that we need a broader definition of security;[34] we do, but the very notion of security is part of the broader relationship between universalising agendas and particularist legacies in which democracy cannot be defined as a gift of the West to the postcommunist world, but as an expanding sphere of political relations. Real dangers of threat and attack do not disappear, but it is precisely the relationship between threat and security that is changing as well as the definition of both.

Conclusion

While for the 'in' and 'pre-in' countries of Central Europe the accession agenda for EU membership came to crowd out all other forms of societal change, establishing a disciplinary framework for fiscal, economic and political change, for Russia and the other CIS states, whose membership in the EU would be a very long-term aspiration at best, the Council of Europe and other 'civilisational' agencies had an enormous impact. While they are 'outs' as far as EU (and NATO) membership is concerned, they are definitely part of pan-European development and as far as civilisational Europe is concerned. Whether this is enough remains questionable: the most effective democracy assistance to Russia would be a credible association with the EU leading ultimately to the guarantee of membership, however far in the future. The EU, however, has proved unable to arrive at a clear and creative view of security arrangements in its relationship with Russia and most other former Soviet states.

Inclusion is always a differentiated process. Europe has long been adept at including ideas and technologies from other civilisations, while denigrating and in some cases destroying the civilisations themselves. The very notion of inclusion contains within itself an accompanying dynamic of exclusion. In keeping with our theme that foreign and domestic policy are intertwined when it comes to these issues, we must here stress that 'in-ness' and 'out-ness' concern domestic processes of inclusion and identity formation as much as they do external integration. In Serbia or Russia today the question of inclusion and exclusion could not be starker. In the case of Russia, we may legitimately ask whether it is a nation-state at all in the conventional sense, and indeed question whether it is even becoming one. While Russia has many an external 'other', it is the many 'others' that it carries within its own traditions and present realities that endows the country with what by any standards is a monumental identity crisis. One aspect of this is the relative failure of the Russian state since the fall of communism, a failure that reflects the lack of political structuration of society itself. The question of who is in or out in domestic politics will determine Russia's external status and policies.

The collapse of the old regime expanded the opportunities for participation everywhere in the postcommunist world. At both the state and the trans-state levels opportunities for inclusion have broadened, but the new citizens, at both levels, still play a subaltern role. Accountable government at both the state and trans-state level may develop or atrophy, but its prospects will depend ultimately on politicising the power relations at the state and trans-state levels. By this we mean providing a forum for negotiation, bargaining and settlements between active constituencies which operate within the framework of universalism and the emerging trans-state political community. Instead of bureaucrat speaking unto technocrat, challenged only by unaccountable pressure groups of one form or another, more formal ways of achieving inclusion for individuals and democratically constituted civic groups need to be found. Only in this way can a genuine politics of transnationalism emerge. Although only fitfully, we are beginning to see what the universalistic keystone in the arch may one day look like.

Notes

1 L. T. H., *The Manchester Guardian* (12 November 1918); reproduced in *The Guardian* (16 October 1999).

2 I. B. Neumann, *Uses of the Other: 'The East' in European Identity Formation* (Manchester, Manchester University Press, 1999), p. 15 and *passim.*

3 S. W. Garnett, *Keystone in the Arch: Ukraine in the Emerging Security Environment of Central and Eastern Europe* (Washington, DC, Carnegie Endowment for International Peace, 1997), p. 135.

4 Garnett, *Keystone in the Arch*, p. 136.

5 Z. Brzezinski, 'The Cold War and its aftermath', *Foreign Affairs*, 74:4 (1992), 49.

6 L. Whitehead (ed.), *The International Dimensions of Democratization: Europe and the Americas* (Oxford, Oxford University Press, 1996).

7 In 1999 Poland had begun to talk of reintroducing a visa regime with some dozen countries to its east, and took practical measures to harden its frontier with Belarus; N. Plotnikov, 'Pol'sha ukreplyaet granitsy s Belorussiei', *Nezavisimaya Gazeta* (21 December 1999), p. 5.

8 R. Sakwa, 'Introduction: The Many Dimensions of Europe', in R. Sakwa and A. Stevens (eds.), *Contemporary Europe* (Basingstoke, Macmillan, 2000).

9 *Financial Times* (2 July 1999), p. 2.

10 For a general analysis and a case study of 'democratic conditionality', see G. Pridham, 'Complying with the European Union's democratic conditionality: transnational party linkages and regime change in Slovakia, 1993–1998', *Europe-Asia Studies*, 51:7 (1999), 1221–44.

11 T. G. Ash, 'Ten years in Europe', *Prospect* (July 1999), 24; and T. G. Ash, 'Catching the wrong bus?', in P. Gowan and P. Anderson (eds.), *The Question of Europe* (London, Verso, 1996), pp. 117–25.

12 M. D. Thurman, review of G. Sanford, *Poland: The Conquest of History* (Amsterdam, Harwood Academic Publishers, 1999), *Nationalities Papers*, 27:3 (1999), 535.

13 Richard Nicolaus Graf von Coudenhove-Kalergi, *Pan Europa* (Vienna, Adel, 1923).

14 J. Checkel, 'Empowerment, ricochets and end-runs: Russia's integration with Western human rights institutions and practices', Program on New Approaches to Russian Security, Policy Memo Series, No. 14, (Harvard University, 1998) p. 1.

15 'Russian nuclear researcher wins key legal victory', The Jamestown Foundation, *Monitor*, VI:5 (7 January 2000).

16 S. P. Huntington, 'The clash of civilizations?', *Foreign Affairs*, 72:3 (1993), 23–49.

17 Neumann, *Uses of the Other*, p. 37.

18 S. George, *An Awkward Partner: Britain in the European Community*, 2nd edn (Oxford, Oxford University Press, 1994).

19 R. Putnam, 'The prosperous community: social capital and public life', *The American Prospect* (Spring 1993), 38.

20 P. R. Newberg and T. Carothers, 'Aiding – and defining – democracy', *World Policy Journal*, 13 (1996), 97–108; and A. Hadenius and F. Uggla, 'Making civil society work, promoting democratic development: what can states and donors do?', *World Development*, 24 (1996), 1621–39.

21 M. W. Doyle, 'Kant, liberal legacies and foreign affairs', *Philosophy and Public Affairs*, 12:3 (1983), 205–35; and B. M. Russett, *Grasping the Democratic Peace: Principles for the Post-Cold War World* (Princeton, NJ, Princeton University Press, 1993).

22 S. Huntington, *Political Order in Changing Societies* (New Haven, CT, Yale University Press, 1968).

23 E. D. Mansfield and J. Snyder, 'Democratization and war', *Foreign Affairs*, 74:3 (1995), 79–97; and E. D. Mansfield and J. Snyder, 'Democratization and the danger of war', *International Security*, 20 (1995), 5–38.

24 M. Weller, 'The Rambouillet conference on Kosovo', *International Affairs*, 75:2 (1999), 211–51.

25 Quoted in RFE/RL Report (18 October 1999), *Johnson's Russia List*, No. 3571.

26 Quoted in M. Kaldor, 'Investing in the future', *Transitions* (August 1998), 5.

27 *New York Times* (17 June 1999), p. A7.

28 George Soros, 'The capitalist threat', *The Atlantic Monthly* (February 1997), 45–58.

29 G. Yavlinskii, 'Condition the cash', *Transitions* (August 1998), 3.

30 Checkel, 'Empowerment, ricochets and end-runs', p. 1.

31 A. Linklater, *The Transformation of Political Community* (Cambridge, Polity Press, 1998).

32 S. Chan, 'Andrew Linklater and the new rhetoric in International Relations', *Global Society*, 13:3 (1999), 370.

33 P. T. Hopmann, *Building Security in Post-Cold War Eurasia: The OSCE and U.S. Foreign Policy* (Washington, DC, United States Institute of Peace, Peaceworks 31, 1999).

34 O. Waever, B. Buzan, M. Kelstrup and P. Lemaitre, *Identity, Migration and the New Security Agenda in Europe* (London, Pinter Publishers, 1993); A. Dorman and A. Treacher, *An Introduction to Security Issues in Post-Cold War Europe* (Aldershot, Dartmouth, 1995); R. Ullman, 'Redefining security', in S. Lynn-Jones and S. Miller (eds.), *Global Dangers: Changing Dimensions of International Security* (Boston, MA, MIT Press, 1995).

9

The challenge of 'soft security': crime, corruption and chaos

Mark Galeotti

At the beginning of the twenty-first century, the very concept of national security is being rewritten. Although Kalashnikovs are being used in anger across the former Soviet south, from Georgia and Chechnya through to civil-war-torn Tajikistan, this is an era of small wars and low-intensity conflicts rather than all-out inter-state conflict. Even Russia's sabre rattling against the Baltic states in a bid to halt or delay their accession to the North Atlantic Treaty Organisation (NATO) is looking increasingly like symbolic politics rather than a serious threat. Ironically, though, this does not mean that the states of the region necessarily feel any more secure.

Moscow's may be a special case, as it must also deal with the legacy of empire and a deep-seated unwillingness to relinquish its claim to military superpower status. For most of the states of postcommunist Europe, however, the issue has simply been a shift in the nature of the challenge facing them.[1] As overt security threats have become less credible, there has been a corresponding rise in the danger posed by non-traditional – 'soft' – security issues relating to economic and political stability, transnational and organised crime, migration and ethnic tensions. To a considerable degree, this reflects both the end of the Cold War and the subsequent transition to free market economics and democratic politics. Rather than being confined to internal affairs or law enforcement, such threats are in many cases becoming a major influence on national security agendas across the region. While some analysts reject the term 'soft security' (pointing out that such security problems pose just as, and sometimes even more, severe challenges to the societies concerned than more traditional political–military security problems) and point out that what constitutes security is essentially subjective, soft security nevertheless provides useful shorthand for the wide range of non-military security problems facing postcommunist Europe.

Reform and transition represent enormous challenges for countries with often unproductive economies, legacies of mistrust between state and society, and traditions of poor, unresponsive and corrupt governance. For many countries of postcommunist Europe, the decade since 1989 will be remembered for hardship, disillusionment with democratic politics, and social, political and economic instability. There has been an obvious if inescapable vicious circle at work, as weak political systems prove unequal to the task of managing reform and combating criminality. The result is a wide variety of problems, from illegal capital flight and increased corruption of state officials to public disenchantment and a distortion of the mechanisms of the market, all of which weaken the state yet further, or at least prevent it from finding its feet. A number of the region's states have managed to run this painful gauntlet.[2] The prevailing pattern, however, is of at best partial success, leaving the long-term stability of many of the new states and their political and economic systems still in question. Furthermore, high levels of instability, uncertainty and overall criminality create public disquiet, perhaps generating support for extremist leaders who promise to apply draconian measures and thereby risk a reversal of the process of democratisation.

The issues

One of the most basic problems to be faced when discussing soft security threats is the high degree of overlap and interplay between separate factors. Terrorism, for example, often shades into organised crime (indeed, many terror groups turn to crime to raise funds) and can – but does not always – also reflect regional separatism or political unrest. In this chapter non-traditional security challenges will be considered by looking at four main issues: the challenge caused by the decay of security forces; the proliferation of weapons and violence, alongside the decay in the state's coercive forces; the threat posed by transnational crime; and the emergence of criminalised or uncontrolled enclaves as state power is undermined.

1   *Hard assets into soft threats.* Non-traditional security threats need to be combated in different ways from traditional ones. To be sure, traditional security assets can play a role – the United States increasingly uses its armed forces to interdict drugs routes, for example – but this is not an ideal or efficient use of them. Traditional security assets can, however, also become part of the problem, posing a political, economic, social or criminal threat to society. In some parts of the world, this has taken the form of political autonomy and their use in coups or repression. In postcommunist Europe, and especially in the former Soviet states, it is instead the case that the morale, discipline and operational effectiveness of armed forces have decayed to the point at which their value as a national security asset is critically low and they are becoming a source of crime and instability.

2   *Proliferation of both weapons and force.* Criminality, instability, state illegitimacy and pressure on security apparatuses and military chains of command struggling to cope with new conditions and political change all

create an environment in which even the most dangerous weapons, materials and technologies are for sale.[3] In this way, the internal problems of postcommunist Europe pose a global proliferation challenge. However, the weapons often simply reflect and exacerbate a wider problem: if states lose their monopoly of the legitimate (or practical) use of violence, then this paves the way for other providers of violence and counter-violence, whether criminals or private security agencies (a distinction all too often of little real relevance in postcommunist Europe), which, in turn, further marginalise and undermine the state.

3   *Destabilisation and transnational crime.* If organised crime is in many ways a corollary of modernisation, so globalisation begets transnational crime. This poses its own problems in policing, controlling borders and protecting national economies. However, it is also important to conceive this as a soft security issue. Transnational crime can emerge in the form of linkages between local gangs, dealing across borders to maximise their profits while minimising their losses, just as many licit companies do. However – again, as in the legal, 'upperworld' economy – it can also involve penetration by foreign enterprises, whose power or effectiveness allows them to take over or destroy local rivals. This carries with it a series of potential dangers, from the destabilising influence of 'invading' criminal groups to the possible colonisation of a nation's underworld by gangs based abroad.

4   *Fragmentation.* Crises of legitimacy and economic dislocation can raise questions about the very boundaries of these new states, or the relevance to local interests of national governments which often seem distant, powerless, corrupt or a combination of all three. More directly, organised crime, often in alliance with separatist elements, can penetrate and subvert political and economic systems and create virtual 'no go' areas for the state, such as Chechnya in Russia and Kosovo in Serbia.[4] There are no real external military threats to the nations of postcommunist Europe outside the former Yugoslavia and, perhaps, the Baltic states. However, fragmentation is already at work, whether in bloodless divorces as in the separation of Czechoslovakia or more violently as in the secession of Chechnya. Even where no overt fragmentation has taken place, regional interests are often able to subvert or ignore legitimate central authority, in a kind of hidden secession.

Rather than as a clear-cut case of peace or war, these non-traditional challenges need to be assessed on a sliding scale, perhaps going from problem through risk to outright threat. All modern states face some degree of organised criminality, for example, but whereas this might be considered merely a problem in, say, France or Canada, the ability of the Mafia to defy the state in Italy might merit the title risk. While there is no fear that the Mafia could topple the Italian state or disrupt the economic or social system, in some parts of postcommunist Europe this may be a very real danger, elevating it into the realms of full-blown threat. This is, of course, still a crude approach, not least because it relies on vague semantics, but it nevertheless illustrates the continuum on which these challenges must be placed.

At their most extreme, these soft threats can translate into military challenges and have a very hard impact on a state. They have fuelled and armed secession movements and war, from the Balkans to Chechnya. They undermine national security assets such as armed forces, both directly (by demoralising and corrupting them) and indirectly (by plundering national budgets). Beyond this, they also have the potential to undermine still-nascent democratic orders. Moscow's invasions of Chechnya in 1994 and 1999, while carried out in the name of the Russian Federation constitution, were characterised by brutal tactics and arbitrary suspensions of constitutional rights. Even relatively advanced and liberal states can be tempted to return to the authoritarian practices of the past by the challenge posed by criminality and disorder. In Hungary, for example, new laws aimed at combating organised crime will dramatically curtail human rights, but Prime Minister Viktor Orbán is unashamed in rejecting what he calls 'the doctrinaire adoption of Western liberal principles'.[5]

The challenges facing Russia, the newly independent ex-Soviet republics (such as the Baltic states and Ukraine), the former non-Soviet Warsaw Pact states of Central Europe and the emerging states of the former Yugoslavia are all linked but distinct. The following sections examine one of the four issues outlined above, focusing on one of these groups of states in each case in order to illustrate both the nature of the problem concerned and the specific challenges facing these different groups of postcommunist states. The rest of the chapter then considers the responses being adopted to these emerging security risks and the prospects for progress.

Russia embattled: when security assets become security threats[6]

In 1994 journalist Dmitrii Kholodov wrote 'our Russian army is sliding down into a world of organised crime'.[7] Shortly afterwards, while following a lead that commandos were working as *mafiya* hitmen, he was killed by a booby trap bomb. The rise of organised crime has been a major feature of Russia's postcommunist development; beset with criminality, violent regionalism, corruption, disillusion and incipient extremism, Russia to many represents a veritable cornucopia of soft threats.[8] As a sprawling and often impoverished land empire Russia has always been prone to explosions of rural unrest and ethnic insurrection – which is one reason why Russia's leaders have historically placed considerable emphasis on maintaining large military and security forces. Today, however, Russia faces a worrying and intractable threat from those very forces, as criminality, indiscipline and disillusion corrode the military chain of command. The danger is not so much from any directed activity, such as a coup, as from the decay of the armed forces into a state of uselessness, creating obvious conventional security threats and providing skills, weapons and other assets to strengthen other sources of threat, whether organised criminal gangs or rebel Chechen fighters (both of whom are armed largely from military arsenals).

It is hardly surprising that the Russian military is in such a poor state. A conscript earns the equivalent of a dollar a week; the officer commanding him will be lucky to pull in as much as a municipal bus driver. Wage arrears are a constant feature of soldiers' lives, and at times when inflation is high that can in effect reduce their income still further. Crime within the demoralised Russian military is rife and growing, as table 9.1 shows. Much of this is a product of internal disorder, engendering a regular toll of desertions, beatings, rapes and killings. In ten years in Afghanistan, the Soviet military suffered just over 15,000 casualties.[9] Between accidents, suicides and killings, the Russian military loses this many men every three years. The seniority-based tradition of bullying known as *dedovshchina* ('grand-fatherism') continues. In practices which originated in the Stalinist era Gulag prison camps, new recruits are frequently forced to work for their seniors, humiliated, even raped and beaten. According to figures dating from 1994, one in four of all conscripts was hospitalised by beating at some point in their national service, and one in twenty suffered homosexual rape. Furthermore, the army is still prone to *gruppovshchina*, a phenomenon equivalent to inter-ethnic violence. Drug abuse within the ranks quadrupled in the twelve months to June 1999 alone.[10]

Figure 9.1 Military crime rates in Russia

Year	Total no. crimes	% change	Crimes/100,000 soldiers*
1995	12,400	+13.5	653
1996	12,300	−0.8	820
1997	18,000	+31.7	1,500
1998	17,700	−1.7	1,770
1999**	17,450	−1.4	1,940

Notes
  * Reflects the shrinking size of the total Russian military.
  ** Provisional projections issued in August 1999.
Source: Russian Ministry of the Interior.

Perhaps even more alarming is the growing involvement of soldiers in Russia's thriving underworld, reflecting the high levels of corruption within the officer corps.[11] In 1998, for example, fourteen generals were jailed for financial irregularities and abuse of office, with another sixteen still facing charges.[12] This does not mean that there is a danger of the Russian *mafiya* controlling the army, however; most organised criminal activity within the military is not especially sophisticated and does not extend beyond moonlighting and embezzlement of (already scarce) military resources.

The relationship between the military and organised crime is rather more complex, and largely takes two forms. There are the so-called 'gangs with shoulder-boards' – criminal organisations which have arisen within the armed forces. They may have links to corrupt local politicians and civilian gangs, but will generally remain separate, concentrating on using the resources and opportunities at their disposal. This is especially visible in regions with high military concentrations and relatively weak civilian control, such as the Kaliningrad exclave and the North Caucasus Military District. These gangs generally confine themselves to profiting at the military's expense. Fuel is often siphoned from aviation and naval units, for example, and sold, while being written off as being consumed in non-existent training exercises. The head of the North Caucasus Military District's armoured forces even wrote off thirty-four trucks and tractors as destroyed during the first Chechen war and then sold them off to local businesses.[13]

More often, the role of the military in the Russian underworld appears to lie in providing services and resources for the *mafiya*. To take one example, military transport and routes are often used for smuggling, whether of drugs from Central Asia brought in by border troops or the Tajikistan-based 201st Motor Rifle Division, or of stolen cars from Europe moved through Kaliningrad.[14] By the same token, the 16th *Spetsnaz* (Special Forces) Brigade, based at Chuchkogo, south-east of Moscow, has acquired a distinctively dirty reputation as a source of contract killers for *mafiya* hits.[15]

The indiscipline and criminalisation of the Russian military are thus a very real security problem, and not just for the Kremlin. First, it leaves Russia with an unstable and unreliable conventional security force, contributing towards a dependency on nuclear weapons to guarantee its security. Second, it undermines attempts to create transparent, democratic and working control over the military. Finally, not only does it generate its own version of the *mafiya* phenomenon which has taken such deep root in Russia, but it may also aid and arm criminals and terrorists at home and abroad. Above all, it permits the spread of weapons – albeit, to date, only conventional ones – into private and criminal hands.

Many other Soviet successor states have problems controlling their armed forces and security agencies. Criminality is rife in their armies, with, for example, Ukrainian border troops involved in smuggling and Belarussian army warehouses used for storing drugs. Russia's inability to restructure its armed forces and reduce manning levels to a manageable and affordable level has, however, left it especially vulnerable.

Proliferation: is the Kalashnikov mightier than the nuclear bomb?

In this context, assessing the relative potency of a weapon is not simply a matter of considering how many people it can kill at once. Nuclear weapons are horrifying agents of mass destruction – or necessary arms of deterrence, depending on your point of view – but for this reason are also rarely usable. They did not deter Argentina from attempting to annex the Falkland Islands, nor Iraq from invading Kuwait, and they certainly have no value in fighting off a protection racketeer or pacifying Chechnya.

While concern over criminals and terrorists acquiring and using weapons of mass destruction from Soviet stockpiles is understandable, it has arguably turned out to be one of the unrealised fears of the post-Cold War era.[16] This may reflect the lack of a market for such weapons: the immediate impact of their use, or even the fear of their use, would far outweigh the potential gains. The major players of the postcommunist underworld are, after all, generally doing very well out of their close relations with corrupt leaderships, and would not want to put this in jeopardy. 'Rogue states' or 'states of concern' so beloved of some post-Cold War security studies may seem an obvious market, but most of the nations which want a nuclear capacity have one, and the main problem is not the warheads so much as the delivery systems. A real and more immediate concern has been the proliferation of conventional weapons allied to a greater will and ability to use them in illegal actions. Proliferation, in other words, not just of guns but of violence.

One by-product of the Russian military's decay is a thriving trade in weapons, equipment and ammunition. In an average year almost 30,000 weapons go missing, and the Federal Security Service estimated in 1995 that 200,000 assault rifles alone were in criminal hands.[17] Only one in three of all illegally held firearms in Russia comes from military arsenals, however, with the rest coming from factories and underground workshops.[18] Thus almost 100,000 weapons flow into private hands every year. Similarly, the collapse of the Albanian state in 1997 saw perhaps 600,000 weapons looted from government arsenals, including 200,000 assault rifles.[19] While many stayed in the hands of Albanian gangs or armed rebels in neighbouring Kosovo, others flowed out, to Europe and beyond.[20]

Postcommunist Europe is thus awash with illegal weapons, many of which are making their way into Western Europe or towards trouble-spots elsewhere in the world. This is one reason why the Russian contract killer's trademark of leaving the gun at the scene of the crime is becoming increasingly widespread – why try to flee with an incriminating weapon when another can be bought easily, cheaply and relatively safely? The age of the disposable Kalashnikov is here.

Underpinning this proliferation in the tools of violence is a proliferation in the agents of violence and also in the demand for their services. One of the most striking features of the postcommunist transition has been the collapse in many countries of the state's monopoly of violence, creating a demand for non-state protection which has been filled by a mix of legal and illegal agencies, from security firms to criminal racketeers. Crucially, this means that organised crime has not just operated negatively, as a parasite on the legitimate economy, but as a positive supplier of services in demand.[21] This role as a provider of non-state protection not only gives organised crime and corrupt officials lucrative sources of revenue, it also opens doors into the legitimate economy and even provides a degree of public legitimacy.

In Russia, an estimated 70–80 per cent of businesses 'buy a roof' – in other words, pay for protection – from the *mafiya*.[22] For this, they expect not just security, but also a range of other 'criminal services', from debt collection to assistance in dealing with corrupt officials.[23] For those unable or unwilling to turn to organised crime, there is a burgeoning and under-regulated private security sector, with around 800,000 licensed staff – compared with a total police strength of 400,000 – and perhaps another 200,000 working for unlicensed firms. However, their services come at a price generally greater than the criminals' cut (typically 30–40 per cent of profit, compared with the usual 10–20 per cent organised crime demands), and they may often prove to be little more than the more respectable face of the mob. In 1996, for example, police raided the offices of the St Petersburg-based firm Skorpion, which they suspected of being a front for the city's dominant *Tambovskaya* gang.[24]

Almost every major Russian firm has a sizeable security department, in some cases a veritable private army. MOST-Bank, for example, reportedly has more than 2,500 armed officers in Moscow alone, equivalent to a regiment of the Kremlin Guard. Even more substantial is the Security Service of Gazprom, the giant gas concern, with 20,000 staff.[25] This reflects a widespread belief by the public and business that the official agents of the state are unable or unwilling to protect them, and that they need and have a right to seek alternative protectors. That this may be illegal is not a key determinant, and even legislators appear to have given up trying to block this process and instead have sought to create legal norms within which it can operate – up to and including wider gun ownership. Parliamentary aide Anatoly Luychenko, for example, one of the drafters of the 1997 Law on Weapons, admitted that there was a direct connection, because 'the state absolutely cannot provide for the protection of its people'.[26]

The correlation of the power of non-state security providers and the limited effectiveness of the state may indicate a serious crisis. The rise of powerful corporate armies cannot be a good sign for democracy, especially when their composition and operation are usually in direct contravention of the letter of the law. Such capitalist warlordism not only contributes to a widespread sense that the Russian new rich live above the law, but it further blurs the already confused boundaries between the state and the private sector. There is clearly a deeply rooted problem with the state's ability to assert its authority and demonstrate one of the essential attributes of statehood and legitimacy.

Again, the question must be asked whether Russia is a unique case. Most of the other Soviet successor states share this problem – indeed, to the east and south the state's grip on security is generally less reliable and alternative sources of violence, from private corporations to local warlords, are more powerful. The situation is particularly unstable in the Caucasus, where 'private security' is often in the hands either of moonlighting police and state security officers or personal armed retinues of central and local political leaders.

In Ukraine, the situation is similar to Russia's, but as one moves westwards the pattern becomes more varied. Private security firms and criminal racketeers are a constant, but in countries at the western extremity of postcommunist Europe greater steps have been taken to control them and alleviate the crisis in state authority. In the Czech Republic, for example, public concern about the so-called 'black sheriffs', as security guards became known, was fuelled by the revelation in 1995 that there were seven private guards in Prague for every one police officer.[27] There has been some success in taming the 'black sheriffs', but they are still a fixture of urban Czech life and, in the words of one Prague police officer, are 'still largely outside the law unless they kill someone – or step on the toes of someone with even more [clout]'.[28] A similar situation obtains in Poland; the early 1990s saw an almost unrestricted rise of private security firms, many of which were criminal fronts or acted as if they were, but there was a partial clawing back of control and authority on the part of the state in the second half of the decade.[29] In South-Eastern Europe, the situation is more problematic. Not only are weapons freely available, but in many former Yugoslav states warlordism has simply taken to cloaking itself as 'private security'.

In short, the proliferation of illegal weapons and sources of armed non-state authority is a common problem across postcommunist Europe. A floating market in illegal weapons (many of the guns used in Kosovo had, for example, previously been used in the anti-Georgian guerrilla war in Abkhazia) arms the criminal and the discontented and encourages 'arms races' between rival groups. This illustrates how soft threats may become or

contribute to hard security issues. Not only does the proliferation of
weapons and violence pose challenges, of varying degrees, to these new
nations, but by creating 'arsenals of anarchy', arming criminals and terrorists elsewhere in the world, it becomes a global problem.

The new Russian invasion?

If the delegitimisation of the state discussed at the start of this chapter is an
essentially internal process, as a state either loses authority or never even
acquires it, then destabilisation, the third key issue to be considered, is an
essentially invasive threat. During the Cold War there was a fear – on both
sides of the Iron Curtain – of the other side spreading subversion. Since
1989, though, a new bugbear has emerged: the fear of a spreading Russian
mafiya that could invade and achieve with drugs, prostitutes and dirty
money what had never been attained by Soviet tanks. This fear is shared –
indeed, in some cases actively promoted – by other postcommunist states.
Yet how realistic is it?

It has for years seemed axiomatic that the spread of organised crime in
Central Europe was predominantly, if not exclusively, because of the influx
of Russian, as well as Ukrainian and other 'Soviet' criminals. When, for
example, the Polish government announced the formation of a new 1,200-
strong organised crime squad, modelled on the US Federal Bureau of
Investigation (FBI), it made it clear that it was primarily to target the
Russian *mafiya*.[30] There are many reasons why Central Europeans might be
expected to talk up this new threat. It chimes with popular dislike of the
Russians in countries which experienced Soviet domination. It allows these
states to shrug off responsibility for domestic criminality, just as the
Chechens have provided the Russians with a suitable target for attack. For
states with an eye to early entry into the European Union (EU) and NATO,
it also provides a convenient issue on which to polarise public debate and
place themselves on the 'right' side of a new European divide, between a
civilised West and a criminalised East.

So is this simply politically convenient moral panic or is the Russian
mafiya really 'invading' Central Europe? Perhaps not surprisingly, both
extremes contain an element of truth. There is considerable penetration of
Central Europe by criminal groups from the former Soviet Union.
However, these are not rigid hierarchical structures but loose networks of
semi-autonomous criminal entrepreneurs; they often include or work with
local criminals, as new members, subcontractors or independent allies.[31]
Indeed there are powerful domestic criminal organisations in Central
Europe, and if anything the tide has turned in their favour. The early years
when Russian and other gangs could roll into these countries and dominate

the underworld have largely passed. Law enforcers have concentrated on these 'invaders' and the local gangs have themselves gone through a Darwinian series of gang wars and takeovers leading to the rise of more efficient structures. As a result, the role of Russian and other 'Soviet' criminals is often as fellow criminal entrepreneurs, working with local counterparts where this is profitable, but exerting no greater control than that provided by the workings of the indigenous underworld market economy.

Consider, for example, the case of the Baltic states. In the immediate aftermath of the Soviet collapse, Estonia, Latvia and Lithuania became staging posts for domestic and Russian-based organised crime looking towards operating within the Nordic region and Western Europe.[32] With their relatively advanced financial services and communications infrastructures, as well as privileged access to the Nordic and European communities, and with policing structures in disarray and sizeable ethnic Russian populations, they represented lucrative and vulnerable targets for expansion and exploitation. At this time, the geography of organised crime in the Baltics was closely related both to the size of states' expatriate communities and proximity to Russia. North-eastern Estonia was especially vulnerable to gangs from St Petersburg; Russian groups colonised the capital, Tallinn, which became a smuggler's paradise and won the nickname 'Metallin' when it became the sixth largest exporter of metals in the world. By 1995, though, crimes once dominated by 'foreigners' – typically Russians or Caucasians – were increasingly being taken over by local gangs, sometimes subcontracting from their former competitors, but increasingly supplanting them.[33] A turf war in Narva in 1995 was won by Estonian criminals and the more sophisticated Russian and Chechen gangs prepared to work with them. Less flexible Russian gangs were in many cases neutralised by physical elimination or by being informed on to the authorities. The use of the authorities to do the gangs' dirty work, for example, appeared to be behind the country's first serious *mafiya* trial, which began in September 1995, with six ethnic Russians in the dock. They were members of a gang from the Russian city of Perm which established operations in Tallinn in the early 1990s and failed to appreciate the changing political climate.[34]

In Lithuania, similarly, there was a shift away from overt gangsterism and towards gangs operating within the economy and with better political links. The violent and effective 'Vilnius Brigade', for example, was largely disbanded after the arrest in 1994 of its self-styled 'commander', Boris Dekanidze.[35] In place of racketeering, money laundering became increasingly important. With so many of their existing laundry routes (through the Chechen State Bank) disrupted by the Russian invasion, in 1995 the Chechens looked for alternative operations. Lithuanian organised crime was one of the beneficiaries, and their proceeds from money laundering assisted their move into legal or seemingly legal business and allowed them to take a more robust line with their Russian counterparts.

This pattern is visible in many countries of Central Europe. In Poland, where there is particular concern about the country becoming a drug-smuggling gateway into Europe, Ukrainians represented the main external criminal threat, but many local operations in Poland are now subcontracted either to Poles or gangs comprising Russians and Ukrainians who have settled there and begun recruiting local 'talent'.[36] In Hungary, for years a favoured haunt of such alleged Russian *mafiya* godfathers as Semen Mogilevich, many Russian-dominated gangs operating at street level have either merged with, or declined relative to, their local rivals.[37]

The problem is thus proving almost impossible to eliminate through purely national efforts. In some cases, policing becomes entangled with politics. For example, the official policy of closer integration between Belarus and Russia has hampered efforts to police the former's eastern borders, especially with the lifting of customs barriers.

Fragmentation: how many Kosovos in postcommunist Europe?

The revolutions of 1989 in Central and Eastern Europe and the fragmentation of the Soviet Union may in part have been a response to rising nationalist pressures, but it does not necessarily follow that nationalism is enough to create nation-states. Indeed, many of the postcommunist states are characterised by a weak sense of ethnic and national identity, arbitrary and disputed borders, and only slow progress in economic and political transformation. Many of these states could be regarded as distinctly 'weak' (in the sense of lacking effective state structures and the social and political cohesion necessary to develop and sustain such structures), as criminality and corruption blur state boundaries, weaken central control, and undermine economic stability and political legitimacy. From such weakness can emerge pressures for fragmentation or even outright secession and the formation of enclaves outside central control.

In early 1998 an Interpol officer made what proved a depressingly accurate prediction: 'Kosovo could become Europe's own little Chechnya or Medellin.'[38] South-Eastern Europe, torn by war, inter-ethnic violence and state collapse, presents yet another challenge, proving that so-called 'soft threats' can be even more horrifying and intractable than their conventional counterparts. Here, low-level conflict between ethnic, religious and political communities is endemic. Attempts at controlling such conflicts by policing, including through the use of foreign and international forces, tend to do no more than impose a temporary and artificial cease-fire. This is even true of the Bosnian-based Multinational Specialised Unit, generally regarded as the most successful such initiative.[39] Arguably, peace of a sort only emerges when one community has been ejected – but even then, this tends only to delay or displace the problem. Ejected communities, as the Palestinians have shown, tend not to react philosophically to their fate. Furthermore, they will usually become refugees, in regions with few resources with which to house, feed and employ them. Such discontented diasporas become fertile breeding grounds for organised crime, political and religious extremism, and uncontrolled migration.

The independence struggle waged by the ethnic Albanian Kosovars against their Serbian occupiers proved a boon to numerous organised crime groups. In particular, the activities of the guerrillas, primarily the Kosovo Liberation Army (KLA), disrupted Serbian police operations and created a new route for heroin smuggled into Europe from Turkey: the entry point for some 95 per cent of the continent's supply.[40] The KLA does not appear to have been directly involved itself in narcotics trafficking, but instead allowed drugs traffickers to cross areas under its control in return for 'tribute' – very occasionally in the form of drugs, but usually as cash or weapons – to fuel its war against Belgrade. Much of this heroin was then distributed in Europe through gangs within the ethnic Albanian diaspora, also a key source of donations for the KLA's war chest.[41] According to a German intelligence estimate, half the funds received by the KLA emanated from the drugs trade.[42]

The refugee camps in Macedonia and Albania themselves also offered prime opportunities for the criminals, who in many cases came to dominate them. Disillusioned young men were easy prey for the criminal gangs, which characteristically first used them as camp enforcers, with the prospect of an eventual transfer to Europe. Many, though, travelled to Europe, either on their own or through the gangs' pipelines, which had developed in the years since the 1997 Albanian collapse.[43] These migrants, especially those who moved illegally, often became prey to the gangs, which demanded further payment or service on pain of being turned over to the authorities. Others were professional criminals, whose discipline, ruthlessness and access to weapons soon made them a serious challenge to European law enforcers.[44] In Italy, 600 extra police officers were deployed to Milan, a city which saw Albanian and domestic organised crime locked in a brutal battle for supremacy.[45] Even in the United Kingdom, the National Criminal Intelligence Service has identified Albanian organised crime as an important and rapidly growing challenge.

As their states and communities collapse around them, it is hardly surprising that many of the peoples of the Balkans have sought to move into the stable and prosperous countries of Europe. Migrant trade has consequently acquired a particularly repugnant dimension. In 1998 it was

estimated that more than 14,000 Albanian women were working as prostitutes in the EU, a figure which may have doubled in 1999.[46] Worse still was
the growth of a child-slavery trade, with children being bought for as little
as $250 to be used in organised begging and pick-pocketing rings or even
prostitution. In 1999, UNICEF warned that growing numbers of children
were being lured and kidnapped from refugee camps in Albania and
Macedonia.[47]

This, further, is more than just a Balkan problem. The war in Chechnya
is, as of 2001, still ongoing and no peaceful solution is likely in the foreseeable future. Chechnya is the most extreme case, but President Putin, in his
July 2000 'state of the union' address to the Russian Parliament, referred
more widely to the extent to which power has flowed out of the hands of
federal authorities to regional elites. In some cases, this is little more than
the predictable politics of a sprawling federal state with still-young democratic traditions. Sometimes, however, it is rather more. The Russian far
east, for example, is drifting increasingly outside of Moscow's control;
corrupt politics and overt criminality have become the order of the day,
and Moscow's repeated efforts to bring the far eastern elite to heel have
met with little success.[48] It is not too extreme to question the cohesion of
the Russian Federation and whether Putin's efforts to restore central
control, through such measures as appointing regional presidential
proconsuls, will prompt a more openly assertive response from local elites
which have become comfortable with autonomy.

Internal ethno-cultural divisions also contribute to the weakness of the
Ukrainian state. While some progress has been made in nation building,
the potential for tension between the 'Russian' Orthodox east of the country and the 'Ukrainian' Catholic west remains a serious concern.[49] Russia is
slowly coming to terms with Ukraine's independence and has withdrawn
from interference in its internal affairs, even to the extent of not officially
regarding the Crimean peninsula as an expatriate province. All the same, in
the Crimea Kyiv's efforts to assert its authority were undermined not only
by its remoteness from the region and by cultural differences between the
Orthodox 'Russians' and Muslim Tatars, but also by the fact that both
communities harboured powerful organised criminal groups.[50] These
groups stoked up local tensions, not least to undermine central efforts to
combat their activities. In 1995, a poll by the Crimean Centre for
Sociological Studies found that only 5 per cent of Crimeans believed that
crime was under control, while Major General Valerii Kuznetsov, the
Crimean Interior Minister, admitted that 'all Crimea is overrun by racketeering'.[51] Crime had also begun to intrude overtly into the region's politics.
In 1994, two successive Chairs of the Christian Liberal Party of Crimea were
assassinated. The presence of the Black Sea Fleet – to which Moscow laid

claim – created a further complication. Officers within the contested fleet took fullest advantage of their anomalous status to develop their own criminal enterprises which were able to play the Russian authorities against their Ukrainian counterparts.

In the more recent period the situation has stabilised, as the position of the Black Sea Fleet has been normalised and relations between 'Ukrainian', Tatar and 'Russian' communities have improved. The police were able to use emergency powers against organised crime to rein in their more overt gangsterism, supported by elite *Berkut* (Royal Eagle) riot police and paramilitary Interior Troops. However, it would be foolish to suggest that this represented more than a partial success. At best, state control of the Crimea has been brought up to the same level as the rest of the country.

Moldova experienced similar problems to Ukraine in the Crimea when trying to incorporate the 'Trans-Dnestr Republic', a splinter state on the left bank of the Dnestr populated by Russian colonists and their descendants. In the early years of independence, Moscow provided overt or tacit support to the Russians' resistance, but even after the Kremlin withdrew its support and subsequently also the Russian troops still garrisoned there, this region remained prone to criminality and resistance to central authority.[52] Moscow was similarly disruptive in Azerbaijan: when the Russian 366th Motor-Rifle Regiment withdrew from the ethnic Armenian enclave of Karabakh in 1993, its entire arsenal was left behind for insurgents to arm themselves.[53] Whether this was an act of central policy or local initiative is still unclear, but if the latter then no charges have been brought against the commanders authorising it. After all, in the countries of the Caucasus, the challenge often comes from rather more overt threats, such as terrorism, regionalism and banditry. Kosovo, Chechnya, Dagestan, Crimea, Transdnestria, Karabakh, South Ossetia, Abkhazia, Nakhichevan – postcommunist Europe is a patchwork of territories with little reason to accept notional political allegiances, and in many cases with the weapons and the will to try to change them.

Responses: think nationally, act regionally?

This chapter has indicated only some of the myriad soft security challenges facing the new states of postcommunist Europe. While they are serious and often seem intractable, it is important to keep them in perspective. One reason why these issues are so important is precisely because – outside the Balkans and Caucasus – the dangers of overt threats have failed to materialise. Russia has neither fragmented nor fallen to a dictatorial demagogue. The other post-Soviet states have not become Russian satellites. Border disputes have largely led to negotiations, not war.

One underlying lesson seems to be that successful resolution of the soft security challenges facing postcommunist Europe depends on two key requisites. First, clear political will. Little can be done while national governments are unprepared to admit to or address the problem or, worse still, are corrupted. Political leaders such as Hungary's Orbán have been active in their desire to combat organised crime and instability, even if there is the fear that this may be at too great a cost to civil liberties. In contrast, while Boris Yeltsin regularly thundered against organised crime, his reign was marked by a steady expansion and consolidation of its power. There was money in the national coffers to fight the Chechens, but the courts and police suffered year-on-year cuts in their funding. The result is that in many towns the police lack the petrol to mount regular patrols, much less the staff and resources to take on organised crime.

Similarly, in 1995 President Leonid Kuchma characterised organised crime as 'the main threat to the creation and development' of the Ukrainian state.[54] Since then, there has been a regular stream of edicts and sound-bites, but few meaningful efforts to combat corruption and clientelism, except when carried out by his political rivals. This is despite the evident negative impact the problem is having on Ukraine, whose apparent stability conceals widespread corruption, insider dealing and capital flight which continue to deter potential investors. A survey in 1998 found more businesses reporting higher (and growing) levels of bureaucratic corruption than in any other country, and the European Bank of Reconstruction and Development put the average cost of bribes to firms in Ukraine at 6.5 per cent of annual company revenue, above the Commonwealth of Independent States average of 5.7 per cent.[55] Between mid 1999 and mid 2000, the Ukrainian police's estimate of the number of firms and proportion of gross domestic product controlled by organised crime rose from 12,000 firms and 42 per cent to 14,600 firms and 48 per cent.[56] This even has a direct impact on weapons proliferation. A parliamentary inquiry found evidence of massive illegal arms sales abroad, especially in the period 1991–96, by official export agencies working with corrupt politicians.[57]

The second pre-requisite for addressing soft security challenges is cross-community and cross-border cooperation. While this cannot substitute for genuine political will, it can provide the necessary tools and intelligence to combat what are, after all, often explicitly transnational challenges. Consider, for example, the threat of nuclear weapons and material proliferation. The fear inevitably arose that criminalisation, military indiscipline and economic collapse plus nuclear arsenals and nuclear power programmes was the perfect recipe for runaway nuclear proliferation. There have been individual attempts to sell nuclear material, although these have generally been small amounts and not of weapons grade. Most of these cases are opportunistic and amateur. On the whole, however, this threat appears to be being tackled by a combination of international aid and pressure and internal controls. Most postcommunist states have tightened up the relevant controls and audit procedures. For example, the Russian Nuclear Energy Ministry claimed in October 1998 that there had been no thefts of nuclear materials in the preceding three years.[58] The Obninsk Methodological and Training Centre now trains inspectors for the police and customs service in preventing proliferation, in part thanks to $30 million provided by the United States to de-militarise and secure Russia's ten 'closed cities' devoted to the Soviet nuclear weapons programme.[59]

The immediate challenges facing both established and emerging democracies are not those of war but of crime, instability and misgovernance. These problems are inevitably of regional, even global, importance. In an age of global commerce, cyberbanking and an enlarging EU, national borders are increasingly permeable, sometimes even irrelevant, and national jurisdictions complementary rather than exclusive. The 1999 Bank of New York scandal not only saw the United States' oldest bank embroiled in the alleged laundering of around $9 billion illegally transferred from Russia as a result of both embezzlement and organised crime, but also involved dozens of other banks around the world, from China to the UK.[60] By the same token, a particular by-product of insecurity, instability and conflict is the displacement of people, whether refugees fleeing persecution or migrants looking for a brighter future. Central and Eastern Europe has been witness to a wholesale reshuffling of peoples, whether ethnic Russians returning to the motherland from Soviet successor states or communities ejected by the ethnic cleansings of the former Yugoslavia. This often has wider implications. Sheltering migrant and refugee communities can be an expensive burden on over-stretched state budgets; it can become a politically contentious issue, fuelling xenophobia and extremism. It can undermine the legitimacy and security of national boundaries, not least as these population movements can also conceal the spread of organised criminal gangs and provide them with a new constituency.

Responses must be similarly transnational. Policing Kosovo, for example, is the job of both a 3,000-strong international police force within the UN Mission to Kosovo and a local force which is being raised under international auspices and trained and equipped by foreign aid.[61] This draws on the success in Albania of the Western European Union's Multinational Advisory Police Element.[62] Beyond this, Interpol and Europol are strengthening their links in the region, while the EU launched a $7.6 million anti-drug project in the Balkans in 1999.[63] Nor is this simply a question of operational cooperation and support. Education, encouragement and the propagation of good governance are as important. The FBI's International Law Enforcement Academy in Budapest trains officers from across postcommunist Europe, just as International Monetary Fund and US government workshops and seminars in Moscow, Kyiv, Uzhgorod and Washington are helping to spread awareness of the dangers of high-level corruption and how to combat it.[64]

Conclusion

It is worth revisiting a fundamental question: is the rise of crime, disorder and ungovernability in postcommunist Europe really a security issue? And, if so, is its importance confined merely to that region? It would be wilfully blinkered not to see these phenomena as challenges not just to regional but global security. Organised crime is a transnational phenomenon, as groups make alliances and trade illicit commodities across national borders and expand their own operations by conquest and coalition. The ready availability and low prices of looted weapons are helping to fuel criminal, terrorist and insurgent violence across the globe. Meanwhile, the routes of the thriving international narcotics-trafficking industry criss-cross the region with little regard to national frontiers, bringing Central Asian opiates and Russian synthetic amphetamines to Europe. Unstable neighbours are unpredictable ones, and also potential sources of refugees and economic migrants.

Besides, for the West, this is also a moral challenge. The temptations to demonise the peoples of postcommunist Europe as criminals, opportunistic migrants and incompetents, and to create some 'fortress Europe', no doubt with the Russians outside the walls, are as inevitable as they are dangerous. After the First World War, the victors responded with a short-sighted vindictiveness which laid the seeds for the Second. After the Second World War, the Marshall Plan helped to ensure that Italy, Japan and West Germany, at least, could emerge as stable, democratic neighbours and dynamic economic partners. An understandable preoccupation with military security issues, however, obscured the softer dangers and helped to create conditions in which organised crime could thrive in both Italy and Japan. Peace in Europe, furthermore, was bought in part at others' expense, as geopolitical tensions were not eased so much as projected into the developing world. The end of the Cold War represents another historical opportunity to learn from past mistakes and successes, and create structures able to manage soft security challenges as effectively as NATO deters the more obvious military threats.

Notes

1 H. Orenstein, 'Crime and punishment: old problems and new dilemmas for an emerging eastern and central Europe', *Low Intensity Conflict and Law Enforcement*, 1:1 (1992), 14–41.

2 W. Miller, A. Grødeland and T. Koshechkina, 'Victims or accomplices?: extortion and bribery in Eastern Europe', in A. Ledeneva and M. Kurkchiyan (eds.), *Economic Crime in Russia* (The Hague, Kluwer Academic Publishers, 2000).

3 A. Musah and R. Castle, *Eastern Europe's Arsenal on the Loose: Managing Light Weapons Flows to Conflict Zones*, BASIC Paper 26 (London and Washington, DC, BASIC, 1998) (www.basicint.org/bpaper26.htm).

4 M. Galeotti, 'Chechnya: the theft of a nation', *Boundary and Security Bulletin*, 2:1 (1994), 69–72.

5 T. Orság-Land, 'Hungary's controversial plan to get tough on organised crime', *International Police Review*, 11 (1999), 20–21.

6 This section draws with permission from M. Galeotti, 'Russia's criminal army', *Jane's Intelligence Review*, 11:6 (1999), 8–9.

7 *Moskovskii komsomolets* (20 June 1994).

8 S. Handelman, *Comrade Criminal: Russia's New Mafiya* (New Haven, Yale University Press, 1995); J. Serio and V. Razinkin, 'Thieves professing the code: the traditional role of the *vory v zakone* in Russia's criminal world and adaptations to a new social reality', *Low Intensity Conflict and Law Enforcement*, 4:1 (1995), 72–88; A. Anderson, 'The red mafia: a legacy of communism', in E. Lazear (ed.), *Economic Transition in Eastern Europe and Russia: Realities of Reform* (Washington DC, Hoover Institute Press, 1995); W. H. Webster et al., *Russian Organized Crime: Global Organized Crime Project (CSIS Task Force Report)* (Washington, DC, Centre for Strategic and International Studies, 1997); P. Williams (ed.), *Russian Organized Crime: The New Threat?* (London, Frank Cass & Co., 1997); M. Galeotti, 'The mafiya and the new Russia', *Australian Journal of Politics and History*, 44:3 (1998), 415–29; and M. Galeotti, 'The Russian mafiya: economic penetration at home and abroad', in Ledeneva and Kurkchiyan (eds.), *Economic Crime in Russia*.

9 A. Lyakhovskii and V. Zabrodin, *Tainy afganskoi voiny* (Moscow, Planet 2, 1994), p. 214.

10 AFP (29 June 1999).

11 G. Turbiville, 'Mafia in uniform: the criminalization of the Russian armed forces' (www-leav.army.mil/fmso/geo/pubs/mafia.htm.); T. Waters, 'Crime in the Russian military', Conflict Studies Research Centre Paper C90 (Sandhurst, CSRC, 1996); M. Galeotti, 'Russia's grafting generals', *Jane's Intelligence Review*, 10:4 (1998), 8–9; and R. Starr, 'Russia's military: corruption in the higher ranks', *Perspective*, 9:2 (1998), 17–23.

12 *RFE/RL Newsline* (31 July 1998).

13 *Kommersant-Daily* (17 July 1997).

14 *Moscow News* (21 January 1993); *Trud* (10 June 1994); and *Literatur'naya gazeta* (25 January 1995).

15 *Moskovskii komsomolets* (19 October 1994); and *Moscow News* (28 October 1994).

16 For conflicting views of the danger posed, see P. Williams and P. Woessner, 'The real threat of nuclear smuggling', *Scientific American*, 274 (1996), 38–42 and 'International: nuclear smuggling', *Oxford Analytica Daily Brief* (18 August 1994).

17 *Nezavisimaya gazeta* (27 October 1995).

18 *Trud* (19 June 1999).

19 C. Smith and D. Sagramoso, 'Small arms trafficking may export Albania's anarchy', *Jane's Intelligence Review* 11:1 (1999), 24–8.

20 M. Galeotti, 'Conventional weapons black marketing: the Albanian "Arsenal of Anarchy"', presentation to FBI/George C. Marshall Center for Security Studies conference 'Organised Crime: The National Security Dimension', Garmisch (Germany), 31 August 1999.

21 D. Gambetta, *The Sicilian Mafia: The Business of Private Protection* (Cambridge, MA, Harvard University Press, 1996); F. Varese, 'What is the Russian Mafia?', *Low Intensity Conflict and Law Enforcement*, 5:2 (1996), 129–38; and F. Varese, 'Is Sicily the future of Russia?', *Archives europeenes de sociologie*, xxxv:2 (1994), 224–58.

22 Williams, *Russian Organized Crime*, 24–26.

23 Galeotti, 'The Russian mafiya'.

24 *Kommersant-Daily* (15 March 1997).

25 *Nezavisimaya gazeta* (6 February 1997).

26 *Austin American-Stateman* (17 November 1997). (http://www.austin360.com/news/11nov/17/russgun17.htm).

27 S. Kettle, '"Black sheriffs" and lawless cops in the Czech Republic', *Transitions*, 2 (8 March 1996), p. 9.

28 Conversation with the author, 12 August 1999.

29 J. Spense and B. Hebenton, 'Crime and insecurity in the new Europe: some observations from Poland', in M. Brogden (ed.), *The British Criminology Conferences: Selected Proceedings, Volume 2* (Loughborough, British Society of Criminology, 1999), 103–32.

30 T. Ország-Land, 'Elite force to target Russian mafia', *International Police Review*, 13 (1999), 24.

31 Galeotti, 'The Russian mafiya'.

32 C. Ulrich, 'Transnational organized crime and law enforcement cooperation in the Baltic states', *Transnational Organized Crime*, 3:2 (1997), 111–30; A. Vilks and D. Bergmanis, 'Global organized crime in Latvia and the Baltics', in E. Viano (ed.), *Global Organized Crime and International Society* (Burlington, VT, Ashgate, 1999), 63–70.

33 'Baltic states: crime centre', *Oxford Analytica Daily Brief* (12 September 1994).

34 *BBC Summary of World Broadcasts: Part 1, Former USSR* (8 September 1995).

35 *The European* (2–8 December 1994).

36 E. Plywaczewski, 'Organized crime in Poland', *Transnational Organized Crime*, 3:3 (1997), 109–25.

37 R. Friedman, 'The most dangerous mobster in the world', *Village Voice* (22 May 1998); A. Wright, 'Organized crime in Hungary', *Transnational Organized Crime*, 3:1 (1997), 68–86; S. Lefebvre, 'Crime and society in Hungary: a survey', *Low Intensity Conflict and Law Enforcement*, 6:1 (1997, 99–110).

38 Conversation with the author, January 1998.

39 P. Valpolini, 'The role of police-military units in peace-keeping', *International Police Review*, 14 (1999), 22–3.

40 M. Galeotti, 'Turkish organized crime: where state, crime and rebellion conspire', *Transnational Organized Crime*, 4:1 (2000), 25–41.

41 G. Xhudo, 'Men of purpose: the growth of Albanian criminal activity', *Transnational Organized Crime*, 2:1 (1996), 18–19; and M. Galeotti, 'The Albanian connection', *International Police Review*, 10 (1998), 1–20.

42 *The Times* (24 March 1999).

43 A. Jamieson and A. Silj, 'Migration and criminality: the case of Albanians in Italy', *Ethnobarometer*, Working Paper 1 (Rome, Ethnobarometer, 1998).

44 Smith and Sagramoso, 'Small arms trafficking may export Albania's anarchy'.

45 F. Sabahi, 'Albanians moving in on Italian organised crime', *International Police Review*, 4 (1997), 15; *Corriere della Sera* (19 January 1999); and *Philadelphia Inquirer* (15 March 1999).

46 *The Sunday Times* (4 July 1999).

47 Reuters (20 May 1999).

48 M. Galeotti, 'Russia's far east–Russian or Eastern?', *Boundary and Security Bulletin*, 601 (Spring 1998), 61–8.

49 A. Krushelnycky, 'East-west split in Ukraine heightened by presidential election', *RFE/RL Newsline* (12 November 1999).

50 T. Kuzio, 'Crime still Ukraine's greatest enemy', *Jane's Intelligence Review*, 9:1 (1997), 10–13; L. Shelley, 'Organized crime and corruption in Ukraine', *Demokratizatsiya*, 6:4 (1998), 648–63.

51 *Krasnaya zvezda* (16 August 1994).

52 T. Waters, 'On crime and corruption in the Republic of Moldova', *Low Intensity Conflict and Law Enforcement*, 6:2 (1997), 84–92.

53 Human Rights Watch Report, *Azerbaijan: Seven Years of Conflict in Nagorno-Karabakh*, (New York, Human Rights Watch, 1994).

54 *BBC Summary of World Broadcasts: Part 1, Former USSR* (5 August 1995).

55 Shelley, 'Organized crime and corruption in Ukraine', 649; P. Goble, 'Overcoming corruption', *RFE/RL Newsline* (16 November 1999).

56 'Ukraine: organised crime', *Oxford Analytica East Europe Daily Brief* (28 April 2000).

57 T. Kuzio, 'Kyiv looks to control runaway arms trade', *Jane's Intelligence Review*, 11:10 (1999), 17–22.

58 *Interfax* (22 October 1998).

59 T. Ország-Land, 'Protecting nuclear materials', *International Police Review*, 13 (1999, 23).

60 *Washington Post* (1 September 1999).

61 K. Nuthall, 'Policing Kosovo', *International Police Review*, 14 (1999), 24.

62 M. Galeotti, 'Turning the corner in Albania', *International Police Review*, 16 (2000), 22.

63 Reuters (12 February 1999).

64 T. Ország-Land, 'Weeding out corruption', *International Police Review*, 15 (1999), 49.

10

Economic security in postcommunist Europe

James Sperling

The traditional separation of national interests into those driving the 'high' and 'low' politics of international affairs is no longer serviceable.[1] That distinction has been rendered obsolete by the changed context of state interaction, driven in large part by the economic and security interdependence of states. The long-lived distinction between the 'high' politics of diplomacy and the 'low' politics of commerce had largely obscured the interdependence between these two fields of action; it removed the need to question whether and how they interact and to what effect. The emergence of economic security as a policy problem is more than a reaction to the absence of military conflict and its diminished prospect in the European area, particularly among the great powers. Rather, it reflects an assumption that in post-Cold War Europe, issues of political economy must be treated as elements of the new security agenda rather than as problems subject to the simple calculus of welfare maximisation and peripheral to the problem of war and peace.[2]

The economic security agenda raises an important question: is the putative threat posed to the systemic or milieu goals of Western European states; to the integrity of European states and authority structures, particularly in postcommunist Europe; or to the societal integrity of the member states of the European security space? Put differently, does the economic security agenda suggest that the threats posed to the contemporary European state system cannot be treated as the relatively simple problem of identifying state-to-state threats that unequivocally represent a state-centric security calculus where the state is both subject and object of the analysis? In this chapter I attempt to answer that question by investigating the structural changes that have occurred in the European state system, the substantive elements of the economic security agenda, and the latent interdependencies of the European Union (EU) and North Atlantic Treaty Organisation (NATO) enlargements.

The new security agenda: the problem of redefining security after the Cold War

The construction of a stable security order in post-Cold War Europe has been vexed by an inability to settle upon a definition of security or a consensus on the security threats posed to the European order. This conceptual muddle has been driven in large part by the expansion of the security agenda, particularly the effort to include and cope with the challenges posed by economic security. Despite growing official and academic recognition that economic security *does* play a prominent role in shaping the contours of the post-Cold War European security space, many security analysts persist in looking backwards. In a recent overview of the nexus formed by the economic and military dimensions of security, Michael Mastanduno emphasised four strands of thought that have dominated the discourse on economic security: the relationship between trade and peace; the impact of security relationships on international economic cooperation and conflict; the use of economic instruments of statecraft; and efforts to establish the links between economic and security factors in domestic and international politics. Yet his overview slights the important contribution made by European scholars working on the multifaceted nature of economic security.[3] The literature reviewed by Mastanduno generally treats the state as the unequivocal and unchallenged actor. Consequently, changes in the international structure of military and economic power are causally linked to changes in the security of the state. This perspective is insufficient to the task of understanding the challenge facing the construction of a stable European security order.

Although there are many definitions of economic security, the evolution of the contemporary European state system suggests that economic security has three identifiable and separable elements. First, economic security reflects a concern over the ability of the state to protect the societal and economic integrity of a society. Second, economic security involves the ability of a state to act as an effective gatekeeper between domestic and international society. Third, economic security requires states, in cooperation with others, to foster a stable international environment in order to reinforce cooperation in the military sector and to reap the welfare gains of economic openness.[4] These three dimensions point to three categories of threat facing European states today: societal security, which focuses on threats to the civil contract originating from external developments ranging from macroeconomic instability to environmental refugees;[5] state security, which reflects the traditional locus of security studies and is preoccupied with the ability of the state to maintain territorial integrity and sustain an autonomy threatened by (in)voluntary regionalisation or globalisation; and systemic security, which is driven by a desire to create favourable external milieu or context of action that facilitates the national pursuit of power and plenty.

Economic security has emerged as *the* security problem for postcommunist Europe.[6] A focus on the economic dimension of security redirects our attention to the consequences of macroeconomic malfeasance by a major

economic power, the collapse of financial markets triggered by a major
debt repudiation, a generalised hyperinflation, or a collapse of currency
markets; these could, singly or in combination, threaten the very survival of
the postcommunist states, nullify the economic clauses of the domestic
social contract, upend the economic foundation of national political stability or reintroduce the corrosive competition between states that preceded
the Second World War. The emergence of economic security as an integral
part of the overall security order raises an important question: Why have
these new security threats risen to prominence in the post-Cold War
period?

The most promising category of response focuses on the changed structure of the European state system and the changing nature of the European
state.[7] The connectedness of European states has been facilitated and reinforced by the success of the post-war institutions of European economic
and political integration. Geography, technological innovations (particularly the revolution in information technologies and the linking of national
economies and societies by the world-wide web), the convergence around
the norms of political and economic openness, and the rising 'dynamic
density' – defined as the 'quantity, velocity, and diversity of transactions'[8] –
of the Euro-atlantic political space have stripped away the prerogatives and
eliminated the autonomy once afforded powerful states by territorial sovereignty. These elements of the contemporary European state system have
linked the states of Europe together irrevocably and now facilitate the
transformation of domestic disequilibria in the postcommunist states into
security threats for the affluent states of Europe.

The 'dynamic density' of the European state system has fostered the
formation of a collective European identity that has cultural, political,
economic and, most importantly, geographic components. The geopolitical redefinition of Europe after 1992 removed a barrier to the westward
projection of economic or political disturbances that may emerge in
Central or South-Eastern Europe. The political commitment of the EU to
the postcommunist states has led to a presumptive membership right in
that important Western economic club at a time when those states cannot
yet be safely assimilated into the institutional arrangements that brought
peace and prosperity to Western Europe. All the states that can be reasonably assumed to occupy a part of Europe have been extended the explicit or
implicit right to 'belong' to the EU. This presumed (and largely acknowledged) membership right has produced a paradox: rather than the boundaries of the European club serving as a fire-wall between the stable and
unstable states of Europe, the expansion of the club has forced the Western
European states to seek mechanisms and policies that ameliorate the
sources of instability these new states will inevitably bring with them.

The political unwillingness to disenfranchise the postcommunist states from eventual membership in the EU, and the structural inability of the EU states to disassociate themselves from the former, have three implications. First, the security threats positioned at the top of the hierarchy of threat in the contemporary European system largely originate within those states with either weak civil societies or weak state structures. In this sense, it is domestic instabilities, either as the sources of conflict and threat or as facilitators of threat, that are projected externally into the wider European political space and thereby threaten the values or stability of specific states or the region as a whole.[9] Second, Europe can no longer be adequately described as a system of discrete states with an 'egotist' definition of security. Europe has been partially, if not completely, transformed into a community of states facing a commonly defined set of threats. The evolution of a community bound together by a common fate thus implies that threats to any society, state or system are easily translated into threats against all, albeit with different levels of intensity and concern. This vulnerability in combination with the evolution of a collective identity has produced an irresistible pressure on the postcommunist states to conform to the norms of the EU/NATO club. This development suggests a third implication: the vocabulary informing the traditional approach to statecraft and defining the problem of security is neither relevant nor serviceable in the changed European context. The state is no longer the sole, or necessarily most important, actor; states no longer perform the relatively simple task of balancing power, threats or interests; and the referents defining the national interest are no longer exclusively national.

The changed threat environment in postcommunist Europe can be ascribed to the *negative* redefinition of threat: European states are no longer preoccupied with the maintenance of territorial integrity or the enhancement of national welfare; rather, states now seek to ensure an absence of migratory flows ignited by economic collapse or environmental disasters. A state-centric approach is no longer viable because, unlike in the past, security threats require joint rather than unilateral action. While a state-centric approach can be salvaged by an analytical sleight of hand – both system-wide goals ('milieu goals') and domestic goals (maintaining societal tranquillity) can be reduced to components of the national interest – there is no easy way to account for the apparent altruism or inattention to relative gains considerations by the NATO and EU states in their dealings with the postcommunist states (with the possible exception of Russia) in the last decade. The economic security agenda suggests that we can no longer fruitfully conceive of security within a framework that is restricted to specific dyads of states. Security threats cannot be simply disaggregated into the capabilities and intentions of states; primacy can no longer be attributed to the state as either agent or object. Rather, security threats have acquired a system-wide significance that requires an alternative conceptualisation. Contagion theory is highly suggestive in this context.

A key insight of contagion theory is that the diffusion of war 'is most likely to operate among those nations that share high levels of *interaction*'.[10] In parallel fashion, the porousness of national boundaries in the contemporary European state system has made it more likely that domestic disturbances – particularly those that are either economic or environmental in origin – are not easily contained within a single state and may well be diffused throughout the European system. The postulated ease with which domestic disturbances are transmitted across national boundaries *and* the difficulty of defending against those disturbances underline the strength and weakness of the contemporary state system: the openness of states and societies along an ever expanding spectrum of interaction provides greater levels of collective welfare than would otherwise be possible, yet the very transmission belts facilitating that welfare also provide the mechanisms of contagion and hinder the ability of the state to inoculate itself against disturbances within the subsystem. The dynamic density of the European system is a double-edged factor in the post-Cold War security order: while the increasing economic, normative and political interdependence between the states of Europe makes cooperative outcomes more likely, reinforces the emergence of a collective identity, and recasts both interests and threats within a collective frame of reference, that very interdependence has embedded within it a network of contagion mechanisms that facilitate the transformation of domestic infirmities into system-wide disturbances.

The threats to economic security are spread by at least four readily identifiable mechanisms of contagion: the dynamic density of the European political space; flawed or underdeveloped civil societies or political institutions of democracy; geographic propinquity; and cyberspace. Geographic propinquity and the ubiquity of cyberspace provide two important mechanisms of contagion in the contemporary European state system because they 'create structures of risks and opportunities that constrain the range of possible inter-nation interactions and make certain types of conflictual behavior more or less likely'.[11] First, the erasure of national boundaries and the potential irrelevance of geographic space are underlined by the growing importance of cyberspace. This mechanism of contagion escapes effective state control and provides the perfect instrument for non-state actors seeking to destabilise the European state system or one of its components. Second, geographic propinquity suggests that domestic disturbances in any of the postcommunist states, from ethnic strife to environmental degradation to the criminalisation of national economies or state structures, could initiate migratory flows leading to the external projection of domestic conflicts that could threaten system stability.

It is the dynamic density of the European security space, however, which provides the most pervasive and nettlesome mechanisms of contagion. Europe's dynamic density gives the European state system its distinctive character, particularly the erosion of meaningful national boundaries and the progressive loss of state control over the decisions of individuals, particularly within the sphere of the economy. The very transmission belts of economic prosperity – largely unrestricted capital markets, high levels of trade and the absence of exchange controls – also provide the mechanisms facilitating the criminalisation of national economies, the erosion of the authority and legitimacy of weak state structures in the states in transition, and exogenous shocks to national economies that states can no longer effectively control, particularly those along the periphery of the EU. Weak civil societies, ineffective or corrupted judiciaries and other political structures, and economies that are either criminalised or escape the effective jurisdiction of national authority plague these states. These states are not only hostage to their interdependence with the rest of Europe, but that interdependence provides a mechanism of contagion that transforms domestic disequilibria along the periphery into potential security threats to the states of affluent Europe. This circumstance underscores the importance of meeting the challenges of economic security in post-Cold War Europe.

The economic elements of the new security agenda

The discussion so far has focused on the structural and contextual changes in the European political space that have made it necessary to redefine security and to treat the economic dimension as a separate and co-equal element of the security calculus. It is generally accepted that systemic stability and the prospect for a peaceful and cooperative pan-European security order are largely contingent upon the successful transition to the market and multiparty democracy in postcommunist Europe.[12] Those transitions, in turn, are contingent upon a stable economic and military environment. Four economic policy areas – the macroeconomy, trade, finance and the environment – constitute the economic elements of the European security order.

The macroeconomic dimension

The security dimension of macroeconomic stability has been given resonance by the marketisation and democratisation efforts of the postcommunist European states. The role of a stable macroeconomic environment in the European security order is indirect, but is nonetheless critical to its stability. Macroeconomic stability and favourable macroeconomic conditions in Western Europe and the United States contributed to the rapid recovery of the postcommunist European economies following their collapse in the early 1990s and retarded the prospects of a return to non-democratic forms of governance. The importance of a stable macroeconomic environment for the success of the transitions in postcommunist Europe reflects the causal connection established in the minds of Europe's ruling elites between the macroeconomic collapse after 1929 and the ensuing political chaos of the 1930s: the competitive devaluations and the rise of currency and trading blocs in the 1930s were an ill-conceived response to the macroeconomic collapse beginning in 1929, facilitated the rise of fascism and provided the basis for the outbreak of war in Europe. The failure to cope with the macroeconomic instability of Europe prior to the Second World War informs the preoccupation with ensuring macroeconomic stability in the post-Cold War Euro-atlantic economy.

Treating macroeconomic policy as an element of the future European security order is not inconsistent with NATO communiqués since the Alliance's London Declaration in 1990 and may be reasonably inferred as a new security concern, albeit one that NATO is ill-equipped to affect. Yet macroeconomic policy remains an ambiguous candidate for inclusion in the security architecture of the post-Cold War world. Prior to 1989, the problem of macroeconomic policy cooperation was linked to the erosion of national autonomy in the conduct of monetary policy: the progressive integration of Euro-atlantic financial markets had amplified the impact of divergent monetary and fiscal policies on bilateral exchange rates and reduced national macroeconomic policy autonomy. Macroeconomic policy has only directly impinged upon security issues, however, when macroeconomic conflicts in the 1970s and 1980s, particularly between the US and Germany, limited political cooperation in the security sphere. Yet the interdependence between macroeconomic policy and security policy was weak and easily by-passed up to 1989: in the 1970s, for example, the Europeans made a successful effort to preclude the linkage of security concerns and macroeconomic policy by the US in the aftermath of the first oil crisis in 1973–74.

Macroeconomic policy stability shapes the prospects for a stable European security order in a number of ways. First, macroeconomic stability was the *sine qua non* for progress towards a single Europe and the transition to a single currency and monetary union beginning in 1999. The criteria of macroeconomic policy stability established in the Maastricht Treaty have become at a minimum the macroeconomic policy criteria for the whole of Europe, West, East and Central. There is, then, a nascent European macroeconomic regime that presents a common standard of macroeconomic performance, acting not only as a potential gatekeeper for future aspirants to the EU (and potentially to NATO as well) but bearing upon the continued deepening of the enlarged EU, particularly with respect to its ambitions in the security and foreign policy fields. Moreover, any future inability of the US and the European Central Bank to coordinate macroeconomic policy may reintroduce an enmity in economic relations that will spill over and corrode efforts at cooperation and integration in the military sphere, particularly on the establishment of a European Security and Defence Identity inside or outside NATO. Such a debate could compromise the security interests not only of the Cold War members of NATO, but place the Central and Eastern European states in the awkward position of having to face the diplomatic choice faced by Germany over the post-war period – choosing between its European identity and the American security guarantee. Unlike the Cold War period, where membership in NATO (and the EU) was largely involuntary for Germany, the Central and Eastern European states have the luxury of choice; so, however, does the US.

The EU, then, has gone the farthest in establishing the criteria for macroeconomic convergence in the Euro-atlantic area. The convergence criteria of the Maastricht Treaty have been embraced not only by the member states of the EU, but also by its prospective members as well. Moreover, the International Monetary Fund (IMF), in its stand-by arrangements with the postcommunist states, has contributed to the adoption and enforcement of the Maastricht norms. The legitimacy accorded the Maastricht norms within Europe faces the problems of enforcement (and free riding) and coordination. The IMF, the EU or the Group of Seven (G7), for example, can enforce these macroeconomic norms with countries that approach either institution as a supplicant for balance of payments or other financial support or, in the case of the EU, seek membership. Consequently, these institutions have exercised leverage over the postcommunist European states, particularly when conformity with these norms is an implicit criterion for EU membership.[13] Within the European context, the limits of macroeconomic divergence have been set by the monetary dominance of the European Central Bank and the fiscal criteria enumerated in the Maastricht Treaty and the subsequent European stability pact. So long as the credibility of the Euro remains at question in the markets, the fiscal criteria will be largely self-enforcing and inescapable for the postcommunist European states seeking full membership in the EU.

The ability of the Euro-atlantic states to expand the zone of security eastwards, therefore, depends upon domestic economic and political developments that are extremely sensitive to the macroeconomic environment that they face. Yet it is also the case that the provision of that macroeconomic environment cannot be guaranteed. Nor do the nations of the Euro-atlantic economy make macroeconomic decisions based upon these impor-tant security considerations. The narrow pursuit of national advantage in the conduct of macroeconomic policy, while it can lead to minor welfare losses for the North American and EU states, could jeopardise the prospects for a stable European security order.

The resolution of the security dimension of macroeconomic policy is located in the acknowledgement of the difficulty of macroeconomic coor-dination and convergence; and in the embrace of a two-speed Europe that is divided between those countries that have met the Maastricht criteria and those that aspire to do so. This solution protects the integrity of European monetary union in its infancy, creates a stable macroeconomic core at the centre of Europe, provides a point of orientation for nations along the European periphery, and fosters greater political balance in the Euro-atlantic economy that could facilitate enhanced US–EU cooperation on macroeconomic and exchange rate policies.

The trade dimension

Trade was treated as a security issue within the North Atlantic area during the post-war period. The first and most sustained security concern was the sale or transfer of military or dual-use technologies to Warsaw Pact member states. The end of the Cold War and dissolution of the Warsaw Pact trans-formed erstwhile adversaries into important security partners of the NATO states. The transfer of dual-use technologies to Central and Eastern Europe is now considered as an additional means for aiding the transition to the market economy, as a mechanism for integrating the postcommunist states into the broader global economy, and as critical to achieving weapons inter-operability between future and present NATO member states.

The second general security concern linked to trade was the vulnerabil-ity arising from too great a dependence upon foreign suppliers of critical raw materials and intermediate or finished goods. Trade vulnerability has receded as a security concern, primarily because commodity cartels have been unable on a long-term basis to set the price or fix the supply of raw materials on the international market. Moreover, dependence upon the foreign supply of intermediate or finished goods no longer poses a credible security threat: the sources of supply are dispersed within the Organisation for Economic Cooperation and Development (OECD), much of the merchandise trade registered by industrial countries is intra-industry and increasingly intra-firm, and the deregulation of national markets reduces both the incentives and opportunities for the restriction of trade for politi-cal advantage between the major poles of economic power, particularly in the European security space.

Yet trade remains a part of the post-Cold War security agenda in Europe. The security dimension of trade flows from the palpable and incontestable welfare benefits attributed to freer trade: trade contributes to the more efficient allocation of resources within and between national economies, to greater levels of consumption at lower prices, to economic growth and development, and to a higher level of employment. The stability of the European political space is partially dependent upon the ability of the Eastern Europeans to exploit market opportunities in the West and thereby lessen the financial transfers required from the West to prepare these states for membership in the EU or NATO.

The welfare benefits and financial savings derived from trade are compounded by the political benefits of closer trade interdependencies: freer trade with the OECD states provides a mechanism for a market-driven restructuring of these nations' economies. Unimpeded trade provides a non-intrusive mechanism for achieving the task of economic transition. Trade delegates the task of economic transition to individual economic agents without entailing the political costs and engendering the political resentments of direct interventions in the economy by Western advisers, bankers and political authorities. The security importance of freer trade between Eastern and Western Europe is located in the contribution it can make to systemic stability via its support of the successful transition to the market and the stabilisation of democracy.

Finally, trade is an element of the European security order owing to the peculiar circumstances of the post-Cold War world: the nations along the periphery of the Euro-atlantic economy have placed a political and security patina on their economic relationships with the industrialised nations. Just as the macroeconomy creates the framework conditions for the transition to the market economy and the support of democratisation, trade (along with investment) is the engine of growth that will consolidate those transitions. If the postcommunist states are denied markets for their goods, the restructuring of their economies will be retarded, their economies will expand more slowly, and their political reform efforts may be severely handicapped. In this respect, trade is a pillar of the European security order and must be considered as such until the transitions to the market and democracy are consolidated and irreversible.

The final destination of the pan-European trading system will reflect some combination of political choice and economic destiny. The political choices facing the nations of the European security space are already embedded in a large number of regional, bilateral and multilateral arrangements governing trade between the prosperous and impoverished halves of Europe. What is incontrovertible, however, is that trade is one of the primary and most efficient transmission belts of economic growth and development.

A dense web of trade interdependencies between the nations of Western, Central and Eastern Europe would contribute to greater amity within the European security space and consequently make easier and more likely the construction of a comprehensive and inclusive set of security institutions. Trade interdependence can create a basis for political trust, an externality supporting cooperation in other areas impinging directly upon or requiring the sacrifice or pooling of national sovereignty. Enhanced trade between the two halves of Europe also carries with it the potential for premature demands for participation in military security institutions such as NATO or the Western European Union (WEU); for the development of trade interdependencies that are not complemented by membership in one of the leading institutions of military security, namely NATO or the WEU; or for the natural regionalisation of the European economy that leads to the alienation or disassociation of Europe and the US.

Trade only poses a danger to the European security order if it encourages the progressive disassociation or even fragmentation of the two pillars of the Euro-atlantic economy. If the progressive openness of the Euro-atlantic economy between 1949 and 1989 was simply a function of systemic bipolarity, then the post-Cold War European security space should eventually be characterised by preferential or regional trading agreements.[14] As a consequence, the decay of multilateral free trade will loosen the bounds that have entwined the security interests of North America and Europe, and regional trading arrangements will inevitably engender conflict between North America and Europe. The self-interest of the major players, particularly the US, Germany, France and the United Kingdom, counsels against that development. Despite the fiasco at the Seattle trade summit, there is ample evidence that multilateralism is not a spent force in the Euro-atlantic area and that the Eastern European states are being slowly integrated into that economy. The extension of the Single European Act norms to the real sector of the European economy has contributed to the integration of the postcommunist states into the Euro-atlantic economy, just as the accession strategy outlined by the EU requires the conformity of the prospective members to the *acquis communautaire*. The normative congruence of the European economy does not suggest that there will be a contiguity of economic and political boundaries in post-Cold War Europe, but it does demonstrate that the EU is uniquely placed to establish and enforce the norms governing economic activity in the European security space.

The financial dimension

The transition to a market-driven and entrepreneurial economy requires large and sustained capital inflows. But capital inflows into the postcommunist states were initially offset by sustained capital outflows, reflecting not only the uncertainty of individual economic agents about the pace and final destination of economic and political reform but also the need to service hard currency debt. The process of correcting the malformation of the postcommunist economies was initially handicapped by the budget deficits of the industrialised West and more recently by the efforts of the EU states to meet the fiscal criteria of the Maastricht Treaty. These two conditions limited the level of financial aid that was made available to the transition states and created a situation where capital flowed from east to west in order to meet sovereign debt obligations. Net direct foreign investment in eleven Central and Eastern European countries by the eleven major industrial countries, for example, amounted to only $36.5 billion between 1990 and 1997.[15] Sovereign debt obligations also placed a privileged claim on domestic savings and export earnings.

The external debt obligations of these states placed a drag on the process of economic reform. Debt service requirements sustained an outflow of capital from these countries, where it was most desperately needed, to Western commercial banks and creditor governments. The geopolitical position and importance of these states to the security of the Euro-atlantic area suggested that their debt service obligations should be treated as something more than the relatively simple problem of protecting the balance sheets of commercial banks – rather, they represented a key element of the new security agenda even though they neither portended the onset of war nor corresponded to the traditional conceptualisation of security.

The stability and solvency of the international financial system is the commonly identified connection between sovereign debt default and national security. Sovereign default by any of the postcommunist European states would not have disrupted the wider international financial system, although it might have created difficulties for German commercial banks in particular. Default, however, would have led to the stagnation of economic and political reform in a number of postcommunist states. The stability of the European security order was not directly threatened by the inability (debt default) or unwillingness (debt repudiation) of these states to service their external debts, but by the economic consequences of servicing external debt with domestic savings. Either debt default or debt repudiation would lower the overall level of investment in these economies because both foreign and domestic investors would have disincentives to invest and incentives to disinvest. Sovereign debt overhang reduced the ability of these states to finance the economic transition and strained the emerging and fragile democratic political fabric in these countries.

The transition to the market was impeded by the burden of debt facing some of those nations, particularly Albania, Poland, Hungary and the

Russian Federation. The primary impediment to the transition, however, was the difficulty of the task itself, rather than debt overhang. The Group of Twenty-Four states have been unable (or unwilling) to meet the investment needs of the postcommunist states. This reflects disputes over relative responsibility for financing the transition – in the US Congress, in particular, there is a scarcely suppressed belief that it is somehow Europe's problem – as well as the constraints imposed by the fiscal criteria of the Maastricht Treaty. Yet the formal international institutions aiding the transition to the market – particularly the G7, the international financial institutions and the Paris and London Clubs – cannot be said to have failed the states in transition. Where the bulk of the debt has been held by governments, as in the case of Poland, the G7 fashioned a rather generous solution.[16] The G7 fear, expressed particularly by the Americans and Germans, that an economically destabilised Poland could disrupt the European security order provides a partial and compelling explanation of the preferred treatment of Polish debt. Nonetheless, Western governments have been unable to find a satisfactory solution to the Russian debt problem even though the aggregate level of debt is a relatively trivial amount if compared either with the annual aggregate defence expenditures of the NATO allies during the Cold War or the debt owed the Russian Federation by the erstwhile client states of the Soviet Union.

The cumulative economic consequences of debt overhang – slower economic growth and a more difficult transition to a sustainable market economy – have been largely absorbed by the Czech Republic, Hungary and Poland. As the case of the Russian Federation demonstrates in particular, however, it is the political consequences of a substantial debt overhang – the potential return to an involuntary economic autarky and to the resurgence of quasi-authoritarian government fuelled by widespread resentment of the West – which pose the greatest risks to the future stability of the European political space. Only in 2000 did the London Club of commercial creditors agree to write off 35 per cent of Russia's $32 billion debt owed to private banks, while the Russian government is still trying to reach agreement with the Paris Club of sovereign creditors to write off $42 billion of Soviet era debt.[17] If Western governments wish to build the future European security order upon a firm foundation, a delicate balance must be struck between guaranteeing that these states service their external debt and ensuring that the debt service burden neither undermines the transition to the market economy nor destabilises these fragile democracies. The failure to devote sufficient resources to the task at hand reflects an irony of post-Cold War Europe: at a time when the economic instruments of statecraft are the most effective and essential to the stability of the European security order, the major European and North

American states lack either the fiscal wherewithal or political will to exploit an opportunity to assure the continuation of the long post-war peace.

The environmental dimension

Even though there is a large and growing literature seeking to integrate transboundary pollution, resource conflicts and environmental degradation into the security framework, there is no commonly accepted definition or conceptualisation of environmental security.[18] Some argue that the environment should not be considered as a part of the post-Cold War security equation, some refuse to dignify the contention with a response and still others view environmental security as a concept for the future.[19] Yet the expansion of the security agenda to include an environmental dimension reflects a growing sense of vulnerability to the consequences of transboundary pollution and the ability to abate that pollution.

The environmental dimension of the new pan-European security order derives its importance from three variables. First, the cost of cleaning up the environmental damage done to the postcommunist states competes for the scarce financial resources necessary to effect the restructuring and transformation of those nations' economies. Second, the unabated and conscious degradation of the environment could cause domestic dislocations severe enough to set in motion equally disruptive migratory pressures that could initiate violent group-identity conflicts undermining civil order and perhaps the legitimacy of existing state institutions.[20] Third, the heavy reliance upon nuclear energy by the former Warsaw Pact states, combined in particular with their dependence upon poorly designed and constructed nuclear reactors, poses the deadly threat of transboundary radiation poisoning that could conceivably engulf the European continent.

The one dimension of environmental security that has salience for the contemporary European security order is the abuse of the regional commons that either starkly reduces the quality of life or jeopardises life itself – security threats that do not necessarily portend or generate violent conflict between states, but are likely to generate environmental refugees or environmentally motivated migration. Such population movements, precipitated by environmental migration within or between states, could strain the economic capacity of political systems or generate violent ethnic conflicts within multi-ethnic societies. Moreover, mass migration from Eastern to Western Europe driven by environmental degradation would portend a lowering of living standards in the West and generate political resentment aimed at those seeking relief from a degraded environment. An inevitable lowering of living standards, probable ethnic or group-identity conflicts and the strain on state capacity to cope with the side effects of migration might have one of two effects on Western European governments. First, it could lower the quality of democracy in the West owing to measures taken to mitigate the effects of accepting environmental refugees. Second, it could reinforce the economic wall dividing Europe with an environmental wall supported by the re-militarisation of Europe's borders on a national or EU basis. Moreover, in those states where an environmental catastrophe occurred, the restoration of state legitimacy or political order could lead to the formation of what Homer-Dixon calls 'hard regimes', defined as regimes which are 'authoritarian, intolerant of opposition, and militarized'.[21] While such a development in the European political space can be safely discounted, its occurrence would nonetheless undermine one of the bases of the European security order, the system-wide establishment of democratic governance, and intensify the security dilemma facing the European states.

Although there are a large number of threats to the European environment, there is at least one environmental threat that unequivocally meets the criteria of a threat to European security: transboundary nuclear radiation poisoning.[22] The safety flaws of nuclear reactors operating in postcommunist states, in both design and construction, threaten societal, state and systemic security. A severe nuclear accident like that which occurred at the Chernobyl power plant would cause not only widespread contamination of large tracts of land but death on a large scale. In many of the countries where those reactors are located, for example Lithuania and Slovakia, the geographic scope of the accident would be large enough to rend the social fabric and produce environmental refugees seeking refuge across national borders. Correspondingly, a nuclear accident that threatened societal integrity could also delegitimise these nations' fragile democracies. Thus a nuclear accident could generate the opportunity or demand for authoritarian governments that would have the collateral consequence of destabilising systemic security. The re-establishment of an authoritarian government in the Russian Federation or Ukraine would intensify the security dilemma facing the states of the European security area. The uncontrolled flow of environmental refugees in combination with the miscarriage of democracy could easily re-militarise Europe's borders and potentially re-divide the continent.

Geography has created a superficial divergence of interests among the nations of Europe. Distance serves as an informal index of the threat posed to the nation and governments appear to treat it as the primary indicator of vulnerability to a nuclear accident. This assessment of risk reflects a narrow definition of national security and ignores the larger contextual consequences of a severe nuclear accident, particularly in one of the postcommunist states. Environmental security plays a contextual role in the European security order, particularly the interrelated threats to societal, state and systemic security posed by an environmental catastrophe. The G7 has proven unable to grapple successfully with as clear cut a problem as that of nuclear safety, although the EU has added the closure of certain Soviet-designed reactors to the list of membership criteria. The G7 established the Nuclear Safety Fund in July 1992 as a multilateral response to this acknowledged problem. While the G7 pledged $700 million to repair nuclear reactors in the region, by 1999 only $260 million had been committed. An additional $257 million was contributed for the Chernobyl Shelter Fund in the late 1990s, although the estimated cost of containing the danger posed by the power plant was put at $760 million. The G7 pledged an additional $300 million to the Chernobyl Fund in March 2000.[23] As in the case of the sovereign debt issue, in a situation where the economic instruments of statecraft have become the most effective means of addressing the security dilemmas facing the industrialised West, the leading Western states are too constrained by fiscal policy or too preoccupied with burden sharing within the G7 to act in order to prevent a nuclear catastrophe.

Conclusion

The enlargements of the EU and NATO underline the interrelationship between these two elements of the emerging security order. The economic security agenda is relevant to the problem of enlarging the EU and NATO: it suggests that the positive externalities generated by postcommunist states' membership in both institutions – greater political-military security within NATO and greater political–economic welfare within the EU – could significantly improve the prospects for capturing and leveraging the security benefits commonly assigned to each institution. Thus any analysis of EU and NATO enlargement is inevitably informed by the need both to meet the economic and military requirements of security and to understand how these two elements of security intersect.

There are good reasons to support the parallel enlargements of the EU and NATO in the future. First, a parallel enlargement of the two organisations largely serves the security interests of the European states, at least from a systemic perspective. Inclusion in NATO will provide states with a reassuring security guarantee. Inclusion in the EU will provide a seal of approval that will transfer economic credibility to the postcommunist states. Second, the parallel enlargement of the EU and NATO would support the three norms that presently suffuse the regimes governing the European security order: democratic governance, collective security and conformity with the market. Finally, the governing norms of democratisation and marketisation (and adherence to the EU's *acquis communautaire*) generate two other important externalities: they create a common frame of reference for identifying and resolving conflicts of interest and a community of interest and values which makes possible a collective security system.

Just as the common command structure of NATO has contributed to the de-nationalisation of security policy within Europe, the EU has facilitated the progressive de-nationalisation of economic policy. NATO has contributed to the creation of a 'security community' within the Euro-atlantic political space just as the EU now serves the broader and pacific function of creating an 'economic security community'. Both NATO and the EU are products and agents of the domestication of inter-state relations in the European political space. The enlargements of the EU and NATO are *de facto* interdependent processes. This interdependence, in turn, argues for their parallel enlargements. The desired geopolitical contiguity of EU and NATO boundaries within Europe, particularly along the eastern periphery, is not simply a function of 'cartographic mysticism'.[24] Rather, it is derived from the real benefits derived from dual membership, particularly the contribution to collective identity formation and the strengthening of a nascent European security community. EU and NATO membership for the Central and Eastern European states offers the best guarantee that we will collectively meet the requirements of economic and military security in the coming decades.

Notes

1 S. Hoffmann, *World Disorders: Troubled Peace in the Post-Cold War Era* (Lanham, MD, Rowman & Littlefield Publishers, Inc., 1998), pp. 110–16; and S. Hoffmann, *Primacy or World Order* (New York, McGraw-Hill, 1978).

2 B. Buzan, O. Waever and J. de Wilde, *Security: A New Framework for Analysis* (Boulder, CO, Lynne Rienner, 1998); J. Sperling and E. Kirchner, 'Economic security and the problem of cooperation in post-Cold War Europe', *Review of International Studies*, 24:2 (1998), 221–37; and J. Peterson and H. Ward, 'Coalitional instability and the new multidimensional politics of security: a rational choice argument for US–EC cooperation', *European Journal of International Relations*, 1 (1995), 131–56.

3 M. Mastanduno, 'Economics and security in statecraft and scholarship', *International Organization*, 52:4 (1998), 825–54.

4 Sperling and Kirchner, 'Economic security and the problem of cooperation', 230.

5 O. Waever, B. Buzan, M. Kelstrup and P. Lemaitre, *Identity, Migration and the New Security Agenda in Europe* (London, Pinter Publishers, 1993).

6 J. Sperling and E. Kirchner, *Recasting the European Order: Security Architectures and Economic Cooperation* (Manchester, Manchester University Press, 1997), chapter 1.

7 W. F. Hanrieder, 'Dissolving international politics: reflections on the nation-state', *American Political Science Review*, 72:4 (1978), 1276–87.

8 J. G. Ruggie, 'Continuity and transformation in the world polity: toward a neo-realist synthesis', in R. O. Keohane (ed.), *Neorealism and its Critics* (New York, Columbia University Press, 1986), p. 148.

9 R. Rosecrance, *Action and Reaction in World Politics: International Systems in Perspective* (Boston, Little Brown, 1963).

10 B. A. Most and H. Starr, 'Diffusion, reinforcement, geopolitics, and the spread of war', *American Political Science Review*, 74:4 (1980), 933; and G. Goertz, *Contexts of International Politics* (Cambridge, Cambridge University Press, 1994), pp. 75–81.

11 Most and Starr, 'Diffusion, reinforcement, geopolitics', 935.

12 J. Sperling, 'Two tiers or two speeds?: constructing a stable European security order', in J. Sperling (ed.), *Two Tiers or Two Speeds?: The European Security Order and the Enlargement of the European Union and NATO* (Manchester, Manchester University Press, 1999), pp. 181–98.

13 M. Huelshoff, 'CEE financial reform, European Monetary Union and eastern enlargement', in Sperling (ed.), *Two Tiers or Two Speeds?*, pp. 63–80.

14 J. Gowa, 'Bipolarity, multipolarity, and free trade', *American Political Science Review*, 83:4 (1989), 1245–56.

15 Deutsche Bundesbank, 'Germany's relative position in the central and east European countries in transition', *Monthly Report*, 51:10 (1999), 21.

16 J. Sperling, 'European security and debt finance in Poland', in E. J. Kirchner (ed.), *Decentralization and Transition in the Visegrad Countries: Poland, Hungary, the Czech Republic and Slovakia* (Basingstoke, Macmillan, 1999), pp. 191–207.

17 *Financial Times* (23 May 2000), p. 2.

18 N. Brown, 'Climate, ecology, and international security', *Survival*, 31:6 (1989), 519–32; B. Buzan, *People, States and Fear: An Agenda for International Security Studies in the Post-Cold War Era* (Boulder, CO, Lynne Rienner, 1991); Buzan et al., *Security: A New Framework for Analysis*; Peter Gleick, 'Water and conflict: fresh water resources and international security', *International Security*, 18:1 (1993), 79–112; T. Homer-Dixon, *Environment, Scarcity, and Violence* (Princeton, Princeton University Press, 1999); N. Myers, *Ultimate Security: The Environmental Basis of Political Stability* (London, W. W. Norton & Co., 1993); and Richard Ullman, 'Redefining security', *International Security*, 8:1 (1983), 129–53.

19 D. Deudney, 'Environment and security: muddled thinking', *Bulletin of the Atomic Scientists*, (1991), 22–8; D. Deudney, 'The case against linking environmental degradation and national security', *Millennium*, 19:3 (1990), 461–76; and Buzan, *People, States, and Fear*, pp. 131–44.

20 T. F. Homer-Dixon, 'Environmental scarcities and violent conflict: evidence from cases', *International Security*, 19:1 (1994), 5–40.

21 Homer-Dixon, 'Environmental scarcities and violent conflict', 36.

22 For a full discussion of the nuclear issue, see Sperling and Kirchner, *Recasting the European Order*, chapter 7.

23 European Bank for Reconstruction and Development, 'Key contract for decommissioning of Chernobyl awarded from EBRD Nuclear Safety Account', *Press Release* (18 June 1999); and *Financial Times* (30 March 2000), p. 2.

24 N. Malcolm, 'The case against "Europe"', *Foreign Affairs*, 74:2 (1995), 53.

11
European security in the twenty-first century: towards a stable peace order?

Adrian Hyde-Price

'When Gregor Samsa awoke one morning from uneasy dreams he found himself transformed in his bed into a gigantic insect.' Thus begins Franz Kafka's surrealist novel *Metamorphosis*.[1] In 1989 an analogous transformation took place, equally suddenly and unexpectedly: the countries of Central and Eastern Europe awoke after a troubled forty year interlude to find themselves transformed from communist allies of the Soviet Union into democratising countries aspiring to 'return to Europe'. The years since have witnessed a process of readjustment and change as the wider European international society has responded – however hesitantly and half-heartedly at times – to the dramatic and largely unexpected transformation in postcommunist Europe.

This chapter addresses the nature and significance of the transformations that have swept the European security system since 1989, focusing primarily on their impact upon Central and Eastern Europe. In contrast to those who suggest that the demise of Cold War bipolarity will mean a return to past patterns of multipolar instability in Europe, the argument developed below is that the years 1989–91 constitute a historical watershed. In what is best termed the 'age of late modernity',[2] Europe is faced with a significantly new security agenda. The emergence of a zone of stable peace in the Euro-atlantic region, with a 'pluralistic security community' (a community of autonomous states for whom war with each other is no longer conceivable) at its core, has transformed the structural dynamics of European order. At the end of the twentieth century, the European security zone has fragmented into three broad zones, characterised by uneven patterns of political democratisation and socio-economic development, and differing attitudes towards international cooperation and conflict. The key to the shaping of a durable and just peace order in twenty-first-century Europe will depend primarily on how these three zones relate to each other.

This chapter also identifies the key questions facing the contemporary European security order. The changes that have transformed many of the established features of European international society pose a new set of questions, the answers to which will determine the nature and character of European order in the twenty-first century. The most important of these questions are: What is the underlying ordering principle of European security? What is the role of military force in reshaping European order? Is there a right of humanitarian intervention? And finally, how can preventive diplomacy and conflict management in Europe be strengthened? The answers to these questions will be central to deciding whether or not the end of the Cold War will eventually give rise to a Europe 'whole and free'.

1989–91: a historical watershed

The events of 1989–91 constitute a profound historical watershed, comparable in scope and significance to the 1789 French Revolution, the outbreak of the Great War in 1914 and the Second World War. 'Events', Fernand Braudel has written, 'are the ephemera of history; they pass across the stage like fire-flies, hardly glimpsed before they settle back into darkness and as often as not into oblivion.'[3] Yet by any but the most demanding criteria, the events of 1989–91 – beginning with the collapse of communism in Eastern Europe and culminating in German unification and the disintegration of the Soviet Union – were much more than the 'ephemera of history'. They signified the end of the bipolar structure of European order that had been a defining feature of international relations for four decades. They have also precipitated far-reaching changes in the wider international system – from the Middle East and Southern Africa, to Central America and South-East Asia. In a number of important respects, too, the *annus mirabilis* 1989 closed a cycle of events in European and global history that opened with the First World War and the Russian Revolution. In this sense, the events of 1989–91 mark a historical conjuncture that constitutes change not simply at the level of events, but at what Braudel called the *longue durée*. For this reason, 1989 can be seen as marking the end of the 'short twentieth century'.[4]

The precise significance of the collapse of communism and the end of bipolar antagonism for the European security system has been hotly disputed. The American neorealist John Mearsheimer famously suggested that with the end of nuclear bipolarity Europe would revert 'back to the future', returning to earlier patterns of multipolar instability and great power rivalry.[5] Mearsheimer's analysis was widely criticised for its lack of understanding of European affairs, and his article stands as a permanent monument to the inadequacies of neorealism. Nonetheless, his prejudices concerning Europe's recidivist proclivities have been shared by some European writers, primarily those of a more realist bent who tend to harbour more pessimistic assumptions about the prospects for moral progress and human development. In Germany, for example, a group of influential conservative historians and political essayists have also argued that Europe is returning to multipolar politics. In a book tellingly entitled *Die Ganz Normale Anarchie* (*The Quite Normal Anarchy*), Jürgen von Alten has argued that in 1990 the world's state system reappeared in the form it was in the year 1910, 'like a Phoenix from the ashes'.[6] Similarly Arnulf Baring has argued that the 'new situation facing the country – and the continent – after 1990 resembles much more the constellations of the late nineteenth and earlier twentieth century than the European structure of the last four decades'.[7]

However, for reasons enumerated below, this chapter takes issue with the conservative emphasis on historical continuity. The argument developed here is that the events of 1989–91 do indeed mark the 'end of the short twentieth century' and constitute an *Epochenwende* – a 'change of epochs'. Neorealist suggestions that Europe's future will resemble its unstable, multipolar past overlook the changed structural dynamics of late modern European order. As Ernst-Otto Czempiel has noted, while states may continue to pursue what they perceive to be their national interests, 'they do so in an environment marked by levels of interaction and communication, and institutions and cooperation that clearly differentiate it from the environment of earlier centuries that gave birth to the seemingly iron concept of *Realpolitik*'.[8] Similarly Michael Clarke has argued that 'Metternich and Bismarck did not have to contend with layer upon layer of international organisations through which their policy would have to pass, nor with any of the other forces which have diversified and diluted sources of political power in the contemporary world.'[9]

To argue that postcommunist Europe will simply return to past patterns of multipolar politics and the balance of power is to overlook the far-reaching and deep-seated changes in late modern Europe. As Robert Cooper, a senior member of the British diplomatic service, has written, 'what happened in 1989 was not just the end of the Cold War, but also the end of the balance-of-power system in Europe'.[10] The change in the structural dynamics of European international society necessitates a paradigm-shift in the way we view security. This point has been underlined by Chris Donnelly, the North Atlantic Treaty Organisation's (NATO's) Special Adviser for Central and East European Affairs. Given that there is no prospect of a general high-intensity war in Europe, he argues, 'we all need to recognise that we have been viewing the world with a hefty residue of Cold War mentality, about Russia, about NATO, and so on. Now is the time to turn the corner and build security in Europe on a brand new basis.'[11]

The Euro-atlantic 'zone of stable peace'

The possibility of building security in Europe on a new basis has come about because of a series of changes that have contributed both to the emergence of a security community in the West and the collapse of communist order in Central and Eastern Europe. These changes include complex interdependence, globalisation, democracy and social market economies. On an international level these changes have led to a significant intensification of global interconnectedness between geographically dispersed societies such that events in one part of the world have effects on peoples and societies far away. 'That this is a highly uneven and differentiated process does not detract from the underlying message that societies can no longer be conceptualised as bounded systems, insulated from the outside world ... In modern society the local and the global have become intimately related.'[12]

In Europe, international society has been transformed not only by globalisation, but also by the consolidation of stable liberal democracies based on comprehensive social welfare systems and social market economics. These domestic developments have been accompanied by novel forms of multilateral interaction and institutionalised cooperation, along with extensive webs of transnational socio-economic interdependence and cross-border transactions. Thus although democratic states in Western Europe today 'still very much *look* like classical modern states, they are qualitatively different, most obviously because they emphasize wealth and welfare rather than warfare'.[13] 'Today's liberal democracies', it has been noted, 'are kinder, gentler things than they used to be, organised as much to provide justice as order or security.' The change in 'what it means to be a state at the end of the millennium' has 'influenced the social interaction among states, including the processes by which international society arrives at its rules, and the nature of the rules themselves'.[14]

The effect of the transformation of statehood and the nature of international society in Western and Northern Europe is that a zone of 'stable peace' has emerged in Western Europe and the wider transatlantic area, with a 'pluralistic security community' at its core.[15] This is the single most important change in the nature of the modern states' system since its emergence in the mid seventeenth century. The defining feature of this zone of stable peace is that the states that constitute it no longer regard war, or the threat of war, as an acceptable means of resolving conflicts within the security community. Thus the spirit of Kant ('perpetual peace') has replaced the spirit of Clausewitz ('war as a continuation of politics by other means'). International relations in Western Europe's *foedus pacificum* have become 'civilianised', and states now operate with a broader range of considerations than the struggle for power, security and influence. Most importantly, they no longer consider using military force or coercive diplomacy in their relations with each other. This is of tremendous significance, for 'if physical violence is no longer a serious option then in practice sovereignty has been seriously weakened, whatever the legal position. In the absence of an effective right to resort to force, sovereignty is, it seems, a very amorphous notion.'[16]

This emergence of the transatlantic security community heralds a profound transformation in the structural dynamics of Western European international society, one that has important and potentially far-reaching consequences for the Westphalian states' system in Europe as a whole. Up until the middle of the twentieth century, all European states were locked into a complex and shifting balance-of-power arrangement, with Germany at its core. These states jealously guarded their sovereignty and engaged in power politics based on *Realpolitik* calculations. Within this *Realpolitik* mindset, military assets constituted the key element in the assessment of relative power capabilities. The emergence of a security community in the transatlantic area, however, has meant that Western European states no longer view their neighbours within this security community as potential threats. Consequently neither the security dilemma nor the balance of power operate among states in Western Europe.[17] Instead, a process of deep integration has transformed Western Europe. Thus, for example, German interests 'are being advanced not in a balance of power clash, but in tedious bureaucratic manoeuvring in the confederation-plus of the European Union (EU) and the confederation-minus of the transatlantic community'.[18]

The emergence of this security community means that realism – particularly in its structural and power politics variants – is of limited analytical utility in understanding the structural dynamics of the Euro-atlantic security community. Realism can provide insights into the functioning of regional security complexes characterised by a high degree of conflict and mistrust, but it is not so useful for understanding international relations in a zone of stable peace.[19] This is because '*where common interests exist* realism is too pessimistic about the prospects for cooperation and the role of institutions'.[20] Similarly, realists stress the importance of relative gains for states in a self-help system, but 'the concern about "relative gains", which is, in general, a consequence of anarchy, is far less among allies than it is between opponents'.[21] Thus 'the constraining effects of anarchy are felt less by liberal democracies enmeshed in complex cooperative networks'. The spread of globalisation and the emergence of 'post-modern states' must increase 'the relative importance of cooperation based on the soft power resources required in complex, plurilateralist networks, and decrease the relative importance of conflict based on more traditional forms of power, especially military power'. Consequently the 'latter form of power is less relevant for the creation of multi-level governance regulating increasingly globalized economies and societies'.[22]

The emergence of the Euro-atlantic security community does not mean that a harmony of interests exists in this region. The distinguishing feature of a zone of stable peace is that conflicts over resources and influence, which remain an indelible feature of international society, are resolved peacefully, without recourse to threats of violence. A 'durable peace' (*dauerhafter Frieden*), Dieter Senghaas has written, involves a structure or political order based upon 'peaceful coexistence and a political order characterised by reliable and civilised conflict-resolution' in which 'constructive conflictive resolution routinely, "unseen", silently and quite naturally takes place'.[23] European international politics – like other politics – is about who governs and by what means, and it therefore raises questions about the process of acquiring, shaping, distributing and exercising power. However, the emergence of a security community changes the relative value of the currency of power. As Stanley Hoffmann notes,

> The structural theory [of neorealism] was geared to a world in which states, as discrete actors, sought power or sought to balance power in a game that entailed the possible resort to war. This limited the importance of variations in state behaviour caused by each actor's domestic regime or politics. Remove that possibility of war or relax those constraints and the nature of the game changes. It is not that the actors will stop seeking power and influence, but rather that the way of acquiring gains, the nature of the desired gains, and the means of provoking international change all will change. In traditional politics, war provided the most visible and often the quickest instrument of change. If war is removed, change in international affairs, or in the pecking order of states, will tend to result either from revolutions or from domestically driven modifications in the goals or in the power of states.[24]

Europe's three zones

The emergence of a pluralistic security community in Western Europe is without doubt the single most important development in the history of the Westphalian system. It has fundamentally transformed the structural dynamics of European order and generated new patterns of international relations that bear little or no resemblance to those of Europe's past. Yet while Western Europe has experienced the emergence of a zone of stable peace, developments elsewhere in the European 'regional security complex' have been less sanguine.[25] The contrasts within Europe were symbolised in the early 1990s by two cities: Maastricht and Sarajevo. The aspiration towards an 'ever closer union among the peoples of Europe' came a step closer with the signing of the Maastricht Treaty of European Union in 1991, even though the subsequent problems of ratification demonstrated that nationalist sentiments remain a potent force within Western Europe. By way of contrast, Sarajevo – in 1914 the flashpoint of the first great conflagration of twentieth-century Europe – came to symbolise the bloody wars of Yugoslav succession that produced a new euphemism for human evil: 'ethnic cleansing'.

Although the post-Cold War situation in Europe was characterised by considerable complexity, ambiguity and contradiction, some broad trends and developments have emerged. Across the continent, the 'most funda-mental paradox of our era' – the 'intense trend towards political fragmen-tation within the context of a globalizing economy'[26] – is much in evidence. The paradoxical coexistence of integration, cooperation and homogenisa-tion on the one hand, and fragmentation, conflict and diversity on the other, is apparent in contemporary Russia or Romania as well as in France or Portugal. Nonetheless, 'there are significant differences among groups of states as to the speed at which they are involved in this process of histori-cal change'.[27] Thus some commentators have spoken of a process of 'uneven globalisation' or 'uneven denationalisation', leading to new cleav-ages between states and groups of states.[28]

As a consequence of this process of uneven globalisation and de-national-isation, the European security system in the 1990s has fragmented into three broad zones or regions, characterised by different patterns of diplomatic and security relationships and different processes of domestic socio-economic, political and cultural development. In contemporary Europe 'three contexts of European change' have emerged in the form of 'concentric circles radi-ating out from Brussels'.[29] These three zones are distinguished by the uneven impact of the manifold processes of change affecting late modern Europe. These 'three contexts of change' bear a striking resemblance to the 'three his-toric regions' of Europe identified by the Hungarian historian Jenö Szücs – namely Western, Central and Eastern Europe.[30]

These three broad zones or regions in contemporary Europe are not clearly delineated geographical areas. Nor are they defined by any single factor or feature. Rather, they can best be distinguished in terms of Wittgenstein's notion of 'family resemblances'. Objects or practices may be most appropriately characterised, Wittgenstein argued, not by 'something that is common to them all' (a single defining feature) but by 'similarities, relationships, and a whole series of them at that ... "family resemblance"; for the various resemblances between members of a family: build, features, colour of eyes, gait, temperament, etc., etc., overlap and criss-cross in the same way'.[31] Europe's three zones or 'contexts of change' are therefore not to be defined by any one factor, but through a series of overlapping and criss-crossing 'family resemblances'. These 'family resemblances' are based on a series of political, economic and socio-economic features, and reflect the uneven impact of globalisation, interdependence and integration on European international society.

The first of these three zones is the *core zone*. It consists of the mature democracies of Western Europe and North America, which together form a zone of stable peace with a security community at its core. This core zone is characterised by responsible and representative government; a high degree of transnational socio-economic interdependence; relatively open and tolerant civil societies; a plethora of multilateral institutions; and a shared set of liberal-democratic norms and values. Nationalism in Western Europe has been tamed and primarily takes the form of civic nationalism. Moreover, national identity coexists alongside other forms of political affili-ation, generating multiple forms of identity – national, local, regional, European, cosmopolitan. This core zone of Western Europe has witnessed the greatest erosion to the pillars of the Westphalian states' system and exhibits evidence of the emergence of elements of a post-Westphalian form of neo-medieval order.[32]

The second zone is the *intermediate zone*, which is largely constituted by the countries of Central Europe. One of its defining features is the region's historic links with Western Christendom, its participation in many of the defining cultural and intellectual movements of Europe (such as the Renaissance and the Reformation), and the influence of German language, culture and economics.[33] In some respects, this zone roughly corresponds to the historic lands of *Mitteleuropa*. However, the defining feature of this intermediate region is not geography or history, but rather the extent to which the 'triple transformation' process has impacted on the everyday life of these countries. In this intermediate zone, political democ-ratisation is well advanced, civil society has developed, and political life is marked by the emergence of pluralist politics and a broad liberal-demo-cratic consensus. Excessive nationalism has been partially tamed and largely replaced by a 'new nationalist myth' which has encouraged the Central Europeans to adopt 'European' norms with respect to individual and minority rights. This 'new nationalist myth' is the 'myth of belonging to European culture, the myth of return to real or imaginary European roots, the myth of normal development brutally interrupted by the Bolshevik experiment or the Russian aggression or both'.[34] In the intermediate zone, the process of economic restructuring and marketisation is well developed; trade has been largely reoriented towards the EU, especially towards Germany; and levels of foreign direct investment are relatively high. Above all, this second region is characterised by an overwhelming desire to 'return to Europe'. This foreign policy commitment to join Western organisations and structures provides the key motor driving the domestic economic, political and societal reform process, and is widely accepted by dominant elite groups and public opinion in general.

The third distinct area within the European security complex is the *outer zone*. It consists of those countries furthest away (politically if not geographically) from the Euro-atlantic security community. This outer zone is constituted by those parts of Eastern Europe and the Balkans where the reform process is less advanced and the relationship with the West more problematical. In this zone, one-party rule has tended to give way to regimes characterised by a mix of authoritarian impulses and nascent democratic structures. Nationalist identity is primarily defined in terms of a 'blood and land' ethnicity and is often intolerant of minority communities. The task of state – and nation – building remains central to the political agenda, and generates uncertainty and instability. Economic reform in this peripheral zone has generally been less thorough and civil society is less developed. In many respects, this region resembles Giselher Wirsings's *Zwischeneuropa*, 'its economies exporting tin saucepans, bottled fruit, cheap shoes, and cheap labour, importing German tourists and Japanese capital. A zone, that is, of weak states, national prejudice, inequality, poverty, and *schlammessel* [a mire or mess].'[35]

These three zones represent ideal types rather than geographically delineated areas. The boundaries between them are not clear cut, and it is particularly hard to distinguish between the second and third zones. This is because processes of economic, political, societal and foreign policy change are not coterminous, either temporally or spatially. Poland, the Czech Republic, Hungary and Slovenia are countries that clearly fall within the intermediate zone ('Central Europe'). Russia, Moldova, Serbia and Macedonia, on the other hand, are countries in the outer zone ('Eastern Europe' and the 'Balkans'). However, there are a number of postcommunist countries that fall between the two ideal types of the intermediate and outer zones (i.e. between 'Central' and 'Eastern' Europe). Estonia and Latvia, for example, are 'Central European' in terms of their economic development, their commitment to 'return to Europe' and their relationship to Euro-atlantic structures. Their political culture is, however, marked by a pronounced ethnic nationalism, and their Western patrons have had to exert a great deal of pressure to ensure that they meet minimum standards of acceptable behaviour in their treatment of the Russian minority communities. Similarly Slovakia is 'Central European' by economic criteria, but politically it still needs to demonstrate that there will be no return to the intolerant nationalism and populist authoritarianism of the Mečiar years.

The dual enlargement process and European order

The crucial question facing European order in the twenty-first century is how the three zones outlined above will relate to each other. While the balance of power no longer operates within the core zone, it continues to operate to some extent within the outer zone. One important question for the future is whether or not relations between the core and outer zones, or between the outer and intermediate zones, will be characterised by balance-of-power calculations.

How relations between these three zones will evolve will depend on an array of domestic and international factors, most notably the success of the reform process, the international economic climate and the policies of the major powers. However, if one factor is of particular importance, it is the dual enlargement process. Following the demise of schemes to build a collective security system based on an invigorated Organisation for Security and Cooperation in Europe (OSCE), the dual enlargement of NATO and the EU has emerged as the primary instrument for reshaping European order.[36] Enlarging these two central institutional pillars of the Euro-atlantic security community will not only change the pattern of international relations in the wider Europe, it will also precipitate far-reaching changes in the policies and functioning of these organisations themselves. The dual enlargement process will therefore have profound implications for the very nature of European international society.

In terms of relations between Europe's three zones, the importance of the dual enlargement process is that it will create new patterns of inclusion and exclusion. Broadly speaking, the aim of much of Western policy since the end of the Cold War has had three dimensions: consolidation of the Euro-atlantic community, which involves deepening of the European integration process (economic and monetary union, building a Common European Security and Defence Policy and strengthening the EU's 'third pillar', that is, Justice and Home Affairs); integrating the new democracies of Central Europe into this Euro-atlantic community through the dual enlargement process; and building a cooperative security system with Russia and the other countries of Eastern Europe.

The key policy instruments currently available to the Euro-atlantic community for shaping new forms of cooperation with Eastern Europe are the EU's Partnership and Cooperation Agreements, together with its 'Northern Dimension' and 'Common Strategies' agreed in the framework of the Union's Common Foreign and Security Policy. In terms of the Balkans, the Stability Pact for South-East Europe is also designed to encourage the emergence of new forms of cooperation and governance in this war-ravaged region. As regards NATO, the key instruments for building cooperation and

security governance in the wider Europe are the Partnership for Peace programme, the Euro-Atlantic Partnership Council and the Russia–NATO
Founding Act of May 1997 (which established the Permanent Joint Council).
With these instruments, Western countries hope they can engage Russia and
the other countries of Eastern Europe in webs of cooperation and governance, in order to reduce the danger of a return to balance-of-power thinking
and a new form of East–West conflict (with the dividing line this time lying to
the east of the three Baltic republics, Poland, Hungary and Romania).

One serious problem facing cooperation between the core zone in
Western Europe and the democratising countries of Eastern Europe is the
legacy of centuries of alienation and cultural prejudice. As Larry Wolff has
written:

> Statesmen, who once enthusiastically anticipated the unity of Europe,
> are looking away from the siege of Sarajevo, wishing perhaps that it were
> happening on some other continent. Alienation is in part a matter of
> economic disparity, the wealth of Western Europe facing the poverty of
> Eastern Europe, but such disparity is inevitably clothed in the complex
> windings of cultural prejudice. The iron curtain is gone, and yet the
> shadow persists.[37]

He goes on to argue that the shadow persists because of the enduring power
of the *idea* of 'Eastern Europe', an idea that is much older than the Cold War
and that can be traced back to the Renaissance. This idea of Eastern Europe
rests on the 'paradox of simultaneous inclusion and exclusion, Europe but
not Europe'. It is defined by the twin formulas of 'between Europe and Asia,
between civilisation and barbarism'. The 'rubric of Eastern Europe', Wolff
suggests, 'may still be invoked to perpetuate the exclusion of the rest, to preserve the distinction that nourishes our own identity'. He thus concludes that
'Eastern Europe will continue to occupy an ambiguous space between inclusion and exclusion, both in economic affairs and in cultural recognition'.[38]

New times, new questions

The watershed years 1989–91 ushered in a new chapter in European history, with new challenges and opportunities. Not only has the existing military, diplomatic and economic status quo been radically altered, a new
security agenda has also emerged in Europe. Many of the questions which
preoccupied strategic analysts in the Cold War – from the esoterics of
nuclear deterrence to forward defence postures and conventional arms
control – have lost their former significance. In their place, new security
'risks' and 'challenges' have emerged, from illegal migration and transnational criminal organisations, to problems of state building and minority

rights. The future of the European security system – and, more importantly, the prospects for a just and durable peace order – depend on
answers given to a raft of questions, questions that barely registered in the
Cold War years. Some of these questions may seem somewhat obtuse and
academic, but they have very real and far-reaching policy consequences
for the future character of European international society.

What is the underlying ordering principle of European security?

Since at least the 1648 Treaty of Westphalia, international relations has
been based on the principle of state sovereignty. This has had two dimensions: the legal equality of sovereign states and non-intervention in the
domestic affairs of these states. Despite changes in the source of legitimate
state power (particularly given the rise of nationalism as a potent political
force at the end of the eighteenth century), state sovereignty has remained
the dominant ordering principle of international politics.[39] It underpins
much of international law and the United Nations (UN) system.

This principle has, however, been significantly eroded in late modern
Europe by two distinct processes. First, the European integration process,
which has led to a pooling of sovereignty within the EU in the framework of
a system of multi-level governance. And second, by the spread of human
rights norms in international society.[40] One of the first manifestations of
this changed approach to the claims of sovereignty was the Nuremberg War
Crimes Tribunal. Sovereignty was also qualified in the Conference on
Security and Cooperation in Europe Helsinki Final Act in 1975, an ambiguous document that both reaffirmed the principle of sovereignty and qualified it by making human rights violations the legitimate concern of the
wider international community.[41] More recently – and more dramatically –
the principle of sovereignty has been curtailed by the Kosovo war, which
privileged human rights above the claims of state sovereignty and drasti-
cally curtailed the principle of non-interference in domestic affairs of
formally sovereign entities. Consequently, a number of commentators have
begun speaking of the emergence of a post-Westphalian system of
European order, in which sovereignty no longer provides the dominant
ordering principle.

The shift to a new system of European order opens up prospects for a
more just security system in which human rights, not the rights of sovereign
states, are accorded primacy. It recognises that the security of individuals
and communities can sometimes be threatened by the arbitrary and brutal
acts of government authorities, particularly in the absence of established
democratic checks and balances and an effective civil society. Yet it also
poses a number of new dilemmas and difficulties. In his reflections on the
Kosovo war, the German Defence Minister Rudolf Scharping concludes

that 'a new balance between two principles of international law, namely state sovereignty and the universal validity of human rights, needs to be worked out'.[42] In particular, three issues need to be addressed.

First, the emergence of a post-Westphalian system poses questions about democratic accountability and responsible and representative government. Since the spread and consolidation of liberal democracy from the late nineteenth century onwards, the nation-state has provided the framework for democratic government and civil liberties. Given the EU's 'democratic deficit' and the lack of mechanisms of accountability and control of other international organisations, curtailing state sovereignty raises serious issues. These were illustrated by the Haider affair in 2000, in which EU governments sought to isolate a democratically elected Austrian government because it contained a far-right party with some obnoxious views.

Second, a post-Westphalian order will be especially problematic for many of the new democracies of Central and Eastern Europe. A number of these states are still engaged in a difficult and demanding process of state and nation building. They have only recently regained their sovereignty and may find it hard to give it up again as a result of joining the EU. Certainly, the Haider affair made many of the EU's applicant countries aware of some of the possible consequences of acceding to the Union. In addition Russia has voiced concerns shared by many others in postcommunist Europe about the implications of Kosovo for state sovereignty.

Europe has thus entered new and uncharted territory, in which the search for a new ordering principle for European international society poses a series of political, legal and moral dilemmas. The answers found to these dilemmas will have a significant impact on the future shape of European security in the twenty-first century.

What is the role of military force in reshaping European order?

The watershed years 1989–91 engendered hopes that Europe would, at last, be 'whole and free' and that a durable peace order would prevail in a continent shattered by two World Wars. This led to a search for a peace dividend arising from the perceived redundancy of arms in post-Cold War Europe. Europe has indeed witnessed a substantial build-down in conventional and nuclear forces – particularly in Central Europe – and a number of important arms controls measures have been implemented. However, the dreams of a peaceful and indivisible European security system have been rudely shattered by a series of bloody wars in former Yugoslavia and around the fringes of the former Soviet Union (notably in the Caucasus and Central Asia).

This has led to a paradoxical situation. The end of the Cold War has certainly led to reduction in military forces in Europe and the effective demise of fears of a continental-wide conventional war leading to nuclear armageddon.[43] Yet at the same time Europe experienced more armed conflict in the 1990s than throughout the Cold War. More recently, the Kosovo war has forced European policy makers and the wider European public to confront a question that many hoped would play no significant role in the new Europe: what is the role of military force in reshaping European order? As Philip Zelikow has suggested, one of the most important security questions in Europe since the early 1990s has been 'whether military power will be readied or employed to influence political developments in or near Europe, especially where the interests of the great powers are not fully engaged'.[44]

This question raises a series of related issues. First, it has led to a rebirth of strategic studies. The essence of strategy is the use, or threat of use, of military force for political ends.[45] This is the agenda of Clausewitz, whose writings on strategy remain the most important single source of theoretical reflections on war and politics. Strategic thinking was greatly distorted, and to some extent neglected, during the Cold War given the centrality of nuclear deterrence. However, the experience of the 1990s has led to fresh thinking about the use of military force for political purposes. One of the most important lessons of operations such as Bosnia and Kosovo is 'the increasing inapplicability of NATO's Cold War war-fighting doctrine ... While NATO doctrine was applicable in the Gulf War, it has had much less salience in the smaller crisis-response operations in the Balkans.'[46] One consequence of this was the British army's establishment of a centre for military doctrine in the early 1990s to address precisely these shortcomings. European armed forces are now called upon to undertake a wide range of military missions, from conventional offensive actions such as the Gulf War or Operation Deliberate Force, to what are sometimes called 'Military Operations Other Than War', and many existing doctrinal and operational military concepts are no longer relevant to this broader spectrum of military missions.

Second, it has led to new thinking about the relative merits of conscription versus professional, volunteer armies. Conscript armies are ideal for national territorial defence or traditional 'Article V' NATO operations. However, for military crisis management, professional forces such as the French Foreign Legion or the British Gurkas are more appropriate. Throughout Europe there is now a debate on military reform, as illustrated in the German case by the May 2000 Weizsäcker Commission report on 'Common Security and the Future of the Bundeswehr'.[47]

Third, the Revolution in Military Affairs poses new questions about military crisis management. The development of precise-guided munitions seems to make the selective employment of military force for political purposes more feasible, given the ability to minimise civilian casualties ('collateral damage', in the language of the military). Yet this in turn raises worries about the increasing use of 'virtual wars' or 'spectator wars' as they have been dubbed, and the emergence of a new form of nineteenth-century 'gun-boat diplomacy' based on cruise missiles and stealth bombers.

Fourth, the question of the use of military force in reshaping European order has been given a new twist by the controversies over US plans for a National Missile Defence (NMD) system.[48] Russia fears that NMD will desta-bilise the strategic nuclear balance and has threatened a new round of arms build-up if the US violates the 1972 Anti-Ballistic Missile Treaty (which limits such defences).[49] Whether or not Russia has the financial and economic resources to engage in a new arms race is a moot question. However, NMD does seem to provide a chilling example of the 'security dilemma' in practice. In addition, Washington's European allies fear that a US missile defence system will lead to a de-coupling of US and European security, threatening the transatlantic alliance and making out-of-area mili-tary crisis management by NATO highly problematic.

The end of Cold War bipolarity has thus posed fresh questions about the role of military force in reshaping European security. Many Europeans are uncomfortable with this. However, the EU's decision to create a rapid reaction corps of 60,000 troops by 2003 in order to give substance to its Common European Security and Defence Policy will necessitate some clear answers to this question. In February 1998, UN Secretary-General Kofi Annan said that 'if diplomacy is to succeed, it must be backed up by both force and fairness'. This poses questions central to strategic theory, namely applying military force within the framework of a political strategy in order to achieve defined political aims.[50] Reflecting on Kofi Annan's words, Carl Bildt has argued that:

> There is no single formula that can guide us through the dilemmas of force and diplomacy. If there is one pattern that we might see emerging, it is of failures of diplomacy being followed by the use of force which, in its turn, is followed by diplomatic attempts to manage the problems which force alone could not solve. Force should never be a substitute for diplomacy – but under the right conditions, it can give strength to the search for political solutions represented by diplomacy.[51]

Is there a right to humanitarian intervention?

The third key question is closely linked to the first two: is there a right to humanitarian intervention in Europe and the wider global system? If one holds fast to the principle of territorial sovereignty, or rejects the use of military force in any circumstances except for the defence of national or alliance territory, then clearly the answer to this question is an unqualified 'no'. At the time of the Kosovo war, there were two clear positions in the British debate that rejected the principles underlying Operation Deliberate Force. On the one hand were pacifists who believed that coercive military force could never be an instrument for just and legitimate political goals. On the other were 'little Englanders' of the nationalist right who believed that sovereignty was sacrosanct. This assumption governed their response to human rights atrocities by 'sovereign' authorities in Kosovo as much as it did their insistence on keeping the pound sterling.

Between these two extremes, however, a wide-ranging debate on the issues raised by the Kosovo war took place. For President Clinton, the Kosovo war was a historic landmark because it established 'an important principle ... that whether within or beyond the borders of a country, if the world community has the power to stop it, we ought to stop genocide'.[52] Many individuals in Western Europe and North America accepted the argument that not to have intervened in Kosovo would have weakened a fundamental principle of international society since Auschwitz and the Universal Declaration of Human Rights, namely that states do not have the right to massacre their own people. However, the Kosovo war also showed that even if this proposition is accepted, humanitarian intervention raises a bundle of complex moral, political and ethical dilemmas to which there are no easy answers.[53] Even if there is a right – perhaps even a duty – to intervene to prevent genocide or widespread violations of human rights, four questions still need to be addressed: intervention by whom; under what circumstances; with what authority; and how?

The case of Kosovo exemplified the dilemmas raised by humanitarian intervention, both because of the lack of a clear UN Security Council mandate and because of the unwillingness of NATO countries to risk the lives of their troops in a ground operation. The dilemmas and difficulties of intervening with military force in order to achieve humanitarian objectives were sometimes lost amid the triumphalism that followed the 'success' of Operation Deliberate Force. Referring to a headline by Stephen Rosefeld in the *International Herald Tribune* of 8 June 1999 – 'Victory for Defence, and by a Margin of 5,000 to zero' – Andreas Behnke comments that the 'obscenity of this triumphalist score-keeping [5,000 dead Serbian soldiers as opposed to no NATO deaths] should be easy to see':

> Firstly, it reduces the complexity of the conflict to a mere body-count. Politics and diplomacy are degraded to mere 'details' to be mastered, the victory of the Western alliance is, in Rosenfeld's view, already assured by NATO's ability to kill a large number of Serbian soldiers without sustaining any casualties itself.
>
> Perhaps even more obscene is the disappearance of the hundreds of Serbian civilian dead from the mental map, produced by a NATO

bombing strategy which willingly accepted their death as 'collateral damage' of its bombing campaign. And finally, the fact that NATO was utterly unable to prevent or end the displacement of the majority of the Kosovo-Albanians from their homes is equally missing from the picture.[54]

The Kosovo war has been the single most important event in European security since the end of the Cold War and its ramifications are still being felt. It has been a key factor in propelling forward EU plans for a Common European Security and Defence Identity and has placed a severe strain on aspirations for a cooperative security arrangement between NATO and Russia. It has therefore had a significant impact on relations between the three zones of the post-Cold War European security system outlined above. A key issue is what lessons the major protagonists in Europe will draw from the Kosovo war. Has a precedent for humanitarian intervention been set as President Clinton suggested, or will Kosovo prove 'an intervention too far'?

In this respect, three points can be made. First, there is a danger in the rhetorical excesses that surround calls for humanitarian intervention. Often what lies behind it is little more than a fear of refugees and unwanted migrants; that is, a fear of 'the other'. Lurking not far from the surface of official justifications for the Kosovo war was a concern to prevent a new wave of refugees arriving in Western Europe. Second, Operation Deliberate Force was frequently justified by reference to the experience of the Holocaust. '*Nie wieder Auschwitz*' was the cry by many in Germany who advocated or sought to defend the bombing campaign. However, this rhetorical excess is a 'perfidious form of relativism which, under the enlightened banner of "learning from history", in fact effects a de-historicisation of the [Nazi] period';

> Furthermore, as recent events in the Balkans displayed, such 'progressive' formulations of foreign policy contain an authoritarian and militarist undercurrent and can be employed to discard international law and the principle of national sovereignty. Within this context, one must question the enlightened intent of those who instrumentalise a 'moral obligation' in order effectively to annul the post-war international arrangements which were constructed precisely as a *response* to the horrors inflicted upon the world by the arbitrary military crusades of the Great Powers.[55]

Third, if Kosovo were in some ways comparable to Auschwitz in its horror and barbarity, why were NATO countries so unwilling to risk the lives of their soldiers in preventing it? As the former Czechoslovak Foreign Minister Jiri Dienstbier commented, 'the international community is not prepared to risk the lives of its soldiers for the sake of human rights'.[56] At the very least, this places a major question mark over the morality of NATO's war in Kosovo. What is certainly clear from Kosovo is that it is not possible to undertake humanitarian intervention by bombing from 15,000 feet. This did not prevent the expulsion of the Kosovars, which was the initial humanitarian aim of the campaign. Although the Kosovars were finally allowed to return to their homes, Operation Deliberate Force could not prevent additional bitter inter-communal conflict and a new round of ethnic cleansing. Thus as Adam Roberts has concluded, NATO's war constitutes a 'questionable model of humanitarian intervention'.[57]

How can preventive diplomacy and conflict management in Europe be strengthened?

While there is little agreement on when or how military force should be employed, there is a broad consensus that more must be done to strengthen the international community's instruments for preventive diplomacy and conflict management. This is the central lesson from the Balkans and elsewhere in postcommunist Europe. 'Prevention', as everyone knows, 'is better than cure'. The problem is how to give credibility and substance to conflict prevention mechanisms.

The key body here is the OSCE, an institution often overlooked in discussions of European security given the attention focused on NATO and the EU. Yet in a number of important respects, the OSCE is the unsung success story of modern European diplomacy. From its inauspicious origins at the Helsinki conference in 1975, the OSCE has come to play six important roles in the European security system. First, it provides a framework for pan-European diplomacy on a comprehensive range of issues. Second, it has codified a series of normative principles governing state behaviour in Europe, from the peaceful resolution of disputes to open market economics. Third, it has institutionalised a set of mechanisms for the permanent monitoring of human rights in participating states. Fourth, it has helped achieve greater military transparency through arms controls agreements and confidence- and security-building measures. Fifth, it has emerged as Europe's primary instrument for conflict prevention, preventive diplomacy and crisis management. Finally, it has acquired new responsibilities for post-conflict resolution.

In terms of its role in preventive diplomacy and conflict prevention, the OSCE has since the early 1990s acquired a number of new institutions and mechanisms. These include the Office for Democratic Institutions and Human Rights, the High Commissioner on National Minorities (HCNM), the Permanent Council and OSCE Missions. Preventive diplomacy, by its very nature, is not very news-worthy (in contrast to violent conflicts); thus its effectiveness is often overlooked. However, it is an essential aspect of the European security system and constitutes a key element of the emerging patterns of security governance in postcommunist Europe. The best illustration of the OSCE's contribution to preventive diplomacy and conflict prevention is the work of the HCNM, Max van der Stoel. With a staff of seven and a tiny budget, his task is to foresee and defuse the ethnic tensions that have become the major source of violent conflict in postcommunist Europe. Despite under-funding and limited resources, he has chalked up some important successes, most notably in the Baltic republics and the Crimea.

One way in which the OSCE can better fulfil its responsibilities for conflict prevention, crisis management and post-conflict rehabilitation is by developing the capability to deploy civilian and police expertise in conflict situations. At the Istanbul summit in November 1999, the OSCE adopted the REACT (Rapid Expert Assistance and Cooperation Teams) concept to develop teams of civilian and police experts drawn from OSCE participating states who could be deployed at short notice to defuse and manage conflict situations. These teams would in effect constitute the civilian component of peacekeeping operations. As experience in Bosnia, Kosovo and elsewhere has shown, civilian and police expertise is often badly needed for tasks the military is not trained or equipped to carry out. Responsibility for giving operational substance to the REACT concept was given to the OSCE Secretariat. In the end, however, the success of the REACT concept will depend on participating states committing their energy and resources to this project. Given the preoccupation of EU member states with creating a 60,000 rapid military corps, and the history of OSCE under-funding by participating staes, there is a very real danger that this important initiative will not receive the material and political support it deserves.

Conclusion

The dramatic and largely unexpected sequence of events that transformed Europe between 1989 and 1991 marks a watershed in the history of European international society. The events of 1989–91 were a watershed in not just that long-established diplomatic practices, institutional structures and strategic thinking were rendered redundant, largely overnight. Rather, they were a watershed because the end of the Cold War coincided with, and laid bare, a series of deeper socio-economic and cultural processes of change bound up with globalisation and regionalisation. For late modern Europe, therefore, there can be no simple 'return to the past'. The Europe of Bismarck, Metternich or Churchill has passed away, and Europe is not returning to past patterns of multipolar instability within a shifting balance of power as some pessimists predicted.

Yet neither has Europe become 'whole and free'. Rather than blossoming into a stable peace order characterised by indivisible and comprehensive security, late modern European international society has fragmented into three broad zones or regions. These zones are characterised by different patterns of security relationships, different political and institutional arrangements, and different cognitive perceptions. The crucial question for the future is how relations between these three zones will develop. Here the dual enlargement process will be of decisive importance. The prospects for a stable peace order in Europe will depend both on the successful integration of the new democracies of Central Europe into the Euro-atlantic security community, thereby enlarging the transatlantic zone of stable peace, and on the consolidation of a cooperative security relationship with Russia and the other democratising states of Eastern Europe. Reconciling these two contradictory goals has proven to be a major challenge for the West, and may in the end turn out to be beyond the political and diplomatic capabilities of Western countries and organisations.

In addition, the nature and quality of Europe's twenty-first-century security order depends on the answers found to a series of key questions. These questions include the future status of state sovereignty; the role of military force; the dilemmas surrounding humanitarian intervention; and the prospects for strengthening preventive diplomacy, conflict prevention and crisis management. In the end, however, developing a just and stable peace order in Europe is not simply a question of institutional architecture, political procedures or military security arrangements. Rather, it involves moral and ethical questions about our sense of responsibility for others. It is a question of building a sense of community (or 'we-ness', in the words of Karl Deutsch[58]) and of enlarging our sphere of moral and political responsibility. At the time of the Munich betrayal in 1938, the then Conservative Prime Minister of Britain, Neville Chamberlain, spoke of the Nazi annexation of the Sudetenland as 'a quarrel in a far away country between people of whom we know nothing' – and, the implication was, about whom we care even less. Such short-sighted, selfish and self-defeating approaches to security problems will not bring peace and stability to Europe. Rather, Europeans should reflect on the words of John Donne in his 1624 *Devotions upon Emergent Occasions*:

> No man is an Island, entire of its self; every man is a piece of the Continent, a part of the main; if a clod be washed away by the sea, Europe is the less, as well as if a promontory were, as well as if a manor of thy friends or of thine own were; any man's death diminishes me, because I am involved in Mankind; And therefore never send to know for whom the bell tolls; it tolls for thee.[59]

Notes

1 Franz Kafka, *Metamorphosis* (London, Penguin, 1915, 2000), p. 1.
2 N. Onuf, *The Republican Legacy in International Thought* (Cambridge, Cambridge University Press, 1998), p. 169 and p. 133.
3 F. Braudel, *The Mediterranean and the Mediterranean World in the Age of Philip II* (New York, Harper & Row, 1973), p. 901.
4 E. Hobsbawn, *Age of Extremes: The Short Twentieth Century, 1914–1991* (London, Michael Joseph, 1994).
5 J. J. Mearsheimer, 'Back to the future: instability in Europe after the Cold War', *International Security*, 15:1 (1990), 5–56.
6 J. von Alten, *Die Ganz Normale Anarchie, Jetzt erst Beginnt die Nachkriegszeit* (Berlin, Siedler Verlag, 1994) p. 306.
7 A. Baring (ed.), *Germany's New Position in Europe: Problems and Perspectives* (Oxford, Berg, 1994), p. 9.
8 E.-O. Czempiel, 'Foreword', in M. McKenzie and P. Loedel (eds.), *The Promise and Reality of European Security Cooperation: States, Interests, and Institutions* (Westport, Praeger, 1998), p. xi.
9 M. Clarke (ed.), *New Perspectives on Security* (London, Brassey's, 1993), p. xi.
10 R. Cooper, *The Post-Modern State and the World Order* (London, Demos, 1996), p. 7.
11 C. Donnelly, 'Defence transformations in the new democracies', *NATO Review*, 6 (1996), 23.
12 T. McGrew, 'Conceptualizing global politics', in T. McGrew and P. Lewis (eds.), *Global Politics* (Cambridge, Polity, 1992), p. 3.
13 P. van Ham and P. Grudzinski, 'Affluence and influence: the conceptual basis of Europe's new politics', *The National Interest*, 58 (1999–2000), 84.
14 D. Armstrong, 'Law, justice and the idea of a world society', *International Affairs*, 7:3 (1999), 559–60.
15 K. Boulding, *Stable Peace* (Austin, University of Texas Press, 1978), p. 17. See also M. Singer and A.Wildavsky, *The Real World Order: Zones of Peace, Zones of Turmoil*, rev. edn (Chatham, Chatham House Publishers, 1996).
16 C. Brown, 'International theory and international society: the viability of a middle way', *Review of International Studies*, 21:2 (1995), 195.
17 K. Deutsch et. al., *Political Community in the North Atlantic Area* (Princeton, Princeton University Press, 1957), pp. 137–8.
18 E. Pond, 'Germany finds its niche as a regional power', *The Washington Quarterly*, 19:1 (1996), 36.
19 A. Wolfers, *Discord and Collaboration: Essays in International Politics* (Baltimore, Johns Hopkins University Press, 1965), pp. 13–19.
20 R. Keohane, 'Internationalist theory and the realist challenge after the Cold War', in D. Baldwin (ed.), *Neorealism and Neoliberalism: The Contemporary Debate* (New York, Columbia University Press, 1993), p. 277.
21 J. Snyder, 'Process variables in realist theory', in B. Frankel (ed.), *Realism: Restatements and Renewal* (London, Frank Cass, 1996), p. 175.
22 G. Sørensen, 'An analysis of contemporary statehood: consequences for conflict and cooperation', *Review of International Studies*, 23 (1997), 268.

23 D. Senghaas, *Frieden Machen* (Frankfurt am Main, Suhrkamp, 1997), pp. 14–15.

24 S. Hoffmann, *The European Sisyphus: Essays on Europe, 1964–94* (Oxford, Westview Press, 1995), p. 271.

25 B. Buzan, *People, States and Fear: An Agenda for International Security Studies in the post-Cold War World*, 2nd edn (London, Harvester Wheatsheaf, 1991), p. 188.

26 K. Holsti, 'International relations at the end of the millennium', *Review of International Studies* 19:4 (1993), 400–8.

27 M. Zacher, 'The decaying pillars of the Westphalian temple: implications for international order and governance', in J. Rosenau and E.-O. Czempiel (eds.), *Governance Without Government: Order and Change in World Politics* (Cambridge, Cambridge University Press, 1992), p. 60.

28 H.-H. Holm and G. Sørensen (eds.), *Whose World Order? Uneven Globalisation and the End of the Cold War* (Boulder, Westview Press, 1995).

29 K. Goldmann, 'Nationalism and internationalism in post-Cold War Europe', *European Journal of International Relations*, 3:3 (1997), 261 and 266.

30 J. Szücs, 'Three historical regions of Europe', in J. Keane (ed.), *Civil Society and the State* (London, Verso, 1988), pp. 291–332. See also K. Kumar, 'The 1989 revolutions and the idea of Europe', *Political Studies*, XL:3 (1992), 439–61.

31 L. Wittgenstein, *Philosophical Investigations* (Oxford, Blackwell, 1953), pp. 66–7.

32 H. Bull, *The Anarchical Society: A Study of Order in World Politics* (London, Macmillan, 1977).

33 A. Hyde-Price, *The International Politics of East-Central Europe* (Manchester, Manchester University Press, 1996), chapter three.

34 V. Zaslavsky, 'Nationalism and democratic transition in postcommunist societies', *Daedalus*, 121:2 (1992), 110.

35 T. G. Ash, 'Reform or revolution?', *New York Review of Books* (27 October 1988), 56.

36 A. Hyde-Price, *Germany and European Order: Enlarging NATO and the European Union* (Manchester, Manchester University Press, 2000).

37 L. Wolff, *Inventing Eastern Europe: The Map of Civilisation on the Mind of the Enlightenment* (Stanford, Stanford California Press, 1994), p. 3.

38 Wolff, *Inventing Eastern Europe*, pp. 7, 15 and 9.

39 G. Stern, *The Structure of International Society* (London, Pinter, 1995), pp. 77–91.

40 T. Risse, S. Ropp and K. Sikkink (eds.), *The Power of Human Rights: International Norms and Domestic Change* (Cambridge, Cambridge University Press, 1999).

41 M. Hanson, 'Democratisation and norm creation in Europe', in *European Security After the Cold War, Part One*, Adelphi Paper No. 284 (London, Brassey's for the IISS, 1993), p. 35.

42 R. Scharping, *Wir Dürfen Nicht Wegsehen: Der Kosovo-Krieg und Europa* (Berlin, Ullstein, 1999), p. 222.

43 J. Dean, *Ending Europe's Wars: The Continuing Search for Peace and Security* (New York, Twentieth Century Fund Press, 1994), p. 384.

44 P. Zelikow, 'The masque of institutions', *Survival*, 38:1 (1996), 7.

45 C. Gray, *Modern Strategy* (Oxford, Oxford University Press, 1999).

46 J. P. Thompson, *The Military Challenges of Transatlantic Coalitions*, Adelphi Paper No. 333 (Oxford, Oxford University Press for the IISS, 2000), pp. 56–7.

47 *Gemeinsame Sicherheit und Zukunft der Bundeswehr* (Berlin, Bencht der Kommission an die Bundesregievung, 2000).

48 I. Daalder, J. Goldgeiger and J. Lindsay, 'Deploying NMD: not whether, but how', *Survival*, 42:1 (2000), 6–28.

49 D. A. Wilkening, *Ballistic Missile Defence and Strategic Stability*, Adelphi Paper No. 334 (Oxford, Oxford University Press for the IISS, 2000); and D. Wilkening, 'Amending the ABM Treaty', *Survival*, 42:1 (2000), 29–45.

50 Quoted in C. Bildt, 'Force and diplomacy', *Survival*, 42:1 (2000), 147–8.

51 Bildt, 'Force and diplomacy', 147–8.

52 *White House Press Release*, (20 June 1999).

53 W. Shawcross, *Deliver Us from Evil: Peacekeepers, Warlords and a World of Endless Conflict* (New York, Simon and Schuster, 2000).

54 A. Behnke, 'The message or the messenger?: reflections on the role of security experts and the securitization of political issues', *Cooperation and Conflict*, 35:1 (2000), 100.

55 K. Wilds, 'Identity creation and the culture of contrition: recasting "normality" in the Berlin Republic', *German Comments*, 9:1 (2000), 98.

56 *The Guardian* (26 March 1999).

57 A. Roberts, 'NATO's humanitarian war over Kosovo', *Survival*, 41:3 (1999), 120.

58 Karl Deutsch, *Political Community in the North Atlantic Area* (Princeton, Princeton University Press, 1957), p. 36.

59 John Donne, *Devotions upon Emergent Occasions* (Oxford, Oxford University Press, 1987), p. 87.

Index

AII
MEMOR

A COLLECTOR'S GUIDE TO

AIR MEMORABILIA

BRUCE ROBERTSON

First published 1992

ISBN 0 7110 2088 4

© 1992 Bruce Robertson

Published by Ian Allan Ltd, Shepperton, Surrey; and
printed by Ian Allan Printing Ltd at their works at
Coombelands in Runnymede, England

Cover: Don Patterson 1988 USA

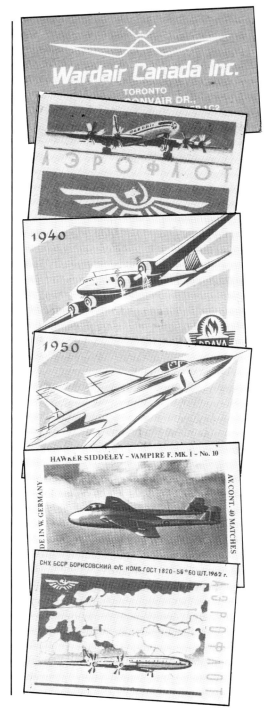

Contents

Introduction

Air memorabilia, or aeronautica as it has been called in recent years, is big business for a few, a collector's realm for many more and a field of fascination for may thousands of air enthusiasts who may acquire odd items of aeronautica without necessarily collecting. This guide has been designed for all.

Many items covered may be well beyond the pockets of the average collector or enthusiast, in particular the veteran and vintage aircraft which are mentioned, but it is deemed a matter of general interest to touch upon the top end of the market. On the other hand it is still possible to acquire some items of aeronautica for a matter of pence rather than pounds. Some, already possessing such items, may at times wish to cash them in for the value that they might hold for others.

Most sellers of valuable items of aeronautica will, in order to gain the highest price, put them to auction. As to which auctioneer or valuer, rather than mention names, the reader is directed to British Telecom's *Yellow Pages*, for the London houses of high repute advertise in the London areas and in the provinces.

For the uninitiated, this means submitting the items to the auctioneer who, having the advice of experts, is the valuer. The item is then recorded in a published catalogue of the forthcoming sale with a suggested price range for prospective buyers. Many catalogues are lavishly produced and may cost £10 or more. They are normally published a few months before the sale, for which it will give details of date, times and location or locations. Notification of sales, availability and price of catalogues, may appear in the national press and aviation magazines.

Since a catalogue cannot describe in detail every item, particularly photo album content, viewing times are given in the catalogue. At the auction the vendor can expect to receive just under 90% of the hammer price — that is of the final bid accepted. Most auctioneers take 10% commission for their considerable effort in promoting the item. The seller can also be expected to pay around 1% insurance and may be liable for VAT. The seller may also have to bear the expense of having his item returned to him if it remains unsold by reason of lack of demand or failing to reach its reserve price, ie the price the vendor can stipulate that he will not sell below.

So it will be seen that auction is a long, involved process and is certainly not for the quick-sale Johnny whose best bet is to advertise in the sales column of an aviation magazine. *Aviation News* has always offered this service free; most magazines usually charge by pence per word or pounds per line, with a minimum charge of five pounds.

From the buyer's point of view, one great drawback of the auction is that items are sold in lots. Many so-called lots may be individual items, but often personal effects, books, flight clothing and the like are lumped together as a single lot. This means that to obtain a single item of his fancy, a buyer would have to bid for the lot. The catalogue will, of course, be the key to this. In cataloguing, auctioneers are circumspect with their wording lest they give false information, so they use words like 'reputed to be' or 'according to information supplied by the vendor' which may or may not be true. In one 1990 auction a Rolls-Royce Merlin cylinder head, valued at a not inconsiderable £250, was said by the vendor to have been removed from a Fairey Swordfish. Surprisingly, the auctioneers, who employ experts, did not appreciate that the Swordfish was never powered by the Merlin. Often pricey items, with reputed special associations, are sold with a letter of provenance.

In general, this book is about articles of the past, then worth pence, that now rate pounds — and which it might yet be possible to obtain for pence. There is the thrill of nosing around today in bric-a-brac markets, secondhand dealers and jumble sales. It is hoped that by this guide you may become more aware of the scope and value of aeronautica.

Above right:
The den of a true collector of aeronautica: machine guns, goggles, paintings, photographs and, overall, books.

Right:
An aircraft almost literally torn in fragments for souvenirs, the wrecked Fokker DRI triplane in which Manfred von Richthofen was shot down. The engine is held by the Imperial War Museum, instruments and parts are in museums in Canada and Australia, while hundreds of fragments of the airframe and pieces of fabric are held by individuals worldwide. Here, its two machine guns are being examined.
Imperial War Museum (IWM) Q10928

Acknowledgements

The publisher and author gratefully acknowledge assistance given by L. A. Anderton, Peter R. Arnold, E. F. Cheeseman, Noel Collier, Peter Cooksley, Andy Doran, Chris Ellis, the late Sqn Ldr E. B. Goldsmith, Jack Long, Glyn Owen, Brian Hansley, Peter McDermott, Colin E. Reed, N. D. Robertson and Alison Scadeng.

Below:
Trophy collecting.

1 Aviation Art

While it is usual to speak of aviation art, the sphere is really aeronautical, for some of the most valuable prints are of ballooning events of the 19th century. Certainly, the Guild of Aviation Artists (GAvA) uses that title as a matter of convenience only, for at some of its annual exhibitions around 10% of the exhibits have been non-aviation , viz, airships, balloons and gliders.

The sphere is wide and there are several facets of presentation such as paintings in oils or watercolours, prints, posters, murals, sketches, cartoons as well as the field of sculpture. Only the subject matter is limited, almost invariably to aircraft or personalities.

PAINTINGS

Ten years ago aviation art was almost an exclusive sphere of its own with the odd exception such as paintings by Frank Wootton that where universally known. Now aviation paintings are attracting the doyens of the art world in general. This is reflected in the valuations during the 1980s which have risen from two to three-figure sums to four-figure amounts. To quote a recent example in auction, Gerald Coulson's impression of a Spitfire Mk IX sold for £6,820. Artists like R. W. Davies, Donald Maxwell, David Shepherd, Charles E. Turner and John Young were among those having valuations in the four-figure class at auction early in the 1990s.

Another surprising aspect of recent auctions is the high prices now being paid for signed prints. Robert Taylor's *The Straggler Returns*, signed by aircrew including Leonard Cheshire VC, had a £250-£280 valuation by Christie's who sold it for £550. Many limited issue prints of around 850-2,000 copies, issued over the last 25 years, are now coming up for sale as their values are realised. As recently as 1980 the Military Gallery advertised prints of Robert Taylor's *Duel of Eagles*, each individually signed by Douglas

Below:
In aviation paintings, aircraft need not feature largely; it is the evocative setting of *On Patrol* (SE5As) that made this painting of Roy Nockold's famous.

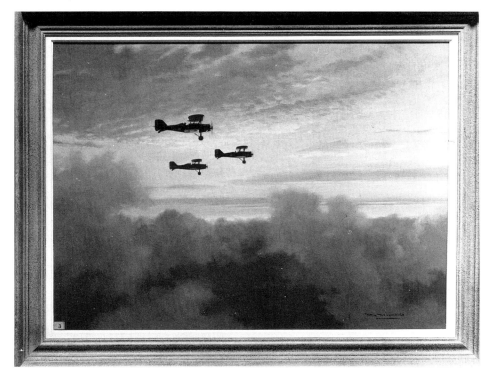

Bader and Adolf Galland, for £7.60 including posting and packing. In the December 1990 issue of *FlyPast*, among 20 advertisers disposing of prints, was *Duel of Eagles* offered at £300.

Paintings that attract could be roughly divided into two classes, those that are evocative of a theme, that may be represented by the titling, or those, usually of aircraft in profile, that owe much to draughtsmanship in presenting a partic-

Above:
A master of service aircraft portrayal, the late Flt Lt J. K. Fletcher's work did not receive the publicity or acclaim that was its due, except in Service circles.

Below:
One famous artist was caught out by the limitations of photography when black did not contrast in shade with blue, making in this case the serial of this FE2A appear as 56, instead of its actual number 5647.

ular aircraft. The latter have often been the result of ex-pilots of World War 2 commissioning an artist to give a good representation of an aircraft that they flew. Belonging now to a passing generation, such works are bound to be coming on to the market in the 1990s. But the paintings that command the really high values are those that combine an evocative background with accuracy of the aircraft subject.

Accuracy of detail will always be important to the majority of buyers and certainly no aviation magazine would commission cover artists who disregarded that important aspect. Even some of the wellknown names in aviation art have not avoided the pitfalls. Bright red roundel centres might add splashes of colour to an aircraft in drab camouflage, but the wartime red was a very dull brick red. In airfield backgrounds RAF vehicles have been depicted in their characteristic blue of pre- and postwar days for World War 2 scenes, when in fact they were in a disruptive pattern of black and green camouflage.

Apart from the proportions of the aircraft which is critical, its markings can cause anachronisms. The proportions of the RAF roundel have been in three different forms of set periods, serial numbers could be wrong for the period as could the wrong camouflage shades for the period depicted.

To many art lovers it is general impression and arrangement that will count, but since some buyers might be put off by lack of technical accuracy it would be best for those buying for investment to seek the advice of an expert. However, with aviation art entering the general world of art, by the aeroplane at last being accepted as an art form, symbolism has become a new aspect.

Aviation is already portrayed in modern art form in Russia, largely due to sponsoring by the national airline, Aeroflot, which is also the world's largest. Its exhibitions and publicity in various countries of the world, including Britain in 1983, brought Russian aviation art under the international spotlight. Aeroflot's next series of exhibitions are due in 1993.

AIR WARFARE ART

Very few contemporary paintings of World War 1 ever come on to the market. Perhaps it is right that those of the masters like Joseph Simpson and Harold Wyllie, with portrait painters like Sir William Orpen who captured on canvas James McCudden VC among other pilots of the period, should be owned by the nation, in these cases the Imperial War Museum. However, works of one artist of the period, Geoffrey Watson, have come on to the market in the 1990s, with one of his works reaching £990 in spite of being catalogued under a re-titling as *First World War Air Battle* which, although descriptive, belied the painter's

dating of his work in 1919 when there was no thought of the World War being the first.

When it comes to the artists of today who wish to recall the first war in which aeronautics played an important part, paintings abound with the biplanes of the period making attractive subjects. Following this in time, the RAF from 1924 introduced distinctive fighter squadron markings, leading to colourful presentations of aircraft like the Hawker Fury which has been described as the world's most beautiful biplane. Here again there are pitfalls for the artist, unaware of the change in the order of colours in rudder striping that occurred in 1931 among other changes.

A vast range of pictures have been executed for World War 2. As early as 1942, colour prints of Roy Nockold's *Some of the Few* were on offer. In 1969 the Kronfield Aviation Art Society, forerunner of the present Guild of Aviation Artists, held a Battle of Britain Collection exhibition with some 50 paintings including original works by Gerald Coulson, Roy Nockold and John Young available in a 12 to 150-guinea range. Since then, paintings of the 1939-45 period have proliferated with many commanding very high valuations.

PAINTING POINTS

The chief showings of aviation art are the annual exhibitions of the Guild of Aviation Artists. For sales by auction, catalogues give an impression of many of the paintings for sale or describe salient details. To help the uninitiated, a few points are given on art catalogueing. Paintings are catalogued by numbers allotted for the exhibition. In order that the exhibitors cannot be said to be giving any precedence, works are usually listed under artists given in alphabetical order of surnames, with each painting listed in numerical sequence. This might be a series number starting at, say, No 501 to take in account numbers allotted in previous associated exhibitions. Paintings displayed will be numbered to accord with the catalogue, but their display is rarely in the same sequence to permit, for example, large paintings to have 'stand-off' viewing.

For each catalogue number the artist's name will be apparent. Names are given by christian name or initials and surname. Neither titles nor professional qualifications are usual, with exception of an RA. Then come the picture title which, particularly with aviation art, may need elucidation. Penelope Douglas's *Pampered Pensioners*, unless seen, would need the explanation that it is of a surviving Spitfire and Hurricane.

Painting valuations, once in guineas, are now more often in pounds, with the exceptions of certain private sales. At most exhibitions where paintings are for sale, the price will appear in the catalogue, not by the painting. Those not for sale will have 'NFS', or similar indication, in lieu of a

Right:
A fine frame can be an aid to presentation as in the case of this study of a Vickers Viscount by David Shepherd.

price. In auction catalogues, issued of course pre-sale, valuations are given in a suggested price range. The lower figure may be the price that the seller was not prepared to go below, and the top figure the highest value the auctioneer expected for the work. This might be exceeded by the hammer price and so increase the estimated value should the buyer sell the picture.

Size is an important factor. Many aviation paintings involve impressive land or sky scapes and combinations of both. Painting dimensions are normally given by depth and breadth in that order, in feet and inches. The art world has yet to recognise the metric system, but auctioneers are now adding sizes in centimetres with an eye to European buyers.

As an aid to authenticity, most artists sign their works or print their names or initials at bottom right or left. A few date their pictures, some by year only.

For the enthusiast who has not the means to buy original paintings or the higher priced prints,

scaled-down full colour representations can be purchased for reasonable sums. Several aviation artists have had portfolios of their works published. One of the latest available in 1991 for £35 was selective works of John Young. Another source is calendars; over the years the productions of firms like Fiat and Fokker have become collectors' pieces. For 1991 the British Airways calendar featured 12 civil aircraft paintings by Roy Huxley. Then there are the greeting cards; the RAF Benevolent Fund in particular has fine reproductions for its Christmas cards including Woottons. Finally there are postcards of aviation paintings available at some museums.

Below:
A Stobart painting of a VC10. The airline QANTAS did much to promote civil aircraft artwork by presenting an annual trophy for the best example.

With old trade posters by chocolate, soap and other manufacturers reaching up to £4,000 in auction and old railway posters much in demand, it is small wonder that over the last 20 years posters featuring aviation subjects have been avidly collected, but only recently have they been reaching high prices in auction.

In the last 30 years the market has been rather stunted by the large range of facsimile posters, in up to 20in x 30in sizing, offered for around one pound apiece by Plaistow Pictorial, Sapphire Productions, through *FlyPast* magazine and other outlets. Added to this the weekly partwork *Wings* presented 12in x 9in posters of the past on its back covers which, becoming surplus when copies were bound up, left the purchaser with an attractive collection of full colour posters.

Particularly attractive are the advertisements for the early flying meetings in England, France and Italy in the 1908-14 period. Such lithographs were being given valuations in the £2,000-3,000 price range at Christie's October 1990 auction of aeronautica at the Commonwealth Institute, at which some 36 lots were of posters.

The range of airline posters worldwide is almost unlimited. It is these for the early 1920s that now reach high prices. Since the range that followed is so vast, later issues are not so valuable, but any well preserved pre-1950 airline posters stand to reach three figures.

Poster artists are not in a class of their own. Some of the most talented painters have turned their hands to posters. For its first posters in 1923, Aeroflot commissioned A. Redchenke, and 60 years later V. Shcherban for its anniversary. Frank Wootton, also noted for his equestrian studies, combined this in his *Fly to Australia by BOAC & QANTAS* poster with a Lockheed Constellation flying over a cattle round-up.

The RAF has engendered a series of recruiting posters dating from the inception of the Force, also wartime 'backing them up' propaganda pictures and air display posters. For the RAF's pre-war annual display at Hendon – called an Air

Above left:
A sketch of Lt Julius Buckler of Jasta 17, 1918, would pass as of little consequence, but its value lies in the artist's signature. Udet was not only the second leading German ace of World War 1, but head of the *Lutfwaffe's* technical services in 1940.

Left:
Eventually the Ministry of Defence must surely put part of its vast holdings of paintings on the market. Over the years hundreds have been presented to units such as this von Richthoften portrait presented to No 209 Squadron, RAF, by Flt Lt D. S. Sykes DFC.

FOR HIGH PERFORMANCE

VICKERS WELLESLEYS

JAMES GARDNER

LUBRICATION BY SHELL

"NEVER WAS SO MUCH
OWED BY SO MANY
TO SO FEW"
THE PRIME MINISTER

Above:
James Gardner was commissioned by Shell for its aviation fuel advert featuring long-range Vickers Wellesleys, 1938. *Shell UK Ltd*

Left:
Typical of the wartime propaganda posters, available from the trade full size or as a postcard from the Imperial War Museum.

Pageant 1920-24 and Air Display 1925-37 – there was a poster competition within the Service. Among those who competed was E. A. Wren who became a famous air cartoonist.

In America, aircraft manufactures and component firms have commissioned artists to present their products for aircraft in appealing settings. So popular were the oil paintings of R. G. Smith, that the MPB Corporation devoted the major part of full page advertising to his impressive paintings, so that a side-line was made in selling poster-size prints.

It is possible for a matter of pence to purchase postcard-size full colour reproductions of wartime propaganda and service recruiting posters from the Imperial War Museum, and of airlines from productions of Drumahoe Graphics. Thus the range in poster collection goes from pence to thousands of pounds. It all depends on rarity and it is possible that the striking posters produced for the Great Warbirds Air Display and the Air Tattoos of the 1980s will be valuable items of aeronautica in the future.

Above:
Wren the famous cartoonist, caricatured by Wren.

Above right:
The last issue of *Tee Emm* with Prune's final words on the cover. *Peter Cooksley*

AEROCARTOONS

Cartoon charters have played a large part in the embellishment of aircraft. The famous characters of Walt Disney are universal and in World War 2 were painted on aircraft of friend and foe alike. But these were, of course, painted by amateurs in the vogue of the masters. Here we are concerned with the masters and their characters.

Of World War 1, the French cartoonist Marcel Jeanjean stands out. Mobilised in 1914 he drew from his experiences in the French Air Service. His *métier* as a cartoonist was not in facial expressions but, typically Gallic, in figure gesticulation that conveyed such meaning that captions were either not necessary or very short. For example his famous portrayal involving the Nieuport Scouts overturned on landing in identical circumstances, showed the two extremes of reaction. In the one case, as the pilot crawls unaided from the wreck, his commandant and superiors are evidently hurling words of scorn for his hamfistedness; in the other, the pilot is aided from

the wreck with those around evidently sympathising with his misfortune. The respective captions are simply 'du Caporal' (the corporal) and 'du Capitaine' (the Captain). His works were published first in 1919 in an album *Sous les Cocardes*, reprinted later and remaindered in 1964, shortly before such items of aeronautica became popular.

Perhaps the most famous of the World War 2 cartoonists was E. A. 'Chris' Wren. As a corporal in the Auxiliary Air Force he designed RAF posters. During the war be became famous for his characterisation of aircraft forms, emphasising pertinent features as an aid to their recognition. At aeronautical functions he sketched personalities with a swift and deft hand. Many of his original sketches were given to those he portrayed and examples abound. At the Empire Test Pilots School at Farnborough, a Wren Room was opened in his memory in 1985.

During and from the war years, cartoonists have contributed to flight safely to a degree that is only now being given its due. In this respect no fictitious character became better known throughout the air forces of Britain and the Commonwealth than Pilot Officer Percy Prune, the clueless clot who continually did the wrong thing that was highlighted as a warning to others to tighten up their flying discipline.

Prune was launched from the very first issue of *Tee Emm*, the phonetic spelling of 'TM' for Training Manual, that ran from April 1941 to March

PRUNE **DILBERT** **PETTIBONE** **SPRY**

Above:
The flight safety cartoon characters over 50 years as portrayed by Bill Hooper, Robert Osborn and Norman Attwill.

1946 with, at peak, 30,000 copies being printed monthly in the UK alone, while copy went to Australia, Canada, South Africa, the Middle East and India for separate printings. Yet it now rates over a pound a copy and a complete set over £100 in the 1980s. It is not yet evident how this pricing will be affected by the publication of a facsimile set. The content was in general related to flying training, aircraft maintenance and administrative matters of which little may now be remembered, but Prune and his ilk live on, part of the nostalgia of Service days (see *The Life and Times of Pilot Officer Prune* by Tim Hamilton, HMSO 1991).

There were Prune's associates; perhaps not so well recalled but worth mention is Flg Off Fixe, he of the RAF moustache, who as a navigator complained that Prune flew him so low that he had to stand up to look over the waves! Other crew members were Sgts Backtune, Straddle and Winde: then there was the attractive WAAF Winsum whose model, like Jane's of the *Daily Mirror*, was a real person. In this case a WAAF at RAF Hornchurch who in 1941 married the talented cartoonist himself – Bill Hooper.

The conception of such a character was the brainchild of Wg Cdr L. H. Stewart OBE, who put the idea to *Tee Em*'s editor, Sqdn Ldr Anthony Armstrong Willis OBE, MC, known as 'AA' for his contributions to *Punch* and as a playwright, in particular his thriller *Ten MInute Alibi*. It fell to Bill Hooper to put such a character on line.

Prune and his retinue, not forgetting Blinder his dog, were essentially a team project. When in 1946 it was suggested that such a character as Prune was purely fictitious, 'AA' was outraged and wrote *Prune's Progress* (now, there's a collector's piece) tracing Prune's ancestry. His father was Peter 'Ropey' Prune who, in World War 1 destroyed 27 aircraft – mainly Bristol Fighters and Sopwith Camels! Postwar, he was posted to

the Department of Aircraft Disposal, more suited to his talents. 'AA' took this theme, supported by the same cartoonist using the pseudonyn 'RAFF', to the Stone Age where a certain 'Proo', was known as 'Proo the Windy' for his continuing absence from tribal mammoth hunts and overindulgence in the subsequent feasting.

Postwar, a new official magazine *Happy Landings* provisionally replaced *Tee Emm*, featuring a number of unhappy landings with caustic comments on the reasons. But its real postwar equivalent was *Air Clues*, the professional official magazine of the RAF, with a Flight Safety section in which the Prune equivalent, if you could dare to call it that, was the staid Wg Cdr Spry, who made a considered comment on damage to aircraft brought to his attention. His words were those of the Squadron Leader holding a particular post in the Directorate of Flight Safety. His person was projected by artist Norman Attwell (nephew of the late Mabel Lucy Attwell) who portrayed Spry on a pedestal – and what better than Nelson's Column, visible to the artist from his studio then situated in a turret of the Old War Office Building in Whitehall.

America had a direct Prune equivalent in Dilbert, conceived the same year by Capt (later Admiral) Austin K. Doyle and portrayed by Lt-Cdr Robert Osborn USNR. Dilbert's bumbling piloting had its counterpart in his groundcrew cousin, Spoiler. Appearing in US Naval Institute's *Proceedings* his antics were extended from World War 2 to Korea.

Cdr Osborn later teamed with Capt Seth Warner USN, who, in 1943, introduced to *Naval Aviation News* Grampaw Pettibone, the elder flier whose caustic comments condemned all who followed the path of Dilberts. He could also give sympathy and praise, in a particularly American way. When a pupil in a Vought A-7E Corsair II suffered a windscreen bird strike, temporarily blinding him, and he was talked down by an instructor, Grampaw Pettibone's comment was: 'Holy low-level braille! This young man nearly bought the farm! A bird in hand sure beats one in the eyes. Thanks to the alert action of a most professional instructor . . .'. Spry would wince!

2 Books and Magazines

Books are the most prolific items of aeronautica as well as being relatively cheap. They are the fuel to the interests of all enthusiasts. They can be acquired from bookshops, libraries, boot and jumble sales, and come in a five pence-upward price range for secondhand examples, and from several pounds upwards for new books. First let us be clear about terms, most booksellers use the term aviation when their scope is aeronautical, because the latter word is rather a long and, perhaps, an off-putting word. In case this is not clear to the reader, it is explained that aviation means powered heavier-than-air flight and thereby by true meaning does not include gliders or lighter-than-air craft like airships and balloons. But the actual scope of aviation bookshops is usually aeronautical and even including astronautical.

Above:
Treasured by an RAF squadron leader. Topping the pile are *Our Atlantic Attempt* by Hawker and Grieve, and *Australia and Back* by Sir Alan Cobham. Most titles are evident except, perhaps, the bound issues of the first two volumes of the *RAF Quarterly* (1930-31) and the total wartime issues of the official *Aircraft Recognition Journal.* At the bottom is Jane's *All the World's Aircraft* for 1932.

FIRSTHAND

For a new book that you particularly require the quickest and surest way is to buy it from a book-shop, but the average bookshop in a small town may well not have the book you require. Most booksellers will be only too pleased to order the book for you, provided you quote the four essentials — title, author, publisher and ISBN number, but there may be a time lapse.

There are only a few bookshops that specialise in aviation books. It has been the dream of some enterprising organisations to open an aeronautical bookshop in the West End or Central London to capture the capital's general and tourist trade. This was attempted in 1946 by the now defunct Harborough Publishing Co which opened such a shop in Hanover Square, London W1, but it failed to pay its way largely due to the high rates of the area. Around the Charing Cross district, the London bookshop area, several shops carry a good stock of aeronautical books, both new and secondhand, but they are not purely aviation specialists, combining their wares with motor, military or general books.

The one London bookshop devoted to all aspects of aviation, dealing in books old and new, magazines with stocks of back numbers and photographs, is the Aviation Bookshop (Beaumont Aviation Literature) of 656 Holloway Road, London N19 3PD (telephone 071 272 3630) open everyday except Sunday. The nearest Underground station is Archway, 10 stations from Charing Cross on the Northern Line (High Barnet or Mill Hill East Sections).

Many enthusiasts, to save travel and money order their books by post, for the additional charge of posting and packing may be less than the cost of travel to a comprehensive bookshop. Shops and dealers may issue catalogues which are advertised in the monthly aviation magazines. Some of these catalogues, issued on a yearly basis, are a book in themselves. More modest, but frequent, are the catalogues of Frank Smith's 'Rare and out of Print Aviation Books' for which 50p sent to 100 Heaton Road, Newcastle-upon-Tyne N6 5HL, will secure the latest. Aeromart of Ipswich is another noted source and the name Falconwood Military and Transport Bookshop at Welling, Kent, hides the fact of its large holding of aircraft books.

Large numbers of the books held by shops are mainly of those published in recent years of which stocks remain available; they are generally referred to as 'still in print', but this may not be strictly correct. Many books only achieve a single

print run and when they are sold out they may never be reprinted. Also, if after a certain time, a book's monthly sales from the publisher go below a certain figure, it may be remaindered, that is sold to a remaindering house for a price less than its marked valve. The reader, will, no doubt, be aware of reduced price books in the shops of W. H. Smith & Son and others. Some people may think that they are getting cut-price books, but

there is no such thing yet, in the general sense of the term, except through membership of a book club. For new books, the Net Book Agreement between the book publishers and authors ensures that their prices will be consistent. Only after remaindering may prices vary. In this respect there may be a wide difference, for while the publishers have sold their stock at cost, which is normally a fifth of the published price, some

Left:
The Mad Major, published by Air Review, is a book to be sought as practically every copy of the single printing was personally signed by the late Christopher Draper, an ace of World War 1, who achieved notoriety by flying under Tower Bridge in 1931 and 15 other Thames bridges in 1962.

Above:
Among the celebrations for the 50th Anniversary of the RAF in 1968, was an exhibition of books on the Force. There, Sir Barnes Wallis examines a book with a photograph of the dam bursting bomb that he designed.

Right:
The Harborough 'Aircraft of the Fighting Powers' series ran to five wartime and two postwar volumes. So collectable did they become that the postwar volumes were reprinted 30 years later. The cover of Volume I of 1940 is illustrated.

booksellers with unsold stocks may continue to sell the same titles at their original published price.

Books today may appear very highly priced, particularly to the older reader who remembers when even large tomes were under one pound, but proportionally, related to average incomes then and of today, book prices are not high.

SECONDHAND

The dealers so far mentioned deal mainly in books of which there are current stocks, but aeronautical books have been published from the early days of the century. Some very fine books have emerged over the years and publishers, now beginning to realise this, are producing a number of reprints. Even so, this is only scratching the

surface of the vast numbers that have appeared. Except in wartime, when vast numbers of books were pulped to make good paper shortages, people tend not to destroy books when they have no further use for them. They are sold or given away to friends or charities, so that large numbers of books of the past are currently in being and may turn up in a variety of different ways.

Most large towns and even some small ones have secondhand bookshops and may well have an aeronautical section. Here is a prime source

Below:
The heyday of Harleyford Publications when 14 titles were on offer, produced at a rate of one per year. Now each title rates over 10 times its original face value.
The Yorkshire Post

for aero books of the past, but they can be pricey in general. On the other hand, few of the booksellers are experts in all aspects of their stock and a particularly rare book may be found on their shelves for a price well below its true value.

LIBRARY SALES

To most enthusiasts there is no limit to their ambitions in owning a large collection of aero books and this can be achieved very cheaply if you are prepared to search. One particularly good source is the library sale. Periodically libraries dispose of stocks when shelf room is getting tight. Some libraries have a permanent section of 'Books for Sale' and, or alternatively, have sales days with literally thousands of books on offer when large libraries are concerned. Of course only a percentage of these will be aero books but here is a chance to buy them cheaply. How cheap? Well, it depends on the locality.

Libraries are run by local boroughs. In a London district like Greenwich, which attracts tourists and has a number of bookshops, prices are much higher than adjoining districts. This is probably to discourage local booksellers from finding a cheap source for new stock. On the other hand at adjoining Lewisham, the same

book would be half the price. At a recent library book sale at Deptford a short distance up-river from Greenwich, prices were paperbacks 10p, hardbacked fiction 15p and non-fiction, which included some aero books, 20p.

There are advantages and disadvantages with library sales. The bad news first. Having been in library circulation, there may be a page torn out or some scribbling and even comments from those who disagree with the author. The writer has often constrained himself on this last issue! On the other hand some library disposals are in almost pristine condition, particularly specialist books in the aeronautical field, which are being discarded for the very reason that there was little or no demand for borrowing them. The great advantage of most library sales over all other sales, is the preservation of the dust cover. Most libraries upon accession of a book, put it in a transparent protective plastic cover, so stopping the dust cover from wearing.

BOOKS AS JUMBLE

There are cheaper sales than some library sales. For example one of the collectable Ian Allan Ltd 'At War' series, the *Stuka at War* originally published at £4.50, was sold by Greenwich Libraries in a reasonable condition for just £1.00. The person who bought it gave it to a Scout's books sale where as a 'used book' it was on the 20p section. Which brings us to general book sales.

Organisations and charities have book sales from time to time. All over Britain Boy Scout groups in particular organise a series of sales. At one recent sale, the bargain basement — a large room full of books on shelves and tables, had everything at 10p. Of course you have to hunt around, but there is no telling what you might find. Also, if you are interested in all aspects of aviation, do not despise general biographical works. The personality concerned may have served in an air arm or have some connections with the industry and the book could contain interesting aeronautical matter. At such sales there is plenty of time to examine carefully and browse.

There are few jumble sales that do not have some books and many have hundreds. Even in the early 1990s there are still such sales in which hardbacks are 10p and paperbacks 5p, although 20p and 10p is the more usual for sales in the London area. Normally there is also a nominal 10p or 20p entry fee. Back copies of aero magazines are also a possibility at this kind of sale. You may be unlucky at several sales, but hit the jackpot with a Jane's at another.

Boot sales are now the rage and books often turn up at these mixed with the variety of goods found in such sales. In winter they are held indoors for which there may be a nominal entrance fee, in this case it is more of a table sale. But in summer these sales abound on commons and market sites up and down the country.

But how do you know when and where book, jumble and boot sales will be held? Well, there is little point in the sponsors holding them if the public are not aware, so they are usually well advertised. You may well be fed up with the increasing number of free newspapers that are shoved through your letterbox. Most of these have a section for local events. To give an example, the freely distributed weekly *Advertiser* in a London district recently had advertisements for 50 such local events due to take place within the next 10 days. A church planning a sale in a heavily populated area, first contacts other churches to avoid having clashing sales on the same day. These sales abound.

There are two other places where aero books may be picked up among others. Most towns and districts have charity shops for Oxfam, Spastics, etc. Most have shelves of books and if you buy there you will be helping a good cause, as indeed you might at some jumble sales. Most secondhand furniture shops are in the business of house clearing to sell the contents. Often these include books and many of those in that line of business, with an eye for antique furniture, do not always appreciate the value of books and aero books may well be among the nondescript works of fiction priced overall at 10p each.

Yet another source is the market bookstall with cities like Cambridge noted for their secondhand books available on the market. Prices tend to vary throughout the country. Apart from Central Lon-

don where secondhand books tend to be priced high, Greater London is the cheapest place in the country for such books and other heavily populated areas come a close second. With a high turnover of house clearances, high density of population donating unwanted books to church bazaars, charity jumble sales and shops, there are more books available than there are buyers. In many London jumble sales, which last about two hours, there is often a large surplus of books left over. Sometimes they may be stored for another sale, but often, as when a hall is hired for the sale, or fire insurance regulations would not permit a large holding of paper, a secondhand dealer is called in to make an offer. Books disposed of in this way rarely rate more than £1.00 per 100. Some dealers sell these to areas of sparse population, perhaps Scotland, Wales or East Anglia where they will fetch many times their London jumble price. Of course, only a small percentage are aero books but the potential is there.

WORDS OF WARNING

Certainly, by careful combing you can add to your collection of aero books for a matter of a few pounds. But a word of warning. Secondhand is just a term for more than one hand. There is no telling where some of the books have been and they may have been through many hands and in homes where there have been infectious diseases — a risk also inherent with any library book. So for book hunting in the secondhand jungle, or rather jumble, take disposable plastic bags, not your household shopping bags. Take at least four, they are no weight and three will fold and go into the other for the outward journey. Nothing is more frustrating than finding a whole run of aeronautical magazines on offer without the means of carrying them away. Make sure you have strong bags, for paper in bulk can weigh heavy. When you get books home wash over the covers with tissues damped with a solution of a disinfectant in water, also wipe the page edges, particularly the top edge on which dust may have collected for years. Glossy and protective covers can be rubbed quite hard; compounded dust makes black marks but is easily dispersed by a dampened tissue. Grease and other marks may be removed by Dabitoff dirt repellent. Shake the container and spray a little on the marks and wipe it off with a dry tissue.

Unprotected dust covers should not be rubbed hard or wetted unless they have a glossy finish. They are the first part of any book to show wear. Often their edges are frayed, particularly at the folds covering the spine of the book. These can

CANADA · AUSTRALIA

GREAT · BRITAIN

R·A·F

· ROOSTERS AND FLEDGLINGS ·

· SOUTH · AFRICA · NEW · ZEALAND ·

The Monthly Journal of the Royal Air Force Cadets, circulating in all Wings of the Cadet Brigade and Schools of Aeronautics.

Vol. I, No. 1   **MAY, 1918**

Above:
For narratives, do not despise the paperback for most are unabridged reprints of hardbacks. All these depicted were bought in good condition as jumble within a 5 to 20p price range.

be reinforced by taking the cover off and putting gummed white paper on the inside edges; plain self-adhesive address labels are ideal for this being thin, strong and highly adhesive. If a piece of the cover has worn away and is repaired as suggested, then the sticky side will be showing at the front. The stickiness can be neutralised by a brush of Tipp-Ex fluid or similar liquid paper which, when dry — and it does dry quickly, can be crayonned or painted over in phase with the cover colouring.

Blemishes in the margins of the pages of a book can be covered by liquid paper and light work with a rubber can erase pencil marks without affecting text. But there is still another warning. You might find that the book is the property of a borough library or school and should not have been sold. Hard luck! Your duty is clearly to return it to its proper owners. Whatever the library concerned, you local library will accept the book for return under the national library agreements, by which any book can be borrowed for a period if you are prepared to go on a waiting list and pay a small fee which varies from different libraries.

To avoid losses by illegal sale, often offered in complete innocence at jumble sales, libraries stamp their books, not only on the initial pages but often on other pages and on some picture pages. When a library sells a book it may not cancel all these marks but imply this by a stamp inside at the front or back 'Sold by . . .' giving the name of the library service, or by a stamp such as 'Permanently withdrawn'. Without such stamps, no book marked as library property should be retained. On the other hand some inscriptions in a book may greatly increase its value. Books given to jumble and charity sales are rarely examined before being sold. Some may bear the author's signature and a book signed by a famous airman could reach a three-figure sum in value.

A recent trend has been the Aerojumble, held at such venues as the Fleet Air Arm Museum, Yeovilton. While unrivalled for their scope, the vendors there know well the value of their goods and price accordingly. But while no great cheap finds are likely to be made, the very close proximity of rival vendors means that competition keeps prices well within reason.

Jane's *All the World's Aircraft* are the prime references. A 1917 copy of Jane's in its original, albeit distressed condition, cloth cover was catalogued in 1990 at £200-300. If you are a collector of Jane's and this one is missing, you may not have a second chance. If you want it for reference then give it a miss. There was scant information and outdated photographs in the World War 1 issues of Jane's due to censorship. It is the 1919 and the 1945-46 issues that are the prime references for the two World Wars, when censorship was relaxed. The difficulty with buying Jane's at auctions is that the seller may have several issues of various years which are lumped together as a single lot. For individual copies required it is worth consulting a specialist book-seller. As a general guide The Falconwood Transport and Military Bookshop, quoted in mid-1992, £120 pre-World War 2, £70 World War 2 and around £40 for post-World War 2 issues. There have been facsimile reprints of some years and while these are not sought by true book collectors, for reference purposes they are ideal and relatively cheap. The prime 1945-56 issue reprint was catalogued by one bookseller at £20 in his June 1990 list which included postwar ex-libris copies at £25.

Overall the scope is wide. Leaving Jane's for Biggles and the like might seem like going from the sublime to the ridiculous. But it is the fictional boys' story books by such authors as

Below:
Now extremely rare is the British equivalent to the prewar American pulp air magazines, *Air Stories*, which had both factual features and fictional stories.

Percy F. Westerman, George E. Rochester, Herbert Strang and the like, in the first two decades of the century, that now rival Jane's in auction prices. The buyers are not necessarily air enthusiasts, but possibly book collectors. And such items could equally come up in your local jumble sale, for who would suspect boys' books of the past achieving high values. Apart from W. E. John's other works, he had 106 Biggles books published by 10 different publishers between 1932-78, so the field is broad.

MAGAZINES

With magazines there is wide scope. Good runs of *Flight* and *Aeroplane* prewar rate hundreds of pounds and of modern aero magazines, it is the No 1 issue that always seems in short supply and is often sought. The old American pulp magazines rate high, for being poor quality paper they were not treasured and few copies exist.

Rare and highly sought are the limited circulation magazines of World War 1 and 2, to name a few: the *Freugh Gazette* of the West Freugh airship station started in 1916; the *Chingflier* of RNAS Chingford was issued 1916-17; *Dope* of No 5 Wing RNAS was being printed during 1917 and *Whitecraft*, the magazine of Whitehead Aviation, started up in September 1917. Similar magazines flourished in World War 2, such as *Atlantic Echo* by RAF Azores and *Gen* of RAF Charter Hall. *V Group News*, prepared by HQ No 5 Group, Bomber Command, containing gunnery, bombing, navigation and engineering progress, was actually classified 'Secret'.

There are endless possibilities of old and new aero books and magazines waiting to be picked up for a few pence at such sales, as have been mentioned. This survey equally applies to paperbacks, in which form many famous works have been reprinted. To achieve results in secondhand book buying you need perseverance and good luck. Do not be too disappointed with unproductive forays, but once you strike lucky — beware. For the book hunt bug will get you and you will become a chaser of aeronautica in one of its most rewarding and cheapest fields.

Below:
Emphasising the vast scope in magazines is this selection of a few of the many house magazines by aircraft firms and airlines.

3 Service Publications

Produced at public expense, often with some security classification, and restricted to those in the Services, are some of the most informative and revealing of all publications. Moreover, their existence is often undreamed of by the average enthusiast whose sphere of perusal is the bookshop, bookstall and public library. But under the 30-year Rule for public records those that have been retained can be perused at the Public Record Office, Kew, and others may be bought at specialist bookshops. Copies of most of the documents that will be mentioned are known to be stocked by such shops in recent years.

WORLD WAR 1 AIR REPORTS

Perhaps the most important air documents of World War 1 are those relating to basic dimensional data and performance. Up to midwar, aircraft were tested by the Central Flying School, but when its experimental flight expanded out of all proportion, this was made into an experimental squadron and later into a complete establishment at Martlesham Heath to where Royal Flying Corps types, previously tested at Farnborough, were sent. A set style of Martlesham Heath reports were issued, numbering up to 250 by the end of the war, prefixed 'M' to denote the series. These reports form the basis of information given in reference works on World War 1 British aircraft.

The Admiralty also sent naval landplanes for testing at Martlesham Heath, which, being inland, was obviously not suitable for testing flying boats, floatplanes and shipborne aircraft, or for flotation test on landplanes which were tested at Grain in Kent where a similar number of reports ensued. These were in three series prefixed 'NM' for type performance tests, 'NE' for engine tests including flying as well as static tests, and an 'NF' for general testing such as airframe and modification or special instrumentation. Additionally the Experimental Constructive Department (ECD) at Grain issued its own series of reports on such matters as modification for shipborne take-off or flotation experiments.

While these reports are regarded as the prime records, and they have been referred to in reference works, the subsidiary reports by Martlesham Heath appear to have escaped notice. A series of reports dealing with propellers, was prefixed 'A' for Airscrews and often involved detailed performance data with comparative trials of different propellers. An 'E' for engine numbered series dealt with anything from a broken gear wheel on static test, to flying trials with various propeller gearings.

Below:
Martlesham Heath reports normally had three accompanying ground views of each aircraft type tested. This is one of the three with Report M195 Sopwith Bomber B1496. *IWM Q67562*

WORLD WAR 1 OPERATIONAL RECORDS

The operations of the British Air Services for World War 1 are undoubtedly the best documented of any of the belligerents. From 25 July 1915 the RFC on the Western Front compiled a daily communiqué and released it to units every few days. At first brief and on field duplicated paper, it increased in size and was printed in large numbers to the end of March 1918. At this point the newly-formed RAF took over, issuing

Below:
A photograph taken in November 1938 to illustrate a report on the Martin Baker MB1. This is one of the RTP photograph series of which hundreds of 8in x 6in prints were on offer for 40p each early in 1991.
Crown copyright

32 weekly communiqués up to 11 November 1918. All these communiqués mentioned units, aircrew, air actions, etc. An edited version of all but the year 1917 has been published in *Royal Flying Corps 1915-1916* (Kimber 1969) and *Royal Air Force 1918* (Kimber 1968), both by the late Christopher Cole. Plans are in hand for a *Royal Air Force 1917* to complete the series.

The Operations Division of the Naval Staff issued fortnightly reports of the Royal Naval Air Service from 26 November 1915 to March 1918 with the appropriate RFC Reports included. From the outset these were in printed form and dealt with activities in all theatres, including units operating on the Western Front and from carriers. A bound copy of these reports weighs over 5lb (2½kg) and is worth a three-figure sum.

The Independent Force issued 15 printed communiqués from 8 August to 11 November 1918. Apart from these main operational reports, the RFC also issued a monthly summary of work carried out and some RFC/RAF Brigades issued their own duplicated sheet communiqués, including the 8th Brigade, forerunner of the Independent Force.

Since the chief published record of the RFC, RNAS and RAF in World War 1 is the six volumes, plus appendices and maps, of the full set of *The War in the Air*, which rates a three-figure sum, the value of sets of unpublished communiqués held by individuals is considerable, even so there has been some traffic in such items in the 1990s.

British naval intelligence was generally reckoned to be the most efficient in the world and by

the amount of publications put out in printed form during 1914-18, both on enemy activities and for briefing officers on their own forces, this can hardly be disputed. Monthly lists gave the stationing of British naval ships by name and aircraft by serial number, giving their stations. The only snag was that, as highly secret documents, they had to be destroyed on receipt of an updating issue. However, a few have survived and have been copied for distribution to enthusiasts on many occasions.

The Air Department of the Admiralty issued reports at periods on aerial activities in home and overseas areas. Maps for airmen were produced in a series known as Air Packets and to effect amendment to these as necessary and broaden the whole field of air intelligence dissemination, the Admiralty's War Staff introduced from 13 March 1916 Daily Aeronautical Reports, known as DARs. They reflected the whole sphere of incoming intelligence with Zeppelin sighting reports not only by ships but by agents in occupied territory, known only be letter and number, eg B309 for agent 309 in Belgium. DARs also gave the British official communiqué for the day, and the translated communiqués for allied and enemy countries. Interest was shown in 1916 in the development of aircraft in America and DAR192 of 20 September devoted pages to the specifications for US naval seaplanes issued the previous 26 August.

BETWEEN THE WARS

Some of the most prized items of aeronautica are the Air Publications (APs) which include the aircraft type handbooks and they cover a multitude of subjects. Up to 1919 the RAF, formed in April 1918, was a new force in name rather than in character. The forms and publications of the RNAS and RFC were still in use, while the new Service planned its documentation for the future. Gradually as the new regulations and equipment were approved, so were the relevant publications written, or incorporated in the new series. They were all numbered for each different title from No 1 upwards in a range that by the end of World War 2 had reached over 4,000.

While numbers in general were allotted in chronological sequence, this was not always the case. The classification of the series was 'For Official Use Only' initially and 'Restricted' later, the lowest security classification which basically meant not for the Press or unauthorised persons to see. Matters of a confidential nature, such as operations in punitive actions overseas, were in a separate Confidential Document (CD) series, but after a period of time many were downgraded and given an AP number, eg CD96 *Report on the Operations in Dir, Bajuar and Mohmand Territory, January-March 1932* became AP1558. A number of former RNAS Confidential Books (CB) were also incorporated, eg CB819 *State of Development of the Airship Service, 1 January 1918* became AP844.

A number of airframe handbooks APs could be bought by the public through Her Majesty's Stationery Office (HMSO) including those for the Bristol Bulldog and the Hawker Hart. In recent years, by arrangement with HMSO, facsimiles of some of the airframe handbooks and in particular their associated Pilot's Notes, have been produced commercially. Among the classic APs are:

Below:
Typical of the illustrations in *Impact* and MAAF Reviews, showing in this case a German hangar being strafed in Yugoslavia. *IWM C4238*

Above:
First of the 11 *Bomber Command's Quarterly Reviews* which all featured a Lancaster in outline on the cover, to the annoyance of Halifax-operating personnel. Page sizes of this and Coastal Command monthly reviews were 8¼x13in (21x33cm). *Peter Cooksley*

AP125 *A Short History of the RAF* which runs to 500 pages in its 1936 final edition, AP129 *RAF Flying Training Manual* with periodic editions from 1920, and AP1081 *RAF Pocket Book* with 300 packed pages on how to run an air force.

WORLD WAR 2 AIR DOCUMENTS

With gathering war clouds and expanding force, the Air Staff at the Air Ministry issued from January 1936 a monthly RAF Intelligence Summary advising new units on re-equipment, operations and events overseas, information on Commonwealth air forces and reports on foreign air forces. Its classification was 'For Official Use Only' and it had a wide distribution and many were retained by individual officers which explains why copies have reached some specialist secondhand bookshops. Its last issue was August 1939.

On the declaration of war came that prime documentation of the war, the Secret AMWIS (Air Ministry Weekly Intelligence Summary) running to 298 issues before the war in Europe ended. With summaries of activity on all fronts, information from captured enemy documents and equipment, inside stories of Germany, illustrated with photographs, maps and charts, its pages per issue increased to 72. Its distinctive overall red cover was changed to blue early in 1945. As a secret document, its movements and eventual destruction was recorded so that few remain, making each surviving issue a highly prized historical document.

Some RAF Commands issued their own reviews. *Bomber Command Quarterly Review* started with the April-June 1942 issue of 22 large format pages of text on four aspects: review of the bomber offensive for the quarter, highlighting of notable flying incidents, miscellaneous articles and enemy reactions; additionally, there were photographic pages and a fold-out map of bomber operations. Ten further issues followed to December 1944 and for the next year there was a single *Bomber Command Review 1945* giving statistics with charts and illustrations for the whole bombing campaign. A surprising number of these reviews have survived. Although secret, there was little of security matter once Germany had capitulated. On the closure of wartime airfields, when much documentation was destroyed officially, many of the reviews were 'souvenired' and the same went for other command reviews.

Coastal Command was first in the field with its large format review first appearing for January and February of 1942. Its text dealt with six aspects: operational activities review, notable incidents, analysis of past operations, technical matters, training features and the enemy. Photographic pages and fold-out maps and charts were additional to its 48 numbered pages. Late in 1942 and for the rest of the war this Command review appeared monthly.

What fascinating books straight facsimile copies of these two Command's reviews would make, with their masses of hitherto unpublished facts, figures and details, as well as many of the illustrations. This is a matter for either HMSO to produce, or for a publisher to approach HMSO for permission to reproduce this Crown Copyright material. This would be an all-round benefit. The Crown, ie the Government, would get the royalties, which is in the national interest, the publisher would have a unique work that he does not have to worry about checking and which can

Right:
Typical of photographs appearing in wartime intelligence reports were views of enemy aircraft brought down, in this case nose and tail of a Heinkel He177 *Greif* that came to grief.

rightly be advertised as detailed and hitherto unpublished material, to the delight of a large readership. But it will not happen. Publishers do not now think that way. You just wait and see: they'll produce another book on the Messerschmitt Bf109 or similar over-written subject.

Overseas commands had their own comprehensive intelligence summaries, but additionally, for those in the Middle East, covering North Africa and later Sicily and Italy, there was the secret *RAF Middle East Review* with the No 1 issue covering May to December in 100 pages, followed by quarterly issues. From No 5 (October to December 1943) HQ Mediterranean Allied Air Forces took over its promulgation from HQ RAF Middle East and, having regard to its wide distribution, downgraded its security classification to 'Restricted — Official Use Only'. Thus, this prime record of Mediterranean operations and activities in its widest sense, more detailed than any commercially published works or official histories on many aspects, came to be hoarded by individuals. While copies have been marketed by specialist shops, due to the initial issues being Secret there are very few sets in existence apart from official archives. A drawback with the *Middle East Review*, like many other documents of overseas commands, is that a very poor quality paper was used which does not wear well. The edges of pages became brown and at worst flake away. However, the 10th and final issue (January–May 1945), running to 220 pages, was printed imme-

diately postwar on better quality paper. Both because it was of better quality and only at Restricted level, so that it was supplied to messes and unit libraries, many copies of this issue were 'souvenired' when units disbanded following the end of hostilities.

AMERICAN RECORDS

Surprisingly, one of the best rundowns on British Air Services World War 1 (RNAS, RFC & RAF) organisation, tactics and intelligence on allied and enemy air forces comes from an American publication, the Bulletin of the Information Section, Air Service, American Expeditionary Force. The Americans coming into the 1914-18 War in April 1917 had much to learn about combat in Europe and sent observers to Britain, France and Italy to learn as much as possible from their allies. By direction of the Chief of Air Service this information was collated under hundreds of subject headings and duplicated in the form of bulletins, with no set frequency. Each Bulletin was marked to the effect that the information was furnished for officers of the US Army and Navy,

Below:
American aircraft reports often included a view from above. The Le Pere LUSAC 11 was the only American-made fighter to reach Europe in World War 1.
US Air Force

authorised civilians and aeronautical students in
the service of the US Government. Copies were
sent to the British Air Ministry which retained
them until the 1960s, when they were destroyed
as not fulfilling the tenets for permanent preservation, being non-British originated documents.
Nevertheless, of the 324 Bulletins issued some
have survived and were in East Anglian dealers'
hands in the 1990s.

As to the overall organisation and build-up of
the Air Service of the AEF, its squadrons, equipment, production, casualties, etc, meticulous
records were kept. With slides of graphs, tables
and charts, the former Chief of Staff of the AEF
Air Service, Col Edgar S. Gorrell DSM, DSO,
LofH, BS, MS, ScD, gave a lecture embodying this
material under the title 'The Measure of America's World War Aeronautical Effort'. This lecture, complete with all the data mentioned, was
published as Norwich University, Northfield,
Vermont, Publication No 6, 26 November 1940.
This booklet running to 76 pages is a very collectable item.

The American equivalent to the British Martlesham Heath and Farnborough was McCook Field.
Not only were all the prototypes for the US Air
Service evaluated there, but also many foreign
and enemy aircraft types. Evaluation was carried

Above:
American aircraft manuals and reports, made in
conjunction with the manufacturers, had much
photographic detail as with this Boeing XP-7 cockpit
installation in 1928.

out by the Engineering Division at the field
which issued Progress Reports and Information
Circulars on aircraft performances and development. On the more specialised aspects, separate
reports were issued by Sections of the Engineering Division.

Effective from 15 January 1920, reports from
McCook Field were no longer promulgated direct
to the service, but were embodied with other
reports from stations and issued as 'Air Service
Information Circulars' with the intention that
they should be seen by all officers. After Issue
No 566 in July 1926, their titling was changed to
'Air Corps Information Circulars' and thereafter
they appeared less frequently until 1937 when
around 700 had been issued. Unlike the earlier
World War 1 publications, which were widely
circulated to Allies and of which many examples
were found in British dealers' hands in the 1980s,
few copies of these circulars appear to have sur-

vived. A near-complete set was preserved by the California Institute of Technology which deposited it with the Durand Aeronautical Museum, Los Angeles.

The tailing-off of the Circulars was possibly due to an *Air Forces News Letter* which ran for some 20 volumes before the Pearl Harbor attack. From late 1942 this was expanded into the monthly *Air Force — The Official Service Journal of the US Army Air Forces* stated to be primarily a medium for the exchange of ideas and information among AAF personnel. Printed in New York and widely distributed, it was roughly the same size as the British *Flight* and *Aeroplane* of wartime and contained illustrated articles on USAAF operations and equipment. As it had no security classification it did not go into detail on operations, but was very informative on technical, training and organisation matters in the USA.

For sheer operational photography of reconnaissance, bombing results and strikes as recorded by camera guns, *Impact* was aptly named. Started in March 1943, it presented monthly 48 pages plus covers of magnificent action photography. The May 1945 issue was a special 72-page 'US Tactical Air Power in Europe' and July 1945 a 64-page 'Strategic Air Victory in Europe'. *Impact* was classified Confidential and was distributed down to squadron level. Some 15 years ago a facsimile version was marketed.

Commands issued their own magazines or news-sheets, but perhaps the most revealing of the printed documents were the intelligence summaries, giving operations with numbers of aircraft despatched, numbers bombing the targets and casualties. These summaries contained articles and notes on their own and enemy tactics, gave details of captured enemy aircraft, armament and equipment. They were all classified Secret, but once the war was over and secrecy no longer necessary, thousands of summaries were taken as souvenirs. Those for the US 8th Air Force, of around 80 different issues and 28 pages per issue, clearly marked 'Secret', were being sold in East Anglian market stalls in 1946!

American service aircraft handbooks were issued from 1916 consisting at first of just a sheet. That for the Curtiss JN4D military tractor gave dimensions, areas, weights and performance limited to speed and rate of climb, Hints on flying were given in just 10 numbered paragraphs. While numbers 6-10 were more detailed, the initial instructions were more brief: 1, Look over machine in a general way; 2, Be sure of gasoline, oil and water; 3, Test motor for revolutions; 4, Be sure controls are working properly; 5, Start off full power directly into wind.

By World War 2 aircraft documentation was meticulous with handbooks more detailed than the equivalent British Air Publications. Whereas the British documents in this field were service compiled, the US handbooks were often manufacturer compiled with service co-operation. In some cases, as with Lend-Lease aircraft to British, the US handbooks were issued with British AP numbers to British and Commonwealth air forces. To make full use of these handbooks, particularly the maintenance sections, it was necessary to have a key link between the US serial numbers and the allotted British/Commonwealth numbers, as the US manuals usually recorded modifications quoting the serial numbers of the aircraft in which they had been embodied.

CANADIAN RECORDS

Canada has been particularly well served with air service journals with some stations providing particularly good newspapers. In World War 2 the Dominion had two operational fronts, West and East; on the Pacific side facing possible Japanese forays and on the Atlantic side playing a very important part in the Battle of the Atlantic. On these aspects the Royal Canadian Navy issued jointly with the RCAF a secret *Monthly Operational Review*, starting early in 1943, running to some 36 pages per issue. This gave anti-submarine warfare tactics and trends, a summary of assessments on all ship and aircraft attacks on U-Boats, discussed new equipment such as ASV radar improvements and charted convoy movement and U-boat attack positions. In addition, the RCAF from June 1943 issued a 44-page *Monthly Review of RCAF Operations — North America* giving their Western and Eastern Air Command Reports and statistics on aircraft availability and flying hours as well as informative articles.

Postwar the RCAF decided to promote a Force magazine unclassified to obtain the widest circulation. This magazine was *Roundel* launched in November 1948 and was highly sought for, in particular, its detailed RCAF squadron histories. Ten issues were produced per year until June 1965 when Volume 17 No 5 was the final issue. Its demise was the result of the amalgamation of the Canadian Forces and the launching of *Canadian Forces Sentinel* which incorporated their Navy's *Crowsnest*, the *Canadian Army Journal* and *Roundel*.

Of all the publications mentioned, examples are known to have been held by UK dealers in recent years.

Right:
A photograph of the aircraft concerned is required for civil registration in certain countries. Facsimiles can be obtained as in the case of this Brazilian Certificate No 41 of a Consolidated Commodore of Panair do Brazil.

Certificado de matricula n.º - 41 -

Marcas de nacionalidade e de matricula : PP-PAJ

Especie (1) Hydroavião.

Classe (2) mercante.

Aerodromo de registro Rio de Janeiro.

Proprietario (3) PANAIR DO BRASIL, S.A., brasileira,

Rio de Janeiro, Praça Mauá nº 7, 11º andar.-

(1) — Avião, hydro-avião, dirigivel, balão, etc.
(2) — Mercante, de recreio ou desporto, ou de instrucção.
(3) — Nome por extenso da companhia. empreza ou particular, seguido da declaração da sua nacionalidade e do seu domicilio e endereço.

GOOD DEALS FOR DEALERS

Acquiring some of the documents listed above can be expensive for enthusiasts. Dealers' prices are high and it will be authors who will be prepared to pay more than the average enthusiast, for they expect some return on the deal. But how did dealers come to get so many historic documents in the first place, and where did they come from?

Items like the the Bomber Command Reviews, *Tee Emm*, station magazines had been collected by aircrew in the same way that at home they had piles of aeronautical magazines like *Flight*. Sadly many were killed and in the years following the war's end families gave away or sold the magazines, completely unaware of the significance of many documents piled with them.

One of the largest air libraries in existence was the old Air Ministry library, known as the Adastral Library for its wartime location in-Adastral House then at the corner of Kingway, London. It moved to the new Ministry of Defence (MoD) building on the Embankment and then to the Holborn area. With each move to smaller accommodation many books including Air Publications were shed. At around the same time, bales of preserved air documents were being sifted through for transfer to the Public Record Office. Many were marked for preservation, others to be destroyed and others for disposal through HMSO. This was at a time before the RAF Museum had become a reality.

Since the war hundreds of RAF and FAA stations have closed and their station or unit libraries broken up with, in accordance with government orders, saleable items sent for disposal through HMSO. Even permanent units dispose of old stocks and thousands of items once in the Royal Air Force College Library, like AP125 *A Short* (500 pages) *History of the RAF* which was once issued one per cadet, have been sold to the public — well, in theory.

HMSO is generally associated with new books and publications on sale to the public at large. But they also traffic in secondhand books initially acquired by the Crown which are being discarded, it being a governmental ruling that all such items should be disposed of through the trade — a logical rule to prevent waste and recoup some value on the articles being discarded. With the majority of government departments disposing of books this way there is little

problem, but from the MoD and the Services, it is up to the department concerned to check on the items being disposed of for security reasons. With very old documents no problem was seen and old bound copies of Air Ministry Orders have been disposed of in this way.

Unfortunately 'disposing to the trade' has not meant to the public at large. HMSO has invited dealers to tender for disposal, since it is more convenient to deal that way, than open shop to the many enthusiasts that would like to get their noses through the door — or rather, into the store. So it has meant a good deal for dealers, and enthusiasts having to pay dealers' prices for the many rare documents and publications that get on to the market in this way.

Because of the high prices dealers put on historic air publications, many more have in recent years come on to the market. This may seem something of a paradox. The reason is that over the years many enthusiasts have acquired such items, not as collectors' pieces, but because of the information they contain. In these cases it is worth their while to go to a library or an estate agent who offers photocopying as an aside, and have the documents copied at 10p a page, so retaining the information and selling the document for many times the overall copying charge, and so going a little way to flooding the market and bringing the prices down.

FINAL WORD OF WARNING

If you traffic or acquire old official documents such as many of the items of aeronautica mentioned here you should be aware that such trading or retention is illegal — well, technically so. Documents produced by the Services are Crown property and are liable to be confiscated on the grounds that you are not an authorised holder or that the documents bears a security classification and has not been officially downgraded.

Of course, the Government would be extremely injudicious to exercise any of its rights in any document over 30 years old in general, but there could be cases in particular where personalities are involved and sensibilities could be affected. Also, apart from officially sold items like Command papers and some Air Publications which were priced, many classified documents have been sold by the Crown, through HMSO as related.

4 Logs and Reports

The prime document of any pilot is his logbook. A pilot of the armed forces, by both Service rulings and the regulations of Aerial Navigation, must log flights by aircraft type and identification letters or numbers, date and times of take-off and landing, with pertinent remarks. These logs provide the key to the flying activities of an airman and are not only collectable, but particular examples are sought as a prime reference by biographers. Such is the general interest that facsimiles of the logs of some well known airmen have been published.

Every air combat had to be reported in detail. In these reports are air fighting accounts, written in detail, within hours of engagement. Apart from being a personal account, often written in freehand, they provide important documentation to those collectors of medals or effects of famous airmen.

LOGBOOKS

A logbook of a famous airman can command a five-figure sum in auctions and the log of any pilot who was one of 'The Few', by combat flying in the Battle of Britain, is now worth several hundred pounds. The names of aircrew serving in Fighter Command during the Battle is contained in Francis K. Mason's *Battle over Britain* (McWirter Twins Ltd, 1969). It is emphasised that the list is of aircrew, for it was not only the pilots of single-seat fighters that fought with the Command, but other aircrew such as the Defiant gunners who had their own form of log. More recently *Men of the Battle of Britain* by K. G. Wynn available from Glidden Books gives details of 2,927 men, plus a supplementary volume published in 1992.

A considerable 'trade' has built up over the years in logbooks and it may come as a surprise to many to realise that this practice is technically illegal; indeed, this applied to all official documents. They were Government property and they remain so unless sold through Her Majesty's Stationery Office, but logbooks have never been a subject matter for formal disposal. Moreover, their content is Crown Copyright. They were, in the case of service airmen, issued as official stationery and they remain Government property. Every word written in them during service was done so while they were servants of the Crown and so the copyright belongs to the Crown, not to the compiler. There is no let-out by claim that the writing up was done at leisure or on leave, for by Queen's Regulations now, and King's Regulations of the past, a serviceman is on duty 24hr a day,

365 days a year. Service pay is calculated on a *per diem* basis. Serving men may be permitted leave as a privilege, not as a right.

Since many ex-pilots still have their logbooks, a fallacy has grown that they are given their logs when they leave the Service. That is not so. There may be security reasons why logs should be impounded. However, regulations decree that 'a pilot or aircrew member may be permitted to retain their logbooks in their possession'. Most take advantage of this privilege for nostalgic reasons or as a reference if applying for civil aviation posts.

Logbooks similar to the RAF pattern were kept by personnel in Commonwealth Air Forces and in World War 2 many airmen with RAAF, RCAF or RNZAF logbooks, serving with the RAF, maintained their original logs. This is unlike personnel of the USAAF who did not have their flights similarly recorded. Logbooks were available commercially from stationers, such as Steele's of Los Angeles with their 200 Series of Pilot Log Books. If a USAAF pilot could get his flying log certified, it would be accepted for a CAA pilot's civil licencse if presented within 60 days of his discharge.

British logbooks have taken various forms over the years. Initially, ruled SO books were used for recording flights. The earliest example believed extant is that of Lt B. H. Barrington-Kennett whose 1911 flying record with the Air Battalion, Royal Engineers, was given to the Empire Test Pilots School in 1953.

From 1915 logbooks were issued much in the same form as they are today. The RNAS Pilot's Flying Log was introduced in February 1915 as Admiralty Form S1516. Pilots who had not previously kept a log were adjured to compile their flights retrospectively as accurately as possible. Columns were ruled for tabulated entries of: date and hour, wind velocity and direction 'machine' type and number, passenger when applicable, time in air, course, height and remarks. In the log instructions on the inside cover, advice was given on points to remark, such as detail of practice flights, first solo, etc. A running total was to be made at the end of each page of flying time, solo and dual or as a passenger. Thus a record was kept of a pilot's experiences by flying time.

Similarly, early in World War 1, RFC pilots had the buff-covered AB425 (Army Book No 425) for recording each flight. These, and the S1516, were used throughout the rest of World War 1. The Army AB425 became the RAF AB425 until the 1920s when the book was re-classified as RAF Form 414 Pilot's Flying Log Book.

Fédération Aéronautique Internationale
British Empire

We the undersigned, recognised by the F.A.I. as the sporting authority in the British Empire certify that	Nous soussignés pouvoir sportif reconnu par la F.A.I pour l'Empire Britannique certifions que

HENRY ALOYSIUS PETRE

Born at INGATESTONE, on the 12TH JUNE 1884, ESSEX.

having fulfilled all the conditions stipulated by the F.A.I has been granted an	ayant rempli toutes les conditions imposées par la F.A.I a été breveté
AVIATOR'S CERTIFICATE.	PILOTE - AVIATEUR.

THE ROYAL AERO CLUB OF THE UNITED KINGDOM.

Mabayon of Tara
PRESIDENT

12TH SEPT. 1911   No 128.

Left:
An airman's 'Ticket': flying badges were purely service recognition of qualification to fly. Prior to World War 1 a pilot needed a Royal Aero Club Certificate as shown, some 863 of which were issued up to August 1914.

Below:
A preserved 'Goolie chit'. Held by pilots flying abroad between the wars in the event of their force-landing in the desert of hostile territory, this explained that the bearer should be well treated and that there was a reward for his safe return.

Right:
Signing the log for North American Harvard, ex-RAF EZ246, as NZ1076 of the RNZAF, which records show flew for over 35 years.

Below right:
Joan Naylor at the controls of a Spitfire. As an Air Transport Auxiliary pilot she filled four flying logbooks during World War 2.

The bearer should be taken to nearest Headquarters. He is friendly, should be well treated and allowed to keep this photograph.

انكليزلرك أسير حرب لرينى فنا معامله ايتدكلرينى حقنده ايشتدبككز:
روايانك يلان اولديغى وبوفطوغرافدن آ كلامه جقندكز كه هركيم بزه
تسليم اولور ايسه بوفطوغرافده كوسترير لن اسيرلركى بياض اتمك وكوزل
طعاملره سيغاره وسائر خصوصاتله تلطيف اولندقلرى كبى كنديلرينه
دوستانه معامله كورهجكلرى شك شبهه سزدر . بوفطوغرافه هر هانكى
انكليز قره غولنه كوستر لديكى زمانده مزاره غايت كوزل معامله ايده جكلر
مركزمزه دوستانه برصورتده كوندرهجكلردر .

بوندن كرهبى كتوران آدمى اك يقين انكليز مركزينه دوستانه

40

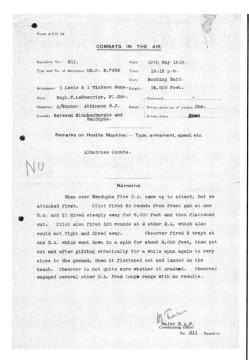

Form A.S.D. 74.

COMBATS IN THE AIR.

| Squadron No.: | 211. | Date: | 19th May 1918. |

Type and No. of Aeroplane: DH.9. B.7638   Time: 12.15 p.m.

Duty: Bombing Raid.

Armament: 1 Lewis & 1 Vickers Guns. Height: 14,000 feet.

Pilot: Capt.T.LeMesurier, Fl.Cdr.   Destroyed

Observer: A/Gunner. Atkinson W.J.   Result: Driven down out of control One.

Locality: Between Blankenburghe and Wenduyne.   Driven down

Remarks on Hostile Machine:— Type, armament, speed, etc.

Albatross Scouts.

No

Narrative.

When over Wenduyne five E.A. came up to attack, but we
attacked first.   Pilot fired 50 rounds from front gun at one
E.A. and it dived steeply away for 6,000 feet and then flattened
out.   Pilot also fired 100 rounds at 2 other E.A. which also
would not fight and dived away.   Observer fired 2 trays at
one E.A. which went down in a spin for about 8,000 feet, then got
out and after gliding erratically for a while spun again to very
close to the ground, when it flattened out and landed on the
beach.   Observer is not quite sure whether it crashed.   Observer
engaged several other E.A. from longe range with no results.

Major R.A.F.
Commanding Officer
No. 211 Squadron.

Above:
A Combat Report by a DH9 bomber crew of No 211 Squadron, RAF, relating to a skirmish with German Albatros Scouts over Belgium on 19 May 1918.

In late 1931 a flying log was extended to aircrew with columns of date and hour, aeroplane type and number, pilot, passenger(s), time (ie, in air), height, course and remarks. Unfortunately there are limitations in the flight records of senior officers. The RNAS decreed that a flying log would be kept by all ranks below squadron commander (ie, lieutenant-commander/major level) so that those of squadron commander and above would consider it *infra dig* to record their flying. In the RFC and early days of the RAF, officers of field rank, major and above, were forbidden to fly operationally and they did not as a rule log their flights. In the 1920s the RAF decreed that logs would be kept by all officers of the General Duties Branch below wing commander, changed to below group captain in 1932.

Pilots may well have more than one logbook. Douglas Bader's first, with an entry on the crash that cost him his legs, sold for £10,000 in 1990, while his later log covering 1939-57 sold for £1,600 at the same time. Photocopies of the logs have since been advertised at £250. Values in general will depend on the pilot's service.

Right:
Lancaster gunner's report for a combat during an attack on Caen the night of D-Day. *Peter Cooksley*

The significance of a logbook needs careful consideration, particularly when valuation may be influenced by inference. The logbook, photo album, certificates, documents and certain books of 2Lt L. F. Lomas were described in a 1990 catalogue with a £1,000-1,500 price tag and made £2,800. Certainly the logbook was worthy of note for the pilot flew in Capt A. R. Brown's flight in the fight with Richthofen — the 'Red Baron' — on the day the latter was killed. An entry in his logbook for 21 April 1918 stated 'Capt Brown shot down down Baron von Richthoven [sic]'. As a result of the catalogue entry, national daily and evening papers suggested that this brought new light on the controversy as to who shot down von Richthofen. Actually it made not one iota of difference, for it is fairly certain that all of Brown's flight would make similar entries in their log's remarks column, knowing that Brown was officially credited with the victory. It alters not the testimony of scores of Australian soldiers, many of whom were firing at von Richthofen as he chased Lt May's Sopwith Camel above the Somme river. They all averred that when the Fokker triplane was seen to falter and fall, there was no other aircraft in the vicinity. Brown's flight was at altitude as Lomas records, at 14,000ft. When Richthofen fell he was sufficiently low to attract rifle and machine-gun fire. Do not be misled by the press who tend to sensationalise events.

The RAF over the years has issued logs for duty and equipment as follows:

Form	Logbook title
68	Watch Log Book
218	Motor Boat (Coxswains) Log Book
219	Motor Boat Engine Log Book
243	Marine Craft Log Book
338	Airframe Log Book
340	Log Book Kite Balloon
343	Compass Log Book
398	W/T Log (Book)
414	Pilot's Flying Log Book
433	Pilot Navigators Log
441	Navigation Log Sheet
778	Log of W/T Flights (Army Co-op)
797	Message Log
813	Log Book for Motor Vehicles
948	Observer's Log Book (RAE only)
1127	Engine Log Book
1139	Accessory Log Book
1319-25	Airframe, Engine and Modification Logs
1507	Parachute Log Book
1767	Flying Log Book, Observers and Air Gunners
2149	Cypher Message Log Book

H.S. Brown.

COMBAT REPORT PRO-FORMA

(Fill in for all "Attacks" and "Combats")

1. Date 6/7 June 1944 Target Caen. Group 5 Sqdn. 106
2. Aircraft type & mark Lanc III A/C Letter & Serial No. "C" LL953
3. Special Equipment carried: ~~AURAL MONICA~~/VISUAL ~~MONICA~~/FISHPOND/~~BOOZER I~~
   ~~BOOZER III/A.T.IV/A.1.V/A.G.L.T.~~
   Say whether serviceable, u/s or not used at time of combat Serviceable
   but did not register the attack.
   Was operator TRAINED/~~UNTRAINED~~?
4. Time 02·37 Height 3500. Heading 050° T Position(Lat.& Long.)49.00 N
5. Outward/~~target area~~/Homeward. On track/~~off track/early return~~.   00.34 W.
6. Weather (cloud, moon & position relative to bomber, visibility etc.)
   Full moon no Stars of A/c Patchy cloud above and below.
7. Searchlight activity, flares, flak etc, prior to or during combat
   small amount light flak.
8. What was first warning? VISUAL/~~FIRE FROM UNSEEN AIRCRAFT/SPECIAL EQUIPMENT~~
9. Which equipment warned? N/A.   Immediate action taken? ____
10. If the first warning was not on special equipment, did it warn later N/o.
11. First Visual; range 500 yds; position ~~PORT/STARBD~~;ASTERN/~~QUARTER/BEAM/~~
    ~~BOW/AHEAD~~:ABOVE/~~LEVEL/BELOW~~: against LIGHT/~~DARK~~ SKY. Light.
    How long after first early warning? N/A.
12. Which member of crew obtained first visual? Rear Gunner.
13. Type of E.A. Ju 188 No. 1 What lights on E/A N/A.
14. Direction of Attack or Approach from astern above.
15. Direction of breakaway of E.A. Astern etc. Range. 250
16. What combat manoeuvre was taken? Port corkscrew.
17. Did fighter fire? Yes. Opening range 500. Closing range
18. Who opened fire first FIGHTER/~~R.GUNNER/M.U.GUNNER/UNDER GUNNER/FRONT GUNNER~~
19.

	REAR GUNNER	M.U.GUNNER	UNDER GUNNER	FRONT GUN.
Name	Sgt. Greenwood	W/O Dixon		
Rounds fired	600	600		
Opening range	500	500		
Closing range	250	250		
Stoppages	NIL	NIL		
Training A.G.S.	Yes	Bristol Court		
O.T.U.& H.C.Us.	17 OTU 1654	17 OTU 1654		

20. Were you able to clear stoppage? N/A
21. Which crew position was searching away from the attack, or in the dark part
    of the sky? Other a/c seen
22. Loss of height during the attack
23. Mechanical defects or damage previously sustained affecting combat
    N/A.
24. Damage to bomber Two holes in Rear Turret Perspex, two in
    Pan Aileron and one in Pan main plane pierced fuel tank.
25. Casualties to crew Nil.
26. Damage to fighter Nil.

27. Fighter claimed ~~Destroyed/Probably destroyed~~/Damaged.

/Over

37497-1

COMBAT REPORTS

From the early days of World War 1, pilots engaging enemy aircraft in combat were expected to give a full report on return for record and intelligence purposes and, not least, to account for the expenditure of ammunition. After 1915, when air combat was becoming common, Army Form W3348 was instituted with an initial print of 50,000. In a further printing of 110,000 in July 1917 the form was revised to categorise the result of the combat and in a final 100,000 print, in January 1918, the foolscap sizing was halved with pilot, aircraft, serial, unit, date, etc, on the front with the back used for the narrative.

Top copies of combat reports are Public Records and not matters for trading. Several copies of reports were made as the unit initiating filed a copy and often an extra copy was made for the pilot concerned. In those days of carbon copies and fountain or dipping pens, pressure could not be made when signing the top copy. This has made an enormous difference to the value of these documents as the pilot and the endorsing officer, often the squadron commander, usually signed in full on each copy. Recently a combat report was valued at £250-300 in auction by virtue of the fact that the counter-signing officer was 'Billy' Bishop VC.

For World War 2, RAF Form 1151 Combat Report did not meet the requirements of Fighter Command which issued Intelligence Form 'F' for details, but unlike the World War 1 forms it did not specify aircraft serial number so that often just the aircraft's letter in its squadron was given. Unfortunately there is no official record of the allocation of individual letters to aircraft. It is the combat reports for the Battle of Britain period that are likely to command the high prices.

Bomber Command had its own proforma for gunners and a stack of such reports for Lancaster gunners of No 106 Squadron were sold to dealers for a matter of pence each in recent years. They had, reputedly, been found discarded at an airfield in 1946.

Over the years various other forms have been used by RAF personnel. In 1918 when Forms W3348 were in short supply due to distribution difficulties, No 1 Air Stores Depot printed its Form ASD24 for this purpose. In No 54 Squadron RAF in Australia in World War 2 the RAAF Form 108A Individual Pilot Narrative Report was used. In the Near, Middle and Far East various proformas were used on a Command basis for reporting air combats. Special forms were also used in all theatres for contacts and air-to-air combat with AI radar, and anti-submarine warfare using ASV, so that the effectiveness of these electronic instruments could be assessed.

5 Photographs

Photographs provide the pictorial evidence of the past. The camera was in existence before aviation so that the scope is almost infinite. It is by photographs that we keep an image of aircraft of the past in our mind's eye.

Collecting aircraft photographs is the hobby of many. For some it is the broad scope of aeronautics, for others only aviation while yet others specialise in periods, nationalities or merely collect pictures that appeal.

COMMERCIAL

The great advantage of photographs, denied to most other facets of memorabilia, is that any number of new prints can be reproduced from the one negative. It was the RAF Expansion Programme of the 1930s, and then the war that sparked off a general interest in aviation which was soon fed commercially. The Ardath Tobacco Co in 1939, as a change from conventional cigarette cards, issued a set of 'Real Photographs of Modern Aircraft'. These 3inx2½in photographs were of high definition and have been used in recent years to illustrate books. A complete set of

the 36 photo-cards are still available for around £10-20.

War brought a general demand for aircraft photographs. Since photography in general was forbidden by servicemen, aircrew bought the commercial prints available to show the type of aircraft they flew. One supplier was the Airplane Photo Supply of Toronto, Canada. Its wartime photographs were stamped 'Passed for Release by the RCAF'. Postwar, to meet an avid demand for all aircraft types, its print range ran into thousands issued in 4½x2¾in sizing.

In Britain it was the Real Photograph Co of Southport, that came into prominence by meeting the requirement of collectors. Its formula was simple: the use of postcard-size prints of 5½inx3½in. Early examples were issued with postcard backing, but this was later abandoned. The series, starting with No 1, the Vickers Vimy

Below:
A Balloon Factory photograph of a Dunne aeroplane chassis in September 1907 incorporated in the Royal Aircraft Establishment Records as negative No 58627 on 7 December 1944. *Crown copyright (RAE)*

H.1552   Cody Biplane, 1912
          (Photo given by N.V. Piper Esq)

Left:
One of Cody's biplanes, photographed by F. Scovell for postcards, taken on Air Ministry charge in its H-series after presentation.

that made the first nonstop transatlantic flight, reached some 3,000 subjects by 1946 and accessions continued postwar.

The Real Photograph series is generally known by the abbreviation RP, often used as a prefix to the number in published photograph credits. The photograph reference number appears in a bottom corner of its photographs, being incorporated on the negative. While this is the number only, for cataloguing the firm used an 'A' for Aircraft prefix to the number, to discriminate from its 'S' for Ship series. While many enthusiasts built up their collection of RPs over the past 50 years,

there were three sources from which they could be acquired in the 1990s. Firstly, collections regularly come on the market from people disposing of their stocks for various reasons. The guide to this is in the advertisement section of the aviation magazines, particularly *Aviation News* with its free 'Wants and Disposals' section. Secondly, the Aviation Bookshop, London, stocked certain numbers modestly priced. Thirdly, MAP (Military Aircraft Photographs, which is a misnomer for their scope is wider) of Aslackby, Lincs, which produces lengthy monthly lists of colour and black and white photographs available in various sizes on a prodigious scale, having also been offering prints from original RP negatives.

On re-issuing RP prints, MAP does not use the original numbering in its lists, but it does keep to the original sizing, now expressed as 9cm×14cm. This, the standard size for postcards, means that they can be filed with the many postcard photographs of aircraft that have been issued over the

Below:
In the pre-World War 1 days when aircraft attracted intense interest, this Blériot monoplane was based at Trengwainton for display flying at Penzance. Examples such as these abound in private albums.

years. While individual RP prints, collectable as they are, rate only a matter of pence, any prewar postcards are a matter of pounds. Their price is inflated by the fact that they are sought by the general postcard collector, for after stamps and coins, postcards come third among the popular collectables.

The postcard craze started before the turn of the century and was at its peak around World War 1. John Drew, a successful photographer whose main business at Aldershot was with the military, extended his business to Farnborough circa 1912, recording some of the early aeroplanes of the RFC. At the same time, the famous military publishers, Gale and Polden of Aldershot, similarly introduced a series it titled 'Copyright Photographic Series' including early military aviation.

During World War 1 when the output of war postcards was prolific, there were few of value as photographs. Raphael Tuck & Sons, well known for the quality of its cards, produced four different series of 'In the Air' but they were full colour paintings. While they were in demand as being in Tuck's much sought 'Oilette' series they had no value as photographs. However, the *Daily Mail* produced some 15 series, some with over 100 different shots of official war photographs. Numbers were of aeronautical subjects, but there again there was a snag — they were in colour. Now this was before the age of the colour photograph; to compete with the Tuck 'Oilettes' its photographs were tinted. Such sets are collectable items of aeronautica, but are not for the reference material-seeking enthusiasts.

Post World War 1 several series of very fine sepia photographs of aircraft were produced as postcards. In the 'Sepia Satin Series' by W. E. Mack of London NW3, the communication part of the reverse side was mostly devoted to detail and data on its aircraft subjects, leaving just a small space for correspondence, at a time when a postcard with address and not more than five words of greeting, could be delivered anywhere in the UK for one penny — similar to the initial cost of these fine glossy photographs. Aircraft firms, *Flight* magazine, the Imperial War Museum (IWM) and the Science Museum, all sold postcard photographs of aircraft. If you acquire any of these or have some in your collection, *Priced Postcard Catalogues and Handbooks*, published yearly, will give a general guide to their values.

During World War 2 Valentine's, famous throughout the world according to its trademark, brought out its 38A series of photograph cards of well over a 100 aircraft types. Today photographs of various sizes are on offer, it only needs a glance at the advertisements in the popular aviation magazines to reveal the range.

Below:
Winston Churchill on a prewar visit to the RFC, one of the remarkable Real Photograph series.
Real Photographs 1665

47

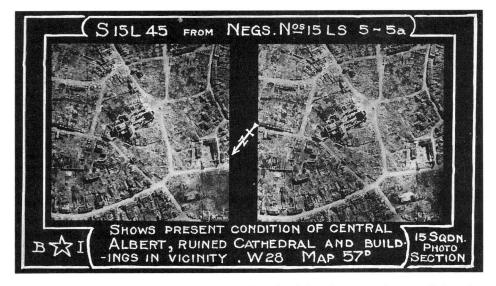

S 15 L 45 FROM NEGS. Nos 15 LS 5 ~ 5a

SHOWS PRESENT CONDITION OF CENTRAL ALBERT, RUINED CATHEDRAL AND BUILD-INGS IN VICINITY . W 28 MAP 57ᴰ

B ☆ I

15 SQDN. PHOTO SECTION

Above:
Stereo-paired photographs, taken officially, were sold in sets commercially in the early 1920s with stereo glasses for viewing. Subjects included captured German aircraft. A full set, once costing a few shillings, could now rate three figures in auction.

Below:
The 'Alpha' postcards of the early 1920s included aircraft photographic subjects, as per No 259 of the series shown.

PRIVATE

Here is a wealth of collectable items of which the extent cannot yet be assessed. Also, many private photographs become commercial. Numbers of the subjects of the postcards of the past were taken privately and sold for publication as post-cards, while today some collectors sell the rights of their photographs of the past for cataloguing by the photograph suppliers of today. In this way, collectors still retain their original copy plus a small amount of cash for each negative loaned out. In some cases this is only £5-10 per print, but when batches of 50 or so are loaned out, there is a reasonable amount of cash in hand for further acquisitions.

Of the snaps taken by serving airmen, there were more taken in World War 1 than World War 2. This disparity is due to the rationing of photographic print paper in World War 2 and the universal VPK used in World War 1. The VPK (Vest Pocket Autographic Kodak) created a revolution in cameras in the late Edwardian era when

Below:
An example of Valentine's real photograph series of the late 1930s and early 1940s.

HANDLEY PAGE "HEYFORD" LONG RANGE BOMBER

photography was becoming a major hobby. When war came in 1914 millions of VPKs had been made and exported worldwide. For servicemen it was ideal, being light (9oz), compact (4¾inx2¾inx1in) and cheap (just over £3). If vest pocket should seem strange to the British reader, it is explained that Kodak was based in America where a vest is a garment similar to a waistcoat.

The 2½inx1⅝in prints of aircraft and airmen from VPKs abound today, loose or in albums. Of course there were other cameras used but such was the popularity of the VPK with 10d film for eight pictures, that thousands of airmen took hundreds of pictures. The vast majority of these have only intrinsic value, monetary value depends on the subject. Famous airmen, unusual aircraft activity or markings, special operations and locations would attract some collectors. As

Below:
Not without flaws, but a rare shot indeed emanating from a Belgian source, of a RNAS BE2a at Ostend in October 1914, before official field photography was organised.

the vast majority of these pictures have never been published, there is the possibility of them attracting reproduction fees. *Aeroplane Monthly* regularly devotes pages to photographs from collections.

It is air-to-air photography, or pictures of aircraft airborne that are the rarities of 1914-18 flying. In 1975 D. Bradford Barton Ltd published *War in the Air 1914-1918* by the late G. R. Duval that had some 150 photographs taken in the air or from the air using the collections of Heinz Nowarra and Bruce Robertson. Photographs of actual air fighting in the period are rarer still, only a dozen or so exist now. Far more were said to exist, but in the mid-1980s the famous Cockburn-Lange collection of World War 1 air warfare photographs were finally exposed as fakes.

So beware the fake. It was in 1932 that the prestigious *London Illustrated News* paid hundreds of pounds to publish 'The Most Extraordinary Photographs ever taken of air-fighting in the War'. In all there were 57 remarkable pictures, published in *The Sunday Pictorial*, on the Continent and in the book *Death in the Air*. For

50 years there was controversy over the authenticity of these photographs of Mrs Cockburn-Lange who maintained that they had been taken by her first husband who had been killed shortly before the Armistice. Actually, Mrs Cockburn-Lange did not exist: it was the pseudonym of Betty Archer whose husband Wesley made models and sets for films in the USA.

In the 1930s the IWM wisely declined a suggestion that the Cockburn-Lange collection should be bought for the nation, but the IWM has been fooled on occasions. IWM negative reference Q27573, published in an IWM handbook, purported to show Bristol Fighters flying over the Alps. Actually it was a montage created by No 139 Squadron. Stills from films are another trap for the unwary, but these can usually be detected for what they are as film makers rarely get the correct markings for a particular aircraft right.

For portrait photographs of the famous personalities of the air, many were recorded on fine glass negatives for it was the custom of the time to go to professional photographers. In the archives of Bassano, F. N. Birkett, Elliott & Fry, Hughes and Mullins, Lafayette and other famous studios, negatives were kept for a generation or longer. F. N. Birkett, in particular, was also commissioned by aircraft manufacturers to record their products.

OFFICIAL

Photographs of aircraft from the early days of flying, right through to today, have been taken for official purposes. Quantities ran into millions of prints as copies were produced for the various departments interested. Many were stamped on the reverse with the organisation concerned and additionally with 'OUO' ('Official Use Only') in rather the same way that equipment bore the crown or arrow stamp of Crown property. While the vast majority were destroyed in normal office clearance, the fact remains that thousands have found their way into private collections.

Early aviation activities were recorded by the Army Aircraft Factory at Farnborough which became the Royal Aircraft Factory in 1912 and the Royal Aircraft Establishment in 1918. There, negatives have been kept since 1912 and earlier photographs of the Balloon Factory were incorporated retrospectively. At the end of World War 2 the negative accession was over 60,000.

At the beginning of both World Wars there was a period of spy mania and ultra-security. A public outcry of the dearth of information about the British Expeditionary Force (BEF) in France in World War 1, led the War Office to accredit correspondents and photographers to GHQ BEF, and to organise official photographers and artists for official use, record and publicity purposes.

The pictures taken for newspapers and magazines went to the publishers and agencies for storage. As this was in the City of London, most perished by fire in the Blitz. Those taken officially were passed to the IWM where they formed the 'Q' prefixed series, with a fair percentage of negatives relating to the air war. Over the years the series has been substantially added to from pictures donated.

Some stations and units had their own photograph sections, but no Air Ministry record was kept of photographs taken although rules were laid down for a standard form of marking. This started with flight letter and squadron number, wing number given in letters relating to its position in the alphabet, the photograph subject number, date in figures and the particular number of that print taken of the subject. For example: A34:AD: 568 19.10.18 5 would be the fifth shot taken on 19 October 1918 of subject registered as 568 by an aircraft (RE8 in fact) of A

Above:
A squadron's photographic section was headed by an NCO. This is No 12 Squadron's section in the Army of Occupation, 1919.

Flight, No 34 Squadron of the 14th Wing. Additionally photographs might have field or trench map references which would vary for different theatres, or focal length of the camera lens in inches sometimes denoted by an 'F' prefix. Maps were orientated by a cross with the top tip pointing north. The flight letter, sometimes omitted, was important for detached flights which might work in isolation.

Perhaps the most sought after prints are those relating to service aircraft under test of which a photographic record was kept, first with the Central Flying School Testing Squadron which moved to Martlesham Heath in early 1917 to become the Aeroplane Testing Squadron in its own right and then, in October 1918, the Aeroplane Testing Station. Postwar, in 1920, the unit was re-titled the Aeroplane Experimental Station and still ran its photograph series which ran into some 3,000 negatives. It was policy to take three or four ground shots of each aircraft type tested. They were regarded as the standard aircraft type photographs. Original prints in the series are hard to come by, but copies are available from the IWM prices on application to the Department of Photographs. Unfortunately there are no references to link the two numbering systems, but fortunately the original series bore their series number etched on the negative, at a bottom corner.

When in March 1924 the Martlesham Heath testing complex became the Aeroplane & Armament Experimental Establishment (A&AEE), the Directorate of Technical Development tasked the

Below:
Typical of the many thousand photographic reconnaissance photographs taken at a high level. At top left, the North indication. Markings on the edge show it was taken by No 3 PRU 16.3.41 with 20in focal length camera. The No 614 is to link the photograph with the sheet of photographic interpreter's comments.
Crown copyright

Above:
For the dramatic action pictures of World War 2 the Imperial War Museum's 'C' series in unrivalled. Here C5721 shows an unescorted raid by Bostons dead on target, a distillery near Furnes, France, on 1 November 1942. *IWM C5721*

station with providing photographs of all types under test both for its own records and as an Air Ministry series. The new series started at No 1 and each print bore an Air Ministry stamp and a date stamp; all were to a 8½inx6½in (165mmx216mm) sizing. In September 1939, when the A&AEE moved to its present location at Boscombe Down, the series neared the 10,000 mark.

In 1940 the series was taken over by the Ministry of Aircraft Production (MAP). Print sizing and the progression of numbers continued as before, but if several shots were taken of the same subject, the same reference number was used with an alphabetical suffix. This brings us to the famous 'round the compass' photographs of British service aircraft of World War 2. For every new type of aircraft, suffix 'A' was head-on, 'B' from 45° to port, 'C' broadside-on port shot, and so on. Moreover, the aircraft type and date was stated on the face of the print.

Unlike the general run of wartime air activity pictures, passed to the IWM postwar, there was no automatic passover of the Ministry's series, largely because many were classified. However, the IWM did get some of these photographs and started an 'MH' series and has added to this by borrowing prints from collectors.

Postwar, the Ministry of Supply (MOS) took over the running of the series. From the 1950s it was no longer the rule to mark detail on the face of the photograph, making it difficult to identify the series except by the reverse side with its stamping, numbering and dating. The series continued in the same form when the Ministry of Aviation took over, to the present MoD when its Procurement Executive took over. At the time the series had reached 40,000 subjects.

Many of this range are held under IWM and RAF Museum reference numbers and in the early 1990s, prints were on offer by Kilbey Ltd of Lichfield at £1.00 per print.

The record and negative holdings of the RAF official photographs taken between the wars disappeared early postwar. The fact that so much coverage does exist is largely due to copying prints from the preserved albums of officers and men that served with the RAF and FAA. In this connection a debt is owned to the late C. C. H. Cole who, as an Air Ministry Information Officer, instituted the 'H' series of photographs, once readily available.

Retired members of the RAF were asked if they would loan prints and albums so that selected photographs could be copied. While the object was to fill the gap between the wars, the opportunity was taken to record new photographs of both world wars. The acquisition of such photographs continued when the Air Ministry was absorbed into the MoD. However, in recent years it has been difficult to acquire prints from the MoD of aircraft and events more than 10 years old. Negatives have been passed to the IWM which now holds much of the collection and later, when the RAF Museum opened, some negatives were passed over.

At the start of World War 2 the Ministry of Information (MoI) took over the control of war publicity. The new Ministry was ready the moment war was declared, until then having been a 'shadow' organisation within the publicity department of the Foreign Office. Two series of pictures were disseminated by the Air Ministry; a 'C' series of mainly action photographs, such as

Right and Below:
Examples from a series of close-up photographs taken by the late C. C. H. Cole of the Martin Baker MB2 private venture fighter. It is shots like these, of little interest to the general collector of aircraft type photographs, that are highly sought by vintage aircraft restorers and modellers alike.

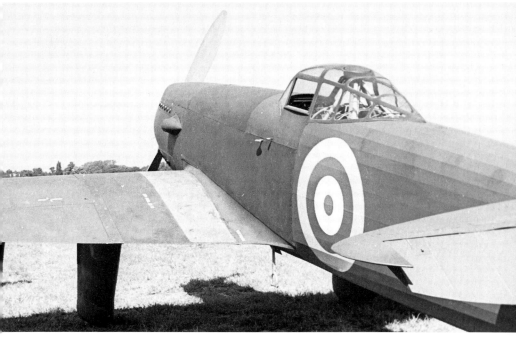

PR and gun camera stills, and a CH general series of air activity. Later came series of CNA and CM series for North Africa and the Middle East, CL for liberation of Europe, CF Far East, CHR Rhodesia, CI India and CR Russia. Negatives of all these series were passed to the IWM from where copies may be obtained.

Unfortunately no catalogue exists of this comprehensive collection of photographs of the war in the air, which over the years has been added to by photographs from individuals. Some aircraft firms donated negatives and prints from their archives to the IWM. Many of these private copyright pictures can be identified by their 'HU' prefix to their series reference numbers.

The series processed through MoI were saved for posterity. But this could not be said of all the station and unit photographs which were regarded as ephemeral and were periodically destroyed, a practice that continued with station photography postwar. The Air Ministry, mindful that wartime photographic records might be destroyed, issued instructions on the classification, storage and disposal of negatives and prints on 21 February 1946 — perhaps a little too late for units already disbanded.

There was adequate provision for the air reconnaissance photographs. A central Film Negative Library was formed at RAF Benson for storing under one roof, in accessible form, all air film exposed 1939-45 by the Empire Air Forces. There was no mention of individual negatives, but the vast majority of PR, strike and camera gun photography was film.

On 1 April 1946, the Central Office of Information (COI) took over from the MoI. Many of the Air Ministry's postwar negatives were passed to the COI where they were re-referenced.

Postwar, the Air Ministry kept a strict register of photographs taken of aircraft and events. From 1946 to 1950 photographs were referenced with an 'R' prefix. A new PRB series then followed, the initials standing for the Photographic Reproduction Branch of the Air Ministry. One confusing element in its referencing was that the original series of PRB reference numbers, which reached to around 40,000 in the early 1970s, was then re-started as No 1, so there is a duplication of numbers of photographs taken up to 1972 with those taken subsequently. At the same time a new numbering policy was introduced whereby the number represented the subject and a suffixed number the separate prints taken of that subject. For example during Operation 'Khana Cascade' of 1973, the largest airlift since Berlin, over 400 photographs were taken, a typical reference was in the form PRB 2690/408.

Dates were marked, usually just month and year, on photograph captions but not on prints. In the 1960s a copyright (©) with the year was included in the PRB stamp, which narrows the field to within a few years, but not necessarily to the year stated as PRB used its 1969 stamps for several years!

One inhibiting factor with official photographs, particularly of aircraft and associated equipment, was that the subject could be secret — using its security classification: Most Secret (changed to Top Secret in 1943 to bring in line with our American ally), Secret, Confidential or Restricted. While in theory holding a photograph with a high security classification, without an official downgrading signature by an authorised person, could infringe the Official Secrets Act, yet thousands are in private hands. Moreover, the security classification may add to its value. What is evident, is that many official photographs are on the market.

6 Recognition Material

Aeroplane spotting has been an activity of aircraft enthusiasts the world over. It reached its peak during World War 2 when it was a functional activity as well as a hobby. There remains a considerable interest in the recognition training material of the past, for it involves wartime publications, posters, postcards, photographs, films and other memorabilia.

WORLD WAR 1

From late 1914, posters and field pamphlets were issued to the Royal Navy and Army since aircraft were being fired upon indiscriminately by friend and foe alike. From early 1915 the first posters were issued for the benefit of the home defences including the police, then came the official service handbooks on recognition produced by most of the major belligerents. Late in 1915 France produced a *Carnet de Silhouettes d'Avions Allemande* (Memo Book of Silhouettes of German Aircraft); however, the aircraft depicted in 1/150th scale were sketches of flying attitudes, not true silhouettes as executed by Etienne de Silhouette. This booklet was followed in 1916 by

Silhouettes d'Avions classes par Analogie of Allied and enemy aircraft in sillograph form to a 1/100th scale. Further editions were issued in 1917 and 1918. Such was thought to be collectors' interest in these publications, that facsimile editions were brought out in Britain in the 1970s.

Perhaps the prime recognition booklets produced by any nation during World War 1 were the newly-formed Air Ministry's Field Service Publications: *Types of British Aeroplanes, Types of German Aeroplanes* and, with coloured content, *Identification Marks on All Aircraft*. These were all of large format with glossy pages, unusual for

Below left:
A poster issued by the Admiralty in January 1915 of which pristine copies were found in a cupboard of the Admiralty Library, Whitehall, in the 1960s.

Below:
During 1915 this poster, prepared by HMSO and commercially printed, was marketed at 2d.

Right:
How others did it: a French aircraft in a German recognition training manual of 1917.

56

Caudron G 4.

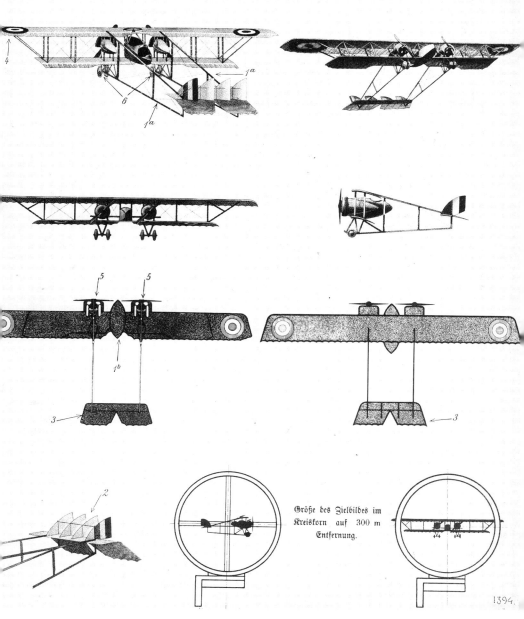

Größe des Zielbildes im
Kreiskorn auf 300 m
Entfernung.

1394.

38A-41   MILES MASTER   REPRODUCED BY PERMISSION
PHILLIPS & POWIS AIRCRAFT, LTD

VOLUME I   NUMBER 8

AIRCRAFT RECOGNITION

THE INTER-SERVICES JOURNAL

APRIL 1943

field service books. The British aircraft volume covered 35 aircraft, each with three photographs, data and sillographs. Postwar, *Types of British Seaplanes, Flying Boats and Ships Aeroplanes* was brought out early in the Air Publications series as AP60.

The RAF expansion from 1936 and then the war itself made the Services and many civilians concerned with aircraft recognition, bringing publishers a ready market. R. A. Saville-Sneath's *Aircraft Recognition* illustrated with official silhouettes and photographs, published by Penguin, achieved a British sales record and was repeatedly re-published. *Flight* magazine issued identification charts, which were reproduced by permission in several wartime general magazines. *Aeroplane* produced booklets of tests, the first coming out when the Battle of Britain was at its height. Early the following year the late Sir Francis Chichester brought out his *Spotter's Handbook.*

Not only the Observer Corps, but many other groups of enthusiasts had formed Spotters' Clubs with some producing their own publications. Probably the best of these was the 'Heaker's Club Bulletin' which, from January 1941, was incorporated in a new fortnightly national publication, an off-shoot of the *Aeroplane* with (now Sir) Peter Masefield as editor, titled *The Aeroplane Spotter.* This ran for seven years, disappearing in the postwar publications slump. It was the demise of such a work that led to the formation of the avia-

tion societies of today, like Air Britain, with their own comprehensive publications. Good condition copies of *The Aeroplane Spotter* are now very hard to come by, due to the newspaper-like format and the use of wartime paper.

Cards played an important part in recognition training. Many were produced in sets and so come within the scope of those with cartophilic interests. Cigarette cards were stopped during the war as a paper-saving measure, but Sweet Caporal Cigarettes got over this by issuing over 100 silhouette and sillograph representations of Allied and enemy aircraft, printed on the push-out section of the cigarette pack which could each be cut out to give 4in x 3in cards. Valentine's 38A series of postcards, also running to over 100 examples, gave standard postcard-size photographs of aircraft, suitable for functional or normal use, followed by its purely functional 'Proficiency Test Series' of recognition cards. Cards of silhouettes for test purposes were produced by both the MAP and later the MoS for use in epidiascopes as tests; thereby the titling was on the reverse of the cards.

Above:
One of the many wartime commercial aids to aircraft recognition.

MANUALS

It was in 1933 that AP1480 *Handbook of Aircraft Recognition* was first issued as an indexed collection of rather crudely drawn aircraft silhouettes. Early in World War 2 this was superseded by a series of loose-leaf volumes, with each leaf

Below:
Q29 in Real Photographs Ltd series of 'Four-in-One' postcard-size presentations. Two numbered series, with 'P' and 'Q' prefixes, totalled 95 different subjects, Douglas Boston is depicted. *Real Photographs Q29*

depicting a three-view (head-on, plan view from beneath and profile) silhouette of an aircraft type, with title and the briefest of detail, but including wingspan and length required for gun setting. Entitled *Silhouettes of . . . Aircraft*, these Air Publication recognition handbooks were issued for countries as follows:

AP No	Countries Titled
1480A	British
1480B	German
1480C	Italian
1480D	French
1480E	Russian
1480F	Japanese
1480G	Netherlands East Indies
1480H	Siamese
1480I	USA
1480J	Polish
1480K	Belgium
1480L	Dutch
1480M	Scandinavian
1480N	Egyptian, Turkish & Iraqi
1480P	Balkan
1480Q	Swiss
1480R	Spanish
1480S	Portuguese
1480X	British (Experimental)

To avoid confusion between letters and numbers an 'O' volume was not issued. AP1480X was the exception in that it was confidential and when not in use was kept under lock and key, whereas all other volumes were only restricted and could be left in crewrooms.

Batches of the pages of these silhouettes have been offered for sale in recent years, but the AP covers are comparatively rare. There is a logical explanation. The volumes were updated regularly, eg by the end of the war in Europe, May 1945, there had been 121 ALs (Amendment Lists) issued to AP1480A alone. ALs would consist of a covering sheet with instructions to remove and destroy certain leaves, replacing then with the appended sheets. Most members of the Observer Corps (Royal Observer Corps from 1941) were devoted aircraft enthusiasts and nothing would induce them to destroy any material relating to aircraft, so the superseded sheets come into personal possession but not the covers.

An anomaly occurred with AL No 10 to AP1480B *Silhouettes of German Aircraft*. Evidently the original issue contained some 'duff gen' to use the expression of the time, for it was followed up quickly in March 1941 by a notice to destroy the whole AL and replace it with the new AL No 10 issued.

Below:
Using a Hampden dorsal turret the A&AEE took aircraft recognition photographs for the British Services. This is Ref 216H, ie view 'H' of their 216th subject, a Beechcraft Traveller taken on 9 May 1944.
Crown Copyright (A&AEE) 216H

РАЗВЕДЧИК
Р-5

(61)

Above:
As others did it in World War 2: page 61 from a Soviet
Red Army Recognition Manual.

Right:
An extract from AP1490X of Experimental Aircraft
No 154, later known as the Hawker Tornado.

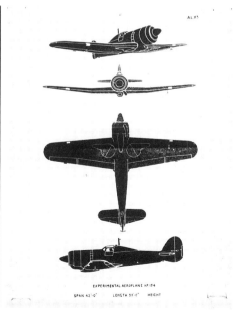

EXPERIMENTAL AEROPLANE № 154

SPAN 42′-0″   LENGTH 31′-0″   HEIGHT

A record of ALs incorporated was made on the
initial sheet of each AP1480, with columns for
date and signature of the person amending. If you
are lucky enough to acquire a complete AP in
this series, this page will provide a guide as to
what period in the war it covers. An AP1480A of
1940 is vastly different from a 1945 issue of the
same AP; the former being of more value.

Additional to the silhouettes, pages of six air-
to-air photographs for each aircraft type were
introduced late in the war. Also the 7in x 5in-
sized sheets were re-issued with new covers to
10in x 5in, the new standard AP size. In the late
1950s the series was declared obsolete, but not
before AP4280 was introduced with its hundreds
of 4in x 3in photocards for test purpose use in
epidiascopes. Individual cards of this series were
priced 20 pence at a Lewisham bric-a-brac market
in June 1992.

Throughout World War 2 a spate of recognition material was issued including posters, wall charts, ciné and film strips. In the RAF's AD (Air Diagram) series, several were devoted to recognition. Among the earliest in World War 2 were AD1340 *Italian Aircraft (Multi-engined)* and AD1343 *Recognition of Italian Aircraft (Single Engined)*. From 1942 Court Cards were issued by the Air Ministry with aircraft silhouette backings; these were colour-coded for different sets.

JOURNALS

Now we come to the most prolific item of World War 2 aeronautical recognition material available today, the Recognition Journals. These abound for while APs and ADs had to be demanded by units, the Journal was sent out automatically to stations and units of all three Services, its full title being *Aircraft Recognition — The Inter-Services Journal* which, with the same basic title and increased content, has been issued monthly from September 1942 to the present day. Wartime copies can still be bought for under £1. The wartime issues were:

Vol I Nos 1-12 Sep 1942-Aug 1943
Vol II Nos 1-12 Sep 1943-Aug 1944
Vol III Nos 1-13 Sep 1944-Sep 1945

Journals, varying from 20-24 pages each, contained features, silhouettes and tests. After the war a vast surplus was held in the Air Publications and Forms Store at 61 Fulham Road, London SW3. The Air Ministry, in October 1946, took the unusual step of advertising the surplus and invited units to indent to make up their sets.

Many of those applying took this up as a free-for-all and for once they were issued unrationed for the object was to completely exhaust the wartime stocks held. The one snag was — as so often happens with commercial journals, it is the No 1 issue that was in short supply and this is the most valuable copy of the set, next in order of scarcity are the July-September 1945 issues which co-incidentally were the only issues classified Restricted.

The publication was re-introduced as the New Series from January 1947 titled *The Inter-Services Aircraft Recognition Journal*. This started at a mere 12 pages and went up to 28 as it took over the function of the AP1480 series. From 1951 the scope was widened to include ships and fighting vehicles under the new title of *Joint Services Recognition Journal*. In more recent years a prime issue was that for April 1968, commemorating the 50th Anniversary of the RAF, with over 150 photographs of RAF aircraft 1918-68.

The Journal was issued to the Royal Observer Corps until the end of 1958, but as it was not concerned with the ship and vehicle element, its own monthly Journal was introduced from January 1959 and continued up to the 1990s. As well as matters of Corps interest it incorporated the air element of the *Joint Services Recognition Journal*. As a postwar publication it is not particularly collectable, the pity is that there was not a ROC Journal during wartime — but there was a monthly *Journal of the Royal Observer Corps Club* circulated privately to ROC personnel only, for one shilling per issue. Starting from October 1941, these 32-page journals, plus covers, are now exceedingly rare. Containing features and letters from members actively concerned with recognition, not available to the public, their content is full of interest.

Aircraft recognition has retained its hold on many air enthusiasts postwar. In the early 1950s Warne's introduced aircraft to their famous 'Observer Book' series. Updated annually, the original editions have become collector's items. In 1990 Frank Smith's catalogue offered 1955-81 copies in a £4.50-7.50 price range.

Since the demand for World War 2 recognition material has exceeded the amount surviving, facsimiles have been offered commercially of such material. In 1977 Warprints of Norwich advertised copies of 1942-44 official silhouette posters.

7 Full Scale Aeronautica

Jet aircraft apart, the three main components of an aeroplane are airframe, engine and propeller, normally built by different manufacturers. All three would have been produced with plates or markings giving a maker by name or code, a serial number and usually a date. But neither engine nor propeller receive any decreed marking to associate them with the particular airframe to which they are fitted. Aeroplanes complete and airframes are well documented, but once engine or propellers are removed the history of these items can become obscure. This is reflected by the lack of background history given in sales catalogues of these expensive items, when their background is of prime importance, both as regards the item's valuation and for the information of the prospective buyer.

The unpalatable fact has to be faced, that for most engines and propellers in isolation, there is no way of tracing the identity of the aircraft to which they were once fitted. If an engine logbook survives, which is rarely the case, linkage might be achieved; but for propellers, not until the sophistication of variable pitch were log books introduced.

Limited documentation of the fitting of engines to airframes exists in the Public Record Office and the Ministry of Defence's Air Historical Branch, but the snag is that it is recorded by airframe serial number, so that no quick trace is possible. Linkage of airframe engine and propeller, each by serial number, were recorded on aircraft acceptance and by maintenance and storage units. Unfortunately their records were not considered to merit permanent preservation and were destroyed. However, a few linkage records are in private hands. As an example, the process-

Right:
A Max Holste Broussard, ex-French Army (as shown) and flying clubs having flown 4,377hr, was valued in a British 1990 auction at £18,000-22,000.

Below right:
This surviving DH88 Comet, one of two remaining in Britain, has been partnered by a third built in 1990 in Australia for a television series on the 1934 Britain-Australia air race. de *Havilland 5367/K*

Below:
In the million-pound class, Spitfire FR14E G-FIRE, of Classic Air Displays, seen before rescue from a scrapyard near Ostend after serving in the Belgian Air Force. It was originally RAF NH904.

ing of Hurricances through a unit in the Far East, 1944-45, was despatched postwar to London for preservation. When, a few years later, papers were selected for passing to the Public Record Office, these were dumped with the bales of paper for destruction. Evidently, someone extracted them, for they have turned up in private hands. It is by such flukes as this that some airframe, engine and propeller linkage documents now exist.

AIRCRAFT

The most desirable and expensive of all items in the field of aeronatica are vintage and veteran aircraft. Some collectors may acquire examples to fly, others for static display. While their price range, which will go higher, excludes all but the wealthy, their acquisition is not without general interest.

66

After both world wars surplus aircraft could be bought cheaply. Alan Cobham (later Sir Alan) bought two DH6s in 1921 for under £23 transport inclusive, and sold them later for £100. Most transactions in aircraft at that time were for commercial reasons. Apart from national institutions, like the Science Museum and the Imperial War Museum, it was left until the 1930s for individuals to acquire old aircraft and build up collections like the Nash and Shuttleworth.

The large number of training and light aircraft built during World War 2 has led to hundreds of Austers, Magisters (Miles Hawk IIIs when civilianised) and Tiger Moths still being flown by clubs and individuals, with changes of ownership through private sales occurring now in price ranges not far removed from those of the more expensive cars.

The rise of aircraft museums, of which there are now over 50 in Britain, has led to a lively market in vintage aircraft for flying or static display. At times the development of display sites has led to whole collections being sold off, heralding the aircraft auction which became a feature of the 1980s. First it was the Strathallan Collection that was put under the hammer, conducted by Christie's, that set the style. The sole Bristol Bolingbroke then in the country, ex-RCAF, made only £18,000 and an ex-RAAF Hudson £16,000, whereas a Tiger Moth and a Harvard in good shape made £19,000 and £20,000 respectively. Surprise came with a Mosquito B35 going to the Weeks Air Museum of Miami for £100,000, indicating foreign competition for British vintage aircraft. However, in this case the balance was maintained as a British restorer had only recently purchased a Mosquito in America. Star of the sale was an ex-Canadian built Hurricane secured by the Sir William Roberts Family Trust for a record £260,000.

When in 1983 Christie's staged the sale of some of the Shuttleworth Collection assets, it brought a spate of other aircraft entries. That same year Philips auctioned the entire contents of the Southend Historic Aircraft Museum. Such was the unpredictability of hammer prices, that it became evident to collectors that while a particular aircraft upon which their sights were set may go beyond their pocket, it was possible to buy an aircraft for the price of a new car. While a post-war Hawker Sea Fury fetched £34,000, twice its estimated value, Air Classics of Germany acquired a Javelin for just £1,000, a Meteor for £2,600, and a Beverley transport suitable for static display went for £3,200.

The scene had been set for the relatively few auctions later in the 1980s, but 1990 proved a bumper year starting with Christie's sale at Duxford, the last Saturday in April, offering inter alia 40 complete aircraft. Unusual was the introduction of a helicopter. Valuation for a Sud SO 1221 Djinn, once with the French Army, was put at £4,000-6,000, but even being subject to a French export licence, bidding reached £18,700. It should be appreciated that the condition of the aircraft were carefully detailed in the auctioneer's catalogue which itself was a work of art. Values and prices paid will always be dependent on the aircraft's state and situation.

The surprising trend of this British auction was that less than a quarter of the aircraft were British and of those half remained unsold. All five French aircraft reached a hammer price: Flamant F-AZEN (£33,000), Broussard G-BJGW (£24,000), Alcyon F-BLXV (£19,250), Pingouin II LV-RIE (£9,350) and another Alcyon F-BLYA (£4,180). The more unusual aerobatic aircraft sell well, a German Jungmeister built for the Swiss Air Force in 1938 reached £66,000.

Most in demand are Supermarine Spitfires and Hawker Hurricanes. It was appropriate that for Sotheby's Historic Aircraft & Aeronautica Sale at the RAF Museum on Battle of Britain Day, 15 September 1990, both a Hurricane (G-ORGI ex-RCAF 5481) and Spitfire (G-IXCC) ex-RAF PL344) were offered under reconstruction at £1,000,000 and £700,000 minimum valuation respectively. That a Hurricane should be valued higher than the popular Spitfire is due to its rarity. Only around 20 Hurricanes exist worldwide to over 160 Spitfires. However, their presentation for sale was perhaps premature with reconstruction incomplete, as both failed to reach their reserve price when bidding ceased for the Hurricane at £790,000 and at £640,000 for the Spitfire. Nevertheless it shows what could be paid and for those interested in the whereabouts of the many extant Spitfires, the book *Warbirds Worldwide Directory* (Midland Counties Publications) gives details.

Replica aircraft that fly are money spinners. Star of the 1990 auctions was Hawker Fury replica G-EKBB; marked as a 1930 RAF aircraft with current permit to fly, it reached a hammer price of £198,000. Replicas of World War 1 aircraft have been favourites, but with original rotary-engined aircraft there is the snag that they would not get a permit to fly with original or replica engines

because of their unreliability, so substitutes have to be used. The flying replica Sopwith Triplane built in 1988 by J. S. Perry, with its taller fin and rudder than the original, was fitted with a cleverly cowled Lycoming 320 four-cylinder engine. In this guise it realised its top estimated value of £22,000 in 1990. At the same auction, a Fokker DrI triplane, originally built for films in the USA during 1958, was sold less engine for £14,300. Several engine types could be adapted and it is imagined that this was in the buyer's mind for it is a heavy price to pay for static display in view of the American market.

For flying or static replicas, America is the country. In the static sphere, Squadron Aviation Inc advertising the 'Big Boys' Toy' in the 1980s offered replica Fokker DVII, Spad XIII and SE5A kits for $6,995, advising 160-200hr completion time. For those requiring replicas and for builders, restorers, modellers, historians or collectors in this field, World War I Aeroplanes Inc is well worth joining. Its sales columns' coverage is from complete aircraft, engines and components down to plans, featured in their quarterly publication *WWI Aero*.

For flying, replica building plans are the key, but in the last few years legal snags have arisen. When, in the 1950s, the late Jack Canary was restoring a Sopwith Snipe to a flying condition, the Air Ministry in Britain was approached for a facsimile copy of the Snipe's manual. This was supplied but with the precautionary proviso that the Air Ministry and HM's Government would not accept any liability for any mishap that might occur from working to the content of the manual. At the time this was considered by some as over-cautious, but in the early 1980s a British firm that had supplied plans to the USA was threatened with legal action from a mishap to a replica vintage aircraft and insurers advised that such material should not be exported. Fortunately this liability does not arise under English law where indemnity can be written into the conditions of supply.

Over the years, hundreds of 'mock-up' full scale aircraft have been built. During World War 2 many were built for display on decoy airfields and subsequently for films, especially *The Battle of Britain* film. Occasionally these are sold for modest sums. Such has been the demand that several firms in Britain now offer to build replicas for museums and individuals. The RAF itself has recently been accused of 'selling the family silver' by replacing its genuine Spitfire gate guardians by fibreglass replicas.

AERO ENGINES

Among the heaviest items of aeronautica, aero engines are a rather limited interest field for collectors. They are chiefly required functionally for airframes or for display. Apart from the many aircraft museums displaying engines, the Derby Industrial Museum has some 20 Rolls-Royce aero engines on display or in hand. In the past, as a consequence of the world wars, there has been more old German engines on display and for disposal than British within the United Kingdom. During World War 1 numbers of German aero engines arrived in Britain as war trophies and immediately after the war hundreds from war reparations went into RAF store for disposal to educational establishments.

Many of the engines distributed around the country went for scrap metal during World War 2, but there was an influx then from German aircraft brought down over Britain. After D-Day a number of engines from enemy aircraft were shipped to the UK for Intelligence to examine after which many became surplus to requirements. This ready availability kept prices down, but they rose in recent years as the numbers of air museums and restorers rose. The main interest now is still with engines of World War 1 rather than World War 2, except in the case of Merlins where there is that popular Spitfire/Hurricane association.

The trend for the older engines is borne out by 1990 auctions where two Bristol Hercules of World War 2, valued at £3,000 upwards, both realised less than £1,000. Even an early jet engine, a DH Goblin 3, expected to realise £1,000 minimum, made less than half that amount. On the other hand, an American Liberty engine, stamped to the effect that it was made in 1918, sold for £9,900, making more even than some Merlins.

PROPELLERS

Perhaps the most aesthetically pleasing items of large aeronautica are propellers whose production is a tribute to fine craftsmanship either in shaping hardwoods or machining metal. Symbolic of the motive power of an airship or aeroplane, before the advent of the jet engine, many are acquired for display in service messes and clubs, while others are kept as reminders of a particular association. There are also some avid collectors and in a few cases propellers are required functionally for a veteran aircraft or to complete a replica aircraft.

Until recent years, a fine wooden two- or four-blade propeller for a World War 1 aircraft would be obtained for around £100. Prices rose steeply in the 1980s and when the largest sale by auction of propellers was staged at Duxford in April

Below:
An ideal way to display a rotary engine. This Oberursel (basic Gnome Monosoupape), housed in its Fokker Monoplane airframe, has had cowling and front plate removed. *IWM H1645*

1990, Christie's estimates averaging around £250, with up to £800 for special items, still proved much too low. Of the 22 propeller lots, all except a relatively late production airscrew from an Anson, were sold at double their estimated prices. Seven went into four figures and a record £2,200 was paid for a laminated mahogany four-blade propeller said to be a from a Curtiss America flying boat.

While most of the well-known auctioneers detail meticulously in their catalogues the markings on the propeller bosses, their remarks can be misleading. In a recent sale a propeller was stated to be from a Sopwith Camel, but its markings were given as 'G1452 N72 P3001 RH 80 Le Rhône D2500 P2400'. In the first place the 80hp Le Rhône was not an engine fitted to a Camel, and secondly the P3001 relates to the drawing number of a propeller designed for the 80hp engine when fitted to an Avro 504 or Bristol Scout C. Incidentally, the initial figures related to the manufacturer's group number, RH to it having been a right-hand turning airscrew and the D and P number prefixes to diameter and pitch in metric measure.

The listings of the significance of the various British World War 1 propeller markings, the makers initials and drawing number applicability, are given in *Aviation Archaeology* (Patrick Stephens Ltd, 1977 and 1983).

For the future, wooden propellers are in the £1,000 plus range and will still be avidly collected. There will be only moderate interest in metal propellers unless there is an association with the Hurricane or Spitfire.

Above:
Of the full scale aeronautica, propellers of the World War 1 period are the most popular, representing symbols of power, being aesthetically pleasing by their curving lines and exhibiting fine craftsmanship. *IMW Q12068*

Below:
Most of the old wooden propellers carried a transferred trademark on the blades, varnished over for protection. Integral of The Hyde, Hendon, was one of over 60 firms in Britain between 1914-18, manufacturing propellers. *B. J. Gray*

8 Aircraft Accessory Acquisition

With the decreasing possibilities of acquiring further complete airframes of veteran aircraft and the almost prohibitive cost of reconstruction, there is now a trend for the average collector to acquire component parts of old, and particularly famous, aircraft. This is a revival of a trend that was rampant throughout both world wars to the dismay of the authorities. At the beginning of this century, souvenir hunting was the craze of the general public. In the pioneer days of flying, if an aeroplane crashed, pieces of wreckage would be avidly sought.

WORLD WAR 1

Plundering of wreckage continued throughout World War 1. When the German Zeppelins L31, L32, L33 and L48 were brought down during 1916-17 in East Anglia, troops had to be brought in to Potters Bar, Billericay, Little Wigborough and Theberton to cordon off the wreckages to discourage souvenir hunters. Much was taken before the troops arrived and after the military authorities had cleared away the main wreckage there were gleaning sessions by villagers and visitors

from towns. Something like a cottage industry sprang up, with pieces of duralumin framework being fashioned into sizeable pieces for sale as souvenirs. Panels were cut into Iron Cross shapes and marked with the identity of the Zeppelin and the date of its demise. Among the more unusual souvenirs existing today, is a gold pendant holding not a precious stone, but a piece of tinted anti-searchlight glass from the central cabin of the L48. Southeby's in 1990 alone had several ex-Zeppelin parts for auction including a brooch, a framed display of parts from the L33 and a section of a Zeppelin frame, none of which were valued under £50. Tucked away in drawers there may well be parts of Zeppelins, their significance long forgotten.

Below:
Aircraft instruments of World War 1: a compass Type 5/17 (No 6077) at top centre, with fuel gauge and altimeter below; left, behind the control column, a luminous air speed indicator and on its opposite side an engine revolutions per minute (rpm) counter. At top right is the clock and below it the Rotax switchboard for the Leitner generator for Sidcot suit and gun heating, navigational lights and Holt flares.

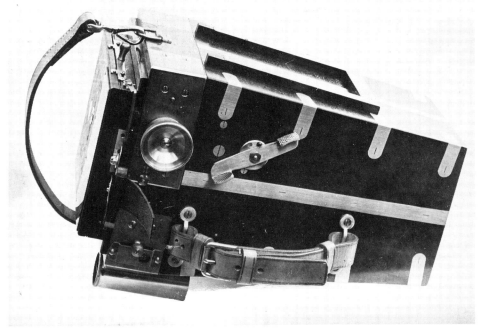

Above and below:
Airborne cameras of both world wars have come up on recent auctions. Here an 'A' Type early standard RFC camera is shown and a captured German photographic reconnaissance camera of the same period.
IWM Q61739/Author

Forced landings through engine failure was a common occurrence in most parts of the UK during World War 1. Aircraft tipping up on rough ground would smash the propeller whereupon the pilot would have first claim to its remains. The blades might be shattered, but the hub usually remained in one piece. The fine wood could make a good setting for a mantlepiece clock and such items frequently come up in auction.

Accidents attracted attention. In the days when an aircraft was a comparative rarity and Britain was far more rural, forced landings often occurred in remote areas. The pilot had to seek means of informing his unit and his aircraft, left unattended, became the centre of attraction from folk in the nearest villages before police or military could reach the spot. The most attractive item from a wrecked or unattended aircraft was its clock, a necessary instrument for calculating flight endurance. The clocks were of high quality and as souvenirs they were also functional. So many clocks were stolen from aircraft that an order went out to all pilots that, if they had to leave their aircraft unattended, they were to remove the clock and keep it in their personal possession until they returned to their unit.

In the early years of World War 1 watches were acquired through the trade. By the end of 1916 eight-day clocks were standard issue, until mid-

1917 when their regular supply from Switzerland became precarious and the RFC decided to make locally produced 30hr clocks standard. The basic design of the clocks remained little changed over the years; numbers still turn up today. Lance's Trading of Boston, Lincolnshire, was offering Mk IIB eight-day clocks in working order for £65 in 1991.

Supply of compasses for the RNAS and RFC was controlled by the Admiralty. In mid-1917 there was standardisation on the Type 5/17 for which the initial order was for 5,000. Later the first aperiodic compass, the Type 6/18, came into use. Under the RAF's classification these became retrospectively Types P1 and P2. There were two series of type numbers, prefixed 'P' or 'O' for pilot and observer positions. The P8 compass in 1940 was common to both Spitfires and Hurricanes among other types.

Many other instrument types and components were plundered, plus many coming from postwar surplus stores. Many such items, that would now have been more valuable in their original state, were fashioned into functional items. Typical

Below:
Camera guns of both world wars are being sought.
Some of World War 2 have been offered commercially and those of World War 1 have appeared in auction. Camera gun as fitted to a Sopwith 1½ Strutter in 1918 is shown.

examples are the nose cone from a Gotha's engine re-modelled with suitable wood to make a biscuit barrel, castings filed down to make teapot stands and instrument parts embodied in plaques.

WORLD WAR 2

Souvenir hunting was still prevalent in World War 2. In general at any accident scene the complex nature of the structure was respected, but not with enemy aircraft shot down. In Southeast England schoolboys collected pieces of Dornier, Heinkel and Junkers aircraft, ranging from instruments to pieces of jagged metal panelling. In theory every piece of enemy aircraft wreckage had to be sifted through for intelligence purposes. In July 1940 the RAF arranged with Section MI9 of the War Office for troops from the nearest unit to be sent to the location of fallen enemy aircraft to guard, among other things, the aircraft from the souvenir-hunting public.

In practice things worked out differently. At the height of the Battle of Britain there were so many wrecks that some were never guarded, the remaining wreckage being eventually salvaged. On some wrecks only a single soldier stood guard. In one such case, standing at an isolated place to guard a wrecked Heinkel, the soldier told the local lads, looking for the chance to sneak a souvenir, to go in and help themselves. Sotheby's during 1990 had a German astro-sex-

73

tant in auction, reputedly removed from a crashed bomber which they valued at £100-150 and a watch from a Messerschmitt Bf109 which reached a hammer price of £198.

Of British aircraft parts in World War 2, people became blasé of collecting anything so mundane. There were, in the later stages of the war, dumps of aircraft fuselages. One, two miles east of Cambridge, had Stirling fuselages stacked three high. At High Ercall fields were covered with derelict Fairey Battle and Lockheed Hudson airframes, left completely unattended although complete with instruments. The opportunities to acquire aircraft parts were boundless, but few availed themselves of this windfall. Eventually metal salvage claimed practically all of them. But in the late 1960s the great craze of aviation archaeology set up teams to unearth the many crash sites and scour remote, particularly mountainous, regions for scattered surface wreckage. Added to this the Ministry of Supply conducted many postwar surplus sales.

As an indication today of material that is available from aircraft of the past, an insight can be gained from advertisements by firms trading in militaria and aeronautica, as well as the 'Wants and Disposals' advertisements in aviation magazines. In 1988 one journal even had offers of a Norden M-9 bombsight and a Ferranti Mk 4E gunsight.

COMPONENTS

A control column is the very link between the man and the machine, so it is small wonder that they are among the most prized of items. Examples of hammer prices in a recent auction of World War 2 control columns show Halifax and Wellington at £154 each; and a Heinkel He111 at £176. A similar item from a Schneider Trophy contesting Supermarine S5, understandably has a higher valuation by both its rarity and association.

The remnants of the control column of Canadian-built Hurricane P5185, dug out in July 1985, came into auction in 1990 with a £400-600 valuation. However, sales of items from digs are not set to occur in general, for their sale is illegal without MoD permission. Crashed British military aircraft and their equipment remain Crown property until such time as the MoD sees fit to dispose of them. Crashed former enemy aircraft and their equipment, lying on or in soil within the UK, are deemed surrendered to the Crown. Crashed US aircraft parts remain the property of the US Government.

Pressings and panels may be cherished as parts of famous aircraft of the past, but they are difficult to display to advantage. The most popular items for collection are instruments. Watches and compasses dating back to World War 1 have already been mentioned. Later came the undercarriage and flap indicators; most of the former had coloured lights, red for the undercarriage

Below:
Aircraft wheels are among the diverse items being offered by traders. Here a Dowty nosewheel unit from a Hawker Hunter shows that wheels can be sophisticated units.

locked up and green for locked down. A few actually had a graphic display in which the wheels on a silhouette frontal view were seen to rise and lower. Dowty produced such an instrument, incorporating an indication of flap movement, for the DH93 Don originally intended as a three-seat general purpose trainer. As a failure in its intended role, 30 were converted for communications duties, a further 20 were delivered for ground instruction and the rest of the 200 order was cancelled after most components and instruments had been made, including the exclusive-to-type undercarriage indicators.

Another highly sought item associated with undercarriages are the micro-switches operated by a plunger depression to very fine limits to give

the up and down locking indications. Not least of their value is that they may still be functional and have been found useful commercially.

Certainly vast masses of small items escaped the postwar reduction to produce of surplus airframes at the two large depots set up for that purpose at Cowley and Eaglescliffe. Ever since, it has been surfacing at bric-a-brac markets and from dealers. But the trickle has not satisfied the demand, for a new trend is the replica. For the aircraft enthusiast the Cliveden Collection offers wall battery clocks modelled in the form of an altimeter and similarly fashioned instruments.

The high and low of instrument sales in recent auction has been £1,650 hammer price for a mounted Spitfire instrument panel to a £20-40

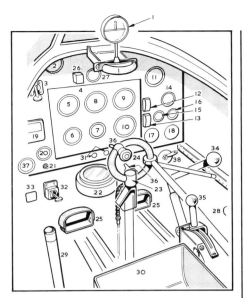

Left and Far left:
Aircraft instruments of World War 2 of which those from Spitfires are the most highly sought. Key to the instruments common to Spitfire Mks I-V as follows: 1, Gun sight. 2, Flap position indicator. 3, Flap lever. 4, Instrument panel. 5, Airspeed indicator. 6, Altimeter. 7, Direction indicator. 8, Artificial horizon. 9, Rate of climb indicator. 10, Turn indicator. 11, Engine revolutions counter. 12 & 13, Oil and fuel pressure gauges. 14, Engine boost gauge. 15 & 16, Oil and radiator temperature gauges. 17 & 18, Fuel gauges. 19, Undercarriage indicator. 20, Flying position indicator. 21, Lights switch. 22, Compass, 23, Control column. 24, Gun firing button. 25, Rudder-bar stirrups. 26, Reflector gun-sight light switch. 27, Dimming switch for 26. 28, Key for recognition light. 29, Radiator flap control. 30, Seat. 31, Floodlight switches. 32, Landing light lever. 33, Throttle control. 34, Undercarriage hand pump. 35, Undercarriage lever. 36, Pneumatic brake lever. 37, Air Pressure control. 38, Fuel cock.

valuation for 12 assorted instruments including an undercarriage position indicator. Trade sales in late 1990 advertised hundreds of items of which a representation selection with approximate pricings follow: Air Ministry Mk II astro-compass — £35; RAF wingtip lamps (Ref 5C/909) — £10; Spitfire/Hurricane applicability gunsight in transit case — £130; wartime Mk XIIID altimeter — £30; and Merlin exhaust stubs — £20 each.

Below:
Be mindful that the instruments of today are the aeronautica of tomorrow. This attractive item is Computing Devices of Canada's projected map display designed for the A-7E Corsair II.
Computing Devices 1691

9 Aircraft in Scale

Modelling aircraft has been a hobby for over 80 years and supplying the kits and materials to effect their building has been, and still is, big business. Several books have been written on the series of some firms, so that this section can be only a brief overall survey. Models can be divided into two main categories, flying and static. Those static, which can be called display models, fall into such a variety of classes that the solid, diecast and tinplate examples and figurines have been covered in the following section.

FLYING MODELS

It was experiments with kites and aerofoils that led to the aeroplane and following the Wright Brothers' first powered flight, the market for powered flying models started. By 1912 the Robie Manufacturing Co of Williamson, New York, offered a rubber strand racer kit guaranteed to fly 1,000ft for a mere dollar. Sophistication was already there with the Model Aero Works of Brunswick advertising their Nomie three-cylinder engines of ¼hp. At the same time, the Co-operative Aero Association of Muncie, Indiana, introduced a cellulose turbine to power models. In Britain, soon after the turn of the century, the *Boys Own Paper* had articles on building model aircraft.

Between the wars, kits for model aircraft abounded. Consisting of balsa wood, fabric, propellers and elastic bands, they could be bought for just a few shillings and the Skyleada range for a shilling. In the late 1930s The Model Aerodrome of 144 Stratford Road, Birmingham, offered Spitfire and Hurricane kits with camouflage tissue finish for 42 old pence. In 1941, with material shortages, Tower Aeroplane Flying Scale Models of Blackpool offered a Hurricane and Skua to HM Forces and Air Training Corps buyers only. There were many other kits such as the Cleveland and Aeromodels series. It is the original boxed items that now rank as worthwhile items of aeronautica, not the made-up models.

Below:
This ¼-scale model of a DH9A by Peter McDermott could pass as the real thing in a photograph with the right setting.

Right:
Cockpit of a Sopwith Triplane in ¼-scale shows the detail that can be achieved. *Peter McDermott*

Below right:
A Supermarine S6B model commissioned in the 1950s by Rolls-Royce.

AVRO BIPLANE, Type 504.

This biplane has been used largely as a standard training machine by the Royal Air Force and by many other air forces. It was also used successfully during the earlier part of the War (1914-1918).

WESTLAND "WALLACE" AIRCRAFT.

This general-purpose biplane was flown over Mount Everest on the Houston Everest Expedition during April 1933, when a height of 31,000 ft. was reached. A "Bristol" Pegasus engine is fitted, developing normally 600 h.p. Model lent by The Westland Aircraft Works.

There were also ready-made flying models. Among the most popular was the 'Frog Interceptor', a sleek, but nondescript, monoplane with detachable wings for neat boxing which contained a geared winder for its rubber bands. A surviving example reached £198 at auction recently.

The building and flying of model aircraft is still a business and a hobby in its own right. Many models are built more for their flying characteristics than accurately depicting a particular aircraft type. Now fully powered and radio controlled they are in a class of their own. At a modest estimate of outlay it needs some £400 for the radio control, engine and materials.

STATIC MODELS

Aircraft modelmaking is a commerical enterprise to meet the needs of airline publiciy, museum display, presentations, a research tool and an enthusiast's hobby. For around £200-300 some

firms will turn out a fibreglass or similar material model to an individual's order. Most airline booking offices display models of their aircraft types, sometimes as large as 15ft long. When an airline replaces its aircraft with more modern types, the discarded models often come on the market. It is doubtful if an airline would sell direct to an individual, but dispose in bulk from their offices directly to a trader. On the other hand air museums could be in a privileged position and might obtain models free, or for a nominal sum, if they were to be displayed in the airline's livery.

Aircraft manufacturers require models for wind tunnel tests, layout discussions as well as publicity. Some of their models are of projects that were never built full-scale. Only in recent years have aircraft firms realised that such models, made by craftsmen within the firm or contracted out, constitute very interesting items of aeronautica. While they are rarely sold direct, being too trivial an item to an aircraft firm, they have been given to directors or senior staff and have then subsequently come on to the market.

STANDARD SCALE

The scale of 1/72nd has become a recognised standard for model aircraft. At this scale a Spitfire's wingspan is just over 6in and that of a Lancaster 17in. Most plans for model building are issued to that scale. For many years Model &

Allied Press has offered a plans service and the fortnightly *Aviation News* frequently lists its plans available, which now runs to several hundred aircraft subjects.

The majority of the vast number of plastic model aircraft kits available are to the standard 1/72nd scale, following the trend set prewar for

Left and below left:
Hundreds of models over the years become redundant to aircraft manufacturers of aircraft that were never more than projects, in these cases the Blackburn B107A and Westland WE-02 transport aircraft projects.
Blackburn Aircraft Ltd/Westland Aircraft Ltd

the solid wood models. The Skybird series of kits from 1932 popularised both the scale and model aircraft construction. Skybird products were boxed with attractive lids for a variety of aircraft types, with contents of fuselage, wings, engine representation, propeller, wheels, etc for a modest 1/6d to 2/6d (7½-12½ new pence) range. Boxed examples, which ran to nearly 100 different aircraft types, with main items of airport buildings and hangars, plus accessories such as bombs and ensigns, are now avidly collected. All these items are now worth hundreds of times their original value.

Other firms soon followed the trend for 1/72nd scale models, including Skyleada of Croydon with a 15d range including a moulded propeller. Truscale, similarly priced, had a range of British, German and French aircraft types. Scalecraft of Southport did a range of German aircraft in the early war years and the National Model Supply

Below:
Typical lid cover for a prewar Skybirds wooden kit. In 1937 it was closely followed by Frog Penguin which introduced plastic to the trade. *Peter Cooksley*

of Huddersfield went to a wartime packaging. Swedish firms, with wood sources at hand, tried to extend their European market to Britain. However, none of the British or foreign firms offered goods as collectable as the Skybirds, with Frog Penguin models a close second. During World War 2, some of the model firms were busier than ever under the national export drive, aided by the Allied blockade affecting the German toy exports.

There was always a plea, as there is today, for more 1/48th scale (¼in to the foot as it is often quoted) allowing for more detail. This was adopted prewar by CMA (Chingford Model Aerodrome) solid scale models while Atlanta Mills of Leeds produced its 'Ace' series aircraft to a 16in wingspan irrespective of type.

Some enthusiasts have built up large collections of model aircraft with storage, dusting and display a problem. Before the plastic kit age Peter Farrer of Torquay had built up 700 models from scrap timber, between 1933-57. After the introduction of Airfix and other kits his total soon topped 1,000 and continued to grow.

In spite of the great variety of plastic kits now available at modest prices, certain types go out of production and become in demand. The advertisements in the 'Wanted' columns of aviation magazines reflect this. It is on the shelves in out-of-the-way village and small town shops that out-of-production kits can still be picked up at their original prices. Most valuable of all are the moulds in which there is now an international market.

SKYBIRDS

BRITISH MADE
A SCALE MODEL
PLANES
of
ALL NATIONS
MILITARY
and
CIVIL
STRONG, EASY
TO BUILD
"SKYJOY" Registered

Price:
12/6

SERIES No. 11A.
FAIREY "HENDON"

CONTENTS
Mainplane
Fuselage
Tailplane
2 Rudders
2 Trouser Sections
2 Trouser Covers
4 Tail Struts (2 Sizes)
2 Airscrews
1 Cabin (Cast)
1 Turret (Cast)
2 Wheels
Envelope of accessories

CONSTRUCTIONAL
MODEL AEROPLANE

10 Miniatures and Figurines

While accuracy in outline, finish and markings in any model is essential for the enthusiast, it is symbolism in hand crafting metal impressions that commands the high prices. To take examples in 1/72nd scale in recent auctions, a finely detailed Fairey Spearfish went for £132, but an aluminium Hurricane made £990 and a hall-marked silver Mosquito reached £1,760, while some aluminium models by Doug Vann went to over £2,000.

METAL MASTERPIECES

Many scale replicas of aircraft have been hand-crafted in metal over the past 75 years for amusement or presentation, particularly by servicemen. Depending on the quality of workmanship, their value in auction can go up to four-figures. Individually made, each model is unique and they are rarely destroyed or thrown away like the production cast models in base metals. They frequently appear in the catalogues of auctioneers.

Cast models of the past, produced in their thousands at one time, can be of curio value today as aeronautica. One of the first large-scale productions of cast aircraft shapes was by Littleover Novelties of Derby in 1940. Benefitting by the interest in aircraft generated by the war, mascot casts of Spitfires and Wellingtons were offered in brass (10½ shillings) and bronze (12½ shillings). Wartime regulations on metal control stopped production in 1941.

Limited issue scale aircraft replicas in silver and pewter have been available in increasing numbers in recent years. To give examples, for the 50th anniversary of the Spitfire's first flight, Franklin Mint produced a mounted, 6¼in-span model of the prototype in pewter for £65. Earlier in 1982, Danbury Mint offered through the RAF Museum, 12 fighter aircraft types in pewter for £24 each. Although limited issues, numbers were not specified: these and similar issues will be coming up for re-sell in the 1990s as many people now buy with the idea of investment in aeronautica.

Now, to consider briefly examples of the top and bottom ends of the metal aircraft type market. Paramount Classics of the USA promoted a 12¼in-span scale replica of the original Wright Brothers' aeroplane in sterling silver; just 1,000 were produced at an individual pricing of $795, making a very worthwhile investment. As recently as 1990, Brass Tacks of Britain offered an 8½in-span mounted Spitfire in brass for £248 in an edition limited to a mere 500. General models in brass on mounts are relatively common and a variety of aircraft types are available from around £10 upwards. In white metal, a wide range of 1/300th scale are offered by Skywarrior Miniatures in a pence to a few pounds price range.

Left:
An example of the many models finely sculptured in metal, a Sea Vixen FAW2 that Gp Capt J. Cunningham presented to RNAS Yeovilton on the delivery of the last Sea Vixen.

Above right:
An example of an aircraft modelled in metal as a trophy, the RAF Aircraft Recognition Trophy of a Victor presented by Sir Frederick Handley Page.

Right:
RAF airfield accessory accurately modelled in metal even to the miniature 'Coles Derby Crane No 1068' nameplate.

BRITAIN'S AIRMEN

Among today's collectable items, model soldiers are among the most prized, particularly the metal products of Britains Ltd. No other firm in this field had such a wide and varied range, running into thousands of different sets, with some boxed sets now worth thousands of pounds. Unfortunately a box of Royal Flying Corps figures was never featured; it was not until the mid-1920s that Britains recognised the flying services with their No 240 set of eight figures titled 'RAF Personnel'.

With cowboy and indian sets made popular by the cinema screen, Britains enjoyed a considerable export market. For that outlet, they produced Nos 330-334 of 'USA Aviation' with officers in dress uniform, overcoats and flying suits as well as enlisted men.

Britains first model aeroplane, cast in 1931, was a nondescript monoplane and the same cast, with revised markings, was used for the American market. To modellers, the lead alloyed monoplane would not rate a second glance but, with the pilot made separate and the boxing designed as a hangar, it is now a much sought item. First true-to-type model aircraft was No 1392 in 1935 when it was assumed incorrectly that the Cierva C30 autogiro would be operated by the Army, but it did have limited use in the RAF as the Avro Rota. This autogiro had a run-down string cable and was boxed with the pilot separate. Two years later came No 1520, a Short Empire flying boat

supplied with launching wheels. The very next issue, a nondescript biplane, was the last of Britains aircraft, but concurrent issues were a 4.5in anti-aircraft gun and the RAF Band in boxes of 11, 12 and 21 figures.

Shortly before World War 2 a variety of anti-aircraft items ensued with range-finders, sound locators, predictors and, prize of them all, a searchlight mounted on a lorry with a battery located on its trailer. There were also searchlights and guns mounted on four-wheel chassis with extendible stays and screw-down legs. Accessories included a spotter's swivelling chair, gunners quarters and Nissen huts. All a delight to youngsters then and valuable items today for a prewar Britains hut sold in 1984 for £700.

In 1939 Britains produced a barrage balloon unit and a box titled 'RAF Fighters' with eight figures in asbestos suits. Early in World War 2 WAAFs featured in a box (No 1894) with six pilots in flying kit. There was even a box of eight *Luftwaffe* pilots and several different boxes of USAAC personnel.

From 1941 there was limited export at the expense of the home market, then came a ban on all metal products until after the war. Postwar, in 1953, the RAF Regiment was introduced in Box

Above:
Skybird figures in a setting of airport building and
hangar, also by the firm prewar. The aircraft are a
postwar Airfix Defiant and Frog Spitfire. All are to
1/72nd scale.

No 2073, to be included later in an 'RAF Display
Box' of 22 figures. Last of the RAF 'lead soldiers'
was a re-issue of the RAF Band of 12 pieces and a
four-piece 'RAF Colour Party'. The range of RAF
figures made postwar was: Air Commodore (cho-
sen for the simple painting scheme to denote
rank by the single large sleeve ring); Officer No 1
Dress walking with sword; airman marching;
pilot with seat parachute; pilot in Sidcot suit;
fire-fighter in asbestos suit; WAAF walking; RAF
Regiment officer; Bren-gunner and rifleman.
Finally, for the display box mentioned, a Royal
Signals despatch rider on a motorcycle was
painted as an RAF despatch rider.

The figures were all to a scale of 2⅛in (5.4cm)
for a normal marching or standing figure, not
including headgear. This became known as 'Standard Size' when a small 'Lilliput' series was
introduced to cater, in particular, with model
railways being marketed in HO and OO gauge.
Even Britains catalogues are now much treasured
as well as instruction sheets which were set out
like military manuals.

SKYBIRDS AND OTHERS

One firm that offered both RFC and RAF figures
was Skybirds, already mentioned in the previous
section. Its figurines were made to fit the 1/72nd
scale of their wooden aircraft and were cast in
metal.

For *Luftwaffe* figurines the Haussman-Elastolin
products excelled. This firm, established in 1904,
was producing some three million figures a year
by the late 1930s. Slightly larger than the Britains
standard, they produced a set of 12 figurines
catalogued as *Flieger*. Star figure of the set was
one of the few of their range that personalised,
being of the chief of the *Luftwaffe* himself, Her-
man Goering. Other sets covered anti-aircraft personnel and equipment which came under the
Luftwaffe.

Skybirds did not trade postwar and under
British Governmental regulations in 1966, forbid-
ding the use of lead in metal 'toys', Britains metal
figures were doomed and the firm went into plas-
tics. Now the metal models produced in the past
are now collector's items and although mainly
militaria there are, as this survey shows, many
items of aeronautica. So far as is known, the
highest price ever paid for a single complete box
of Britains metal products was £7,200 in 1985.

DINKY TOYS

A product of Meccano Ltd, Dinky Toys were first
produced in 1932 as accessories for Hornby railways, but from 1934 they branched out into general metal models, including aeroplanes, sold for

Above:
The famous Crossley tender of the RFC and the early days of the RAF seen for real. 'Models of Yesteryear' series by Matchbox first featured this vehicle in 1974.

a matter of pence. Even its Flying Fortress (No 62g) brought out in 1939 only rated one shilling (5 new pence). Now, the Fortress, among some other of their models, are valued around £100 each, with boxed gift sets in good condition worth hundreds of pounds. Essentially, values now depend upon rarity and timescale. Few pre-war models have survived, but production continued for some lines up to 1980. It may come as a surprise to some to learn that one of the rarest aircraft models of the range is a comparatively

Below:
Tin toy aeroplanes have been fetching three-figure sums in auction, but for around £6 you could buy this toy, based on a 1922 design, from the Museum of Science and Industry in 1990-91.

modern aircraft — the Avro Vulcan; this is due to the fact that only around 500 were cast.

Designed to match the original Dinky aeroplanes in 1/200th scale is a 2,000-sets edition of airshow miniatures of the Battle of Britain Memorial Flight's Lancaster, Spitfire and Hurricane. These sets were offered by Skytrex Ltd of Loughborough for just under £50 during 1990-91.

To a smaller scale than Britains', Dinky Toys prewar produced various anti-aircraft vehicles including a towed Bofors gun on a four-wheel chassis and a searchlight vehicle, the latter now valued around £150. A postwar Dinky RAF pressure refueller, sold for pence in 1957-62, now rates nearly 100 times its original price.

OTHER DIE-CASTS

Various RAF and airfield vehicles have been produced by other die-cast model toy manufacturers. Spot On in 1965 made an RAF Land Rover which is now classified as 'not common' with a trader's price of £60. Among its vast range, in 1978 Matchbox produced small model airport coaches in American Airways, British Airways, Lufthansa, QANTAS and TWA markings, all still available for a few pounds in model marts. But its earlier RAF 10-ton pressure refueller, dating back to 1960, would be difficult to obtain under £25. One item that stands out for its excellence, is the RAF 1918 Crossley tender in the Models of Yesteryear series, first issued in 1974 with a colour change in 1976. Prices for this tender are now soaring with the latter version the most valuable.

Corgi, like Spot On, produced an RAF Land Rover and additionally did an RAF Vanguard staff car. Among other Corgis was Bloodhound and Thunderbird surface-to-air missiles on trolleys; it also produced two US Army helicopters, a Bell Iroquois and a Sikorsky Skycrane.

11 Flying Equipment

Early flying clothing was made by commercial firms as aviator suits for private sale. When World War 1 came and the RNAS and RFC expanded, the Admiralty and War Office placed contracts to standard patterns. Flying kit was issued on loan and replaced for fair wear and tear, otherwise they were charged to a scale which, by listing, gives the standard flying kit for 1915-17:

Item	£	s	d
Jacket, leather, RFC	5	8	0
Boots, knee, RFC, pair	2	18	4
Cap, fur-lined	1	9	0
Gauntlets, pilot		17	6
Gauntlets, observer		9	11
Goggles, pilot, Triplex		6	6
Leggings, leather, brown		8	0
Suit, Jean combination		6	6

The importance of Jeans, like flying overalls to follow, was that it obviated the danger of carrying items of intelligence interest to the enemy in the event of landing in enemy territory. Any one item of such early equipment is now of value; in recent auction an RFC leather flying jacket was given a £400-500 valuation.

CLOTHING

As the ceiling and endurance of World War 1 aircraft increased, so came the need for light heated clothing. Excessive wrapping, to ward off the intense cold in open cockpits, inhibited movement. Contracts were arranged for electrically-heated flying suits in mid-1917 on the basis of 20 suits per squadron. Early examples were the Holinguist 14Volt overalls and mittens; Dowsing 12Volt front and rear chest warmer with heated gloves and soles; and Amleto Selvalico 14Volt gloves, soles and helmet.

The need for batteries to heat the clothing led to a change in aircraft systems design. Already batteries or accumulators were in use for wireless, navigational lights, gun heating and in some cases plus Holt flares and Klaxon horns. A generating system had to be introduced to cut down the bulk and weight of batteries. Lucas in mid-

Below:
The first Aviator Suit Combination, lined with Kapok, made by G. H. Leavey & Co, under test in August 1918. The suit weighted 9lb.

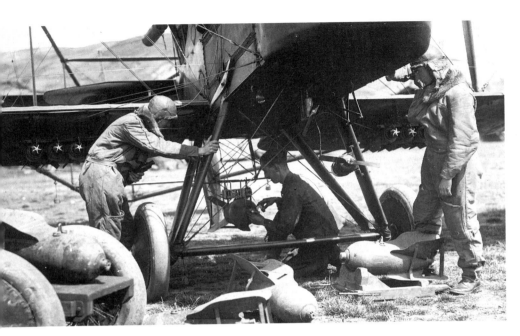

1917 produced a propeller-driven generator, soon followed by a Leitner model, both of which went into production. Secured to struts outside the fuselage the propeller was turned by the slip-stream.

Later in 1918, the electrically-heated Sidcot flying suit, named after its designer Sidney Cotton, was introduced. Two types of Sidcot fire-proofed and non-proofed, became standard in the 1920s. New patterns of flying clothing were introduced by decades, becoming a 1930 and 1940 pattern series. During World War 2 several new series were introduced, including a dark blue series for the Royal Australian Air Force, referenced in the RAF's Section 22C; these suits were also issued to Allied personnel serving in the RAF.

For a detailed listing of RAF flying clothing the reader is referred to *Flight Equipment of the RAF, 1920-1945* (Acme Publishing Co), price £10.95. Although only of 40 pages, it is of large format, contains 72 photographs of flying suits, helmets, goggles, boots, gauntlets, etc and it lists, by RAF Section 22C with brief descriptions, over 850 items of RAF flying clothing items by stores reference numbers from 22C/1 Belts, life-saving, self-inflating, Type 'A', to 22C/ 1070 Backpack for overalls, flying, lightweight. More general in its treatment, including civil airlines, is *Flying Clothing — The Story of its Development* by Greer and Harold (Airlife Publications, 1979).

For functional use, which may of course become collector's items later, RAF Mk 10

Immersion Suits and Mk 14 Normax flying suits can still be obtained for around £50.

Unlike general utility equipment, there were series of variations to flying equipment apart from the different patterns. Suits were issued in a dozen different sizes, variations that also applied to gloves and boots with the addition of right and left items. Also, aircraft electrical systems were either 12V or 24V, so heated equipment to suit both had to be available. Each size, side and other variation was separately referenced in Section 22C which, as an RAF system, did not cover Fleet Air Arm home water and tropical items or army aeroplane and glider pilots.

HELMETS

Pioneer airmen like motorists of the day, wore caps reversed or used the commercial helmets made for the motoring industry. Some early helmets were quite literally motor-racing crash helmets. Not until 1915 was there RFC standardisation on helmets. During 1918 a Mk I helmet for the RAF was introduced based on the proven fur-lined leather RFC helmet.

Between the wars a Helmet Type 'A' of twill-covered cork was issued for aircrew in Egypt and all points east. Helmets of the period were designed for fitting in Gosport speaking tubes, the World War 1 Le Vaillant and Standard tubes by then having been discarded. By the 1930s there was a need for the incorporation of earphones in helmets and microphones in masks with all the complications of electrical equipment and wiring.

Oxygen systems had been introduced from late 1917 and early 1918 Specification G8 was raised for the Aero-oxygen breathing mask Mk I, followed later that year by G30 Flying helmet with detachable breathing mask. These original standard oxygen masks are not only rare but, issued before the RAF referencing system, bear no type identification. Later oxygen masks vary considerably in current availability and thereby in value; in fact from £20-250, dependent upon the different types of rubber masks, with canvas masks going higher. Mk XIIIA masks are available from ex-RAF stock for under £36.

The flying helmets of the 1930s, like the Type 'B' with zip-on ear pieces, were used throughout the Battle of Britain; any extant examples in reasonable condition should now rate £100 at least. The improved Type 'C' was notified to the Service as available from 16 March 1941. This was modified during production, leading to descriptions of the type as early or late pattern. Meanwhile the Type 'D' helmet of cotton drill was introduced for overseas commands, again with a

Above:
The RFC fur-lined helmet with its all-round fur fringes when strapped as shown. The heavy flying gauntlets, essential for slipstream protection, were unsuited for gun manipulation. *IWM Q27564*

Below:
By May 1918 these No 32 Squadron RAF pilots flying SE5As, had standardised RFC pattern helmets, shown unstrapped, and Mk I goggles with fur-lined masks seen lifted for map reading. *IWM Q12042*

Left:
A highly sought souvenir from captured German airmen of World War 1 was their ribbed crash-cum-flying helmet.

Below left:
The leather flying jacket in general use during the early years of World War 2. This observer is seen receiving an F24 vertical camera aboard his Blenheim IV.

Right:
'B' Type flying helmet with zip-on headset lobes and Mk III goggles of an air gunner, 1940, who is also wearing a 'Harnessuit'.

Below:
Ready for a dogfight. With sheepskin-lined leather Irvin jacket, 'B' Type helmet, showing headset phone hanging from a lobe and Mk III goggles. *IWM CM2423*

later pattern. Last of the wartime RAF helmets was the Type 'E' Airtex model. In general, RAF flying helmets were produced in four sizes.

GOGGLES

As with helmets so with goggles, Early aviators used the eye protectors already marketed. There was virtually no RNAS or RFC standard goggles, those required being supplied by contracts with the trade, Triplex in particular. It was not until mid-1917 that the views of the RFC in the Field were sought as to the ideal goggles. From the feedback, working drawings were prepared in August 1917 for the Goggle Mask Mk I, but it was early 1918 before they became general issue.

Goggles Mk I and the tinted Mk II continued to be used postwar, while the RCAF continued to use seasonally the special glasses issued in 1918 to RAF (Canada) with amber tints to reduce snow glare. The Mks III and IIIA of the 1930s had an improved field of vision and, since they were in use during the Battle of Britain, are likely to command the higher prices. It was during the Battle that the complex Mk IV goggles were evolved, replaced in 1944 with the Mks VII and VIII which remained in use postwar. The intervening mark numbers related to specialist-use goggles.

A buyer of aeronautica, advertising in *The Daily Telegraph* in 1990, offered from £25 to £100 for old RAF goggles and this pricing has stood up in auctions. Replica Mk VIII goggles, produced for Ford Halcyon Ltd of Hertford, were available in 1990 for £31.

BOOTS AND GAUNTLETS

Seemingly only with aeronautical connections would old boots command worthwhile prices, but there is a functional market in that pilots of vintage aircraft may wish to completely dress the part. It was the VC, Maj Lanoe Hawker, who ordered thighboots from Harrod's both for himself and his pilots which the firm registered (No 376623) as 'Charfor Boots'. Known to pilots as 'Fug Boots', they became so popular that the RAF later made them standard as Boots, thigh, flying. Between the wars a series of electrically-heated boots were produced for 12V and 24V aircraft systems, in sizes 7 to 10, but during World War 2 the size range was from 5 to 12.

As to values, a pair of unused sheepskin flying boots, wisely catalogued by size (9), reached a hammer price of £143 in auction in 1990. Michael Young (Aviation) at the same time was offering up to £90 for leather and £25 for suede World War 2 flying boots and a £15-25 price range for gauntlets of the period.

In auction, gauntlets have tended to be valued at around £50 but, inconviently for collector or pilot, lots have often consisted of two or more pairs, making them too high a valuation to obtain the one pair that might be required.

MISCELLANEOUS

Various items are associated with pilot comfort, safety and operation that could fill a reference book on its own. Some of the most valuable of these items would be examples of the original early marks.

Being of the pre-RAF referencing era, they are listed here by their specification numbers. They were also known by their 'T' prefixed drawing numbers, but as some were composite items, having several numbers, they have not been given.

G3 Oxygen regulator
G10 Case for goggles, flying
G11 High pressure oxygen cylinders
G13 Goggle mask, flying, Mk II
G22 Aero urinary apparatus, Mk I, re-issued as Aero latrine, Mk I
G24 Aero feeding flask, Mk I
G25 Aero Protractor and chart board (Bigsworth type)
G26 Aero bearing plate with ground speed sights, Mk I
G36 Course and distance calculator
G41 Observer's fighting harness

There was also the Mks I, II and III (Sutton Type) of pilot harnesses attached to aircraft by sorbo-rubber in the first instance, but replaced by rope in some cases by deterioration of the rubber.

Below:
The Mk IV angled lens goggles. Aircraft rear-view mirrors, fitted from 1940, have also become collector's items. *IWM CH6459*

Bottom:
The most valuable preserved flying boot in the world, that worn by Manfred von Richthofen when he was shot down in April 1918.

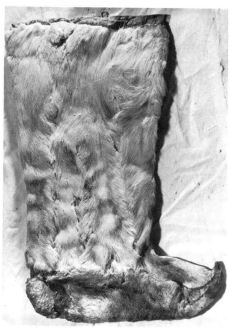

12 Emergency, Escape and Survival Equipment

Equipment to aid airmen in evading capture in the event of landing in enemy territory has had a particular fascination for collectors and museum display alike. Most of the less perishable items, like silk maps and button compasses, were considered unique at the time and became highly prized souvenirs. For this reason many examples have survived, putting them in the more moderately priced class of item. One trader recently offered £12 for such maps and £30 for buttons, but it is to be expected that they would raise more in auction where, a silk escape map of Italy sold at £33.

Below:
While the parachute itself may be an uninspiring package, the pack and harness is almost a dress item. A postwar Irvin PB6 pack and harness are shown.

Below right:
The space needed for full parachute exhibition is demonstrated by this prewar display at Seletar, Singapore. *IMW H2264*

Survival equipment goes back to the early 1920s when RAF aircraft in overseas commands, likely to patrol desert or jungle areas, carried emergency equipment. A standard pack included three days' flying rations (sealed flat tins with concentrated food that would keep indefinitely), tropical medical outfit, water purifying tablets in a phial, haversacks one per crew member, water bottles, axe, knife, flotation waistcoats and a pocket or wrist compass.

Parachutes and lifejackets do not usually command high prices except by association with a famous airman. The British Mae West lifejacket remained standard throughout most of the war. Not until April 1945 was the improved Mk II introduced, identifiable by a less bulky collar and adjustable straps with buckles replacing the securing tapes. A wartime *Schwimmvest*, the *Luftwaffe's* equivalent of the RAF's Mae West lifejacket, valued at £200-250 in recent auction, failed to achieve its reserve price. But when it comes to the exclusive club badges held by those who used such equipment, these small items command high prices. One dealer in the 1990s

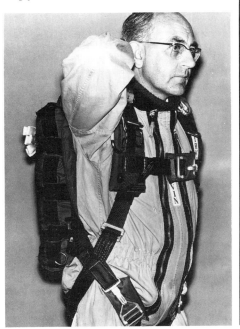

offered as follows: Caterpillar Badge (those saving life by parachute) £90; Goldfish Badge (for those forced to ditch) £75; and the Guinea Pig Badge (for those undergoing burns surgery) £150.

DINGHIES

The inflatable aircraft dinghies engender a certain fascination, both for their serious use in saving the lives of ditched aircrew and their pleasurable use by the numbers that were sold off postwar for use on rivers and at seaside resorts. As perishable items, unless well looked after, few wartime examples survive; but later examples continue to come on the market. Too bulky for the average collector, they are attractive items for museum display as they justify a pool setting to ring the changes of presentation.

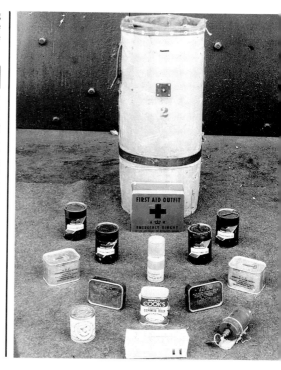

Right:
Emergency equipment of a Lindholme dinghy container shown with contents that include a first aid pack, Cook's corned beef, Services and RAF flying rations, rum and cigarettes.

Below:
In spite of Dunlop producing over 100,000 wartime dinghies they are now rare, but collectable for the drama that they evoke.

ATP 83

98

Above left:
Early postwar sea survival demonstration at Middleton St George with 'J' Type dinghy, survival suits, beacon, transmitter and poster information.

Left:
Three marks of airborne dinghies were produced between 1942-52 and were sold off later for pleasure use; a Mk 1A is depicted.

Above:
The postwar RFD MS9 liferaft (RAF Ref 27C/2426), seen demonstrated here by WRAF members, was carried by RAF Comets, Hastings, Shackletons, Valettas and Varsitys.

RAF dinghy types were classified by letter, allotted alphabetically. The first Type 'A', of triangular shape, developed circa 1925 as an inflatable seaplane tender for three to five persons, was operated by foot bellows. Type 'B', the first emergency dinghy, was for three persons and had a motor blower, while the improved Type 'C' featured gas cylinder inflation. For the flying boats of the 1930s, Type 'D' was both a tender and for emergency use taking the normal crew of five for the period, but reverting to foot bellows for inflation.

In 1935 the Youngman dinghies were introduced for aircraft operating over water. The initial Type 'E' was followed by Types 'F' and 'G' for single-seat and up to three-man crews; all were hand-pumped. Of circular shape, adapted from the Youngman, was Type 'H' issued to Heyford, Harrow and Whitley squadrons, followed by a modified form in 1941, with carbon-dioxide bottle inflation, for issue to Hudson, Hampden and Wellington squadrons. The large circular Type 'J' was introduced to accommodate eight men for the four-engined bombers while, at the other end of the scale, the boat-shaped Type 'K', introduced in 1941, was designed for single-seat fighters. However, possession of a 'K' does not necessarily imply a wartime souvenir, as its replacement in the RAF, by the RDF SS Mk 3, did not start until 1957. Also introduced in 1941 was the light Type 'L' together with the Type 'M'; the latter was a scaled-down 'J' to replace the 'C'. Some specialist types followed in 1942 with limited use until 1943 when the Type 'Q' bomber crew dinghy was first issued to Halifax squadrons.

The RAE had designed a dinghy to replace the 'J', provisionally designated the Type 'R', but it was discarded in favour of the 'Q'. Finally, of the wartime dinghies, the Type 'S' sailing dinghy, virtually a scaled-down 'Q', was introduced. Postwar, several commercial type dinghies came into RAF and airline use and have been appearing in ex-service equipment sales since then.

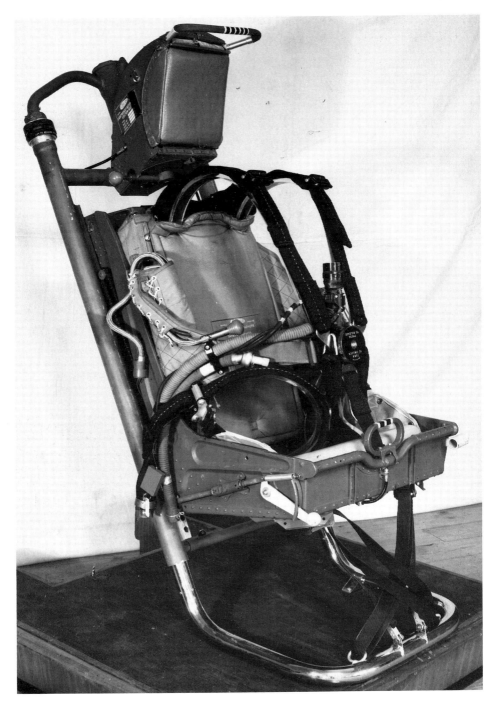

EJECTION SEATS

Looking to the future, it seems certain that ejection seats will attract increasing interest. An early Martin Baker type, dated 1956, fetched £176 at auction in the early 1990s. Certainly the acquisition of a Mk 1 would be an attractive display item for any museum. Such seats date from September 1945 when the Ministry of Aircraft Production ordered 'two pilot ejection units'. Later after being put into production, the first emergency use of such apparatus was made on 30 May 1949 when J. O. Lancaster ejected hurriedly, but safely, from the Armstrong Whitworth AW52 which had suffered from uncontrollable oscillation. The first automatic ejection was by Lt Bushe who abandoned a Supermarine Attacker at 2,000ft on 7 July 1953 in a Mk 1A seat, which brings us to ejection seat type classification.

Types are designated by mark number in Arabic figures with the adaption of that type for a

Left:
Folland Mk 4 lightweight, fully automatic ejection seat as fitted to the RAF's Gnats are now coming on to the aeronautica market with the boost of 'as used by the Red Arrows'. *Folland Aircraft Ltd*

Below:
An early German ejection seat from a Heinkel He162A (as shown) sold for £880 in a British auction in 1990. This is believed the highest sum yet paid for an obsolete ejection seat.

particular aircraft model given by a suffix letter in capitals. Thus for the first service production type in 1947 (initial experimental units were unclassified) the application was Mks: 1A Supermarine Attacker, 1B Westland Wyvern, 1C EE Canberra, 1D Hawker Sea Hawk, 1E Gloster Meteor. The Mk 2 was similar, so that some Mk 1s were later modified to Mk 2 standard. Basically it differed by the face blind and drogue stowage housed in the seat headrest. Suffix letters were not always allotted alphabetically in chronological sequence, but selectively, so that 2H was for the Hawker Hunter and 2J for the Gloster Javelin.

The Mk 3 was the first major re-design and the first to have sub-sub type designations, for example the Mks 3A1 and 3A2 were for Vickers Valiant pilot and co-pilot respectively, and 3K1 and 3K2, and 3L1 and 3L2, were similarly for the same crew positions in Avro Vulcans and Handley Page Victors respectively. A basic mark was not exclusive to a particular type of aircraft; late production Hunters and Javelins, for example, had 3H and 3J seats fitted.

The Mk 4, about half the weight of the Mk 3, was first fitted in the Hunter T7 and Fiat G91 and is still in use today in various aircraft types. Other types that followed by Martin Baker, the experts in this field, were the Mk 5 for some 20 types of US Navy aircraft, the Mks 6 and 7 for the Hawker-Siddeley Kestrel (forerunner of the Harrier) and F-104 Starfighter respectively, the Mk 8 for the BAC TSR2 (doomed to cancellation), and the Mks 9 and 10 for the modern aircraft of today such as the BAe Harrier.

13 Uniforms and Dress

That many people are interested in military dress is evident by the many books on the subject. Few of those consider airmen on their own, but even this aspect is vast. The actual numbers of collectors is relatively few, for each item needs a tailor's dummy for realistic display and these can take up considerable space. For this reason alone, display of uniforms is largely a matter of museums. There are those who trade in this field, but chiefly as an adjunct to other items of aeronautica.

The vast majority of people in this field are enthusiasts seeking and collecting information on uniform and dress regulations. In the air sphere, RFC and RNAS dress regulations were a matter of War Office and Admiralty strictures. All RAF uniform and dress regulations have come from the Air Ministry from 1918 to 1964 and the Ministry of Defence subsequently.

RAF REGULATIONS

When the RAF was formed on 1 April 1918, by the amalgamation of the RNAS and RFC, the effect was purely administrative. Dress was not initially affected, in fact the only immediate change to personnel was that the RNAS was forced to adopt army ranks. Not until August 1919 were RAF ranks introduced.

From 1918 regulations regarding dress were issued in a series of Air Ministry Weekly Orders (AMWO) with reference Nos 83, 99 (paras 8 & 9), 101, 111, 125, 331, 502, 526, 585, 617, 727-8, 1024-5, 1066, 1175, 1217, 1268-9, 1318-9, 1365, 1578, 1579, 1623,1668-9, of 1918; and 82 of 1919; plus Air Ministry Monthly Orders 162 and 747 of 1918. Orders remaining relevant were all incor-

Below:
Examples of RFC and RNAS uniforms posed in front of a Sopwith Camel.

Right:
WAAC driver serving the RAF wears her former RFC badge and titles for driving her P&M motorcycle. *IWM Q12291*

Below right:
An RAF group of 1918 in which only the officer has partial RAF dress. An NCO and three airmen retain their RFC uniforms and the ladies their WAAC dress with RFC shoulder titles. Centre, rear, is an attached Royal Engineers signaller.

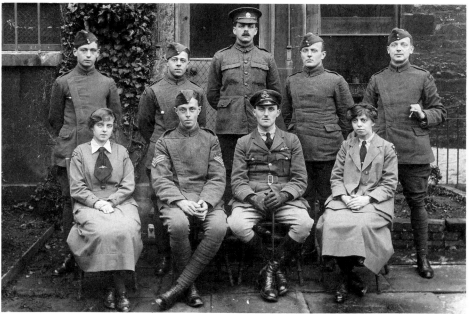

porated in AMWO 783/19 (ie No 783 of 1919) issued that July pending the issue of dress regulations as an Air Publication manual. An original copy of this order was in stock in 1991 at the Falconwood Transport & Military Bookshop.

Although regulations up to the issue of AMWO 783/19 were cancelled, they are nevertheless individually important to enthusiasts tracing the stages of dress changes. AMWOs 617/18 and 728/18 are significant by detailing the short-lived light blue RAF uniform that never featured in any manual. With its light shade and badges of rank in gold braid instead of the usual worsted mate-

rial, it horrified some senior officers by its 'Ruritanian' appearance. The light blue was also inappropriate for those working in the proximity of oil-throwing rotary aero engines of the period. Surprising were the associated regulations with latitude in the shades of shirts worn by officers — blue or silver-grey with the option of white.

The comprehensive AMWO 783/19 made it clear that at the time there were only three patterns of service dress: khaki, blue and tropical; it then went on in 13 pages with 30 tables to give dress items and classifications. Khaki was still very much an alternative to the new grey-blue brought in to replace the light blue. Khaki as an alternative was even allowed for cadets, to use up existing war surplus stocks of khaki dress. Later, in the 1920s, came full dress and mess dress.

In the 1920s AP1358 (Air Publication No 1358) was issued as the manual of dress regulations and was re-issued over the years, the fourth edition coming out in the mid-1970s. Copies of the old AP1358s now rate some £50 each, but even possession of each edition does not give the full picture. In the 12-15-year gap between editions, changes have been introduced and cancelled through the medium of Air Ministry orders. Among many items introduced and cancelled before the issue of the first AP1358 were the regulations for wearing war service chevrons and field service equipment, using up army stocks of 1908 pattern webbing and 1903 Pattern bandoliers.

Left:
An RAF uniform medley of late 1918 as represented by the officers of No 208 Squadron. Maj 'Chris' Draper (with dog) wears his RNAS uniform, two officers wear the short-lived light blue uniform and the remainder varying degrees of RNAS and RFC dress and badges.

Below left:
RAF Cadet summer dress featured khaki shorts and socks, with white cap-bands and white-blancoed belts. This photograph was taken on Hastings promenade in 1918. *IWM Q12260N*

Below:
Battle of Britain period RAF and WAAF dress, posed in front of a Hurricane.

It is only by individual orders, not by the manuals, that the dates of introduction of changes are given, as well as temporary or specialist items such as armlets. To give an example of a temporary wear item, AMOs A900/46 and A289/47 allowed Air Training Corps cadets, awarded the pale blue proficiency badge of a four-bladed propeller or its similar advanced training badge featuring additionally a four-pointed star, to wear these badges during the period of their RAF recruit training only.

Reflecting the jet age at the start of the 1950s, AMO N880/50 introduced 'Overalls, Anti-kerosine', as protective clothing for airmen refuelling and servicing jet aircraft. These were in small, medium and large sizes (Ref 22G/1204-6 respectively) with associated 'Boots, Ankle, Anti-kerosine', in sizes 5-12 (Ref 22D/797-804 respectively). The order also gave sketches of the overalls and boots.

When it is appreciated that around 1,000 orders in the AMWO, AMO 'A' and 'N' series appeared per annum — many of them relating to dress — it will be seen that, overall, they are a more valuable record than AP1358. Scrap-books of uniform orders, kept by some servicemen, have now become highly prized items. They are

Left:
Prepared for chemical warfare in 1940 by RAF-issued protective anti-gas clothing. *IWM C1162*

Below:
A great many World War 2 RAF uniforms were needed in 1968 for filming *The Battle of Britain*. Here ACM Dowding and AVMs Leigh Mallory and Park, left to right, are posed by Sir Laurence Olivier, Patrick Wymark and Trevor Howard.

Above:
An unusual uniform feature was the RAF side-hat as worn by officers of air rank, in this case ACM Sir Arthur Tedder, as he was then.

the key to many confusing uniform issues, such as the inverted chevrons for denoting NCO ranks postwar and the reversion to the more usual display in 1963. The ranges of Air Ministry orders and the RAF Equipment Code are explained in Chapter 17.

WRAF & WAAF

The Women's Royal Air Force had its own problems of the medley of dress in 1918 for, in addition to direct entry, there were transfers from the Women's Royal Naval Air Service, Women's Auxiliary Army Corps and Women's Legion Motor Drivers to the new service. The transferees could retain their former uniforms until the clothing was condemned. By early 1919 some 40 items of clothing were applicable to the WRAF, many with alternatives of khaki or blue. The light blue RAF uniform was not considered for the WRAF, possibly because it was deemed a wartime-only organisation. In fact, it was disbanded in April 1920 so that its dress regulations were never included in the AP1358.

COLLECTING CLOBBER

Surviving RFC uniforms will always command good prices by their rarity. An RFC jacket, belonging to a pilot of no special significance, sold for £400 in 1985 putting the price of a complete uniform of the period in the four-figure class. But RAF uniforms in general, largely because there was little change in the pattern over a wide period of time, rate only moderate prices. Recently a trader was offering £25 for a World War 2 RAF uniform and £15 for an officer's peaked hat of the same period. Many ex-ser-

Left:
The RAF in kilts! Pipe band of the Central Flying School, Little Rissington, saluting and RAF Kinloss Pipe Band seen at the halt.

vicemen held on to items of uniform and these turn up today in secondhand shops which do house clearances, and in jumble sales. While picking up such items in a jumble sale is a matter of pure chance and luck, the serious collectors contact the house clearers who advertise regularly in the weekly free newspapers, asking for first refusal on such items when they turn up. For modern service dress there are frequent disposal offers in RAF station magazines.

Those with old uniforms for disposal may well find a market for them at theatrical costumiers to meet film and TV wardrobe requirements. But those who acquire a uniform as a form of fancy dress, should take heed that it is an offence under the Uniforms Act 1894 to wear service uniform without authorisation. In 1990 a publican was fined £250 with £1,100 costs for wearing an RAF wing commander's uniform at a fancy dress

Below:
The RAF in skirts! Men of No 94 RAF Malayan Field Regiment at Butterworth in the 1950s, being inspected by AM Sir Frederick Scherger RAAF.

evening raising money for the RAF Benevolent Fund.

TIE MART

The RAF tie worn with uniform was black from the inception of the Force, when for officers it was specified as of silk or poplin and of cotton for all other ranks. So there is little interest in this tie, but off-duty association ties are sought by some collectors. The Royal Flying Corps tie with its stripes on a large sky-blue field has been worn with pride for over some 70 years. Since its wearers are now on the wane, it was suggested that the colours be adopted by RAF Halton trainees, but some veterans were justifiably loth to see its exclusiveness disappear within their lifespan.

Perhaps most familiar today is the RAF tie with its broad red and navy blue stripes, denoting its origins in army and naval arms, and with a thin sky-blue stripe representing its element. This off-duty tie did once feature on uniform when, in 1932, a flash was introduced for the drab or white-covered Wolseley pith helmets issued overseas. Pending production of the flash, it was advised that a strip of the RAF tie would suffice. Similar to the RAF tie is the RAF Volunteer Reserve tie with shade variations, while the Fleet Air Arm tie combines Royal Navy colours

109

Above:
An RAF Regiment member of the Arabian Gulf detachment in the late 1960s.

A modern dress mode of the 1980s, continuing into the 1990s, is to wear a flying jacket in the style of the 1940s. This had been made popular by films of World War 2 and by the re-introduction of the bomber jacket in the USAF. Now, Aviation Leathercraft of Thruxton Aerodrome near Andover, Hants, has been producing flying jackets to old RAF and USAAF specifications. RAF Irvin sheepskin flying jackets, made by this firm to the original Irvin design, have been supplied to the RAF's Battle of Britain Memorial Flight and they have also marketed them individually tailored to the general public. The USAAF's A-2 leather and B-3 sheepskin flying jackets are produced by both Aviation Leathercraft, and Eastman of Ivybridge, Devon, retailing at around £200-300; while MBI Flight Gear of Chessington, Surrey, offers a genuine Cooper A-2 US military issue jacket for around £230. The US Navy's leather jacket with mouton lamb collar and the later A-10 jacket are also produced in Britain for general sale.

Many of the prewar RAF and Auxiliary Air Force officers were gentlemen of means and had dress accessories such as tie-pins and cuff-links specially made. Most such items being sold today come up in jewellery sales, but there are occasions when they appear in auctions of aeronautica. One such item was a pair of cuff-links bearing RAF wings and badge, made by Asprey & Co circa 1940, which had a £600-800 auction valuation just 50 years later.

Below:
Sporting caps in the aviation field range from this rare RFC Rugby Cap to baseball caps of the 82nd Airborne Division, currently being sold commercially for around £6. *Brian Hansley*

with a sky-blue stripe. The Army's Parachute Brigade tie is also truly symbolic, being of maroon to match the airborne troops' beret, with parachutes winged in blue to accord with the parachute proficiency badge.

Considerable variety exists in the formation ties. The No 1 Group Bomber Command tie, instituted in 1958, bears panther heads rather lighter than the black panther of the group's badge, on a field of Lincoln green symbolic of the location of its main stations. Squadron ties abound and there are also service aircraft type ties, that for the Nimrod being dark blue with the aircraft flying over light blue wavy lines. Among those entitled to wear it is the former Minister of Defence, Michael Heseltine, who flew back from the Falklands in a Nimrod.

For casual wear by anyone, a large range of ties has been promoted by *Aeroplane Monthly* depicting aircraft, including the Camel, Lancaster, Spad and Spitfire. Similar ties are available commercially from firms like International Leisurewear of Nottingham. During the late 1950s, an American gimmick for air enthusiasts and ex-servicemen was to have the aeroplane of their choice painted on a plain coloured tie. One can also wear a tie in a worthy cause by becoming a Friend of the RAF Museum.

14 Medals and Medallions

Although a specialist range of items, with a price range now reaching six figures for prime items, there are still some items available for a matter of pence. Also, since the demand steadily increases, pushing up prices, most purchases in this field will increase in value.

MEDALS

Medals are in a class of their own. Collections in this sphere are on the increase and represent big business to some dealers, since a VC holder's medal can now command a six-figure sum. Some collectors are interested in an example of each medal, naval, military and air, but some collect air medals on their own or only medals awarded to airmen — there is a difference. Up to June 1918 personnel of the air arms — RNAS, RFC and RAF, were awarded the medals of the Royal Navy and Army; not until June 1918 were specific air awards, like the Distinguished Flying Cross (DFC) and Distinguished Flying Medal (DFM) — awarded to officers and men respectively — instituted. In the USA it was July 1926 before air medals were instituted.

Some collectors are interested in collecting medals in clutches, that is all the medals awarded to a particular individual. Most recipients of gallantry awards will also have qualified for the more mundane campaign and war service medals and these will complete a clutch. In general, the higher the gallantry award, the pricier the medal and with clutches value will increase greatly if the original recipient had more than one gallantry award. Most gallantry awards bear an indication of the recipient and cannot be substituted, but war medals and campaign stars are not marked in any way. On the other hand the General Service Medal for participation in peacetime troubles such as the pre-World War 2 Palestinian disturbances or the post-World War 2 Malayan Emergency bear, on the rim, service number, rank, initials, name and service.

Collectors interested in clutches are generally concerned with the background of the recipient, with documentation such as logbooks copies of citations, record of service, letters and photographs. In this respect air enthusiasts can increase the value of clutches of medals by hundreds of pounds. A recent clutch, undocumented and bought for £300, was valued at £600 after a competent enthusiast had researched the airman concerned. Photographs can be a stumbling block, for museums and archives can rarely offer more than the most famous personalities. However, newspapers of the time may help, obtain-able from libraries, but the quality of wartime newspaper printing was not good. For World War 1 many airmen's portraits appear in the weekly *War Illustrated*, copies and bound volumes of which can still be bought from second-hand dealers. Of this magazine, the weekly issues were bound in volumes with red covers, but the content in a slightly rearranged form was also printed on better quality paper, giving much better reproduction and bound in a blue binding. A complete set 1914-18, running to nine volumes, was sold in the 1980s at a church 'in the weekly table sale' for a mere £8.

If newspapers and magazines fail in the quest for photographs, then school Roll of Honour books might help. After both world wars many public, grammar and a number of other schools, as part of their war memorial funding, produced Roll of Honour books of old students who participated in the wars, quite often containing photographs and records of service. Tonbridge

Above:
The medal ribbon clutch of Gp Capt P. Raw, RAAF emphasises the point that awards like the DFC and DFM (the diagonally striped ribbons), campaign and war medals are essentially British Commonwealth medals, not just British medals; also that foreign medals may be worn, in this case the Polish Cross of Valour (bottom right ribbon).

School, for example, presented hundreds of photographs of 'old boys' who served in World War 1 with a resumé of their service; among them was the elusive 'ace' Maj T. F. Hazell DSO, MC, DFC & bar.

Replica air medals in the £25-upward price range have been marketed as items of aeronautica, which are of course much cheaper than the genuine articles. This is mentioned in case some replicas are marketed as genuine, for in the past there have been rackets in this line. The markings on the rim are one way of checking. One particular individual advertised widely in

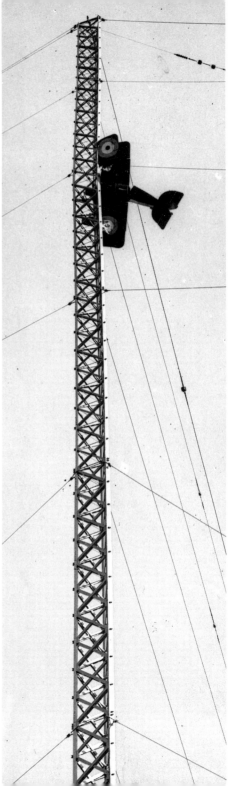

the American, British and Canadian aviation press of his stock of 'Genuine Iron Crosses'; such was the response that his presses had to work overtime to meet the demand!

The awards of the Victoria Cross to airmen, head the lists of high prices paid for war medals. It was a record when Glendining & Co sold the sole Battle of Britain VC, awarded to Flt Lt J. B. Nicolson, for £110,000. Previously the VC of Flt Sub-Lt R. A. J. Warneford, the first man to shoot down a German Zeppelin, was sold for £55,000, the buyer being the Fleet Air Arm Museum. But when in September 1990 the first VC to be awarded to an airman, Lt William Rhodes-Moorhouse, came to auction it reached a record £126,000 paid by an anonymous telephone bidder. At this same auction clutches were reaching high prices for famous airmen of World War 2. The DSO with bar and DFC plus a Czech award to Gp Capt P. C. Pickard, who was lost on the Amiens prison raid, reached over £50,000 and those of Sqn Ldr J. (Ginger) Lacey, who fought in the Battle of Britain, topped £30,000. Next to Battle of Britain, it is Dambuster raid participants' decorations that command high prices at auction, while DFMs were selling at £350, that awarded to Sgt D. Webb, who flew in the raid as Flt Sgt Bill Townsend's front gunner, sold in 1989 for £6,160, three times its estimated value.

The connotation of 'RAF' seems to give an impetus to VC prices, but it is not generally realised that not all serving RAF VC holders won their award for deeds in the air. In 1925, the peak year for the number of VC holders serving in the RAF, only five (Barker, Insall, Jerrard, Rees and West) gained their awards for deeds in the air. The other six had won their VCs before transfer to the RAF; they included Wg Cdr F. H. Kirby OBE, DCM, whose VC was Gazetted in 1900; and the fire-eating Plt Off A. O. Pollard MC, DCM.

Because of the specialist interest in collecting medals, they are not always sold as part of the sales of aeronautica or other aeronautical interest, but are included with specialist sales of coins, decorations and medals. For those collecting medals associated with the flying services, many such awards included with military and general awards may not be evident unless the citation is known. There were, for example, some 25 awards of the Albert Medal for gallantry in saving life on land or at sea in World War 1 that were directly concerned with the flying services.

Perhaps the most spectacular awards of the Albert Medals (now ranking with the George Cross and Medal) were to three seamen who climbed a Poulsen mast to rescue a pilot thrown unconscious on to the wing of his Sopwith Baby floatplane which collided and became impaled on the mast. Photographs of the recipients, an adjunct to medal sales, might be obtained through family or press photographs, but rarely is

Above:
In World War 1 many Americans joined the French Air Service before the USA came into the war, transferring later to the USAS, resulting in 'mixed clutches'. Left to right, below US Army wings: Distinguished Service Cross with bronze oak cluster on the ribbon and Field Service Medal from the USA; French Legion of Honour and Croix de Guerre with three bronze palms and silver star on the ribbon.

a photographic impression of the deed available as in this case.

In a rescue attempt of an RAF corporal from a bomb crater in June 1918, both Pte Arthur Johnson and Brig-Gen Alfred Burt DSO were among the recipients of Albert Medals. Although most of these were for saving life on land, several RNAS personnel were recipients of the separate medal for saving life at sea. One such case was when Sopwith floatplane No 58 had a bomb prematurely explode, causing it to drop 150ft into the sea, during November 1914. On that occasion the observer, CPO J. C. S. Hendry, received the award for extricating the pilot from the wreckage, although badly shocked by the fall.

The Albert Medals have been replaced by the George Cross and Medal, the latter two having been instituted on 24 September 1940. At that time 18 Empire Gallantry Medals had been issued to RAF personnel and 16 of these recipients survived to relinquish those medals for the George Cross. The new awards were issued throughout World War 2 and subsequently for gallantry, and were primarily awards for heroism by civilians, many of whom displayed gallantry whilst under air attack; but they were also issued to service personnel for gallantry in cases where there was not a suitable service award. A number of RAF and WAAF personnel received such awards for rescuing aircrew trapped in aircraft after they had crashed.

George Crosses and Medals now coming up to auction are reaching the five-figure mark. In the 1980s, British Airways paid £9,900 for the George Cross awarded to Miss Barbara Harrison, an air hostess who died at Heathrow Airport in April 1968 whilst trying to save passengers from a burning aircraft. Some airwomen have been awarded the Military Medal which was instituted in March 1916. The conditions of eligibility stated that under exceptional circumstances it may be awarded to women. Six Military Medals were awarded to WAAFs during World War 2, three of them for devotion to duty during the bombing of Biggin Hill on 1 September 1940.

RAF personnel can compete for various awards of prize money, trophies, cups and swords of honour. In other cases medals so-called have been issued regularly. In 1921 the RAF instituted what was intended to be an annual Force sports event and medals were struck for the winners in various classes. An RAF cadet is selected each year on passing out at the RAF College, Cranwell for the award of the Queen's Medal; in 1964 two cadets were selected. Over the years RAF personnel have won the North Persian Forces Memorial Medal, the Gold Medal associated with the Chadwick Prize and the Lady Cade Medal. Quite regularly there has been an RAF winner for the Royal United Services Institution Prize Essay Gold Medal. These medal awards and others have sufficient prestige for the medallists to be recorded in the appropriate issues of the Royal Air Force List.

RIBBONS AND CLASPS

Ribbons in themselves make an attractive item for collectors. Most of the usual medal ribbons are held by military tailors. RAF ribbons are all classified by RAF stores reference numbers, for example the Ribbon, Air Crew Europe Star is 22A/767. An RAF officer in 1965, cleaning out an RAF store, came across some old medal ribbons

Right:
Obverse and reverse of a medallion struck in Germany during World War 1 in honour of Rittmeister Manfred von Richthofen, the leading ace of World War 1.

which started him off as a collector and by 1973 he had collected, worldwide, some 28,000 different examples. Of course, not all were concerned with the air, but several thousand were, giving some idea of the scope in this field alone. His more recent additions related to the ribbons of awards to astronauts.

Various clasps to ribbons have been issued throughout the years, such as a bronze oak leaf worn with the appropriate campaign medal for a mention in dispatches. Perhaps the most prized clasp is a silver-gilt rose emblem for wearing with the Ribbon of the 1939-45 Star, to denote service in fighter aircraft during the Battle of Britain. Air Ministry Order A544/46, issued on 24 June 1946, gives areas, date and units concerned for those entitled to campaign medals. This 28-page document includes Battle of Britain personnel eligibility, for aircrew service in 62 squadrons and the Fighter Interception Unit between 10 July and 31 October 1940. The rosette (RAF Stores 22H/820) was issued on the basis of two per claimant and a similar silver rosette (22H/725) was issued for certain campaigns to adorn the Africa Star medal ribbon.

MEDALLIONS AND COINS

Although often called medals, medallions are an entirely different matter. They may be struck commercially for sale as souvenirs, or ordered from a public mint to honour a famous person or event; many have aeronautical connections dating back to the Montgolfière and Charlière balloon ascents of 1783. Other medallions ensued from France and Germany and the following century such as a souvenir could be purchased in Britain, included in the passenger purchase price of a balloon ascent.

The range is broad and values go from a matter of pence. A coin with a Blériot monoplane in flight with 'Louis Blériot — 1909' on the obverse (front) might on the face of it seem valuable by commemorating Blériot's epic cross-channel flight — as indeed it does. But the reverse of the coin, with a large Shell trademark, reveals it as a petroleum company's giveaway. In fact, in the early 1970s Shell produced 16 such coins, depicting 'Man in Flight' with coin subjects ranging

Right:
Limited edition medal holders: a distinguished gathering assembled on 18 January 1988 after receiving their Sir Thomas Sopwith Centenary Celebration Medallions.

Above:
The clutch of ACM Sir Thomas Pike KCB, CBE (top two ribbons), included a bar to the DFC (middle left), represented by a silver rose on the ribbon, and an oak leaf on his 1939-45 Medal to denote that he was 'Mentioned in Despatches'.

from Icarus to Apollo 11, plus a display card with insets for the coins and captioning on the rear. An instructive collection for the schoolboy and one apt to be disregarded by adults simply because it was a giveaway then. Sets were being sold in the 1980s at jumble sales for as low as 10p. However, this in no way alters the fact that the set is an attractive item of aeronautica, yet it would be despised by many because of its pecuniary cheapness.

At the other end of the scale is the 'Man in Flight' legal tender crowns issued by the Pobjoy Mint Ltd for the bicentenary of manned flight, commissioned by the Isle of Man Treasury. The four crowns bearing the Queen's head on the obverse, depicted the Montgolfière balloon, Wright Flyer, Gloster-Whittle jet and the Orbiter space shuttle. Limited issues ranged from 50 to 50,000 in platinum, gold, silver and cupro-nickel editions in a price range from £3,900 town to £17.

Attractive and legal tender is the Isle of Man Double Crown the size, shape and value of a mainland 50p piece. For Christmas each year the Isle of Man issues a Double Crown commemorating different events. That for 1985 marked the 50th anniversary of the official airmail service to the island. The obverse features the scene of mailbags being unloaded from a DH Dragon at Ronaldsway Airport in 1935.

One of the most recent medallions struck, given to 176 guests at a celebratory luncheon to mark the 100th birthday of Sir Thomas Sopwith on 18 January 1988, bore the head of Sir Thomas as an air pioneer. Of 2in diameter, created by John W. Mills, this very limited item, each one of which was numbered and given to associates of the late Sir Thomas, will become highly prized and valued in the years to come.

As the anniversary of the famous dam-busting raid approaches in 1993, a 10-dollar, 50,000 edition, brass coin has been struck depicting this event by Lancasters on the night of 16 May 1943. This was being advertised as a legal tender coin, as indeed it is — in the Marshall Islands.

15 Badges

Like most aspects of aeronautica, badges take many forms but can be divided into two main categories — official and non-official. Those official are decreed in Service orders or manuals and are worn by service personnel in uniform. This has given rise to a host of badges that have been called 'sweetheart badges'. These are the commercially produced badges in the image of official badges that service personnel might give to their girlfriends and families as souvenirs. Their variety is infinite as is their value, for they range from mass-produced brooches to specially commissioned works in gold and studded with diamonds. They are, therefore, considered jewellery rather than aeronautica.

Unofficial and semi-official badges take on many different forms, such as embroidered patches both aeronautical and astronautical, unit and station badges, wings, etc, all available for a pound or two. Just 30p in stamps to Stewart Avi-

ation at Market Harborough, Leicestershire, would, in 1991, secure a comprehensive catalogue with hundreds of representative badges displayed. For lapel badges, brooches, badges on tiepins, ear-rings, cuff-links, pendants and keyrings, in aircraft shape forms or motifs, the Clivedon Collection of Witham Friary, Frome, Somerset, offers a wide range at moderate prices. The advertisements in current aviation magazines will tell you more.

Age and number produced is always a factor in determining values. Cheaply produced brooches for the 1929 and 1931 Schneider Trophy contests, being made for limited periods, with £40-60 catalogue valuation, made three-figure hammer prices recently. One range of lapel badges now highly sought after, are those issued in both world wars by aircraft firms to their workforce to show that they were engaged on work of national importance.

Service buttons are another aspect of badges for many uniform buttons bear the badge of the arm of the service. Since it was usual for servicemen to have spare buttons to hand, it was these that were so often given out as souvenirs.

FLYING BADGES

Of particular interest are the flying badges, usually known as wings. In British service there have been the RFC pilots' wings and the winged 'O' of observers, the RNAS and FAA flying badges, RAF pilots' wings and a range of a dozen or so aircrew badges. Most of these can be bought in accurate replica form today for a few pounds each. The scope widens with the Master Aircrew, Aircrew I-IV and aircrew cadet badges brought out just after World War 2 and the 1949 preliminary flying badges.

All RAF badges, ground and air, were given reference numbers in the equipment vocabulary, Section 22H, which runs to four-figures for the separate subjects. Outside that scope are the colourful British Army pilots' badges past and present and the glider plot badges of the past.

In the US Services, flying badges have been worn successively by the Signal Corps, Air Service, Army Air Corps, Army Air Force and Air Force with a whole series of changes over the years. Rarest of all is their 14 carat gold Military Aviator badge that was issued to just a few pioneers. It was in August 1917 that wing-form badges in silver bullion were adopted by the army in three forms for military aviator, junior military aviator and observer, followed two months later by the first silk badges for enlisted

Above:
Rank badges in general are too well known to detail, but less well known are the bars each side of an RAF cap badge used to denote ranks below major in 1918 only. This officer has retained his former RNAS wings on his cuffs while adopting RAF wings on his breast.

Above:
Apart from the many air forces' flying badges there are the flying badges of army pilots of the world, not forgetting the British Army's former first (top) and second glider pilots' badges.

Right:
Shoulder flashes, both official and unofficial, abound.

pilots. From the end of World War 1 there was as division into aviator and aeronaut for heavier and lighter than air (ie, aeroplanes and airships) flying operators. During World War 2 flying badges proliferated with crew badges including flight surgeon and flight nurse.

The US Navy adopted wing badges from September 1917. With various changes of pattern they go up to the astronaut wings of today. The initial issues of wings had clasps on which it had been intended to identify each pilot by engraving has service number, but there was only room for three digits. A precedence list was then compiled from the date of passing out as a pilot and these early badges were numbered 1 to 282. Records have been preserved by the US Navy so that the identity of the original recipients can be traced if any of these numbered wings should turn up. As well as changes to pattern, badges have diversified to include such items as flight surgeon and tactical observer.

Flying badges of Commonwealth countries in general follow the British pattern, while most

European countries tend to follow American styling. Russia has pilot brevets for 1st and 2nd class pilots and for three classes of pilot-instructors; all bore the inevitable red star. Most East European countries followed the Russian pattern for their flying services badges. Worldwide the range of service badge variations runs into thousands; then there is the civilian flying badges.

There is a large range of wings applicable to the flying personnel of airlines, usually full wings in two different stylings for Captain and 2nd Pilot, and half-wings for navigating, engineering and radio officers, bearing an indication of their functions. Similar half-wings may also be applicable for air hostesses and other cabin staff. Multiply these for the various airlines of the world which have their own styling, and some idea of the vast range will be apparent. When British Airways introduced new insignia for hats and

tunics in 1975, its initial order was for over 50,000 pieces of embroidered insignia.

Finally there is the range of wings produced commercially for individuals to indicate an aerobatic, microlight, helicopter or commercial pilot, as well as other flying categories available in the 1990s for around £2.

SQUADRON & UNIT BADGES

Squadron badge images have become popular items for collection. For many years attempts have been made to produce a book of RAF badges in full colour, but so far it has not proved commercially viable. Although RAF Squadrons adopted crests from the 1920s, it was not until 1936 that the present form of badge was officially approved. The original badges, arranged through Chester Herald and approved by the Sovereign, are public records. It is the reproduction of these in colour or line that are collected. Player's Cigarettes gave an early impetus to RAF badge collection by its full colour card set of 50 RAF Squadron badges issued in 1938. Sets have risen in price over the last 25 years from £1 to £20.

Below:
Dakota badge on the sleeve and air despatch wings on the cuff for Royal Corps of Transport NCOs flying in aircraft and supervising air drops.
Crown copyright PRB 24455

MIDDLE EAST COMMUNICATION SQUADRON · ROYAL AIR FORCE

WE TRAVEL THE HORIZON

OXFORD UNIVERSITY AIR SQUADRON · R.A.F.V.R.

Dominus illuminatio mea

ΑΕΡΟΒΑΤΩ ΚΑΙ ΠΕΡΙΦΡΟΝΩ ΤΟΝ ΗΛΙΟΝ

SINGAPORE SQUADRON · MALAYAN AUXILIARY AIR FORCE

USQUE AD ASTRA

427 SQUADRON · 427 ROYAL CANADIAN AIR FORCE

FERTE MANUS CERTAS

Left and Far left:
RAF Squadron badges had a standard frame, but the crown varied according to period, the Imperial Crown being used up to 1952 and the St Edmund's Crown (as per Oxford UAS shown) subsequently upon Queen Elizabeth's accession the throne.

Bottom left and below right:
Commonwealth air forces unit badges had frames varying from the standard RAF form as examples show.

Right:
Additional to Caterpillar and Goldfish Club badges is the Late Arrivals badge for those tramping in form forced landings in the desert, to which the AOC-in-C Middle East, RAF, gave permission to be worn by entitled personnel.

Below:
Squadron shoulder badges, here shown worn officially, are sold commercially throughout the world to meet the needs of collectors. In this case, even ground crews have squadron-numbered caps.

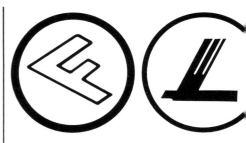

Above:
Trade marks on aircraft parts — An Aircraft Co Ltd motif on a Henri Farman biplane strut made by the company circa 1915. *B. J. Gray*

Some sets have been seen recently in bric-a-brac markets, mounted in a frame and as a background to glass-topped trays.

Full colour posters have been issued with selective badges; in 1985 a poster of 48 badges of fighter squadrons that participated in the Battle of Britain sold for £2.50 a copy. For line impressions of squadron badges, James J. Halley's *The Squadrons of the RAF & Commonwealth 1918-1988* cannot be equalled. Therein are representations of 386 RAF squadron badges, inclusive of Allied forces units operating under RAF control, plus 95 badges of Commonwealth squadrons. The point should be appreciated that no-one can collect the badge of every RAF squadron because a number of squadrons, particularly those raised in the latter part of World War 2 and disbanded immediately after the war, did not have a badge issued.

While most people speak of squadron badges, the official RAF badge range runs to thousands with all the various command, group, wing, station and unit badges in the same basic form as squadron badges. Many units were flying organisations, such as experimental establishments, operational training units, flying training schools, etc.

BADGES GALORE

Most airlines adopt an attractive insignia for marking their aircraft and equipment. With over 900 main, feeder, cargo and taxi airlines worldwide, which may at times have changed their motif, there is a large and colourful range. Some idea of their attraction can be gained from aircraft and engine manufacturers, or oil combines, whose advertisements have shown displays of airline motifs. Individually the motifs are worthless, but collected over the years and placed in albums they have appeared in auction and from secondhand booksellers.

Aircraft manufacturers from before World War 1 have used trade motifs. Armstrong Whitworth embossed 'AW' on engine cowlings, many other firms used transfers for placing their trademark (a badge in effect) on aircraft wing struts. Their trade-mark was included in their letterheads and adverts which too, have become collectors' items. Some collectors of old aircraft magazines have, to make them less bulky, removed the advertisement pages where they were numbered separately from the text pages, thereby considerably reducing the value of the magazines.

Badges that were reaching four-figure sums in recent auctions of aeronautica were those relating to cars: one such was a Brooklands Aero Club coloured enamel badge. Perhaps more common is the Royal Aero Club car badge and that of the Pathfinder Club, but there are many others.

Association and society badges range from the Royal Aeronautical Society to the badges of the various air enthusiasts' organisations. Certainly, aero badges abound.

Above and right:
Aircraft trade badges of German firms in 1938, left to right: Fieseler, Focke-Wulf, Heinkel, Henschel, Junkers and Messerschmitt; the photograph shows the Junkers product badge on a Ju90.

JUNKERS JU90

16 Aeronautical Artefacts

Some people refer to the associated items of aeronautica as ephemera, but since that word is used to describe short-lived or quickly passing interest it is not deemed suitable for items that have survived from the long past. Hence they are referred to here as artefacts, which can be divided into three main classes. First come the genuine relics of aircraft such as nameplates, pieces of structure, fabric with insignia or motifs, and items of equipment used on airfields. Secondly there are the goods fashioned from relics, such as walking sticks made from aircraft struts. An example of this is Battle of Britain keyrings, recently offered by Aviation Artefacts, made from parts of Hurricane W6670 of No 79 Squadron which was shot down during the Battle. Thirdly, comes the mass

Right:
C. H. Price of 62 High Street, Croydon, was well placed to take and publish airliner postcards at a penny a time. This original Handley Page W8F photograph is now worth a few pounds, both to air enthusiasts and postcard collectors.

Below right:
Also based at Croydon, Pamlin Prints has re-issued airliner and other postcard photographs, like this Handley Page HP42, available now for a matter of pence.

of commercial items that commemorate aeronautical events in various materials over the last 200 years, many now classed as *Objets d'Art*.

Among the first of the aeronautical *Objets d'Art*, is a dressing table ornament reputedly made for Marie Antoinette, in which bottles of scent were enclosed within a model of a Charlière balloon, circa 1784. Early balloon ascents in France, the marvel of their time, brought forth

Below:
Airline memorabilia examples: Air France book matches, British Airways boarding card with an Aeroflot sugar lump cover, a Japanese airline motif and airline postcards of prewar Imperial Airways and postwar Continental Airlines. *Peter Cooksley*

1 IMPERIAL AIRWAYS "HERACLES" AT CROYDON 1939

Pamlin Prints,
Croydon

Above left:
Over the years 1927-75 there have been some 25 sets of cigarette cards concerned with aviation. The cards shown are from Player's 'Aircraft of the RAF' issued in 1938 with an album priced a penny.

Left:
Cigarette cards are no longer issued as part of the anti-smoking drive, but trade cards may still flourish. Cards shown here were free issues by team importers in the postwar years. The lady shown is Amy Johnson.

Above:
Troops were avid trophy and souvenir hunters, in this case from a wrecked Japanese Kawasaki Ki-61 'Tony' fighter.

Below:
A jewel box carved from propeller wood, lined with velvet and bearing the RNAS badge on the lid.
Brian Hansley

trinket boxes, pendants, fans and even buttons decorated with scenes of ascents during the latter part of the 18th century. Military use of balloons was apparently first represented on a snuff-box of the period, with an oval lid depicting a captive balloon over the Belgian battlefield of Fleurus in 1794 during the French Revolutionary wars.

In all three cases the range is almost infinite.

AIRLINE MEMORABILIA

Aircraft finishes have always attracted keen interest and among the most colourful and decorative schemes have been the liveries of the airlines. These have been illustrated in colour in series articles in British, American and Japanese magazines in particular. A noticeable feature of recent

Above left:
A World War 1 propeller blade as a picture frame for photographs of a lady serving with the RFC, with an RFC badge and button inset in the centre.
Brian Hansley

Left:
Top: aircraft type picture set example by Solo Matches and the two sides of Wardair airline book matches. Middle: matchbox top varieties produced for Aeroflot. Bottom: selection of aeronautical history matchbox tops by Drava of Yugoslavia.

Above:
Not generally realised are the number of private museums around the country which are run by military units. This was No 56 Squadron's memorabilia room at RAF Wattisham in the 1960s. *Crown copyright*

auctions was the amount of artwork originally produced for publications, that was now being sold off. In due course, much airline artwork will come on to the market.

Associated with airlines is a whole range of memorabilia, not least attractive the postcards of their aircraft; some airlines included flight menu cards with postcard backing. Such cards were selling for as little as 10p each during the 1980s, but prewar airline postcards of Imperial Airways,

Sabena and the like now measure in pounds each.

Boarding cards, baggage tags, beer mats, sugar and condiment packs are all collectable provided they bear the name of an airline. There are those who collect court cards and in this field a whole range exists with airline motif backings. Book matches are another collector's line, evinced by the boxes of book matches at some bric-a-brac markets, where a search may reveal some from the smaller airlines. Apart from the hundreds of different airlines, there is great variety in the packages themselves. Alitalia had black matches with red striker heads, whereas Swissair had similar matches with white heads and cover titling was according to the route. BOAC had matches individually named with a series of destinations for its network. Air France, with titling as the 'World's Largest Air Network', had double standard-size books with each match proclaiming its quality with 'Bryant & May' printed. The variety is almost endless.

Albums of airline memorabilia, covering a number of different airlines, were in the stocks of a specialist bookseller in 1992.

SIGNATURES

The signatures of famous people have always attracted some collectors and the aviation field offers rich pickings with pioneer airmen, fighter aces, aircraft manufacturers, designers and test pilots as well as those responsible for famous flights. In late 1990 a collector using Box 154 of *FlyPast* magazine was offering £100 each for signatures of George Bulman, Sidney Camm, Geoffrey de Havilland, Guy Gibson, 'Sailor' Malan and R. J. Mitchell.

One of the largest collections of autographs of airmen ever offered for sale was of around 1,000 amassed by Wg Cdr W. J. Cleasby during World War 2, including 200 of fighter aces; Sotheby's in 1990 put an £8,000-12,000 valuation on this unique collection. With an eye to the future, a collector obtained several hundred signatures at annual Battle of Britain reunions during 1968-81 which, placed in auction in 1990, were valued at up to £1,000.

Menus at aeronautical functions are a good source for signatures. The dinner on 12 July 1920 to the first 100 British aviators (by Royal Aero Club licence number) and pioneers, with 220 guests, provided a spate of valuable signatures. In modern times, many menus were signed at the dinner in celebration of the 100th birthday of Sir Thomas Sopwith, on 18 January 1988, which had an assemblage of some 200 of his associates.

Autograph books were more common in World War 1 than World War 2; their values go from a few pounds to hundreds depending on who signed them and the quality of the content. Signatures in books and on documents have been covered in other sections.

CHINA & GLASSWARE

Aeronautical artefacts in china exist in many forms, official and unofficial. Certain RAF mess china bore the service badge as did chamber pots in some married quarters. A whole range of semi-official, specially commissioned, china existed in some station messes and items, like tureens, were often presented with inscriptions.

China miniatures of the kind produced as souvenirs of seaside resorts from the beginning of the century, were also produced for shops near principal RAF stations like Cranwell and Halton with suitable pictorial representation and name. Many commemorative plates relating to events in aviation have been issued over the years and among the bric-a-brac sponsored by airlines are ashtrays, mugs and plates decorated with aircraft in the livery of the line.

Engraved glassware such as wine glasses and decanters with RNAS or RFC crests is a possible pick-up, but a rare one since glassware is all to easily broken. Glass paperweights with aeronautical subjects is also a possibility, but those depicting the old ballooning days would be more valuable as general antiques than as aeronautica. However, sturdy and functional glassware with aeronautical connections has been available in recent years. To mark the opening of the Bomber Command Museum, a one-pint glass tankard was produced, price £22.50 with the Command badge. For a few additional pounds, ranks, names and decorations could be marked.

In 1984, for the 40th anniversary of D-Day, genuine lead crystal whisky decanter and tumbler sets, wine decanters and tankers by Heritage Crystal had an RAF section that included RAF and Bomber Command badges and a Hurricane flown by 'Johnnie' Johnson. The price range was under £10 for a tankard and £60 for engraved decanter and wine glasses. There were similar offers before and others will follow. Such items, aimed at serving and ex-service personnel, might well be bought by young collectors with an eye to sale in the future. Since all such items are of limited production, with their rarity increasing year by year, their value will increase.

AERIAL LEAFLETS

Advertising leaflets dropped from balloons were a feature of the last century, but few have survived. For Manchester Lifeboat Day in 1902, in conjunction with the Post Office, 4,000 postcards were dropped from a balloon as souvenirs. Only two copies appear to have survived, one in the Science Museum and the other which sold for £1,525 in 1983. Many of the early aviators, as a publicity stunt, dropped a form of visiting card. One, based in Wales, had cards printed 'Dropped by Vivian Hewitt from his Monoplane'; these he signed and dated by arrangement with the Rhyl town authorities to draw crowds to that resort. Cards liberally thrown from his Blériot were collected by people, unaware that in years to come each one could be exchanged for many pounds. These are only examples of hundreds of events.

Military use of leaflets from balloons go back two hundred years, while drops from aeroplanes date from Italy's operations in Tripolitania during 1912. It is from World War 1 that propaganda leaflets survive in quantity. From 1914 the *Daily Mail* office in Paris was contracted to produce leaflets exhorting Germans to desert to the Allies, while the Germans first tried to suborn Indian troops on the Western Front by similar measures.

Between the wars leaflets were dropped by the RAF for air control overseas. When it comes to World War 2 the production figures for propaganda leaflets is truly astronomical. Hundreds of millions were dropped by RAF Bomber Command and for South-East Asia Command alone,

Right:
A propaganda leaflet of World War 1, dropped by the Belgian Air Corps over their homeland to encourage their kinsmen suffering the occupation by German forces.

AVIATION MILITAIRE BELGE

La puissance allemande arrive à son déclin.

Le colosse aux pieds d'argile chancelle.

Courage ! chers amis de Belgique ! L'Armée Belge pense à vous. L'Armée Belge lutte pour vous.

VIVE LE ROI !
VIVE LA BELGIQUE !
VIVENT LES ALLIÉS !

全日本軍ハ問フ

我ガ航空機及ビ大砲ハ

何處ニアリヤト

己達の持物は之れだけだ

之だけで戰爭に勝てやうか

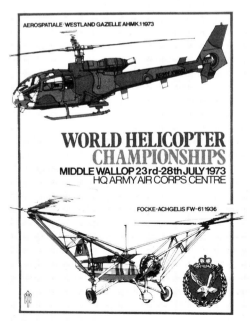

AEROSPATIALE/WESTLAND GAZELLE AHMK.1 1973

WORLD HELICOPTER
CHAMPIONSHIPS
MIDDLE WALLOP 23rd-28th JULY 1973
HQ ARMY AIR CORPS CENTRE

FOCKE-ACHGELIS FW-61 1936

BRITISH LEGION

3P

50TH Anniversary

ARMY AIR DAY
3&JULY73
BRITISH FORCES 1973 POSTAL SERVICE

Comd.
A Avn Centre
Middle Wallop

Left:
Obverse and reverse of Leaflet SJ/11 dropped over Burma asking the Japanese infantry where their air force and artillery support is, and pointing out their only help was a spade with which to take cover.

Below left:
Typical of the many special postal covers is this issue of Army Air Day 1973 with, appropriately, a World War 1 airman included in the stamp.

their dropping return for just December 1944 was 4,528,300 leaflets and 1,099,100 news-sheets. Each different propaganda leaflet was numbered in a series according to the intended recipients, the series being denoted by code letters as follows: B — Belgian (aeroplane and balloon dissemination); C — Czechoslovakia; CF — Occupied France (Canadian sponsored); D — Danes; F — French (UK sponsored); G — German forces and civilians; H — Dutch; I — Italians; J — Chan-

Below:
Where railwaymania merges with aeronautica. Engine nameplates and plaques of British Rail 'Battle of Britain' Class locomotives have been avidly sought. Names include commands, stations, squadrons and personalities of the Battle. Illustrated is the engine *Royal Observer Corps. National Railway Museum 393/77*

nel Islanders; L — Luxembourgers (limited and now vary rare); N — Norwegians; P — Poles; SB — Burmese; SJ — Japanese in SE Asia; SS — Siamese; USF — French (US sponsored); USG — German forces and civilians (US sponsored); WG — Germans in West (Post D-Day); XA — Special packaging of cigarettes and crop seeds for Burmese, Kachins and Shans; XF — French (regions still occupied post D-Day).

Leaflets were dropped by the RAF in the Falklands War, but few of those dropped survived due to high winds causing widespread scattering. One of the most recent leaflet drops was from a light aeroplane over Greenham Common, Upper Heyford and Welford bases in May 1984. Since such droppings are now illegal the pilot was fined. These leaflets have no value as it would be difficult to tell them apart from other anti-nuclear leaflets simply handed out. On the other hand wartime leaflets are of the same value whether dropped or taken direct from the press, with the exception of certain 'G' series leaflets of which whole packs survived. In general, wartime leaflets were tightly controlled and, surprisingly for papers being given direct to the enemy, were classified 'Secret' to Allied personnel. Any unreleased leaflets had to be returned for pulping. Perhaps the most valuable leaflets of all the wartime releases are examples of 'double-cross' — leaflets dropped by the Germans over their own occupied territory purporting to be of Allied origin.

AERONAUTICAL PHILATELY

Philately, the collection and study of postage stamps is the world's most popular hobby. Stamps with aeronautical connections can be divided into two main series. Some countries, like the USA, have issued stamps specially for air transit. But most countries who issue stamps that can be used for air or surface transit have issued special stamps with aeronautical connections. These might be to commemorate a special flight, the opening of a new airport, anniversaries such as the Battle of Britain, air strength propaganda or just featuring aspects of flying for an attractive presentation.

The Aero Philatelic Club was founded in Britain as far back as 1923 and still flourishes. Over the years hundreds of different types of aircraft have appeared on stamps. As a challenge to the reader, where else could you turn up an image of a Schwarz airship of 1897 or a PKZ-2 helicopter of 1918 except in a modestly priced packet of Hungarian stamps. The fact that French aerophilatelic history can be traced back to 1783 and that there has been some 20 editions of a Zeppelin post catalogue, will give some idea of the scope by taking in account all that has happened in aviation since.

Specially marked envelopes have always been sought by collectors, but it is only in the past 35 years that first day covers have been so widely collected. Add to these the special event covers and thousands will be found to have aeronautical connections; as an indication of scope a few are tabled as representation of the many:

REPRESENTATIVE COLLECTABLE POSTAL COVERS ON AERONAUTICAL SUBJECTS

Issued	Description by Country, Subject and Details
04:04:62	San Marino. Vintage aircraft. Set of 10 stamps on large cover, with stamps depicting aircraft of Glenn Curtiss 1908, Alliott Verdon Roe 1909, etc
20:09:69	British (RAF Museum SC6). Battle of Britain Anniversary 1969. Cover has a painting of Sopwith Camel B7270, bears a 1968 one shilling RAF 1968 50th Anniversary stamp and certified as

flown from RAF Coltishall to RAF Biggin Hill in Spitfire Mk 19 PM631

10:12:69	Australia. 50th Anniversary of first flight from England. Cover shows Vickers Vimy G-EAOU and bears the three different stamps issued commemorating the occasion; Pakistan also used a cover and stamp 02:12:69 for the 50th Anniversary of its staging at Karachi
10:06:72	British (RAF Museum SC21). 60th Anniversary of the Central Flying School. Cover depicting a Gloster Gamecock bears certification of being flown in Vickers Varsity T1 WJ945 on a training flight, bearing a 3p British Legion Stamp
28:03:73	Italy. 50th Anniversary of Military Aviation. Cover with six stamps depicting S-55 flying boats, Campini-Caproni jet, Fiat Cr42, G91 and G91Y and F-104S Starfighter
02:12:73	Italy. Stamp Day. Cover with 25 lire stamp of Alitalia Sud Caravelle
15:01:74	Qatar. Arab Civil Aviation Day. Cover with set of four stamps depicting Gulf Air BAC VC-10 and Doha airport together with flags of Qatar and Arab League
03:02:75	Britain. Royal Aircraft Establishment 21st Anniversary of first pilotless target drone sortie at Llandebr. Cover certified flown in Canberra PR3 WE146 on its last sortie by Sqn Ldr D. E. Betts. Jindivik on cover which bears a Welsh stamp
20:05:77	USA. 50th Anniversary of Lindbergh's lone transatlantic flight with stamp of the 'Spirit of St Louis'
01:04:78	Isle of Man. 60th Anniversary of the RAF. Set of four stamps depicting Short 184 over HMS Ben-my-Chree, Bristol Scout and HMS Vindex, a Defiant over Douglas Bay and a Jaguar over Ramsey
13:04:78	Eire. 50th Anniversary of first East-West transatlantic flight with attractive cover sponsored by Aer Lingus and stamp depicting D1167, the Junkers W33 concerned
24:04:79	Jersey. 25th International Air Rally. Set of five stamps featuring a Tiger Moth, Harvard, Mew Gull, Chipmunk and Turbulent on an attractive cover

17 Identifying Aircraft Parts

As emphasised in Chapter 7, it has to be appreciated that airframes, engines and propellers, each with their own identity systems, hold no indication of their relation together on a particular aircraft. Thus there is no means of telling which individual aircraft any isolated assembly or part came from, although it may be possible to identify which manufacturer or aircraft type that the part came from. Major components did have identity nameplates, but as these are among some of the most highly prized items of aeronautica, they were often prised off by collectors, isolating the component from its own identity.

INSPECTION STAMPS

Aircraft component makers may be identified from their inspection stamps. All parts for aircraft must be inspected and, if practicable, marked with a stamp exclusive to a particular individual. Important assemblies may be stamped by an AID (Aeronautical Inspection Directorate) inspector with the letters AID and the individual's identity letters and numbers. But the vast mass of compo-

nents are inspected by works staff who have AID approval. These stamps bear prefix letters indicative of the firm. While the aircraft design and construction firms may have coded letters, most other firms had a direct abbreviation of the firm concerned, for example 'PSC 25' would indicate Inspector No 25 of the Pressed Steel Co.

Inspection stamps have been in general use since 1914. One difficulty in using them for aircraft type identity is that only a fraction of the aircraft that have been built have been constructed by their design firm. In World War 1 only about 10% of all Sopwith Camels were built by Sopwith Aviation, the majority being built by 10 different firms. There has been large-scale sub-contracting in the industry ever since, to the extent that, apart from the prototype, the whole production of Hawker Hectors was by Westland Aircraft.

Below:
Aircraft type and mark can be ascertained from the airframe serial number. On RAF aircraft this number is normally in 8in high black digits. ZA322 is a Tornado GR1. *Peter Cooksley*

PART NUMBERS

British aircraft parts are all item numbered as far as is practicable. Castings and mouldings normally have their part numbers embodied; on most machined or pressed parts the number was stamped. On instruments a type number normally appears on the face. In general, part numbers are derived from their drawing numbers. As early as 1916 aircraft manufacturers were allotted code letters to prefix their numbers, from allocations by the Air Board.

Some firms retained their original code letter prefixes to post-World War 2, others used a numbering system in which the first digits related to the aircraft's type number. Most firms numbered parts in groups according to main assemblies. Finally, to cater for modifications, for which revised drawings would be issued, suffixed let-ters were allotted alphabetically. For example, 57685/14B related to the 2nd (B) drawing revision of Part 14 in Assembly 685 of a Halifax (Handley Page Type 57).

Code letters issued to manufacturers appear in *Aviation Archaeology — A Collectors Guide to Aeronautical Relics* (Patrick Stephens Ltd 1977, Revised 1983).

RAF EQUIPMENT CODING

The RAF calls its part-numbering system as referencing. Numbers from 1 to 99 are given to various ranges of equipment, followed by a suffix let-

Below:
With Fleet Air Arm aircraft the digits were normally displayed half RAF standard size. EK746 was a Firebrand Mk IV.

Above:
The key to American aircraft identity is the serial number where the first digit refers to the last digit of the fiscal year in which it was procured, in this case 6 for 1956. The other numbers relate to its allocation within the fiscal year, in this case to an F-100 Super Sabre. Books giving the range of numbers are available commercially.

ter denoting the type of equipment within that range. As an example armaments are Range 12, with 12A-C relating to bombs, practice items and ammunition respectively.

Like the army, RAF stores description is, to normal usage, about-face — to partially express it! To give an example of RAF stores referencing and description:

Ref 1A/3716 Box, tool, large
Ref 1A/3717 Box, tool, small
Ref 1A/3826 Box, tool, medium

The first Vocabulary of Stores, as the RAF chose to call their stores listings, was FS133 (Field Service Publication No 133), available from April 1920. This was provisional, being replaced by AP809 *Priced Vocabulary of Stores* and other Air Publications.

A major change came to referencing in mid-World War 2, when American equipment began to be taken on charge in large quantities. While American equipment was categorised under the appropriate range and section, 100 was added to the range number. For example British aircraft compasses had been referenced 6A in the manner 6A/473 for a Type P6 Compass. For American compasses the numbers would start at No 1 under the range 106A in the manner 106A/1. Section 26 related to special aircraft type equipment, with the suffix letters relating to the particular type of aircraft. Since the reference was usually marked on the equipment it has helped aviation

archaeologists in establishing aircraft type identity. Section 126 similarly related to American aircraft types in British service. The letters concerned and the aircraft types into which they referred are given in the guide mentioned earlier.

Classification of equipment in RAF parlance had nothing to do with referencing, but related to replacement. Stores were divided into Class 'A', 'B' or 'C'. An 'A' store could only be replaced by the return of the original issue, Class 'B' related to a store where the original was required to be returned or its disposal certified by a unit or station commander and 'C' concerned stores that were consumed in normal usage, like oil.

AIRCRAFT AND ENGINES

The type, mark and contractor of a British service aircraft can be ascertained if the airframe serial number is visible or known. Then it is a simple matter of looking it up in a register. Only one full range register has so far been published — *British Military Aircraft Serials*, first published by Ian Allan Ltd in 1964, of which the sixth and current edition for 1878-1987 is published by Midland Counties Publications.

For the history of individual RAF aircraft, the published registers of Air Britain (Historians) Ltd are the most comprehensive and they plan, eventually to cover the whole range. Up to mid-1992 separate volumes have been issued for serial ranges prefixed as follows: J, K, L, N, P, R, T, V & W and X & Z in combined volumes, AA-AZ, BA-BZ, DA-DZ, EA-EZ, FA-FZ, HA-HZ, JA-JZ, KA-KZ, LA-LZ, MA-MZ, NA-NZ, SA-VZ in one volume; WA-WZ and XA-XZ.

For British and foreign civil aircraft there are several published registers giving registrations, aircraft type and current owner.

Aircraft engines are recorded individually by maker's number. From 1916 those in RFC and RNAS service, and later those of the RAF and FAA, were also given an official identity number. Up to April 1918, the official numbers, allotted consecutively, were prefixed 'WD' and by 'A' subsequently.

Engine numbering systems by firms varied. Some, like Hispano, used by the RAF and other forces, had blocks of numbers accorded to the 10 different manufacturers. Other manufacturers used different batches of numbers according to left- or right-hand rotation of their engines. Although a listing of aero engine types by official numbers exists for 1920-60, it has never been published.

OFFICIAL ORDERS

For the introduction dates of the main items of equipment, from aircraft and engines down to radar sets and flying helmets, this information is to be found in Air Ministry Orders. They also contain various administrative changes and in uniform, badge and medal introductions and changes. Copies can be perused in the Public Record Office and some museums; they occasionally come up in sales.

The main orders for the RAF from 1918 were Air Ministry Weekly Orders (AMWOs). Following the pattern of existing Admiralty Fleet Orders and Army Orders, they were numbered from No 1 upwards on an annual basis. Reference to a particular order was made by number and year, eg AMWO No 291 of 1919 (incidentally relating to Mess Dress for Officers) would be given as AMWO 291/19. For a time, from 1918, there were also Air Ministry Monthly Orders and Confidential Communication Orders RAF, also issued monthly, but the latter was later embodied in Air Ministry Confidential Orders that continued to post-World War 2. There was also a series of Air Ministry Technical Orders (AMTOs) dealing with equipment and modifications.

At the end of 1930, AMWOs were discontinued and three new series evolved. These were Air Ministry Orders 'A' series of general matters which included dress, markings of aircraft and vehicles, 'N' series so-called Temporary Orders and Notices, but which gave notice of introduction and obsolescence of equipment, unit badges approved, etc. The third series, Air Ministry Equipment Orders, replaced AMTOs and was later discontinued with their information embodied in Air Publications. In 1964 all were replaced by Defence Council Instructions (Air) series.

Top right:
Up to 1949, RAF vehicles were numbered with an 'RAF' prefix. When the six-character Joint Services numbering was introduced of two numbers, two letters and a further two numbers, the first letter as 'A' identified RAF vehicles.

Above right:
Panel identity markings, where PSC relates to Pressed Steel Co manufacture for Hawker (Code 41H) of assembly and part 407222. DTD relates to the cellulose (C) finish to Directorate of Technical Development (DTD) Specification No 308 of matt cellulose finish and primer.

Right:
An example of an inspector's stamp. Aeronautical Inspection Directorate approved inspector No 58 of Percival Aircraft Co.

18 Aeronautica Ubique

Aeronautica abounds. As well as watching it on TV or reading it in your armchair, you can indulge it in travelling and on holidays in Britain and abroad. There are vintage and veteran aircraft on exhibition at over 100 sites in Great Britain. There are books about them modestly priced. Local tourist offices will have details. Most of the air museums supply tourist offices in their district with brochures giving times and prices. The Patrick Stephens Ltd 'Action Stations' series of books cover, by areas, all used and disused airfields in the United Kingdom with a write-up on their past history. Some local history groups have covered airfields in their particular county. Just walk into the locality's public library and ask for details.

Visit local museums, secondhand bookshops, libraries and in particular churches where a plaque may relate to an airman. For example in St Nicholas Church at Moreton, Dorset, incidentally not far from Lawrence of Arabia's grave, there is a memorial window engraved by Laurence Whistler dedicated to an airman killed in the Battle of France 1940. Postcards of the window are available in aid of the church funds, as are cards of the RAF memorial windows in Ely, Lincoln and Guildford cathedrals.

AERO PUBS

Many public houses contain items of aeronautica exhibited in the bars, particularly those with aeronautical names. There is the 'Comet' at Hatfield, home of the de Havilland works where Britain's first jet airliner evolved, although the name was derived from the earlier Comet that won the 1934 England-Australia air race. Both are worth drinking to! Additionally, Eric Kennington designed the stone column outside the pub, dedicated to flight. A replaced, slightly weathered inn sign 'The Flying Boat', circa 1945, depicting a Sunderland flying along a coastline of cliffs, was valued by Sotheby's at £450-550 for auction in 1990.

Other famous aircraft have the attribute of an inn sign in their honour. Ind Coope's 'The Britannia' at Hackney, London, displays the aircraft in BOAC livery. An appropriate painting appears on

Below:
Around the UK's libraries, thousands of postcard photographs of local history are on sale. This No 10 'Historic Thanet' postcard shows a *Daily Mail* Blériot monoplane at Margate. *Kent County Library*

'The Lancaster' at Desford, Leicestershire, and 'The Swordfish' at Newlyn, Cornwall. In 1970 when the 'Coronation Arms' was given a renovation, it was appropriately re-named 'The Harrier', being close both to Hawker Siddeley's Hamble factory and the College of Air Training, and for which a suitable inn sign painting was made. Currently 'Concorde' and 'Spitfire' are the most popular aircraft names for inn signs.

As a modern version of the 'Pig and Whistle', there is a 'Jet and Whittle' at Tuffley, two miles south of Gloucester, not far from where the first British jet aircraft was conceived. The Fleet Air Arm is recognised in 'The Ark Royal' at Alton. Perhaps not immediately recognised as having an aeronautical connection is 'The Guinea Pig', but its location at East Grinstead is close to the hospital where so many airmen received plastic surgery under the care of Sir Archibald McIndoe and his dedicated team whose work has been chronicled in a book titled as the inn name.

Apart from such pubs, there are those with more conventional names that have a place in aeronautical history, such as the 'George Hotel' at Grantham and the 'White Hart' of Newark, haunts of bomber crews during World War 2, or the village pubs around famous fighter stations. These were not necessarily the nearest pubs; for Biggin Hill "The White Hart" at Brasted, some eight miles away, was the favourite. It was here that many famous fighter pilots chalked their names on a board, that has been subsequently presented to the RAF Museum and preserved. It is said that the inn retains an atmosphere of the past to this day.

During the Battle of Britain No 1 Squadron identified itself with the 'True Briton' inn at Tangmere, Sussex. Many other squadrons later operated from the airfield which in late 1918 was being prepared for American Expeditionary Force airmen flying American-built Handley Page 0/400s. But in 1964 the run-down of the station started and local pubs lost trade. When the 'True Briton' was closed its inn sign was presented to No 1 Squadron at West Raynham, thus making such a sign an official item of aeronautica.

Hostelries in Cambridge, Ely, Lincoln and York — all in 'bomber country' during World War 2 — had their share of pubs, some that became famous throughout Bomber Command and the US 8th Air Force. It is said that one of the most nostalgic things that returning American and Canadian airmen notice is the famous brewers' signs, such as the elephant trademark of Fremlin's ales. Certainly it was the quality of the ale that largely influenced the selection of the airmen's favourite haunts.

CAPITAL AERONAUTICA

Many aircraft enthusiasts will at some time, for business or pleasure, be visiting the capital cities of Europe. For London the Royal Air Force Museum at Hendon, the Imperial War Museum at Lambeth and the Science Museum at South Kensington are a must for those interested in aeronautics. To the stranger to London, there are simple guides. The Geographers' *A-Z London Street Atlas and Index* is indispensable; fortunately it is cheap and comprehensive, dealing with a large amount of Greater London. But make sure that you get the paperback edition, not the large and more expensive hardbacked edition. The softbacks are on sale throughout London for a couple of pounds. They have an Underground railway map on the back or inside, but being in black and white in the cheaper edition it is rather difficult to differentiate between the different lines. However, most Underground station book-

Above:
At the outset of your journey abroad you can use your camera to record the Alcock and Brown statue at London-Heathrow Airport.

ing offices and tourist centres will supply a coloured chart free.

For the RAF Museum take the Northern Line (Edgware Section), do not get out at Hendon Central but alight at Colindale, the next stop, turn left when you come out of this station and at the roundabout take Grahame Park Way almost opposite, named after the air pioneer Claude Graham-White. The museum is on the right along this road.

The Imperial War Museum is a fairly easy walk from the Charing Cross area across Waterloo Bridge to the South Bank by the aid of your A-Z, or Lambeth North station is only three stations from Charing Cross on the southbound Bakerloo Line. From Waterloo mainline terminus it is only a 10min walk. South Kensington for the Science Museum is on the Circle, District and Piccadilly Lines, westbound from central London. From the station there is an underground walkway to the museum.

If you cross the Channel for the Continent at Dover, with its long association with cross-Channel shipping, you may well forget that once it was a town with three air stations. On the downs behind the castle a Royal Naval Air Service aerodrome had a nearby Royal Flying Corps one and below them on the sea front was the seaplane station. The whole area behind the cliffs abounds with sites of the military installations, many of them related to the air war — radar, searchlight

and anti-aircraft gun sites. In the town and at the castle you can buy a moderately priced booklet *A Handbook of Kent's Defences* giving map references for these sites.

Paris, like London with its RAF Museum out at Hendon, has its main air museum out at Chalais Meudon. In central Paris there is only limited aeronautica in the Army Museum in the Place des Invalides, but it is different on the streets. Paris is a centre for postcard collectors. Apart from the typical tourist views of famous edifices, and the views of old Paris which are in the majority, are cards of railway, ship, vehicles and aircraft subjects of the Grand Age and more moderately priced than at collectors' fairs in Britain.

Brussels has become the stamp centre and those seeking air mail stamps should not be disappointed. Antwerp, too, is a good place to start with 100 different stamps of air subjects still available for around £2.50. Bookshops in Belgium in general, and in Ostend in particular, are worth browsing in. Often you can pick up books that are out of print in Britain. While Belgium does not have aviation magazines like Britain, air matters have been well covered in its general illustrated magazines. Their *Illustré* was published monthly in Brussels, even during German occupation throughout most of World War 1. Among others an October 1916 issue, originally sold for 20 centimes, containing items of Austrian, German and Swiss aeronautical interest, was bought in the 1980s for just 100 times its face value, ie 20 francs. But at 75 Belgian Francs to £1 at the time of writing, the equivalent of 27p, it was still a cheap item of aeronautica. At the same time pre-World War 2 copies of *La Patriote Illustré*, also with items of aviation interest, were selling at the same price.

At Portugal's capital, Lisbon, the secondhand bookstalls near the main station were selling copies of Portugal's main illustrated magazine going back to pre-World War 1 with illustrations of pioneer flying in that country; certainly, rare items of aeronautica, again at around 25p in British currency. Some of these copies have found their way to British dealers in the late 1980s. No doubt they keep their eyes open when holidaying abroad, so why don't you?

While in Lisbon the Naval Museum is well worth a visit. Where else could you see a Fairey IIIC floatplane and an FBA flying boat? From the coastal railway nearby trains go to Cascais, a pleasant resort with a large park and a small one dotted with anti-aircraft guns, sound locators, range calculators and predictors of World War 2 and postwar patterns, plus a suspended pilotless target aircraft.

Some European cities can be disappointing in respect of aeronautica. Bonn, a recent capital, seems to offer little and Luxembourg, a country without an air force, even less. One of the fascinating aspects of Switzerland is the ability, by means of mountain railways, to reach vantage points from which aircraft can be viewed flying below.

As a small defence-conscious country there is a relatively high rate of military aircraft flying to be seen and, being centrally placed in Europe, considerable civil aircraft traffic. The shops have much to offer in books and models, but the drawback is that because of its high standard of living the country is more expensive than most.

AERO ITALIA

No-one should miss the Queen of the Adriatic coast — Venice — when visiting Italy. The beauty of the city has been extolled for centuries and here is the site of so much history. It was in 1849 when this city of canals was besieged by the Austrians, that their first bombardment from the air came, by explosives dropped from 3,320cu ft hot air balloons. In the naval base at the tip of the main island, an air station was established on the north side before World War 1.

Above:
The gaunt windowless warehouses of Venice, abandoned after Allied bombing in World War 2, viewed from the Canale della Guidecca. *N. D. Robertson*

As you enter Venice on the road viaduct, built between the wars, you are parallel with the railway causeway, target of the Austrian Lohner flying boat attacks from May 1915 when Italy came into World War 1. From the Piazzale Roma road terminus, you may well take the river bus down the Grand Canale to St Mark's Square. About 50yd past the Rialto Bridge on the port side, there is a break in the ancient architecture, the result of a World War 1 bomb. Once at St Mark's (Piazza San Marco) you will be aware of the magnificent tower, and on the opposite side of the canal the spire of St Giorgio. You can ascend to the top of each and actually stand where the air-raid sentries stood in those early days of air warfare to warn of approaching Austrian raiding aircraft.

Further toward the tip of the main island, in the old naval base history was made in anti-submarine warfare. Here the British submarine B10, under repair, was sunk by bombs from Austrian aircraft in August 1916.

The Venetian Lagoon is steeped in aeronautical history. It was here in 1917 that chains of barges carried balloons to lift screens of netting to create the first balloon barrage. Italian Macchi flying boats and French FBAs took of from the Lagoon waters to fight off the Lohners, or to bomb them in their lair at Pola. Landplanes were brought in to operate from a strip on the Lido which, even now, has an airstrip for light aircraft. The island of St Andria became an air base and on Poveglia slipways were built for RNAS Short 320s, but they were used by the Italians as a sub-station.

Between the wars, the Lagoon was the venue of the 1927 Schneider Trophy Contest. The old seaplane slipways and sheds on St Andrea had become a civil seaplane station as Aeroporto Guiseppe Miraglia. Here were housed the Macchi M52s of the Italians and the Supermarine S5,

Gloster IVA and Short Crusader of the RAF High Speed Flight, while the Trophy itself was exhibited in St Mark's Square, one of the priceless treasures that has not been retained in Venice. Stands were erected on the Lido for the great event and for watchers of the practice flights. They witnessed the dramatic plunge of the Crusader into the waters of the Lagoon at 150mph up-side-down. Fortunately the pilot escaped and the seaplane was salved minus a float which eventually surfaced in the Grand Canal.

Then World War 2 when the harbour, just behind the main coach and car park, was subjected to a precision bombing attack by Mustangs and Kittyhawks of the Desert Air Force while Thunderbolts and other Mustangs attacked the anti-aircraft positions on the Lido and other islands. You can still see the old anti-aircraft gun sites on former coastal fort gun positions on the Lido. But most impressive of all the relics of air warfare are the tall gaunt skeletal remains of the warehouses on Giudecca, lining one side of the Canale della Giudecca, burnt out after an attack by B-17s and B-24s of the US 15th Air Force and abandoned to this day. And the guidebooks tell nothing of all this; their compilers have no sense of history.

The Italian lakes, Como, Garda and Maggiore, are noted for their beauty, peace and tranquillity, shattered only by the occasional low pass of a Tornado, F-104 Starfighter or Macchi 326. These calm inland waters are rarely ruffled except by chugging motorboats, the ferries that stage along lakeside villages and the hydrofoil expresses that do the full-length routes; also, in certain areas of the lakes, floatplane landings are permitted.

In Austria and Italy, if you travel by train — and to some degree if by road — then there is hardly a major bridge that has not been a former target of Mediterranean Allied Air Forces; and they are still finding unexploded bombs along the road and rail routes. At San Marino, that independent republic within Italy, you can still buy their famous aviation pioneer stamps on a first day cover. If you have not figured out how they have catered for selling these to the daily coachloads of visitors extending for over 25 years since the covers were issued, and still maintain stocks, then your guess is as good as the writer's!

On to Naples — there may be a carrier of the US 6th Fleet in the bay. En route, along the motorway, the white walls of the Monte Cassino monastery on the Abbey Hill, standing 1,700ft above Cassino, dominates the view to the left for some 10 miles. It was on 15 February 1944 that the decision was taken by Allied Command that this main foundation of the Benedictine Order, started by St Benedict in 529AD and then occupied as a German stronghold, must be destroyed if the hill, dominating territory for miles around, was to be taken. After due warning to the monks

a massive air attack was launched by 142 B-17 Fortresses dropping 287 tons of 500lb GP bombs and over 66 tons of 100lb incendiaries. There were also 47 B-52 Mitchell and 40 B-26 Marauder sorties dropping 1,000lb bombs. The buildings, courtyards and the outer walls, in places 10ft thick, were devastated. The white structure now visible is the rebuilt monastery. It may be visited by means of a winding access road. Enthusiasts touring in their own cars are advised that it would be prudent to remove those 'Save a Fortress' stickers.

Naples was vigorously attacked during the invasion of Sicily to disrupt reinforcements reaching the island through the port. The harbour and marshalling yards were repeatedly attacked by USAAF B-17s by day and RAF Wellingtons at night. When the 7th Armoured Division entered Naples on 7 October 1943, the largest enemy city captured up to that time, there were 145 German and 45 Italian aircraft found abandoned on

Below:
Many plaques on the Continent have some relevance to aviation such as the one that marks the birthplace of Italy's leading ace of World War 1, Franceso Baracca, at Lugo di Romagna.

Above:
Even when visiting the Great Pyramid in Egypt, you can figure out the actual site of this RAF radio relay station for the November 1943 Cairo Conference. *IWM CM5614*

Capodichino and Pomigliano airfields, including many Junkers Ju52/3ms and Messerschmitt Me323s. In Naples the wife or girlfriend may, unlike you, think that she has had a surfeit of aeronautica and readily fall in with your suggestion to visit the ruins of Pompeii, secure in the knowledge that a town overwhelmed and buried by an eruption of Vesuvius in 79AD would be as far removed from aviation that she could get. She's wrong again! Since the middle of the last century this Roman town has been meticulously excavated, revealing magnificent structures; but an area of Roman villas was blasted out of existence during World War 2 by bombing. Even the guidebooks mention this, but not how it happened. The story is of a US 15th Air Force pilot,

briefed to bomb installations near Naples, failing to find his primary target as Vesuvius was belching smoke. Coming low over Pompeii and observing the vast area of ruins, he exclaimed to his crew, 'Gee! Look at that! Musta been one hell of a vital target' — and made it his secondary. If he did not have any sense of history, at least he left his mark upon it.

You're now quite near to Sorrento for visiting Capri which you can do on a Russian 'Kometa' Class hydrofoil. 'Kometas' also abound along Russia's Black Sea Coast, so we shall move on to there.

UBIQUE

As a tourist you can now visit Russia with Moscow, St Petersburg, Yalta and Sochi the main centres, travelling on international and internal routes by the largest airline in the world — Aeroflot. You will also get an awareness of why it is such a vast organisation. With some railways, like the main line down the east side of the Black Sea going into Georgia and serving Sochi with its three million annual visitors, being only single track, and with distances so vast, air travel is essential. In parts of Russia you are hardly ever out of earshot of the whine of Kuznetsovs or the drone of Ivchenkos, but not in Moscow where, still following Stalin's decree, the capital must not be overflown.

A package holiday in Romania gives you the opportunity to fly in a TAROM Ilyushin Il-62, but aeronautical activity is very limited in this country with its fuel problems. Which seems strange for a country with the Ploesti oilfields, one of the most important World War 2 targets and subject of a famous massed raid by USAAF B-24 Liberators. You fringe the oilfields and pass through the rebuilt town on your way to Piana Brasov, the Romanian mountain centre resort. Those taking a beach holiday at Mamaia, the principal resort of the country, will be close to Constanta, the chief seaport where the naval museum, while having no aircraft to offer, has a large collection of anti-aircraft guns in its grounds from light to heavy calibres.

Yugoslavia, once the most popular of the former Communist countries for tourists offered more freedom of movement. Here, immediately outside the main airport at Ljubljana, was full-scale aeronautica in an array of a selection of discarded Yugoslav Air Force aircraft types.

Wherever you go, keep an eye open and note what you see. Look at memorials, visit churches — it was in a church in Florence that the writer bought one of his aero first day covers! The main centres of aeronautical exhibits you will know from books and magazines. In general they are few and far between on the Continent, but aeronautica can abound — anywhere.